Regional and Sectoral Development in Mexico as Alternatives to Migration

Series on Development and International Migration in Mexico, Central America, and the Caribbean Basin

Sergio Díaz-Briquets and Sidney Weintraub,
Series Editors

Volume I
*Determinants of Emigration from Mexico,
Central America, and the Caribbean*

[JV 6493.D48]

Volume II
*Regional and Sectoral Development in Mexico
as Alternatives to Migration*

FORTHCOMING

Volume III
*Migration Impacts of Trade and Foreign Investment
in Mexico and Caribbean Basin Countries*

Volume IV
*International Migration, Remittances,
and Small Business Development in Mexico
and Caribbean Basin Countries*

Volume V
*Small Country Development and International Labor Flows:
Experiences in Central America and the Caribbean,*
edited by Anthony P. Maingot

Volume VI
Receiving Country Policies and Migration Flows

Regional and Sectoral Development in Mexico as Alternatives to Migration

EDITED BY
Sergio Díaz-Briquets and Sidney Weintraub

Westview Press
BOULDER • SAN FRANCISCO • OXFORD

Series on Development and International Migration in Mexico, Central America, and the Caribbean Basin

This Westview softcover edition is printed on acid-free paper and bound in library-quality, coated covers that carry the highest rating of the National Association of State Textbook Administrators, in consultation with the Association of American Publishers and the Book Manufacturers' Institute.

Copyright © 1991 by Westview Press, Inc.

Published in 1991 in the United States of America by Westview Press, Inc., 5500 Central Avenue, Boulder, Colorado 80301, and in the United Kingdom by Westview Press, 36 Lonsdale Road, Summertown, Oxford OX2 7EW

Library of Congress Cataloging-in-Publication Data
Regional and sectoral development in Mexico as alternatives to
  migration / edited by Sergio Díaz-Briquets and Sidney Weintraub.
    p. cm.—(Series on development and international migration
  in Mexico, Central America, and the Caribbean Basin ; vol. 2)
  Includes bibliographical references.
  ISBN 0-8133-8143-6
  1. Mexico—Emigration and immigration. 2. United States—
Emigration and immigration. 3. Regional planning—Mexico.
4. Mexico—Economic policy—1970–   . I. Díaz-Briquets, Sergio.
II. Weintraub, Sidney, 1922–   . III. Series: Series on development
and international migration in Mexico, Central America, and the
Caribbean Basin ; 2.
JV7401.Z79U557 1991
338.972—dc20   90-25257
                                                            CIP

Printed and bound in the United States of America

The paper used in this publication meets the requirements
of the American National Standard for Permanence of Paper
for Printed Library Materials Z39.48-1984.

10   9   8   7   6   5   4   3   2   1

Contents

Series Preface

The Immigration Reform and Control Act of 1986 (IRCA) was a manifestation of widespread public concern over the volume of undocumented immigration into the United States. The principal innovation of this legislation—the provision to impose penalties on employers who knowingly hire undocumented immigrants—was a response to this concern.

This effort at restriction was tempered in IRCA by other provisions permitting the legalization of two types of undocumented immigrants—those who had resided in the United States since January 1, 1982; and what were called special agricultural workers (SAWs), persons who had worked in perishable crop agriculture for at least 90 days during specified periods from 1983 to 1986. Approximately 3.1 million persons sought legalization (what is popularly referred to as amnesty) under these two provisions. The breakdown was roughly 1.8 million under the regular program and 1.3 million as SAWs. Mexicans made up 75 percent of the combined legalization requests.

Two elements—punishment and exoneration—were essential ingredients of the compromise that made possible the passage of IRCA, but they also had the effect of working at cross purposes, at least temporarily. For a time, many persons who might have crossed the border without papers took the opportunity to regularize their status and thus enter legally. In our research we discovered many non-farmers who had not earlier considered temporary migration but who obtained papers as SAWs to enter the United States. Officials of the U.S. Immigration and Naturalization Service (INS) asserted that there was widespread fraud under the SAWs program for applicants from Mexico and elsewhere. We verified from the Mexican side of the border that, indeed, there was fraud, but our evidence does not permit making an estimate of its magnitude. The two provisions together did not slow immigration but instead permitted some switching from undocumented to documented border crossing. During the period that legalization applications could be submitted, therefore, data showing a decline in unauthorized border crossings (apprehensions) were deceptive.

In due course, however, undocumented immigration began to pick up again, and apprehension data and other evidence now indicate that it is at a level similar to that before enactment of IRCA. There is ample proof of the production of fraudulent documents permitting immigrants to show employers that they are "legally" in the United States. It is probably impossible to end this entrepreneurial document production short of instituting a foolproof identity card, assuming the word "foolproof" is an accurate characterization of technology. The idea of Americans having to show an identity card when seeking employment has not been accepted.

It is an overstatement to say definitively that IRCA has failed to accomplish its main task, to staunch the flow of undocumented immigrants by means of penalties on employers, but that is the initial conclusion one must reach. Its failure means that the available options for reducing the inflow of undocumented immigrants—assuming this is still the U.S. goal—are reduced by the one option that was earlier considered the most promising.

An identity card is not acceptable. A high fence, patrolled by armed guards keeping persons without papers from entering the United States, would be unacceptably obtrusive and also alter the relationship with Mexico. It would be anomalous to forcefully close the border to people at the same time the United States and Mexico are planning to open the border to the free flow of goods and services.

There thus remains only one feasible option—short of leaving bad enough alone and letting those who wish to come do so—and that is to foster the economic development of those countries that send the bulk of undocumented migrants to the United States. If punishment is not the solution, then perhaps development is.

We did not know development was really the only option when this research project was started. However, IRCA had a little-noticed provision that established the Commission for the Study of International Migration and Cooperative Economic Development with the following mandate:

> The Commission, in consultation with the governments of Mexico and other sending countries in the Western Hemisphere, shall examine the conditions in Mexico and such other sending countries which contribute to unauthorized migration to the United States and [shall explore] mutually beneficial, reciprocal trade and investment programs to alleviate such conditions.

THE RESEARCH PROGRAM

The research program of the Commission focused on two broad themes: why people emigrate from their own countries to enter clandestinely into the United States, and what cooperative development measures are most appropriate to reduce the economic incentive to emigrate. More emphasis in the research was placed on the second of these two issues, particularly job creation in migrant-sending countries, because there was already ample scholarly literature on the motives for emigration. These motives are not solely economic, but evidence from years of research demonstrates clearly that the economic dominates.

We have culled the research supported by the Commission to sort out those essays that we think make valuable contributions to the literature on the relationship between development and migration. The authors of the essays are experts in this field from migrant-sending countries, Europe, and the United States. The essays selected are organized into six volumes, each dealing with a specific aspect of the development theme; each volume is therefore self-contained. In our judgment, the six volumes together make the most original contribution that exists to date on the development-migration relationship. We are gratified that Westview Press reached a similar conclusion and wished to publish the series.

Both editors were involved in the research program of the Commission: Sergio Díaz-Briquets as research director and Sidney Weintraub as senior research adviser. Our motive in bringing out the series is to provide scholars with a base of research from which they can delve further into the development-migration nexus.

As the listing of the series shows, one volume (Volume II) deals exclusively with Mexico, and three others (Volumes I, III, and IV) with Mexico and with other countries in Central America and the Caribbean. For the sake of convenience, we use the phrase Caribbean Basin to refer to the collectivity of countries in this region. The emphasis on Mexico is warranted by the evidence that Mexicans constitute about 70 percent of the unauthorized immigrants in the United States. Volume V deals with Central America and the Caribbean, and the final volume (Volume VI) with U.S. policies relating to development in and emigration from Mexico and other countries of the Caribbean Basin. Although we take responsibility as senior editors for all the volumes, the editor for Volume V is Anthony P. Maingot. The final volume contains the executive summary of the report of the Commission submitted to the Congress and the president.

The essays deal mostly with migrant-sending countries in the Western Hemisphere because that was the Commission's mandate and because the bulk of undocumented immigrants into the United States come from Mexico and other countries of the Caribbean Basin. However, the Western Hemisphere emphasis is not exclusive, and several comparative essays on receiving-country policies in Europe are included in Volume VI.

KEY OVERALL FINDINGS

Although research conclusions in the specific areas are discussed in each volume, some overall findings merit emphasis. The most important is the one already stated: that no viable alternative to economic development seems to exist that would significantly reduce undocumented immigration into the United States. It is hardly original to state that as a country becomes better developed, the economic pressure to emigrate is likely to be reduced. Historically, the development thesis has been demonstrated, particularly in Western Europe where countries of emigration became lands of immigration. Western Europe is now coping with its own undocumented, or unwanted, immigrants. Ireland, which has not enjoyed as much sustained growth as other countries in Western Europe, is still a country from which people emigrate. We observed, over time, that domestic economic well-being in European countries overcame the strength of networks in perpetuating outward migration.

Skeptics (including us) acknowledged the need for development, but they argued that it took too long to be relevant for dealing with current problems of undocumented immigration or, indeed, with anticipated migration movements over the next several decades. We do not know what income differential stimulates undocumented migration; nor do we know how much narrowing of this differential is necessary to deter emigration. We do know, however, that the difference between $1,900 and $19,000 a year—which are the respective 1990 per capita incomes in Mexico and the United States—is a stimulant to emigration. Completely closing this gap, even under wondrous estimates of Mexican economic growth, is apt to take more than 100 years. This is not the kind of assessment a policy maker likes to hear.

Yet, it is to this advice that our research leads. Sherlock Holmes was fond of saying that if all explanations but one to a conundrum must be discarded, then that one must contain the answer. This is the conclusion we reach. If emigration cannot be curtailed by other means, then the remaining viable option must be exploited; and it really does not matter if policy makers and legislators with a short-term outlook grumble at this conclusion.

The saving grace is that incomes do not have to be identical to act as a deterrent to clandestine migration. There is a natural desire of most persons to remain at home, which can be reinforced if economic hope is offered to would-be migrants and their children. We suspect, based on the research contained in the series, that absolute income differentials may matter less in the migrate-stay calculus than the direction of economic hope (that is, whether economic conditions at home are improving or deteriorating). We are not referring here to improved economic conditions for one year or two, but sustained over a decade or so.

The importance of sustaining economic growth over some unquantifiable time period must be emphasized. What we found in study after study was that a short-term increase in income, over one or two years, leads to increased emigration. We came across no study that contradicted this finding. The reason, presumably, is that a modest increase in income makes it possible for people to afford the trip. If, as in the Mexican case, income per person increases by, say, 3 percent after inflation, this adds only $57 to the annual income of the average Mexican. Even this overstates the case; the "average" Mexican, some 50 percent of the population, earns much less than $1,000 a year. An increase in income of $57 or less is not enough to deter the economic incentive to emigrate. But adding 3 percent a year, compounded over 10 or 20 years, might make a difference.

The conclusion that it requires continued economic growth to have a meaningful influence on curtailing emigration has as its corollary that the "cooperative" U.S. policy contained in the Commission's mandate must also be sustained. Although development is essentially an internal responsibility, and Mexico and other countries in the region are taking many needed steps to restructure their economies, the external environment plays a decisive role. This is not the place for a detailed discussion of U.S. economic policy except to note that if sustained economic growth is required in sending countries to reduce emigration pressures, then U.S. measures that frustrate this growth (particularly trade protectionism but also U.S. macroeconomic policy that slows U.S. growth or pushes up the interest rate that sending countries must pay on their foreign debt) will stimulate undocumented immigration. If the current push toward free trade between Mexico and the United States serves to augment the growth of income and employment in Mexico, it will also have a long-term effect of curtailing emigration pressure. Free trade between the United States and other countries of the region is a less immediate prospect, but it too may eventually help to stimulate the growth of income and employment of these nations.

One other overall conclusion that emerges from the research is that the economic development process as it has been pursued, certainly in the period since World War II, has stimulated internal migration. In country after country, the rural-urban population relationship has shifted in favor of the urban part of the ratio. Cities have burgeoned as the relative role of agriculture has diminished. Manufacturing and services have grown in importance compared with agriculture. This is the normal pattern of development, as witness the historical experience of Europe and the United States. Habits of migration have thus become commonplace in sending countries in the Western Hemisphere, as elsewhere. Although it is more traumatic to pick up stakes and leave one's own country than to shift within the country, the difference is a matter of degree. Once networks, or ethnic diasporas, have been established in the United States, as they generally have for migrant-sending countries in the Western Hemisphere, even the difference of degree between internal and external migration diminishes. Thus, the number of undocumented immigrants to the United States should not be expected to diminish for the foreseeable future; and this fact increases the importance of sustained economic growth to keep people home.

The relative importance of Mexico as a sending country may decline in coming decades because its economic prospects are more auspicious than those of other countries in the region, particularly in Central America. In addition, migrant networks in the United States have now been established for Central American countries.

Populations in the migrant-sending countries are quite young, and none of these countries is creating enough jobs to satisfy all persons entering the labor force. This situation, once more, points to the primacy of economic growth as the necessary deterrent to emigration.

We have been struck in our investigations by how extensively people in the world are on the move. Our studies concentrated on the movement of people in the Western Hemisphere to the United States, but there are large migrations within Africa and Asia, and into Western Europe from the east (the former Communist countries) and the south (such as from North Africa into France and Italy). It is easier—not easy, but easier—to control immigration into Western Europe than it is into the United States, to which migrants can come across a large land border with Mexico. Yet the West Europeans are not having much success either in dealing with their immigration problem. As with the United States, the key to control is development in the sending countries. We are dealing, in other words, with a global phenomenon. The subject presents itself as a migration issue, but at its core it is a development matter.

WHAT COMES NEXT

The proper approach to development must differ from country to country—even apart from the conceptual or ideological model that is used. Mexico is a large, populous country in which there is scope for regional differentiation. This approach is not available to any meaningful extent for other countries in the Caribbean Basin. Mexico has a substantial industrial structure on which to base export-led growth, as it is now doing. The industrial structure is more modest in Central America and hardly exists in much of the Caribbean.

Overall findings of the type set forth in this preface can take a policy maker only so far. Understanding the link between development and migration, and then making policy to influence both phenomena, requires intimate knowledge of conditions in sub-regions and in each country. This is provided in the six volumes in this series.

Our objectives in bringing out these volumes are twofold: to augment understanding of the development-migration relationship based on the extensive research that was carried out; and, much more importantly in the long run, to stimulate further scholarly research about this theme.

Sergio Díaz-Briquets
Sidney Weintraub

Introduction

Sergio Díaz-Briquets
and Sidney Weintraub

The durable abatement of undocumented immigration into the United States from Mexico depends ultimately on a steady improvement of Mexican living conditions and a narrowing of wage differentials between the two countries. Greater economic opportunity at home can decrease the appeal of the U.S. labor market for Mexican workers. It will take considerable time to narrow the large wage gap—now at about a ten-to-one ratio—between the two countries. The influence of cross-border social networks driving migratory flows cannot be modified in the short term. Conditions in the U.S. labor market that provide a welcoming environment for undocumented labor migrants will not alter in the near future. These features of job markets and social networks between the two countries are well entrenched. Changing them will take a long time. In the interim—ten years, twenty years, or however long—migration pressures will persist.

Mexico is now making decisions that will have great bearing on the employment and migration choices of future generations of workers. Mexico's structural economic changes—opening the economy to foreign trade and investment, reducing the role of the state, and increasing that of the market—will result in winners; but there will also be losers who bear the major cost of adjustment. This restructuring is what makes possible Mexican consideration of a free trade agreement (FTA) with the United States. An FTA would make the two economies even more interdependent than they are now; an FTA would lead to the transformation of many sectors of the Mexican economy. These changes will be felt nationally and at the regional level.

The authors of the chapters in this volume examine a number of regional and sectoral developments in Mexico and assess how they are related to undocumented migration to the United States. The fundamental premise driving their analyses is that greater regional and sectoral development constitute the best antidote to undocumented migration. The chapters, which reveal a complex scenario, have several common threads. These threads include the excessively intrusive role of the Mexican state based on a highly centralized structure of government and uneven regional economic opportunity. Mexico's state-led development model can claim major accomplishments, but it endured well past its time. The rural economy has suffered for the benefit of a few large cities. This development asymmetry led to immense urban problems—overpopulation, ecological damage, and traffic gridlock, to cite just a few—and to the deterioration of many rural communities, many of which are now dependent on emigration to the United States for their economic survival.

Jesús Tamayo and Fernando Lozano provide a comprehensive examination of policy actions that emigrant-sending states and regions in Mexico could take to enhance their development and thereby reduce economic pressures to emigrate. Their study focuses on Zacatecas, one of the poorest Mexican states and traditionally an important source of undocumented immigrants into the United States. The authors contend that the highly centralized Mexican political system, in which state governments have limited authority, penalizes states such as Zacatecas. National resources—including those generated within the state—are allocated based on decisions made almost exclusively in Mexico City. Many states receive from Mexico City only a small portion of what they contribute to the national coffers. One option for Zacatecas—and other states—is to demand at least that federal expenditures in the state be more in line with the contributions made by the state. In principle, poorer states should be net recipients of national resources.

Tamayo and Lozano found that most undocumented migration originates from some of the poorest regions of the state. They conclude that it would be futile and costly to seek to promote the development of regions in Zacatecas that have little economic growth potential. Instead, they urge that a new policy be designed that includes mutually reinforcing municipal, regional, state, and federal initiatives. They analyze strategies for the development of Zacatecas's agricultural, mining, industrial, and service sectors, and note that different policy interventions have varying time frames. The policies recommended by Tamayo and Lozano would build on the considerable financial resources Zacatecas receives from migrant remittances and on the state's locational advantage at the crossroad of Mexico's major economic regions and most populous cities.

Jesús Arroyo Alejandre, Adrián de León Arias, and Basilia Valenzuela Varela consider the question of emigration and development from the regional perspective of the state of Jalisco. They contend that "it is possible to influence the magnitude of the migratory flow to the United States through the development of regional centers that serve as hubs after having defined their potential and identified their geographic integration with the regional economic system." These regional centers would be able to attain the economies of scale and specialization needed to achieve self-sustained growth. They could serve as alternative destinations for migrants originating from areas in Jalisco and nearby regions with limited development potential who would otherwise migrate to one of Mexico's large cities or to the United States.

Like Tamayo and Lozano, Arroyo Alejandre, Arias, and Varela conclude that an attempt to promote the development of migrant-sending regions with limited development possibilities would waste resources and distract attention from the development of regional centers with better potential. They believe these promising regional centers can base their development on regional and export-oriented expansion of agribusiness, light manufacturing, and services. These policies, they believe, would generate jobs and contribute to the diversification of regional labor markets.

Arroyo Alejandre and his colleagues also view the extreme concentration of authority in Mexico City as an impediment to balanced regional development. They are encouraged by the current tendency of Mexico's political and economic policies toward decentralization and by the government's encouragement of more active participation by the private sector in the country's development. They believe these policies will enhance the prospects for further regional development. Arroyo Alejandre and his colleagues advocate fostering small and medium-sized businesses; expanding the communications infrastructure; increasing investment in promising secondary cities; promoting credit instruments attuned to local needs; and reorienting education to serve regional needs. Their premise is that as these initiatives begin to take effect, and as regional development occurs, increasingly fewer workers would rely on the extraregional emigration option. This outcome, however, is not guaranteed. The authors note that it is difficult to integrate rural communities into wider urban systems and that, just as local conditions can encourage emigration, emigration can hinder local development.

The emigration-development issue is also addressed by Wayne A. Cornelius. Cornelius and his colleagues conducted surveys in 1988–1989 in three migrant-sending communities, one each in the states of Jalisco, Michoacán, and Zacatecas, which they also had studied earlier, before the passage of the Immigration Reform and Control Act (IRCA). The policy question posed by the emigration-development dilemma is how to create a viable local alternative to undocumented migration. The answer, Cornelius finds, is complex because there is a deeply ingrained emigration tradition that pervades the culture of many communities. The solution to economic problems is almost always sought in the United States and emigration "becomes a complete substitute for local economic activity." There is little incentive to invest resources in communities of origin, which many migrants visit only for short periods of time. These attitudes can be changed only if local opportunities are available.

Those surveyed stated that what was needed were more and better jobs, particularly factory jobs, and an improved social and economic infrastructure. Few cited the need for improvements in agriculture, an indication of the widespread despair about upgrading this activity. Migrants who have worked in higher-paying jobs in services and manufacturing in the United States reject agricultural work.

There were striking differences in responses from persons with different status. Persons who had legal access to the U.S. labor market were more concerned about local infrastructure improvements and better social facilities than those who could not legally cross the border, while undocumented migrants were preoccupied mainly with finding jobs. Cornelius concludes that the residents of the labor-exporting communities are seeking "the creation of permanent, nonagricultural employment opportunities, preferably in small-scale manufacturing enterprises [and that] such nonagricultural microenterprises may be the *only* strategy to appreciably reduce future migration flows from them."

Cornelius argues that the viability of small rural industries can be enhanced by providing them with specialized support services, relatively easy access to credit, and the cooperative purchase of inputs and marketing of outputs. Under these circumstances, rural industries would help retain some prospective emigrants, but even then it is doubtful that a policy of promoting small rural industries would significantly reduce undocumented migration. These industries, mostly microenterprises, are not known for their durability. They are vulnerable to economic downturns.

Arroyo Alejandre and his colleagues favor fostering the establishment of larger manufacturing facilities—not in small rural communities from which many people emigrate, but in more dynamic and larger communities nearby that could serve as alternative destinations to potential migrants; Cornelius, however, is skeptical of this approach. His reservations are based on research findings that indicate that migrants from rural communities do not even consider going to nearby cities with relatively good employment prospects. Arroyo Alejandre and his associates recognize this problem. In order to overcome this obstacle, they recommend establishing employment information services to guide prospective migrants to alternative destinations within their own regions.

Cornelius recommends that because of deeply ingrained patterns of behavior in many rural regions of Mexico, policy should focus on finding alternatives for "would-be, first time migrants to the United States, rather than try to persuade already experienced individuals and families to abandon this source of income."

Mexico's northern border cities are experiencing extremely high demographic growth rates. These cities, while relatively prosperous in Mexican terms, are much poorer than localities on the U.S. side. This difference, coupled with the high cost of health and human services and an aging population in the United States, led David C. Warner to conclude that both countries would benefit if more U.S. citizens could receive these services in Mexico. The health services in question include nursing home care, extended hospital care, care for the mentally retarded, for head-injured persons, and for the chronically mentally ill. Warner believes these services could be provided at low cost to U.S. nationals at convenient locations in Mexico near the U.S. border. Mexico would gain foreign exchange and many new low-skilled and semiskilled jobs.

The costs for many of the health services under discussion are covered by U.S. federal and state programs, such as Medicare and Medicaid, and regulations would have to be changed to permit Mexican providers to be reimbursed for providing care to U.S. beneficiaries. Warner notes that use of these services in Mexico by Americans would have to be on a strictly voluntary basis. Health care providers would have to meet U.S. standards, and in some cases facilities would have to be operated jointly by service providers from both countries.

Although benefits accruing from the growth of maquiladoras (plants in Mexico, mainly near the U.S. border, which complete labor-intensive operations on materials sent largely from the U.S.) have been significant— in the form of employment creation and foreign exchange earnings— many Mexicans are uneasy about them. They are concerned that the maquiladoras are in Mexico only to take advantage of the country's cheap labor. Although the maquiladoras are in Mexico, critics note, they are not part of Mexico's industrial structure. If wage rates in Mexico were to rise more rapidly than in other countries, or protectionist sentiments in the United States to prevail, maquiladora operations could suffer.

Sidney Weintraub argues that the promise of the maquiladoras extends beyond their demonstrated capacity to bring in billions of dollars in foreign exchange and create hundreds of thousands of jobs. They are best viewed "as a transitional phenomenon, as a source of wages and employment in the process of moving to a higher level of development, when other more secure jobs will be available." If the promise of the maquiladoras is to be realized, and if Mexico is to become an efficient industrial competitor, the country must continue to upgrade the quality of its labor force and take steps to integrate the maquiladora industry into the national economy. As this occurs, the maquiladora plants will cease to be enclaves and will contribute to the diffusion of modern technology. This process will accelerate dramatically if the United States and Mexico enter into a free trade agreement. In the absence of tariffs and other trade barriers between the two countries, the maquiladora plants would lose their current tariff advantage but, on the positive side, would become part of the industrial structure of the integrated market.

Patricia A. Wilson's survey of over seventy maquiladoras in Guadalajara, Monterrey, Juárez, Nuevo Laredo, and Tijuana, is the basis for her examination of spatial and organizational features of the industry. The industry today has few links to domestic suppliers of material inputs, so the larger part of Mexico's value-added inputs comes from labor utilization. The share of domestic inputs used by maquiladoras in Mexico's interior, though larger than those in towns near the border, is still small.

Wilson's principal finding is that the higher percentage of domestic material inputs in interior locations corresponds to the utilization of preexisting capacity. In their search for markets during the economic crisis of the 1980s, domestic suppliers directed some of their output to the maquiladora sector. In Guadalajara, many suppliers to maquiladoras started from a tradition of craft manufacturing; most of these producers still direct part of their output to domestic users, including maquiladoras. This has not been the case, however, for electronic maquiladoras established by foreign firms. The percentage of Mexican inputs used by these maquiladoras is much lower than among crafts manufacturers, but by virtue of their size the volume of inputs purchased by electronic maquiladoras is important.

The wholly foreign-owned electronic maquiladoras acquire some inputs from Mexican firms and have contributed to the establishment of several local companies as suppliers. They also frequently use local service firms for their tool and die needs, metal stamping, and plastic molding needs. Many auto parts firms that produce primarily for the domestic market also function partially as maquiladoras and use many Mexican inputs. They are able to do so thanks to a strong local metalworking industry that has an experienced labor force. The availability of these workers was one reason why these firms located in Guadalajara. Monterrey's large industrial groups began producing for the maquiladora sector as a way to utilize idle capacity when domestic demand for their output declined during the 1980s.

Wilson's main conclusion is that the obstacles and opportunities of the maquiladoras are specific to the sector in which they operate and where they are located. Wilson recommends that, in regions of Mexico where feasible, steps be taken to encourage local links among clusters of related industries to achieve greater integration. This was the path followed by crafts industries in northern Italy and other countries that have become internationally competitive. The firms in a cluster reap benefits from working together while still retaining flexibility. This development would be in keeping with the transitional role for the maquiladoras foreseen by Weintraub as Mexico continues its march toward modern industrial development.

One sector that is generally believed to hold promise for absorbing much Mexican labor is fisheries. Because Mexico has extensive coastlines along the Gulf of Mexico and the Atlantic and Pacific Oceans and exclusive access to major fisheries, it has been assumed that the sector would flourish if Mexico devoted more resources to its development. The findings reported by Alejandro Nadal Egea, however, cast doubt on this assumption: Nadal Egea gives evidence of the limits to development of Mexico's coastal resources, which, he argues, are being poorly managed. He also criticizes current policies in the sector. Because of price controls, there is little incentive to invest in modern canning facilities to process valuable sardines caught in Mexican waters. Instead, much of the catch is processed into animal feed despite strong domestic demand for human consumption and the high price fetched by many varieties of sardines in international markets.

Furthermore, concentration on a few species such as shrimp is leading to their being over-fished, while many other species are only sparingly fished. Nadal Egea urges that, in Mexico's prevailing climate of deregulation, attention be given to respecting natural catch limits in order to sustain renewable resources.

Nadal Egea argues that by and large employment potential in the fishing sector is modest. For example, Mexico has one of the world's most modern tuna fleets. However, relatively few jobs are generated and the cost of creating each job is high. Links between tuna fishing and other economic activities are limited. If traditional fishing methods were improved, employment prospects would be better in the harvesting and marketing of coastal species. Aquaculture, particularly for shrimp, has the potential for substantial growth because of prices and demand in international markets. Employment generation in relation to investment is relatively high in shrimp aquaculture.

Agriculture, Mexico's economic mainstay for much of its history, has stagnated or has been in decline for decades. This deterioration can be attributed partly to the industrial bias of Mexico's modern development strategy, which was financed at the expense of agricultural investment. Agricultural output has failed to keep pace with population growth, net exports have declined, as have rural employment and real wage levels. A decline in rural employment is not necessarily symptomatic of agricultural stagnation because modern farming implies the introduction of labor-saving technology. In addition, a shift away from agricultural to service and industrial employment is the most visible and inevitable consequence of modern economic development. Nevertheless, Mexico's agricultural policy has been wanting, and production has not been optimal, nor has the employment potential of the rural sector been fully exploited. These themes are addressed by two independent teams of investigators.

Antonio Yúnez-Naude and Ramón Blanno-Jasso examine foreign trade trends in agricultural products and the impact of official policies on these trends. Agricultural stagnation, they conclude, is the result of the price-distorting effects of urban-biased state interventions. Traditional peasant producers of basic grains in rain-fed land were penalized by support policies that set prices too low, while modern producers were given the incentive to specialize in noncontrolled crops whose prices for inputs—water, fertilizer, seeds, pesticides—were subsidized. Yúnez-Naude and Blanno-Jasso argue for agricultural policies that combine market incentives and state interventions to maximize output and employment. Liberating the prices of nonstaple crops would allow efficient producers to benefit from market opportunities, and the state's limited resources could then be devoted to small producers of staple crops. Also, the small producers could be protected and encouraged by state-funded price supports and regulation of imports of staple commodities. Yúnez-Naude and Blanno-Jasso conclude that further deregulation of Mexican agriculture should take place only within the context of a more open international trading regime. Under the current circumstances of state intervention elsewhere, they believe that state intervention is necessary in Mexico as well.

Amado Ramírez Leyva, Marcos Portillo Vázquez, and Celia Sánchez Solano, a team from the Autonomous University of Chapingo (a leading Mexican agricultural, teaching, and research center) examine the export potential of Mexico for many commodities traded in international markets. Their analysis is based on an evaluation of data from the Food and Agricultural Organization of trends in world export volumes and prices and on an assessment of market responses to these trends by producing, exporting, and importing countries. In their detailed analysis, the Chapingo investigators identified those crops that offer promising international marketing opportunities for Mexican producers. They believe that Mexico is well suited to develop a diversified agricultural export profile because it is blessed with ecological and climatic diversity. In their view, Mexico can diversify its agricultural exports without compromising production for internal consumption. To this end, they examined the potential of many crops for which world marketing conditions are favorable and which could be produced on underutilized Mexican lands.

The Chapingo chapter evaluates the global agricultural export potential of the various Mexican states, and also gives the results of a pilot study assessing opportunities and constraints in three rural development districts in Zacatecas. Both evaluations considered the availability and current use of productive resources, crop composition, and local production limitations. The methodology took into account marketing bottlenecks, existing development programs, and tradeoffs between income yields and job creation. In the view of the editors, this is a path-breaking study whose methodology could usefully be replicated in many regions of Mexico.

The employment potential of the tourist industry is significant, and tourism is likely to absorb a rising share of Mexico's labor force in the 1990s. Because the industry relies heavily on unskilled and semiskilled workers and is geographically dispersed, tourism is a high-priority sector for Mexico. In 1988, the industry created 650,000 direct jobs and many more indirect jobs. However, Daniel Hiernaux Nicolás and Manuel Rodríguez Woog argue in their analysis that the strategy followed to promote the sector's overall growth has failed to maximize its employment generation potential.

Until recently, Mexico's tourism development strategy was based on considerable capital investment by the state, particularly in modern beach resorts such as Cancún and Ixtapa. Three main objectives were behind this approach: the generation of foreign exchange; the promotion of regional development; and job creation. The strategy was generally successful, although the achievements were below expectations for the last two objectives. Tourism has become one of Mexico's main sources of foreign exchange. However, although the areas immediately surrounding the main resorts experienced economic growth, this development was uneven and of only limited benefit to the population of the region. Many of the gains accruing from links between tourism and other sectors of the economy continue to flow to the economically more advanced regions of Mexico.

The strategy entailed a high opportunity cost in that the cost of each job created in large, modern, and heavily capitalized resorts is far higher than in smaller, less costly, and more geographically dispersed resorts catering to national as well as international tourists. Although smaller resorts generate fewer direct jobs than do larger resorts, indirect employment is greater in the smaller resorts because of their economic links with other sectors in the region, including informal activities. In this respect, the tourist industry is different from the fishing industry, which has fewer regional links. Hiernaux Nicolás and Rodríguez Woog recommend that the issues of cost per job, regional development, and economic ties be kept in mind as Mexico formulates policies to encourage greater private sector involvement in tourism development.

Nature-oriented tourism, which relies on natural areas and outdoor recreational activities, is a specialized but growing branch of the industry. Although limited in its job-creation potential, nature-oriented, or ecological, tourism is ideally suited for rural and isolated areas with restricted development potential. However, as Art Pedersen and Héctor Ceballos-Lascurain show in their evaluation of the nature-oriented tourism potential of the state of Guerrero, there are obstacles to the development of this specialized branch of tourism. These obstacles are related to how the local population is incorporated into the process, the need to preserve the natural appeal of tourist sites, and the difficulty of coordinating the activities of different government entities. In Guerrero, there is also a security problem in some sites with great potential. Nature-oriented tourism can also serve an important environmental preservation function.

In the concluding chapter, Jesús Tamayo and Fernando Lozano review how different Mexican administrations have viewed undocumented immigration to the United States. They evaluate the government's attempts—usually as part of national or regional development initiatives—to influence the determinants of undocumented migration. These include the Programa de Inversiones Públicas para el Desarrollo (PIDER), Coordinación General del Plan Nacional de Zonas Deprimidas y Grupos Marginados (COPLAMAR), Sistema Alimentario Mexicano (SAM), Programas Regionales de Empleo (PRE), and Programas Regionales de Desarrollo (PRD). Tamayo and Lozano conclude that although these rural development programs may have had political and symbolic value, they had little effect on regional development and the employment needs of the Mexican countryside.

Taken together, the analyses in this volume suggest that more can be done to promote the development of the regions of Mexico from which many undocumented migrants depart. This is not always true in particular communities of origin, but it does apply generally to the broader economic regions in which these communities are found. The contributors argue that the role of the central government in Mexico City—almost the only major force in setting regional development policy—should be reduced, and that greater authority and resources should be given to state and local governments for their own development. But even under the best circumstances, achieving balanced regional development is a difficult task. The policies most appropriate for one region may be inapplicable in others.

Despite the infrastructural and environmental problems associated with rapid growth along the border, this region, due largely to its proximity to the United States, has considerable advantages in attracting investment and in generating employment. Although much attention has been focused on the maquiladora industry, the potential for expansion in services is significant and has been only partially exploited. Regardless of what transpires with respect to the free trade agreement negotiations, the border is likely to continue to be an important center for Mexican manufacturing and spinoff activities.

The potential for labor absorption in many sectors of the Mexican economy is impressive. Maquiladoras, or their successors, are likely to continue to generate many new jobs, particularly if these plants are incorporated into the national economy. With the proper policy framework, the agricultural sector can make a greater contribution than it does now to the alleviation of rural poverty. Tourism already generates significant employment, but it could provide even more, given policy adjustments favoring less grandiose projects. Even in fisheries there is room for growth in employment, though less than in other economic sectors.

The contributors of this volume provide support for their policy recommendations. However, there is no simple way to significantly increase regional employment; and, even if the number of jobs increases, a corresponding slowdown in undocumented migration may be some time in coming.

1

The Economic and Social Development of High Emigration Areas in the State of Zacatecas: Antecedents and Policy Alternatives

Jesús Tamayo and Fernando Lozano

I. INTRODUCTION

In 1980, the state of Zacatecas provided the largest contingent of Mexican migrants to the United States. Situated in the arid north-central region of Mexico, Zacatecas is an old mining enclave that has been in decline since the end of the last century. It has sent its surplus population to the United States ever since. Ten years ago, official statistics ranked it as one of the poorest states in the Mexican federation.

Municipalities with the highest emigration rates were determined by a procedure based on returning migrants identified by the 1980 census. According to our analysis,[1] most of the migrants came from 25 of the state's southern and southwestern municipalities. These municipalities are characterized by scattered communities in which most people are employed primarily in agriculture and livestock and where unemployment rates are high. The market economy is not well developed in these communities and standards of living are low.

On the basis of an analysis of economic, physical and human characteristics, this paper evaluates the effects—at the regional and state levels —of a series of policies that could be carried out to promote employment and improve living conditions in the state. While the measures we propose are certainly not the only ones likely, we feel that they are among the most important. They might constitute a central core of a concerted strategy for developing those regions of Zacatecas subject to the most intense migratory pressures.

II. REGIONAL ECONOMIC DEVELOPMENT POLICIES AS A STRATEGY TO REDUCE MIGRATORY PRESSURES

These policies, if successful, may have some direct effect in reducing undocumented migratory flows. We do not claim to have discovered novel actions or policies unknown to the officials in charge of economic policy in the state government. We do claim to have systematically explored and evaluated opportunities and constraints for economic development in the state in light of Zacatecan emigration patterns. This evaluation can be compared with the state's present development project[2] and hopefully will assist in the selection of development policies.

We have taken account of the peculiarities of the Mexican political system. There are a number of corporations, agencies and "decentralized" and state-owned organizations which, at least theoretically, provide support to the states or to regional development programs.[3] Thus, in our policy proposal, we have attempted to keep in mind the government agencies that may be involved in any specific proposal.

Taxonomical Foreword

To organize our discussion, we have classified potential interventions along several dimensions. There are those that restrict or facilitate private investment. These are differentiated from direct government investment. Some of the latter, in turn, are geared toward creating social capital (or social assets) or toward more narrowly defined productive activities. Our interest is not focused on this functional classification of policies, but on those elements that enable us to differentiate time, space and the agents involved in them.

Any approach to socioeconomic development issues enables us to distinguish different types of problems and, consequently, to think of different types of "corrections" or policies. Thus, for example, some problems are amenable to short-term interventions through the adoption of some simple measures. Others, on the contrary, demand complex strategies that will produce results over the medium- or long term. Thus, from a temporal perspective, we assess the effects of policies over the short- medium- or long term. Policies can also be differentiated according to the political scope or level of the executing agency. In Mexico, this refers to the federal, state or local authorities. Finally, from the point of view of spatial specificity, the differentiation is not clear. Therefore, to explore this matter in some detail, we provide below a taxonomical exercise.

Let us differentiate economic policies according to their origin. First of all, federal policies, frequently of a macroeconomic nature, are the reflection of a strategy designed to achieve a national objective (fiscal policies, for example). Federal policies can be distinguished from those designed by state governments and which seek to accomplish state, as opposed to national, objectives. A good example is the successful petition of a fiscal, sectoral state policy by the Zacatecan government to Mexico City to consider state mining operations as local business entities for taxation purposes. Similar policies could originate at the municipal or regional level and be formalized by the central political system[4] (the policy of "free trade areas," in force in the extreme north of Mexico, is a good example of a successful regional policy).

Apart from "territorial" origins of certain policies (an origin that lets us see who it is probably addressed to), their effects often extend beyond the intended boundaries. They presumably will affect the economic space its promoters intended (in the desired sense, if we are lucky), but it is possible that they may impact other economic spaces coterminous with the area for which they were designed; some of these effects may even be contrary to those anticipated. It is also possible that they may have undesirable effects on neighboring economic areas. In addition, some of the policies that are regarded as specific to some region might be relevant to other parts of the country, while other policies which are viewed as national may be useful only at the regional level.

A diagram of these relationships might be posed as follows:

Origins of the economic policy	National (NE)	Expected effects at the State (SE) -levels-	Regional (RE)
Federal (FP)	direct	uncertain	unpredictable
State (SP)	?	direct	uncertain
Municipal (RP)		?	direct

Attempts to influence regional development are thus not limited to the proposal of *regional* or *municipal* policies. It is also crucial to study external influences on regional development. These include *national* (explicit in the state and federal actions or policies) and even *international* policies.

Scope or Coverage of This Section. Here we assess the PxRE vector; that is to say, the policies that affect the region. In particular, we are interested in those policies that could have, in the short- or medium term, an impact on the emigration of workers from the state or from the high push area (HPA). We propose some federal and state policies (FP and SP), exogenous to the RE region. We point out some of their effects and, if necessary, suggest modifications. In this exercise, we deal only with those federal or state policies whose effects on the region seem to us to be proportionally more important than on the state, or on the country; that is to say, when: RE/R > SE/E, or RE/R > NE/N.

We are aware that, in the Mexican context, state policies are almost nonexistent. So-called state policies are frequently only local expressions or adaptations of federal policies. It is optimistic, therefore, to propose modifications to many of these policies.

Regional policies are not frequent in the Mexican context either. A certain level of political development, not yet present in Mexico, is necessary for the design of these policies. Regional policies, up to now, have frequently been limited to the formal or rhetorical expression of the geographical distribution of federal spending and investment. It has not often responded to the strategic will to concentrate efforts to develop certain parts of the national territory.[5]

III. NOTE ON THE BINATIONAL CONTEXT: U.S. AND MEXICAN INTERESTS

The New Circumstances

Thanks to the work of innumerable specialists on the subject, the real dimensions of Mexican migration are beginning to become clear to both governments. This better understanding ranges from its historical roots to its present relevance in terms of national labor markets and monetary remittances. It is likewise beginning to be clear that the migratory flow cannot be stopped by police measures. However, the ways of influencing this demographic phenomenon, either in the medium- or the long term, remain rather obscure. Fortunately, it would seem that the present binational scenario favors the design and implementation of economic development policies for areas of high emigration to the United States.

The migrant-receiving country's interest in finding viable alternatives to control the flow of Mexican workers is obvious, especially at the highest levels of government. Indications of this interest are the Immigration Reform and Control Act of 1986 (IRCA)—better known in Mexico as the Simpson-Rodino Act—and the Commission for the Study of International Migration and Cooperative Economic Development, an offshoot of IRCA. The very name of the commission reflects the level of understanding among enlightened members of the U.S. political establishment with regard to immigration to their country.

Official Mexican interest is more vague and depends a good deal on U.S. attitudes. The Mexican concern for the economic development of high "push" regions dates back several decades. However, it has always stemmed from leftist groups (which, in the United States, would correspond to the ranks of liberal Democrats), both inside and outside the government. Perhaps for this reason, this concern has found no echo in the highest decision-making circles to concrete demands for support of broad, rural development policies. In the last 30 years, while agricultural and agrarian policy were adrift, Mexican emigration to the United States became a permanent reminder of the system's weaknesses—the ultimate test of the system's honesty and administrative efficiency. Finally, the reality of labor emigration became obvious to Mexican government officials, while the intellectuals of the system created an "ad hoc" rhetoric, rich in half truths. According to them, the emigration of workers, although undesirable, was of little significance (at least it was not as sizeable as the United States said it was); it was urban (and, therefore, not due to poverty in the Mexican countryside); it was of people who had jobs in Mexico (therefore, not because of local unemployment); and, finally, it was "structural" (impossible to change in the short- and medium term).

The above perhaps explains why Mexican official interest in altering the migration *status quo* was far from overwhelming. Certainly, there is an inevitable diplomatic response to U.S. approaches, but frequently Mexican government officials do not wish to waste time and effort in trying to "manage" the flow of migration, either directly or indirectly. The political costs of trying to contain it directly are so high that these officials would argue in favor of the constitutional right to move about freely.[6] Besides, in general, these officials are skeptical about the effectiveness of regional economic development strategies. Maybe they are right. Indeed, they have been witnesses—if not managers—of numerous plans and programs that, while contributing to economic development, have not helped the social groups for whom they were presumably intended. In spite of these antecedents, we think today there is reason to be optimistic.

The economic depression in Mexico has probably speeded up the pace of migration and made it more sizeable. It is also likely to have increased the will of Mexican government officials to avoid unnecessary bilateral frictions and to satisfy the requirements of U.S. policy. In this sense, comments from our neighbors on the limited local effectiveness of regional development programs will now be listened to with greater attention.

Foreseeable Difficulties

We are not totally optimistic. On both sides of the border, it is difficult to accept that any strategy for slowing the flow of migrants could act only indirectly and would show results only in the medium- and long term. It is equally difficult to assume the existence of a tradition that continues to encourage migration, even if differences in income and standards of living were nil. One must also recognize the efforts to control migration go against the grain of the increasing liberalism that seeks to eliminate barriers to the free flow of goods and capital, although still not of labor. If we Mexicans do not soon find better formulas for development and distribution of the social product, we shall have to get used to the constant drain of our best labor force, and the Americans will have to resign themselves to living besieged—if not invaded—by their starving neighbors.

The opportunity is now opening again to try different strategies of regional development, once again with international, technical and financial aid. In view of this situation, we should keep in mind the obstacle that the present Mexican centralistic political structure presents. We should recall the background of some regional development efforts. In similar programs, the Mexican government has always administered the funds and kept international inspectors at arms' length. The administrative antecedents of the present Mexican authorities suggest, however, that for the implementation and supervision of regional development programs, it might be necessary to create an autonomous organization or agency.

Whatever form the administration's development strategies take in Mexico's areas of high emigration, we must now begin to define such strategies. This exercise attempts to make a contribution to this objective. The proposals are ordered sectorally; the ordering does not reflect the relative importance attributed to them.

IV. AGRICULTURAL AND LIVESTOCK POLICIES

We do not pretend to describe the enormous problems of Mexican agriculture. Neither would we dare to suggest any strategy for restructuring it. Nevertheless, we can neither ignore the sector's difficulties nor overlook the ongoing liberal restructuring of the economy, a process which includes a restructuring of agricultural policy. This is not merely a buzz word; it is part of the overall restructuring of the national economy that started in 1982 and was speeded up by the present government. The National Development Plan, in May 1989, stated clearly that change is inevitable and:

> " . . . (5.3.1.) . . . the basic objective is to increase the output and productivity of the countryside . . . [and that] in order to achieve this it has been decided to carry out a firm policy for promoting efficiency in production."[7]

Because of its neoliberal orientation, the restructuring (which is highly necessary) will probably include measures of which not everyone will approve. For example, the border has already been opened to imports of grains used for animal fodder;[8] attempts have been made to tax the predominantly poverty stricken farmers.[9] It is likely that private investors will soon be allowed to purchase agricultural land. Although we share the present administration's desire to modernize agriculture, we doubt that the problems of Mexican agriculture can be solved merely by the market. It is not wise to overlook the economic and political interests of peasants and poverty stricken *ejidatarios* and end the government's tutelage of the last 60 years. Regardless of this polemic, we will suggest some measures specific to the state of Zacatecas. Running the risk of appearing naive in a liberal and anti-state-ownership environment, we suggest five basic actions that might be useful in promoting the development of agriculture and livestock in the state. Some explicitly link rural development to regional/state, development. All of the proposals may contribute to the reduction of emigration flows. Some are premised on the increased use of the state's natural resources or the more effective utilization of seasonal workers' or emigrants' remittances. They are:

1) Reactivating the National Commission for Arid Areas (Comisión

Nacional de las Zonas Aridas, CONAZA);
2) Providing special guaranteed prices for the production of basic grains in high emigration areas;
3) Encouraging increases in fruit production;
4) Promoting a pilot plan for increasing value-added in cattle raising; and
5) Reviewing other rural development experiences.

Each of these proposals will be examined.

V. AGRICULTURAL POLICIES

Agriculture in Zacatecas is a good reflection of Mexican agriculture in general: small islands of activity afloat on a sea of underdevelopment. Its most general characteristics are:

1) Shortages of land suitable for agriculture;[10] agricultural lands are dispersed within regions of widespread aridity.
2) Low levels of technical development in association with excessive population pressure; this translates into a relatively low agricultural product per capita.[11]
3) Disinvestment in agriculture.
4) A precarious social organization for production.

Geophysical Constraints and CONAZA: The Need for Technical Assistance and Financing for Agricultural Research and Development

The physical and environmental limitations of the state of Zacatecas lead us to a discussion of soil technology, its uses in arid and semiarid lands and its potential for Zacatecan agriculture. No one could deny the advisability of improving present agricultural techniques, that is to say, of channelling resources toward the cultivation of certain products according to modern techniques, or identification of new agricultural products well suited to local products or conditions. To a great extent, these have been the objectives of a government agency: the National Commission on Arid Areas (CONAZA). CONAZA has its headquarters in Zacatecas and was set up several administrations ago. The results of its efforts are largely unknown.

It is not our aim here to discuss why numerous government agencies created with valid objectives have survived despite their limited achievements. Our interest lies in taking advantage of their structure, however weak it may be. Therefore, we propose to reactivate CONAZA. This should include redefining its objectives to support its research and development actions and increasing its rural extension functions among rural producers, especially those from Zacatecas.

It would be unrealistic to expect that measures to increase the productivity of agriculture (through research for improvement of soil, seeds and production processes) could bear fruit in the short run. This would limit their attractiveness to those who want immediate and spectacular results. However, it would not be sensible to fail to grasp that present technological investment will set the tone for future agricultural development.

Aid to agricultural research and development opens the door for international collaboration. The state of Zacatecas, on its own, should make efforts to obtain or increase assistance from the international community, such as the United Nations Development Program (UNDP) or from developed countries with similar geophysical conditions (Israel, for instance). Measures should be taken to institutionalize these initiatives to ensure that they do not come to an end when the present governor's term of office comes to a close. These measures fall within a general rural development strategy and will have an impact on migration only over the medium- and long run.

Economic-Political Constraints: Disinvestment in Agriculture

Background. Impediments to rural development are more closely related to economic policies than to social organizational features or productive techniques. In our opinion, economic policy constraints have had the most adverse effect on rural production.[12]

For example, the limited investments in the Mexican countryside reflect the unintended consequences of political decisions made in the 1940s to speed up Mexico's urban industrial development. The import-substitution development strategy, in effect since then, implicitly required the transfer of resources from the countryside to the cities.[13] Public investments were also sent to urban areas; additional resources were transferred through a policy of "guaranteed prices" for agricultural products, one of the main instruments of Mexico's development strategy. The latter process affected some sectors and regions more than others, but frequently led to the impoverishment of small holders and *ejidatarios* (small farmers, producers of stable grains).

Agricultural prices were brought down by politically and economically controlling the producers of staple grains. The government, through the National Company for Popular Foodstuffs (Compañia Nacional de Subsistencias Populares, CONASUPO) became the main purchaser of agricultural goods.[14] This policy, designed to favor urban consumers, progressively made the rural producers poorer and very often made productivity stagnate.[15]

Zacatecas, an agricultural state and a large producer of basic grains, was also the direct victim of these processes, although it should be remarked that, from the outset, its population had a survival strategy—the tradition of its farmers migrating to the United States.

Problems Stemming from Current Neoliberalist Economic Development Strategies

In recent years, the constraints imposed by a recessive economic policy have further damaged small farmers. It would seem that the political system is today trapped in its liberal rhetoric. Because of the Mexican farmers' lack of international competitiveness, it seems more logical, from the point of view of Mexico's leaders, to import relatively cheap grain instead of buying it from inefficient domestic producers.[16] Refusing to modify its macroeconomic policies, the government has up to now resisted increasing prices to domestic producers. This may have some economic logic, but it does not seem to be politically sensible. This policy has made the production of basic agricultural staples plummet.[17] The inevitable rise in imports and the associated political crisis have reached a point that is undesirable for everyone. Recently, a "high level" source finally announced the future rise in guaranteed prices,[18] although other signs indicate that they will not rise very much.[19]

Zacatecas is a good example of the weakness of price policy in agriculture. The state has an important number of producers who, overcoming geophysical constraints, have become significant producers of basic staples, mainly beans.[20] Some of these producers have joined forces and have developed defense mechanisms to fight official coercion. This has led to some minor problems and has made the relationship of the producers with the state government somewhat difficult. But the biggest difficulty is the very low prices that the government purchasing agency pays for their products.[21] The "Guillermo Aguilera Cabrera Ejidos Union" of Fresnillo is a good example of regional impoverishment brought about by low agriculture prices. In January 1989, some of the farmers belonging to the Union were getting ready to migrate north as seasonal workers. Their purpose was to earn money and make up for the losses they were sure to incur during the winter's planting cycle.

This policy urgently needs to be reversed. Sooner or later the government will have to confront the economic and political consequences of removing agricultural subsidies to urban consumers. Other analysts concur with this view.[22]

Regionally Differentiated Guaranteed Prices. Aside from gradual modifications in the *national* guaranteed price policy, we would suggest setting differential guaranteed price scales to favor Zacatecan and HPA farmers. We propose a pilot program that will provide higher guaranteed prices for products originating from high emigration areas.[23] The results of the pilot program would be evaluated by independent specialists after two years, or four consecutive agricultural cycles, and its results would be compared with those in other high emigration areas following different migration-reducing strategies or in areas not pursuing any particular development program.

It should be noted that, in an informal talk, the Secretary of Planning and Comptrollership of the state government came out against a regionally differentiated guaranteed price policy. He argued that cereal production would shift to the favored areas. Instead, he outlined a strategy for direct technical assistance to producers to be provided by extension agents whose compensation would be linked to the economic success, or failure, of the farmers under their advice. His proposal is attractive to the extent that it would depend on the political commitment of the state and not on the federal government. But, we have more faith in the direct response of farmers to better prices for their products.

Development of Fruit Production in the State

In recent years, many high emigration municipalities of Zacatecas have increasingly been growing commercial fruit, mainly guavas (in Apozol and Jalpa) and peaches (in Jerez). According to local observers, this process has been accelerated by migrant remittances. This is a logical sequence for the region: once basic family needs are met, remaining resources are used to buy cattle or land. The planting of fruit trees is ideally suited to the migrant laborers or farmers of the region since it is an investment that has to be looked after personally only once a year.

The increase in fruit growing has attracted various agroindustrial plants, a development of which the state government is very proud.[24] These include peach or guava packers in Calera, Chalchihuites, Jerez, Jalpa and Apozo[25] and a canning plant in Huanusco. These agroindustries are good examples of the productive use of workers' remittances. These initiatives deserve additional support.

Policies to Encourage the Further Growth of Fruit Production. We propose a program of technical support to increase the quality and quantity of fruit production in the state and another to promote the marketing of Zacatecan fruit products in neighboring urban markets.[26] Support for the first of the programs would come from CONAFRUT (Comisión Nacional de Fruticultura-Nacional, The National Fruit-Growing Commission), and for the second program, from CANACO (Cámara Nacional de Comercio—National Chamber of Commerce), CAMPECO (Cámara Nacional del Pequeño Comercio-National Chamber for Small Scale Commerce) and the trucker associations. In a second stage, the producers' organizations should be encouraged by the state's development agencies to establish more ambitious agroindustrial projects and to penetrate the markets of Mexico City, as well as those of Texas and California.

VI. LIVESTOCK POLICY

Traditionally, the arid northern areas of Mexico, including Zacatecas, have been oriented toward open range cattle raising.[27] Cattle raising in Zacatecas is recovering from a severe drop in production experienced during the late 1970s. This recovery seems to be associated (at least in the "canyons area") with remittance income.[28] One analyst has indicated that it "would be hard to find an explanation for it [the recovery of the sector] in a change in the (traditional) way in which the sector grew since the current growth seems to derive from the greater profits yielded by export activities."[29]

It has often been noted that this activity is weakly linked to the rest of the national economy. Under present conditions, cattle raising is far from labor-intensive. These criticisms also apply for cattle raising for export in the state, even though it contributes 50 percent of the state's agricultural and livestock product.[30] This situation highlights the need to increase value-added south of the border and not only in Zacatecas. This matter falls within the jurisdiction of the Undersecretary for Livestock in the Ministry of Agriculture and Water Resources.[31]

The recent liberalization of Mexican cattle exports,[32] which did away with the practice of assigning some cattle raising areas for export and others for domestic production, might harm Zacatecas if the state's cattle raisers do not increase their competitiveness *vis-á-vis* their counterparts in southern and southeastern Mexico.

Pilot Plan for Increasing Local Value-Added

We propose a pilot program to *increase value-added* and *promote exports* within the state government's Special Livestock Program. Like the overall program, the pilot program would be sponsored by the Ministry of Agriculture and Water Resources, in conjunction with the state of Zacatecas' Ministry for Development and the state's livestock associations. Mexican cattle raisers, and not only those from Zacatecas, should evaluate the feasibility of having Mexican feed lots and of increasing their output of dressed carcasses and ground meat for the American market. The export promotion plan would provide fiscal incentives for the establishment of feed lots in Zacatecas.

The value-added plan would further encourage the planting of pastures and feed grains. It would first foster—through tax credits—linkages between feed lots and producers of cattle fodder in Zacatecas. In a second state, the plan would enhance linkages between local tanners and suppliers of hides with the shoe making industry in the nearby city of León, Guanajuato and with manufacturers of leather garments, both locally and in Mexico City.

VII. ORGANIZATION FOR AGRICULTURAL AND LIVESTOCK PRODUCTION

There have been numerous attempts in Mexico to create independent organizations to promote agriculture. Of particular interest are those that seek to bring technology and organizational skills to the countryside. There have been successful experiences, such as those of the Mexican Foundation for Rural Development, The Rain, Communal Labor and Food Programs sponsored by the International Labor Organization (ILO) and the United Nations Development Program (UNDP) in the state of Oaxaca,[33] and the Service, Development and Peace (SEDEPAC A.C.). Still others, such as Cooperative Without Frontiers, with headquarters in Querétaro, start off by organizing migrant workers into labor unions and seek to channel savings into productive uses in Mexico.

Aware of the importance of the seminal accomplishments of these organizations, we suggest that their experiences be subjected to detailed analysis. Many of those experiences are surely applicable to Zacatecas and to many other regions of rural Mexico.

Overview of Experiences in Rural Organization

It is essential to take stock of the experiences of rural development organization in other states of the country—especially those with large peasant populations (Tlaxcala or Oaxaca), or with significant migrant flows to the United States (Jalisco or Michoacan). A comparative perspective of the experiences of these states in promoting rural development would constitute an indispensable input for similar efforts in Zacatecas.

VIII. POLICIES FOR THE CONSERVATION AND RATIONAL USE OF WATER RESOURCES

More than half of Mexico's territory is arid or semiarid. As a result, it is essential to formulate policies for the conservation and efficient use of water resources. The north central region of Zacatecas is desert-like and the regions with the highest migratory rates are semiarid. Zacatecas should be one of the main targets of a national water policy.

A policy to enhance agricultural and livestock production (labor-intensive or not, whether or not intended to keep labor within the state), is unthinkable in the absence of minimal water resources. Even those minimal levels are lacking in Zacatecas.[34]

The paucity of rivers has limited the construction of large dams and irrigation works, although there are some small dams along the southern canyons. For that reason, the pumping of underground water is an important element in the state's rural development projects. The drilling of numerous wells has permitted the rapid expansion of irrigated agriculture. In fact, the irrigated area, which from 1960 to 1970 remained stable at 50,000 hectares, has tripled in the last 20 years. In the three years of the present administration, it has grown by 26,000 hectares. This constitutes a major effort, but one that may carry serious implications for the future. We wonder (in light of the experience of the neighboring La Laguna region) if studies have been made to determine suitable rates for pumping underground water.

Limits to Growth in Zacatecas

A first step in assessing the agricultural potential of the state consists of determining the extraction and replenishment rates of the state's aquifers. Technicians from the Ministry of Agriculture and Water Resources, the National Water Commission and the FICAR, already active in Zacatecas, could advise the state government and—if they have not yet done so— recommend suitable rates for extracting underground water.

A second stage would consist of contrasting the state census of water resources with the census of soil resources, in order to derive a first approximation of the theoretical limits to agricultural exploitation according to region and existing technology. The exercise would provide probable agricultural production and employment "ceilings". It might also be possible to evaluate the maximum extent of industrial activities, as well as the potential for urban growth. What we are proposing, in brief, is a far-reaching study of the possibilities and limitations of the state's growth.

It has been asserted that a good deal of the rain that falls in Mexico drains off into the sea without being used and that the infrastructure for retaining, storing and distributing it for use is lacking.[35] It is important that Zacatecas make efforts to reverse this situation.

Evaluation and Possible Broadening of the Program to Build Drinking Troughs

The state government has long had a program for building drinking troughs, many of which are visible from the state's highways. The Ministry of Agriculture and Water Resources, the municipalities and the cattle raisers all take part in this program. The present administration claims to have built 1,660 drinking troughs (one for every four rural communities).[36] We wonder if there has been an independent evaluation or a cost-

benefit analysis of this program. If not, we propose that such an evaluation be made to decide if it is desirable to continue the program.

Attention to Other State Conservation and Use of Water Programs

The Government of the state of Oaxaca (as Zacatecas, one of the poorest
states in Mexico) has initiated a program called "Rain, Communal Labor
and Food."[37] Although its results have yet to be evaluated and the social
structure in Oaxaca is considerably different from that in Zacatecas, the
Zacatecan government should give careful attention to the preliminary results of the Oaxacan program.

IX. MINING, INDUSTRIAL, AND SERVICE POLICIES

Mining

Mining, as the rest of the national economy, is undergoing a restructuring process. We will point out some measures that might be encouraged
by the state government without interfering with the restructuring policies of the federal government.[38]

Mining in Mexico has functioned as an economic "enclave". Zacatecas
is no exception to this rule. Zacatecas or this state have not benefitted
from mining operations but have endured many of its negative effects.
Even high levels of economic activity have not generated self-sustaining
growth of regional demand.[39] The challenge for sectoral/regional policies
is to develop mechanisms for integrating the mining sector into the
regional economy.

In Mexico, the mining sector is part of an exceptional juridical regime.
The Mexican constitution grants the nation direct control of underground
resources. The federal government is the owner/administrator of these
resources and has discretionary authority to grant private entities permission to develop them.

This *sui generis* interpretation of national ownership does not extend to
the state governments which, for their part, are careful to avoid conflict
with the federal authorities over mining. The forced silence that state governments maintain, vis-á-vis the federal government, would not be of
great significance were it not for the fact that the benefits arising from the
activity bypass the producing states as well as the miners themselves.
The benefits accrue to prosperous firms and entrepreneurs, as well as the
dominant economic centers in Mexico or abroad.

Renegotiation of the State's Share of Revenue Obtained from the Mining Sector.
The state government of Zacatecas has begun to negotiate to correct this
situation. It has managed to register in the state firms with mining operations there. Hence, these firms contribute a portion of their taxes to

Zacatecas, rather than paying their full tax obligation to the central government. While this was a beneficial first step, there is still a need for further negotiations with the business sector and the central government (the latter to bring in line federal spending in the state to Zacatecas contribution to the national real product).

Policies to Encourage Greater Participation of the Mining Sector in the State's Development: Encouragement for Linking Mining and Other Complementary Activities. Through negotiation with the federal government, it might be easier to increase its share in mining tax revenues than to increase tax rates for mining firms active in the state. This might be difficult to accomplish from a legal standpoint. Nevertheless, we feel that marginally increasing tax rates for mining operations in Zacatecas would not unduly compromise their profitability. Through their fiscal contributions, mining firms could assist the development of Zacatecas.

The aim of the negotiations to be conducted between the state and the mining companies is to find ways to get them more involved in the Zacatecan economy. The first stage would be to encourage them to establish smelting and refining processes in Zacatecas. Options would have to be studied for locating metal processing facilities in the regions where the metals are mined.[40] In a second phase, the state would undertake a revision of its economic policies toward the sector with a view to creating the necessary conditions to promote forward and backward linkages. This might require an assessment of potential markets, although there are reasons to believe that potential linkages could be forged with such activities as apparel making and the manufacture of simple mining tools. There are fewer options for forward linkages, but the state may want to consider promoting coining money or producing jewelry for the export market. Training would be a necessary component of these efforts.

The task of finding productive linkages for the state's mining sector might not be so difficult. Contrary to what theory on the localization of industry might predict, the minerals mined in Zacatecas are smelted outside the state.[41] The state's strategy should be to increase value-added for the metals mined in the state. A suitable combination of tax incentives and disincentives premised on nonsubsidized mineral transport fees should reorient smelting and refining activities "toward raw materials".

X. RENEGOTIATION OF THE AMOUNT OF FEDERAL INVESTMENTS IN THE STATE

The state's finances are extremely precarious. In fiscal year 1988–1989, total revenues (in U.S. dollars) were not more than $126 million. Of these, $65 million were direct state revenues (the federal government's contribution, which is, allocated to current spending) and $61 million from the

Convenio Unico de Desarrollo (CUD),[42] a development fund vested by the federal government, as well as its beneficiaries.

But federal injustice toward Zacatecas is even more evident when the state's contribution to the current balance of payments is taken into account. This contribution is estimated at some $200 million a year and is made up of migrant remittances. These more than triple the total investment made by CUD. Zacatecas' contribution to the federal government is significantly higher than its tax revenues or its domestic product. The state's claim on the federation is more than reasonable: federal spending in the state should be in proportion to Zacatecas' overall contribution to capital formation in Mexico, in order to reduce the unfair exchange between the state and the federation. The federal government continues to ignore this claim, at its peril.

XI. POLICIES FOR THE EXPANSION OF THE STATE'S INDUSTRIAL INFRASTRUCTURE

As an old mining enclave, Zacatecas experienced an unhealthy process of capital accumulation. In the view of some, no savings were generated in the region. As a result, a manufacturing industry geared to satisfy regional needs did not evolve because mining did not encourage associated industrial activity.[43] Given the functional nonexistence of local investment capital, the timidity of national investors (which at times has bordered on abdicating historical rights) and the almost inevitable local dependence on outside investors, it seems logical to analyze the potential for promoting industrial enclaves which might gradually emerge as export platforms.

Industrial Feasibility Studies

It is necessary, first of all, to evaluate Zacatecas' advantages and disadvantages with regard to this type of industrialization: that is, to carry out industrial feasibility studies. Whether or not to initiate promotional policies would depend on the ratio of expected employment benefits to the social and environmental costs. If the decision is to go ahead, consideration would have to be given to the construction of the industrial, communications and service infrastructure needed to promote the location of in-bond industries. It would also be necessary to establish training programs for industrial workers. Skilled labor and a suitable infrastructure would have to compensate for Zacatecas' distance disadvantage in relation to other states closer to the United States.[44]

Designing Sectoral and Regional Specialization Policies

It would be essential to fashion a sectoral specialization strategy to identify the type of in-bond plants the state would like to attract. This would include industries more prone or with more possibilities of promoting local development or with low water requirements, for example. At the same time, it would be necessary to select the best site(s) for the proposed Zacatecan export platform(s). For these activities to prosper, secondary and higher education should be reoriented toward training activities relevant to the new industry.

Note on the Maquiladora Project

In recent years, reference has often been made to the possibilities offered by export platforms as elements in development strategies. In Mexico, these notions have become a new rhetoric. It would seem that every investor or producer wants to be part of the *maquiladora* industry, but without considering the requirements for exporting from specific regions. It is natural that many regions with stagnant economies seek the *maquiladora* industry as a development alternative. Some regions, however, may not be capable of achieving that objective under present conditions. They are far from the producers of components, their communications are deficient, they are unfamiliar with distribution circuits or their labor forces may be inadequate. Some of these regions should reconsider their real prospects of becoming export platforms and instead focus their comparative advantages on producing for the domestic market. Zacatecas may be one such region.

XII. POLICIES WITH RESPECT TO MIGRANTS IN THE UNITED STATES

In the past 80 years, the state's excess labor has eliminated itself by migrating to cities within Mexico and to the United States. Many workers still emigrate from Zacatecas; the latest census shows Zacatecas to be one of the states with the highest migration rates.

The state government, therefore, must have policies on this matter. They should have at least two components: "external" and "domestic"— the former toward emigrants who reside in the United States; the latter toward seasonal migrant workers who usually make their home in Zacatecas.

The state government can no longer disregard its migrant workers. The present administration has designed a plausible "external" policy. It does not, however, have a similar "domestic" policy. Migrant worker policies should be intended to reassess their social significance. Zacatecas would have much to gain if state authorities were to acknowledge the personal sacrifice made by the migrant workers, as well as their contributions to the state's economy. The state should also implement policies to maximize the benefits of migration while reducing their negative consequences.

Maximizing the Use of Remittances

Bureaucratic inertia and the guilt feelings with which the federal and state governments deal with the migration of Mexican workers to the United States have prevented the design of simple local strategies to benefit from utilization of migrants' remittances. Some initiatives could be oriented toward:

1) reducing the leakages of migrant workers' remittances;
2) organizing social networks to channel remittances from abroad; and
3) promoting the allocation of remittances to productive uses.

Reducing Remittance Leakages

Various estimates suggest that Zacatecas' share in Mexican migration to the United States is about 7 percent. It is reasonable to assume that the state holds a similar share of the remittances sent by the migrants to their families in Mexico. If this is so, the Zacatecan economy receives approximately 200 million dollars each year. Remittances account, therefore, for about three times the state's tax revenues and the state's investment through the CUDs in 1989 (in 1987, they would have been 40 times greater).[45]

It would be in the best interests of the state and federal governments of Mexico for U.S. agricultural wages to rise and for the emigrants' propensity to save to increase. While these factors cannot be manipulated, measures can be taken by the state government to try to reduce the flow of remittance income toward unintended beneficiaries and to keep it within the state. It is known that undocumented workers are subject to extortion by the police.[46] Postal Service employees take advantage of the naivete of some migrants and steal cash sent through the mail. It is also in the interest of Zacatecas that remittances do not end up in other regions. Remittances ideally should be used (in as many transactions as possible) for the purchase of locally produced goods. In other words, the state should attempt to take full advantage of the multiplier effect of income earned abroad. One alternative is to gradually develop an attractive line of locally produced goods and services (agricultural and livestock inputs such as seeds, fertilizers, cattle, simple tools) and marketed at the right time. The state planners should consider incentives for marketing these inputs in "*tianguis*" (local markets) or regional fairs.

The question of who handles foreign exchange in the region is also relevant. In Zacatecas, the regional banks are at a disadvantage with the money exchange houses and even with private individuals. If the intention is for dollars to enter the local banking system, or even to stay in Mexico, the banks should be allowed to offer a premium for the dollars sold in the region.

Organizing Social Networks to Channel Remittances

The state government should allow—if not encourage—church organizations to serve as a conduit for the transfer of remittances from Zacatecans residing abroad. The U.S. government worked with church organizations to process visa applications for the Special Agricultural Worker (SAW).[47] It makes sense to cooperate with the Catholic Church for the reliable transfer of foreign remittances to rural families. There seems no other comparable organization in Mexico that can undertake a task of this nature. If the government does not take the initiative, sooner or later the Church will do it on its own; in some cases, it already does.

Promoting the Allocation of Remittances to Productive Uses

The amount of money spent by migrants upon their return or when visiting Zacatecas is significant. Some of the migrants openly squander their savings. Regional and national businesses strategically organize "fairs" or festivities at certain times of the year. They thus encourage nonproductive consumption without counter-measures to encourage the useful or rational spending of remittances. Community organizations, be they religious or not, should be asked to advise emigrants to use their remittances for productive purposes. The efforts of these institutions should be decisively supported by the state's educational and social agencies.

XIII. TOURISM POLICY

Zacatecas has some features that make it particularly attractive for national tourism. The whole state, especially its colonial capital, which has been splendidly restored, has numerous sites of historical interest. In addition, as the birthplace of the poet Ramon Lopez Velarde, it represents the quintessence of "Mexicanness". This makes Zacatecas a special cultural attraction.

Some nearby cities have made use of their relative advantages. For example, the San Marcos Fair in the neighboring state of Aguascalientes generates considerable economic activity. Another example is the Cervantino Festival in Guanajuato. The former is a popular fair, the latter a cultural event. Zacatecas could organize an annual literary fair, for example, that offers a substantial monetary prize.

Comprehensive Use of the Tourism Potential of Zacatecas' Unique Features

Mexico is engaged in an ambitious program for the promotion of international tourism. Recent studies have suggested, however, that the multiplier effects of domestic tourism are far greater than those of international tourism.[48] This suggests that a study to promote domestic tourism ought to receive the support of the tourist authorities.

There is already a festival in Zacatecas. It should be made bigger, and should seek to motivate Zacatecans living in the United States to visit their friends and relatives, even if for a few days.

XIV. POLICY FOR SELLING PRODUCER SERVICES

The national railroad network has its nodal points in Zacatecas-Aguascalientes. This was evident even at the time of the Revolution: Zacatecan towns became strategic sites for controlling the flow of arms and merchandise. The national railroad company has recognized the centrality of the region by locating its main workshop for repairing railroad cars in Aguascalientes (100 kilometers from Zacatecas).

Taking Advantage of the Central Location of Zacatecas

With a scenario of increased trade and travel to and from the United States, the "centrality" of Zacatecas should not be overlooked.[49] In the *long term*, a regional development strategy might consider providing maintenance services to airlines and trucking and bus services from a strategic location in Zacatecas. The state could also serve as a distribution (warehousing facility) point for firms marketing their products throughout Mexico. Presently, most central facilities are in Mexico City. This subject deserves specialized attention.

XV. EDUCATIONAL POLICY: REORIENTATION OF REGIONAL EDUCATION

The role of education in the development process has always been emphasized. It has always been understood that the payoff of education will come over the long term. Recently, Mexico assigned a privileged role to investment (the right investment at the right time and in the right place), hoping to accelerate the development process. This is now being reassessed, and education has again come to the fore as a catalyst for development. We also realize that the long term is not as far away as we once thought.

Technical Training and Education for Water Conservation

The poorer Mexican states, Zacatecas included, face the challenge of improving their educational systems to match national standards and the need to revise their high school and university curricula to bring them into line with their development needs. In this regard, the need for strengthening agrotechnical training in the state of Zacatecas is evident, as is the urgency of promoting water conservation for environmental and economic reasons. This should be accompanied by a strengthening of technical-industrial education if Zacatecas is to succeed in developing a *maquiladora* industry. Technical-agricultural schools and the Centros de Educación Técnica Industrial (CETI) must, therefore, be strengthened.

XVI. SOME FINAL REMARKS

To summarize, the measures proposed here are ranked and classified in this concluding section. We do so, first of all, according to geographic specificity (Table 1), i.e., according to whether the proposed measures have direct or indirect effects on emigration areas. In that way, we further distinguish between the measures likely to have an impact on high push areas or on Zacatecas as a whole. We further differentiate policies according to whether they should have an effect over the short- medium- or long term. Finally, we also identify the source—state or federal—of the final decision pertaining to the policy in question. When appropriate, we name the agencies directly responsible for the decision.

The organization of the proposals enables us to identify some obvious relations. There is a group of proposals directed toward the HPAs that are handled by the state and whose effects are short term. They have to do with remittances and their productive use. Other short-term policies specific to the region, but dependent on federal decisions, are likely to be the most significant. These include, for example, changes in guaranteed prices, federal investment in Zacatecas and the protection of migrant workers upon their return to Mexico.

State support for fruit growing and the organizing of fairs and *tianguis* (markets) to maximize multiplier effects of emigrants' remittances are also specific to the HPAs. Responsibility for their implementation falls to the state and their effects would be felt over the medium term. Although some of the proposals are specific to the whole state, they will also benefit the migrant-sending regions within the state. There are three proposals that fall within the state's domain. Two would require close collaboration with the private sector. These are the state tourism project and the shared contribution that mining firms could make to the development of Zacatecas. The third is completely within the state's domain—that of

TABLE 1

ZACATECAS: STRATEGIES FOR REACTIVATING THE REGIONAL/STATE ECONOMY, ORIENTED TOWARD BRINGING DOWN THE EMIGRATION RATE

Policies or policy actions	Spatial specificity	Expected effects	Decision-making level	Collaboration level
Remittances: Encouraging their productive investment	HPA	ST	state	business
Remittances: Channels for sending them	HPA	ST	state	church
Remittances: Reducing leakages outside the sector	HPA	ST	federal	
Remittances: Reducing leakages outside the region	HPA	MT	state	business
Federal investment: Negotiating higher federal spending in region	HPA	ST	federal	
Agriculture: Special guaranteed prices for regional production of staples	HPA	ST	federal	state
Agriculture: Engouraging regional production and distribution of fruit	HPA	MT	state	
Water: Evaluating and enlarging water trough program	ZAC	ST	state	
Tourist Services: Using the exceptional character of Zacatecas	ZAC	ST	state	business
Mining: Negotiating business' share in development	ZAC	ST	state	business
Education: Reorienting agrotechnical and industrial education	ZAC	MT	state	federal
In-bond: Designing strategies for sectoral specialization	ZAC	MT	state	business
In-bond: Designing strategies for regional specialization	ZAC	MT	state	
Mining: Encouraging linkages between mining and other activities	ZAC	LT	state	business
Producer Services: Taking advantage of Zacatecas' central location	ZAC	LT	state	fed-business
Agricultural: Pilot Plan for increasing local value-added in Zacatecan cattle raising	ZAC	LT	state	federal
Agriculture: Reactivation of the National Commission on Arid Areas	ZAC	LT	federal	state
Water: Far-reaching study on limits to state's growth	ZAC		state	
Agriculture: Analysis of experiences in organizing production	ZAC		state	
Water: Other state programs on the use of water resources	ZAC		state	
Business: Feasibility studies for independent industry in the state	ZAC		state.	

HPA: High-push areas
ZAC: Zacatecas
ST: Short-term
MT: Medium-term
LT: Long-term

broadening the program for building drinking troughs.

The table also identifies other medium- and long-term measures. These refer to the possible promotion of the maquiladora export industry and to the reorienting of the state's agrotechnical and industrial education. Long-term measures include the plan for increasing value-added in cattle raising, developing linkages between mining and other productive activities and making use of the "centrality" of Zacatecas. The proposals for concrete studies, although relevant and potentially quite important, have no specific time horizon.

We have identified what, in our opinion, are viable initiatives for the development of Zacatecas. They are surely not the only ones, but certainly are the most important; they could become the central core of a formal development strategy for developing what we have called the HPAs.

Independent of how well we achieved our task, the most complicated assignment lies ahead of us: putting the proposals into practice. And this can happen only if there is the necessary political will.

NOTES

1. Center for Social Research on Regional Development (CISDER), "Zacatecas: áreas de expulsión de fuerza de trabajo" (Report prepared for the Commission for the Study of International Migration and Cooperative Economic Development, Washington, D.C., January 1989, mimeographed).

2. Constitutional Government of the United States of Mexico/Constitutional Government of Zacatecas, *Zacatecas Plan 1986–1992*; Genero Borrego, State Governor, *1st, 2nd and 3rd Annual Reports on the State* (1987, 1988 and 1989)

3. It is not sensible to recommend, for example, how best to use land in Zacatecas and ignore the existence of the National Commission on Arid Areas (CONAZA). This institution may now perform more of a political than a technical function though.

4. In a presidential system like Mexico's, where the municipal authorities are deprived of resources and political power, the policies, if they are to be effective, must almost always stem from the federal government.

5. David Barkin and Timothy King, *Desarrollo Económico Regional*, 3rd ed. (Mexico City: Siglo XXI, 1978), chapters II, III, and IV.

6. In recent months, on the pretext of pursuing drug traffickers, but perhaps testing the public's response, the police were used to limit the flow of migrants. Rejection of this policy was immediate.

7. The orientation of the proposed change was anticipated when it was asserted that: "1.3. . . . various sectors of production have shown deficiencies in their dynamism or even have stagnated or shrunk. In agriculture, there are many holdings of less than 5 hectares, mostly on land of poor quality. This situation makes it difficult to adopt modern and efficient techniques." *National Development Plan*, 1989–1994 (Mexico City, May 1989).

8. "While we are fighting for better and more realistic guaranteed prices, the government upsets our hopes by opening the borders to imports," said the members of the National Peasants Confederation (CNC) in their last Ordinary Congress. "Estímulos y precios justos buscan productores: Autosuficiencia en maíz en, tres años, prevé la SARH," *La Jornada*, 17 December 1989.

9. Last November, the Secretariat of Finance proposed to the Chamber of Deputies a Federal Revenue bill that included, as part of the tax "adjustments", the elimination of the special tax treatment for agricultural producers, an exceptional fiscal privilege they have enjoyed since 1955. The political opposition as a whole and some of the official party's members rejected the proposal. The political cost of the initiative was very high.

10. Despite its aridity, only 1.5 percent of Mexico's agricultural land was irrigated in 1980. With even less water, only 1 percent of Zacatecas was irrigated (3 million and 50,000 hectares, respectively). Instituto Nacional de Estadística, Geografía e Informática (INEGI), *Manual de estadisticas basicas del estado de Zacatecas* (Mexico City, 1984).

11. Zacatecas' per capita output is the second lowest in the country. Agricultural and livestock activities in 1980 contributed 23 percent to the State's product and employed nearly half of the economically active population. See INEGI, *Estructura economica del Estado de Zacatecas, Sistema de cuentas Nacionales, Estructura Económica Regional* (Mexico City, 1986).

12. In this statement, we are in agreement with all the specialized literature on Mexican agriculture. José Luís Calva, *Crísis agrícola y alimentaria en México 1982–1988* (Mexico City: Fontamara, 1988); Antonio Yunes, *Crisis de la Agricultura Mexicana* (Mexico: FCE/El Colegio de México, 1988), pp. 184–200; Fernando Paz, "Problemas y Perspectivas del Desarrollo Agrícola," in *Neolatifundismo y Explotación*, (Mexico City, Nuestro Tiempo, 1975), 4th Ed., pp. 56–104; Thierry Linck, *El Campesino Desposeído* (Mexico, CEMCA/El Colegio de Michoacán, 1988), pp. 17–37; Gustavo Esteva, *La Batalla del México Rural* (Mexico City: Siglo XXI, 1980); Cynthia Hewitt de Alcantara, *La Modernizacion de la Agricultura Mexicana, 1940–1970* (El Colegio de México, 1988), pp. 17–30; Michel Gutelman, *Capitalismo y Reforma Agraria en México* (Mexico City: ERA, 1979), pp. 241–256.

13. This interpretation is shared by the National Development Plan 1989–1994, which states that one of the nation's most serious problems is the consideration of income. "(1.3) . . . which to a great extent was the result of the industrialization strategy followed for many years, and which favored capital at the expense of labor, industry at the expense of agriculture, the city at the expense of the country. . . ."

14. According to press information, until 1987 Compañia Nacional de Subsistencias Populares (CONASUPO) held a 49.9 percent share of the marketing of corn, 80 percent of powdered milk, and 12.3 percent of beans and soya. However, in the last few years, CONASUPO's shares have dropped drastically. "Aumenta la Producción de ICONSA," *La Jornada*, 6 November 1989.

15. The case of corn is exemplary. Until 1972, Mexico exported corn and, for a few years, exported more than a million tons per year. During that period, national producers supplied more than 99 percent of national consumption. Since 1973, there has been a major drop. In 1980–1986, purchases of corn amounted to 25 percent of total agricultural imports. Since 1986, CONASUPO has imported on average 2.5 million tons of corn a year. In 1989, imports of corn accounted for 21.5 percent of national demand. In the last decade, corn imports totaled 23 million tons, according to the State of Jalisco's Research Institute on Forestry and Agriculture. "La comercialización del maíz no logra el ajuste para elevar la oferta," *La Jornada*, 16 December 1989.

16. Aside from the low productivity of Mexican farmers and the subsidies granted by foreign governments to their producers, their production costs and final domestic prices, like those on all the goods produced in Mexico, decline from day to day vis-á-vis that of foreign producers. This is due to the sliding peso-dollar rate and progressive overevaluation of the peso in relation to the dollar. It is, therefore, not surprising that Mexican cereals are increasingly unable to compete with imports.
   A recent study, comparing the evolution of domestic prices to "real guaranteed price" (average international price, plus transport, plus protection to domestic farmers), concludes that guaranteed prices have lowered national producers' in-

come and redistributed it to urban areas and industry. Quoted in Fernando Cal-
zada and Francisco Hernández, "Descapitalizacion Agrícola," *La Jornada*, 7
November 1988.

A few months ago, the domestic scandal about guaranteed prices made it clear
that they are one product of an agreement between the technico-political authorities of some ministries, which frequently compete among themselves. The
technocrats act under a constraint: the government's agreements with the IMF,
which force domestic prices into line with international prices. In the interministerial discussions, some groups are supposedly more radical than the Fund;
others seem to act on the assumption that the constraint is more formal than real.
Yet others feel that guaranteed prices should ignore this constraint and that prices
be fixed on the basis of domestic production costs. No one could fail to share the
intention of getting the economy and public finances back on sound footing. But,
many of us disagree with the treatment given to some sectors of the economy,
especially agriculture, where the poorest sectors of the population are found. Our
planners, in their search for macroeconomic equilibrium, at any cost, have made
agricultural production plummet.

17. There is abundant documentation for this statement. Here we mention just a
few examples. According to the National Agricultural and Livestock Council
(Consejo Nacional Agropecuario, CNA), in 1988, between 7.5 and 8 million tons
of basic grains were imported. It is anticipated that, in 1989, imports will reach 12
million tons. Since the guaranteed prices do not cover the producers' expectations, the CNA states that sowing for this cycle has declined because there is no
confidence of obtaining a good price for the harvest. "CNA: Se deberá importar 12
millones de granos básicos," *La Jornada*, 11 January 1989. The President of the National Federation of Bean Producers (Federación Nacional de Productores de Frijol), when demanding 1,711,000 pesos for a ton of beans (now paid at the rate of
760,000 pesos), warned that the output deficit is already 200,000 tons. He demanded that the two million pesos per ton that the government pays to foreign
farmers should be used to encourage national production. "De no más del 17 percent será el alza para frijol, trigo y arroz," *La Jornada*, 8 November 1989. According
to figures from the Bank of Mexico, between January and August 1989, agricultural imports recorded a 36 percent increase in comparison with the same
period the year before. "Déficit de 8 millones 196 mil dolares en la balanza agrícola
en el lapso enero-agosto," *El Financiero*, 21 November 1989.

Some readers might believe it useless to demand higher guaranteed prices. Recent events, unfortunately, prove that it is not. A year ago, on a working trip
through Zacatecas, we witnessed the disgust and disillusionment of the Fresnillo
bean producers. It is now known that bean production in Zacatecas during the
spring-summer cycle declined by a third and that the authorities, with the help of
the army, forced the producers to sell their scant production to CONASUPO.

18. The same "highly placed" source announced that guaranteed prices for corn
and beans for the present agricultural cycle should be 435,000 and 930,000 pesos a
ton, respectively. "Aumentos de 41.69 y 17.9 percent para maíz y frijol," *La Jornada*, 31 October 1989.

19. The Subcommission for an Agreement on Agricultural and Livestock Products (Subcomisión de Concertación de Products, Agropecuarios) announced that
the new guaranteed price for beans will not be more than 17 percent higher. "De
no más de 17 percent será el alza para frijol, trigo y arroz," *La Jornada*, 8 November
1989.

20. At the end of the 1970s, Zacatecas was already a big producer of basic staples, especially beans. The 1980s confirmed its specialization, thanks in part to the weak growth of national production: in 1985, a third of the beans produced in Mexico were from Zacatecas. See following table, taken from Raül Delgado Wise, "Consideraciones sobre la crisis y orientación del crecimiento en Zacatecas," in *Diálogo*, Revista de la UAZ, no. 4 (November–December 1987) p. 46.

21. Everyone knows that official purchasing prices are today even lower than so-called "production costs." The latter are really the costs of the for-production inputs, since they do not include labor costs. Ignorance on the part of producers and the way official credit is handled have made this situation possible. The peasants are in debt to the official banking institutions; they, in turn, operate permanently in the red, but the producer remains tied politically. From time to time, the government grants credits, thus enhancing the president's image.

22. An economist has recently proposed an emergency strategy for overcoming stagnation in agriculture. It is oriented toward the small farmer under the leadership of the state and involves the reincorporation of "vast agricultural areas and large segments of the rural population displaced by the modernization process that went hand-in-hand with Mexico's entry into the world market." The reincorporated peasants would produce for the domestic market. In brief, his proposal is to foster the production of basic foodstuffs on rain-fed land that is presently idle. The key element of his program is to "raise the price of corn to a suitable level, so as to guarantee a minimum wage . . . to the producers who cultivate medium quality land in the rain-fed areas." The higher prices for the agricultural products would be made up for by subsidies to the most poverty-stricken sections of the population and by the direct and indirect effects that the increase in the farmers' income would have on the whole of the Mexican economy. He backs his arguments with an econometric model that estimates the multiplier effects of each peso paid to the sector. The author even finds his proposal compatible with the Mexican government's macroeconomic adjustment strategy. David Barkin, "La económia de guerra: una estratégia rural frente a la crisis," *La Jornada*, 10 April 1989. Another version of this proposal was published under the title, "El sector social, al rescate de México," *El Sector Social de la Económia, Una Opción ante la Crisis*, A. Labra, coordinator (Mexico City: Siglo XXI Editors/UNAM, 1988).

23. This proposal is not a novel one. In fact, some farmers requested it a year ago. "Piden campesinos fijar por region precios de garantía," *La Jornada*, 22 December 1988.

24. Borrego, *First, Second and Third Annual Reports* (1987, 1988 and 1989).

25. Notice the agroindustrial orientation toward the Guadalajara urban market.

26. Zacatecas' peculiar central position or "centrality" is an advantage for marketing this type of article. Its producing regions are located at 310 and 450 kilometers from the second and third biggest urban markets in the country, Guadalajara and Monterrey. This does not include other neighboring urban markets which are significant in size: Aguascalientes (131 kms.), San Luis Potosí (190 kms.), and even Durango (22), Saltillo (365), and Torreón (378).

27. Cuauhtemoc Esparza, *Historia de la Ganadería en Zacatecas 1531–1911* (Zacatecas: UAZ, 1988); also, Pedro Martínez, "Transformacion de la ganaderia en

TABLE 1

EVOLUTION OF THE MAIN AGRICULTURAL PRODUCTS IN ZACATECAS 1970–1986

	Beans		Corn	
Year	Tons	National %	Tons	National %
1970	85,477	9.2	291,133	3.3
1975	67,100	6.5	85,300	1.0
1976	77,800	10.5	236,800	2.3
1977	119,000	15.5	257,049	2.5
1978	163,923	17.3	351,817	3.2
1979	84,381	14.0	139,206	1.4
1980	106,704	11.5	194,635	1.6
1981	297,006	19.4	399,028	2.7
1982	201,704	21.0	243,788	2.4
1983	363,793	28.7	459,475	3.5
1984	295,100	30.3	357,172	2.8
1985	302,203	33.4	295,744	2.1
1986	298,089		252,493	

los ochenta," in *Primer Informe de Investigacion Sobre el Estado de Zacatecas*, LII Legis-latura, Zacatecas, 1989.

28. Delgado Wise, Raul, "Consideraciones," 1987.

29. Delgado Wise, Raul, "Consideraciones," 1987.

30. Borrego, *Third Annual Report*, 1989.

31. We are not unaware of the existence of feed lot operations in the north of Mexico. This is not the case for Zacatecas. The owners of feed lots in northern Mexico are oriented toward the U.S. market and used for higher profit margins that the urban markets of central Mexico cannot provide.

32. Last November, the Secretary of Commerce announced the liberalization of cattle exports, bringing to an end a long period in which cattle raisers in northern Mexico required export permits. These were assigned annually and at the discretion of the Secretariat of Agriculture and Water Resources.

33. Ma. Antonieta Benejam, "Lluvia, tequio y alimentos: Un camino para combatir la pobreza" (November 1988, mimeograph).

34. The lack of water resources is a nationwide deficiency, although official concern is directed more to urban areas. For example, in late 1989, the deputy director of the National Water Commission announced that 24 million Mexicans had no piped drinking water in their homes. "Se estudia una inversión de 23 billones para cinco años—CNA," *La Jornada*, 20 December 1989. The following day he was removed from his post for "giving wrong information."

35. A former undersecretary for Planning in the Secretariat of Agriculture and Water Resources recently commented that there is a lack of rain water reservoirs. Approximately 75 percent of rainfall flows unused to the sea. "Faltan obras para captar y aprovechar el agua de lluvia," *La Jornada*, 20 December 1989.

36. Borrego, *Third Annual Report*, 1989.

37. Benejam, "Lluvia, tequio y alimentos," 1988.

38. An example of the policy "restructuring" was the recent decision to sell the Minera Real de Angeles, located in the Noria de Angeles municipality, Zacatecas. This is one of the biggest open seam gold and silver mines in the world. According to some reports, its starting offering price was extraordinarily low.

39. Various studies document the history of mining in Mexico. See: C. Velasco, et al., *Estado de la Minería en México (1767–1910)* (Mexico City: FCE/SEMIP, 1988); Miguel Othon de Mendizabal, *La Minera y la Metalurgia (1520–1943)* (Mexico City, 1943); D.A. Brading, *Mineros y Comerciantes en el México Borbónico (1763–1810)* (Mexico City: FCE, 1985); J.L. Sariego, et al., *El Estado y la Minería Mexicana: Política, Trabajo y Sociedad Durante el Siglo XX* (Mexico City: FCE/SEMIP, 1988). For Zacatecas, see Harry Edward Cross, *The Mining Economy of Zacatecas, Mexico in the Nineteenth Century* (Ph.D. diss., University of California, Berkeley, 1976); P.J. Bakewell, *Minería y Sociedad en el México Colonial: Zacatecas (1456–1700)* (FCE, 1984); Arturo Burnes, *La Minería en la Historia Económica de Zacatecas (1456–1876)* (Zacatecas: UAZ, 1987).

40. "The mining industry is an integrated process consisting of various basic stages: extracting, smelting and refining." "Zacatecas, because of its historic and economic phenomena . . . concentrated on the tasks of extracting, which are the ones with least value-added in mineral production. This limits the regional multiplier effect as far as production of value and employment is concerned. Miguel Ochoa Santos, "La Minería Zacatecana en los Ochenta," *Díalogo, Revista de la UAZ*, no. 10 (March–April 1989).

41. The concentrates are sent to Belgium, Greece, the United States and neighboring Mexican states for further processing. According to a report by the Commission for the Encouragement of Mining in 1988, more than 31,000 tons a day of Zacatecan concentrates are sent to San Luis Potosí, Coahuila and Chihuahua. Ochoa Santos, "La Minería Zacatecana," 1989.

42. Borrego, *Third Annual Report*, 1989.

43. Sariego, et al., *El Estado y la Minería Mexicana*, 1988.

44. The case of Ciudad Juarez is a good example. In the 1960s, federal officials and private entrepreneurs designed a regional policy directed toward converting the city into an "export platform." They may not have had a strategy for training the labor force, but did channel resources into the productive infrastructure and into promoting their project with U.S. businessmen.

45. Center for the Research and Teaching of Economics (CIDE), Regional Studies Program, "Importancia de la ejecución o puesta in march de las modificaciones a

la Ley Migratoria Estadounidense (enmiendo Simpson-Rodino): algunas respuestas políticas posibles" Brief Report (Document for restricted circulation, prepared for the Secretariat of Planning and Budget, Mexico City, August 1987, photocopy).

46. This is a national scandal. However, it is no different from what the English, for example, did last century to the Irish or their own compatriots emigrating to America. At the end of 1989, the Secretariat of the Interior put into effect a program known as "Paisano", to protect emigrants visiting Mexico. We are not aware of any prosecutions yet.

47. Two offices in the diocesan headquarters in Zacatecas and Guadalajara, and a third in a parish in the "Los Altos" region (in Pegueros, Jalisco) were providing this service throughout the region until late 1988.

48. Daniel Hernaux Nicolas and Manuel Rodriguez Woog, "Tourism and Absorption of the Labor Force in Mexico," Chapter X of this volume.

49. Economic geography uses some notions of the network analysis to study the characteristics of the road and rail systems. In them, the localities are linked together by roads and the whole set of junctions and roads makes up the network. Some junctions are more "accessible" than others, according to their relative position in the system. Thus, we understand "centrality" to be a topological characteristic of some junctions in the system.

2

Patterns of Migration and Regional Development in the State of Jalisco, Mexico

Jesús Arroyo Alejandre, Adrián de León Arias, and Basilia Valenzuela Varela

I. INTRODUCTION

Most research on migration to the United States has taken place in rural and semiurban communities in the states of Jalisco, Zacatecas and Michoacán. The resulting case studies have focused on, among other factors, the profiles of migrants, their motives for emigrating, their insertion into the U.S. labor market, the characteristics of their communities of origin and migrant remittances and their disposition.[1]

This paper features a regional analysis of the state of Jalisco, with respect to migration to the United States. It is assumed that migratory patterns are a geographical phenomenon related to inequalities in comparative socioeconomic levels in populated areas, and that both patterns and levels of migration are products of economic, social and political processes. This paper also explores ways to influence these patterns, with special reference to migration to the United States. Thus, this research is policy oriented.

The focus of this study is on the rural and semiurban population of an area in Jalisco where there is a strong "push" factor that impels people to migrate to the United States. We selected 42 municipalities with a total population of 710,000 (see method of selection in the methodological appendix). We then selected a sample of 574 families in 69 rural and semiurban communities (the sampling method is explained in the methodological appendix). The sampling is representative of the population of the area, and the units for analysis were the family and the individual, particularly the migrant. We also interviewed "key informants" in the communities where the survey was taken and in the principal towns of the municipalities where these communities were located.

This essay is a summary of a longer essay on the results of this research.[2] Here we report only the most important findings of the fieldwork and of a regional analysis of the state of Jalisco that we undertook in an effort to relate it to migration to the United States.

II. RESEARCH ON MIGRATION OF MEXICAN WORKERS TO THE UNITED STATES

We begin by outlining some of the generally accepted conclusions of scholars who have done research on the migration of Mexican workers.

Various studies agree that many migrants to the United States have traditionally come from the western region of Mexico.[3] The states of Jalisco, Michoacán[4] and Zacatecas are particularly noted for their volume and continuity of migration. With the exception of Baja California and

Chihuahua,[5] these states have the highest push indexes in the country. A fact that has been amply documented is that the migrants come mainly from rural and semiurban areas,[6] although in the last decade a greater number have come from the medium-sized and large cities.[7] It has been noted that rural sending communities can be either underdeveloped or developing; over time their conditions have changed, but not enough to stem the flow to the United States. This flow is composed primarily of male temporary workers between the ages of 20 and 28, a large proportion of whom lack legal permission to work in the United States.[8] Approximately half are married, and most have had more schooling than the Mexican national average. These migrants do not always belong to the lowest-income families in their communities; many belong to families with medium to low income.[9]

The main destinations for this type of migrant are the American states along the Mexican border, specifically California and Texas,[10] although there are also concentrations in more distant states such as Illinois and Washington, among others. The migrants generally work in agriculture, but recently increasing numbers are employed in urban production sectors.

Some scholars assert that migration presents a problem for the local communities because the flight of young, skilled men has adverse repercussions on local development. This opinion is not shared by other scholars, nor by the migrants involved or their families, who generally consider migration to the United States beneficial rather than problematic, especially when it is from places with a high rate of unemployment and underemployment. It has been shown that remittances relieve economic pressures on families since most of this money is devoted to current household expenses.[11] However, it is widely accepted that the migratory flow implies a drain of population from some rural communities because it rapidly becomes a permanent feature as a result of the establishment of migratory networks.[12] Another widely accepted view is that undocumented immigration has been beneficial to the U.S. economy.[13]

It is not yet possible to know what the long-term effects of the reform in U.S. immigration law (Immigration Reform and Control Act of 1986, IRCA) will be. However, in migrant-sending regions, particularly in Jalisco, younger people and individuals who apparently had not previously thought of abandoning their local communities have joined the migratory flow. In that sense, migration increased due to IRCA, which has also served as a mechanism for many individuals and even families to take advantage of the legalization program to obtain documents for possible future use.[14]

Although the exact number of migrants who take part in the annual flow is unknown at the present time, methodologies for estimating them are being tested. The International Labor Organization's (ILO) 1987 report estimated that the number of undocumented migrants in the United States was somewhere between 4 and 5 million, half of whom were Mexicans.[15]

The most important changes in the migratory flow are the incorporation of new areas of origin (including medium-sized urban areas and state capitals); more migrants with higher levels of training, including skilled workers, technicians and university graduates and an increased number of women. In general, women tend to form a specific migration pattern in which a large proportion are unmarried, they have higher levels of education than men and they concentrate in urban labor markets, particularly in California.[16]

III. LITERATURE ON THE LINKS BETWEEN MIGRATION AND REGIONAL DEVELOPMENT

Massey[17] reviews an extensive literature on development and migration, which looks principally at the experience of European migration to the United States and its relationship to economic cycles in both sending countries and the countries of origin. In his own study of Mexico he concludes that economic development is an incentive to international migration from poor countries to industrialized ones, particularly the United States and especially in the short term. However, Massey does not define the short term, and the regions he analyzes are large and heterogenous, so this linkage is not at all clear. He mentions that the main cause of migration is regionally uneven economic development during industrialization, a process that requires territorial concentration of capital and economic grouping in order to achieve growth of economies of scale.

Martin[18] agrees with Massey's conclusion from what he calls the "vast literature on migration and development." In areas of origin, development does not slow migration, at least in the short term. Moreover, Martin asserts that the remittances and the skills learned in receiving countries are not used to promote economic development in the communities of origin. Remittances are used, according to Martin, to buy durable consumer goods, such as houses and cars, whose economic multipliers have limited effects and can, instead, produce local inflation, thereby worsening the conditions of the inhabitants in the communities of origin in poor countries. Martin does not define short term either, nor does he see a positive effect on the areas in which the goods and services bought with remittances are produced.

Gregory[19] concludes that measures to promote development in poor sending countries have unforeseeable short-term effects. To lessen income differentials between the countries of origin and the United States, far-reaching efforts in economic development would be required to achieve small reductions in migration, at least over the short term.

Gregory is one of the few authors who implicitly takes into account trends in the world economy and Mexican macroeconomic policy in suggesting that strategies for opening up the economy and increasing exports, as a basis for growth in countries such as Mexico, may reduce emigration to the United States. Like the authors mentioned above, he studies the links between economic development and migration at the aggregate national level, but also fails to define the short and the long term.

Perhaps the most comprehensive study of the relationship between regional economic development and rural-urban migration is that carried out by Rhoda,[20] based on a review of extensive literature and on the experiences of economic development projects in Third World countries. This study is important because we believe that within Mexico such rural-urban migration is similar in many ways to that from Mexico to the United States. What changes are the "economic and cultural distances." The author's firm conclusion is that:

> in almost all cases, development activities in rural areas cannot be justified by the argument that they will diminish rural-urban migration.[21]

Arroyo's[22] study shows empirically that poor rural areas with small farms (*minifundios*), few natural resources and population pressures suffer substantial emigration. Emigration increases as these areas move into agribusiness and become part of broad national and urban markets. On the other hand, when agribusiness develops in fertile areas that have less population pressure, it is likely that the hub urban community of such areas experiences economic growth in nonagricultural activities and retains and attracts population. In general, the author states, the need to increase agricultural and livestock productivity requires concentration of resources—mainly land, mechanization and modern technology—in that sector to obtain economies of scale. Consequently, the use of manual labor is constantly reduced and rural emigration continues. However, this agricultural growth is permitting urban development in cities that are regional centers, many of which have potential for attracting migrants.

We also know that Mexican migrants' opportunities for employment and income in the United States may decrease because of IRCA.[23] Furthermore, we assume that large reductions in the income differences between Mexico and the United States are not required to achieve a slight reduction in emigration. We believe that marginal increases in opportunities for employment and income, principally in medium-sized regional cities in Mexico which have an "economic base in a stage of self-sustaining growth," may retain their population and attract some people from the countryside, thereby decreasing international migration.

The main hypothesis of this paper is that from the perspective of potential rural and semiurban migrants, the greater the distance factor (all other factors remaining constant), the less their migration to the United States. In other words, those who are most able to pay for the trip, who have greater contact with friends or relatives (information) and who have less aversion to cultural adaptation, would tend to migrate to the United States and to Mexico's metropolitan areas. Those who perceive greater distances in these areas would tend to move to the closest city that serves as a hub for most of the socioeconomic functions of these migrants' region of origin. Such migrants normally have enough information and family and friends in these cities, which from the migrants' point of view can offer greater access to job opportunities and income if the cities are dynamic and experiencing sustained growth of their economic base.[24] This kind of economic base is one which produces mainly for markets outside its region, of which it is the center, so that much of the profit is reinvested in the city, producing multiplier effects and self-sustaining growth.

We believe that it is necessary to define short term and long term to determine the effects of regional development on migratory patterns. Economic theory establishes that the short term is that period of time during which the capital equipment of productive units does not change. The long term is when changes in fixed capital are possible. We obviously cannot apply this analysis to regions or locations. Therefore, we propose a geographic definition in which the time period is implicit: the short term is when the economic base of a region or an urban center has not yet achieved self-sustaining growth; the long term is when it has reached this stage.

Since the distance factor, as well as other psychological costs due to leaving the family, are greater for migrants to the United States than for those who stay within Mexico, especially in rural-regional hub migration, international migration could decrease more rapidly if there were a more equitable geographic development within a macroeconomic growth policy based on exports. This assumes that exporting firms would not locate in large cities and could instead stimulate regional development, since exporting firms do not depend on concentrated markets.

IV. PROFILE OF JALISCO MIGRANTS TO THE UNITED STATES OVER THE PERIOD 1978–1988

To better understand the relationship between migration to the United States and development in the migrants' home communities, we have tried to develop a current profile of those individuals who leave the rural and semiurban environment. The family sample survey shows the presence of very young people in the migrant flow: 17.56 percent are between

16 and 20 years of age. On the other hand, it is notable that only 7 percent of migrants to the United States in the last decade have been over 40 due to restrictions in the U.S. labor market.

The presence of young people in the flow is an indication of how quickly people from a rural or semiurban environment acknowledge the lack of opportunities in their home communities or region. This situation is undoubtedly attributable to the stage of local development and opportunity, as well as to the local educational system, which does not give rural youth the specific skills necessary to compete in the national market. The average educational level in rural and semiurban areas with a strong push factor is six years, that is just through primary school. However, there are indications that people with more education are also starting to migrate, particularly from Guadalajara.

Nearly half, 42.35 percent, of the migrants are unmarried and three quarters of them are men who are younger and have a higher level of education than the women. The presence of women migrants should be noted in that it indicates the possibility of a mass migration and, consequently, a more rapid depopulation of the communities with the strongest push factors.

One of the problems found was the lack of diversification of the productive structures of the communities, despite the population's capacity to adapt to greater job diversity. This capacity is a wasted potential, as can be seen from the way in which migrants fit into the labor market in the United States. Although the largest group of migrants, 18.13 percent, are employed in agricultural jobs in the United States, this number is small when compared with the 48.38 percent of nonmigrants who have agricultural jobs in Mexico (see Table 1).

It is worth reflecting on the need for diversification of the labor market at the regional level in high-sending areas and the policies needed to achieve this objective. If regional development is to incorporate workers to reduce the migratory flow, then the type of jobs migrants perform in the United States could serve as an indicator of the employment potential for Mexican workers that could be encouraged in Mexico, i.e., jobs in agroindustry, manufacturing or service industries.

According to our field work, the labor market in high-sending areas is monoproductive in activities of minimal productivity, mainly agriculture and livestock. There is also little occupational mobility from the first job a person has in the labor market and that in which he may be working several years later. For example, the number of people who said they were working in agriculture was only 4 percent below the number whose first job was in that particular sector (see Table 2).

Sixty-nine percent of migrants send money home (remittances), which reduces the economic pressure on their families. The disposition of the remittances has not varied. They are spent primarily on household

TABLE 1

PRESENT OCCUPATION OF TEMPORARY MIGRANTS TO THE UNITED STATES
AND NONMIGRANTS IN THE REGION OF JALISCO WITH STRONG
"PUSH" FACTORS (1989)

Sector	Occupation of Migrants in the United States	Occupation of Nonmigrants in Mexico
	(percentages)	
Agriculture & Livestock	18.13	48.38
Peddling	0.14	2.19
Stores	1.98	13.05
Government	0.00	3.62
Transport	0.14	4.00
Domestic service	5.67	2.86
Restaurants	17.42	7.52
Handicrafts	0.00	2.38
Construction	6.94	5.24
Manufacturing Ind.	12.75	4.38
Pensioners	2.41	2.57
Agroindustry	0.00	0.10
Unemployed	0.85	0.00
Not specified	33.57	3.71
Total	100.00	100.00

Source: Family Sample Survey, 1989.

Note: Total number of temporary migrants: 511
     Total number of nonmigrants: 1,050

expenses and secondly on housing; we believe the latter is one of the unspoken reasons for emigrating, since housing is an essential objective in the lives of individuals and families.[26]

The recent changes in U.S. immigration law have had an important impact on communities with strong push factors. Our family survey showed that 40 percent of the migrants interviewed had legalized their entry into the United States, most under the Special Agricultural Worker program (SAW). Having secured their right to enter and leave the United States at will, a larger number of migrants than in former years set off for home. This phenomenon was widespread throughout the state of Jalisco. Even persons with no previous migration experience returned to their places of origin after having gone to the United States to obtain their documentation. Twelve percent of the interviewees in our case study[27] had made their first trip in the period 1986–1988.

From the above, we can infer that IRCA will have the direct effect of enabling migrants to return home with greater regularity and the indirect effect of increasing economic activity in their places of origin. Legalization

TABLE 2

OCCUPATIONAL MOBILITY OF THE WORKFORCE IN THE HIGH EXPULSION
AREA OF JALISCO TO THE UNITED STATES
1989

Employment of Nonmigrant	First Employment	Principle Employment (Actual) *(percentages)*	Secondary Employment (Actual)
Agricultural Workers	54.25	50.20	11.86
Street Vendor	2.37	2.27	4.05
Retail	8.00	13.54	1.19
Government	2.27	3.75	0.20
Transportation	2.08	4.15	0.40
Domestic Services	2.67	2.96	0.89
Restaurant	5.43	7.81	1.19
Handicraft	0.49	2.47	0.10
Construction	4.25	5.43	1.19
Manufacturing	4.55	4.55	0.69
Retired	2.57	2.67	1.28
Agroindustry	0.30	0.20	0.00
Nonspecified	10.77	0.00	76.98
Total	100.00	100.00	100.00

Source: Family Sample Survey, 1989.

Note: Number of total migrants: 511.

may be a means for migrants to obtain more stable work, but it may reduce wages received, above all in traditional labor markets. On another level, it may strengthen migratory networks since those who have obtained documents may feel they can better help friends and relatives.

The new legislation affects the labor market by inducing a surplus of labor in nontraditional activities, such as skilled or semiskilled jobs in the urban sector. Recently legalized migrants feel they have greater opportunities for better paid jobs which, in turn, require a better quality of work. At the individual level, this law brings expectations of greater freedom of movement between the two countries and of obtaining fringe benefits and jobs that require less physical labor. However, there is also the possibility of more competition for jobs.

Many who did not obtain documents believe they may continue to migrate illegally, and their job expectations in the United States have not diminished.

IRCA has also affected migrants' decisions about residence in the United States. Three quarters of those who recently received amnesty as residents since 1982 said they intended to live permanently in the United States, and half of those intended to become citizens. The SAW workers intend to continue to migrate seasonally to the United States, although a large number of them are also considering settling there permanently. California continues to be the main destination for migrants from Jalisco: 83.77 percent of the sample families.

Lack of work is one of the principal reasons people migrate for the first time (19 percent); 14.3 percent migrate to increase their wages and 9.4 percent want to get to know the United States (see Table 3). The persistence of these initial objectives is notable since many continue to migrate to seek a higher socioeconomic level in Mexico.

The largest families with the most economic dependents do not have any migrants. These families have about eight members, only three of whom work, although their educational level is similar to that of families with migrants. The migrant families, with about six members, were created during the demographic boom of the late 1960s and early 1970s; so that today large families have about six members.

The effects of the economic crisis on migration were an important ques-

TABLE 3

REASONS FOR TEMPORARY MIGRATION FROM HIGH-SENDING AREAS
OF JALISCO TO THE UNITED STATES BASED ON FIRST AND LAST TRIP, 1989

Reasons for Migrating to the USA	FIRST TRIP TO USA			LAST TRIP TO USA		
	Main Reason	Secondary Reason	Other Imp. Reason	Main Reason	Secondary Reason	Other Imp. Reason
	(percentages)					
Unemployment in Mexico	19.0	5.5	0.4	31.1	6.5	0.6
To set up business in Mexico	2.3	3.1	0.2	5.7	4.1	0.4
Higher wages	14.3	11.9	0.4	26.8	19.8	1.2
Travel and adventure	9.4	4.9	0.8	10.6	6.3	1.0
Not able to support the family	9.2	5.3	0.8	12.9	10.0	1.0
To obtain money for agriculture	0.4	1.2	0.4	1.4	1.2	0.6
Other	1.6	0.8	0.4	8.4	5.1	0.6
Did not reply*	43.8	67.3	96.7	3.1	47.2	94.7
Total	100.0	100.0	100.0	100.0	100.0	100.0

Source: Family Sample Survey, 1989.

Note: *This high percentage is due to the fact that, in most cases, the person interviewed was not the migrant himself.
Total of Temporary Migrants: 511.

tion for our study. Most of the families in the sample who perceived a positive change in their economic position were families with migrants. They attributed this change to the employment of more members of the household both in their local community and in the United States. Some family strategies to maintain their standard of living have changed and others persist. The migration flow to the United States has continued and some new people have joined the flow, while in nonmigrant families women have had to go to work.

V. MIGRATION AND REGIONAL DEVELOPMENT IN JALISCO

To our knowledge, the only available indicator of migration from the various municipalities of Jalisco is the municipal index of migration to the United States which, however, was drawn up in 1984 from data on the number of people detained and deported (see municipal index in the methodological appendix). According to this index, the state's high-sending municipalities contained 16 percent of Jalisco's total population and 27 percent of its rural population in 1980. If we plot the high-sending indices of the 42 municipalities on a map of Jalisco, migration to the United States is shown to be geographically widespread.

If we also use an index of comparative regional socioeconomic development[29] and relate it to the municipalities with strong push factors, it becomes apparent that migration to the United States originates mainly in areas with comparatively low- to medium socioeconomic levels.

As has been previously suggested, the link between development and migration has not been satisfactorily explained. One reason for this is that specific development situations and the geographic position of the communities of origin, vis-à-vis the nearest hub urban center, vary considerably, making it difficult to explain the relationship in general terms.

A characterization of the functional relationships between the communities studied and the larger urban centers, both at the municipal and the regional level, can be made based on a study by the National Population Council (CONAPO) in conjunction with the well known Mexican firm INESER.[30] It relates selected features of the population's geographic distribution to transportation networks, consumption patterns, marketing, employment, main migratory flows and the possibilities of access to a better general standard of living. The study also analyzes the geographic function by applying the gravitational model, the flow of telephone calls and the results of a survey of key informants.

This study shows that Jalisco has experienced unbalanced socioeconomic development; opportunities for economic development and personal advancement are concentrated in Guadalajara, although some regional centers have taken on urban functions that enable them to supply goods and services to their region. There are distortions that make it difficult to achieve greater regional integration among the urban, semiurban and rural towns. Throughout all regions resources move in a vertical ascending pattern, from the smallest, most isolated rural communities to the largest city. Such supply mechanisms perpetuate situations of scarce productivity in poor rural communities and regions, with increasing imports from areas with greater comparative socioeconomic development. This syndrome also results in minimal local investment of savings, which find their way to the financial centers of the biggest cities through formal banking procedures and migration.

Based on the characteristics of the communities, the equipment they possess, the social, political, administrative and economic functions they perform and the influence they exert on other localities, we identified 40 regional centers of different sizes in Jalisco's system of cities. We also identified nine urban hubs that, defined through their socioeconomic functions, delineate more- or less fixed regional areas.

Three typical regional situations can be singled out for analysis from the nine regions into which we have divided Jalisco: a) those with an economic base for self-sustaining growth—Guadalajara and Puerto Vallarta; b) those with a potential for achieving that base—the regions of Lagos de Moreno, Tepatitlán, Ciudad Guzmán and Ocotlán; and c) those with no present potential for achieving self-sustaining growth—the regions of Colotlán, Ameca and Autlán.

In the first situation, both Guadalajara and Puerto Vallarta are capable of incorporating their populations, as well as immigrants, into dynamic economic activities: industrial development and diverse services in Guadalajara, as a great regional center; and tourism, agriculture and agroindustry, with the opening of new irrigated lands in the Vallarta region. According to our information, these regions send relatively fewer migrants to the United States. Although this migration has practically the same characteristics as in the rest of the state, there is a segment of population in this flow that uses migration more as an opportunity to increase income rather than to escape from unemployment. The impact of remittances is internalized in the economies of Guadalajara and Puerto Vallarta where they are used to buy goods and services, causing multiplier effects in these cities because of their diversified production (see Table 4).

From the results of our fieldwork that are detailed in our research report,[31] we outline some findings that describe the characteristics of migration to the United States from the nine above-mentioned regions.

Migrants from the regions of Guadalajara and Puerto Vallarta are relatively younger and there are more women among them; their families have fewer economic dependents; and most are more skilled, particularly

TABLE 4

USE OF REMITTANCES FROM TEMPORARY MIGRANTS, (MAIN DISTRIBUTION AND FIRST TRIP, BY REGION OF ORIGIN) STATE OF JALISCO, 1989

	Colotlan	Lagos	Tepatitlan	Ameca	Ciudad Guzmán *(percentages)*	Guada-lajara	Vallarta	Ocotlan	Autlán
Current household expenses	50.0	7.5	57.8	60.7	52.4	36.8	30.0	52.5	90.0
Housing	38.9	9.4	15.5	10.7	24.6	21.1	10.0	26.3	10.0
Furniture & domestic appliances	—	6.2	2.2	3.6	3.3	10.5	10.0	—	—
Investment to set up a business	—	—	2.2	3.6	3.3	—	—	5.2	—
Land, vehicle or agric. machinery	11.1	—	6.7	10.7	1.6	10.5	20.0	—	—
Savings	—	3.1	—	7.1	11.5	—	—	—	—
Entertainment	—	6.2	8.9	3.6	3.3	21.1	—	16.0	—
Others	—	—	6.7	—	—	—	30.0	—	—
Total	100.0	100.0	100.0	100.0	100.0	100.0	100.0	100.0	100.0

Source: Family Sample Survey, 1989.

Note: Total of temporary migrants: 511

those from the Guadalajara region. A high proportion (one-third from the Guadalajara region) are employed in small service businesses, manufacturing and handicrafts, generally as a strategy to become self-employed at home. Fewer people expect to emigrate (only 10 percent in Guadalajara). An outstanding fact is that remittances are spent overwhelmingly on housing (building and improvements). Because many urban families need more living space, it may be feasible to satisfy this need of the migrants' families and at the same time create jobs locally. Thus, the economic activities of some cities could be revitalized.

Of the regions with potential for strengthening their economic bases, Lagos and Tepatitlán are agroindustrial, while Guzmán and Ocotlán have agricultural and manufacturing bases. All of these regions need to expand their urban areas in order to attract and concentrate an increased population.

The flow of remittances tends to generate a demand that, at least in part, could be satisfied by promoting activities based on small- and medium-sized businesses. This commercial activity could also absorb workers who might otherwise emigrate to the United States. Our fieldwork showed evidence that remittances tend to be invested in the more dynamic economic activities, although the amount and their effect seem limited. For example, some are invested in poultry farming, a basic and dynamic activity in Tepatitlán.

In general, migration to the United States from this typical regional situation can be characterized as strong both in magnitude and tradition, particularly in the regions of Lagos de Moreno and Tepatitlán which form the area known as "Los Altos" of Jalisco where well-known migration research has been carried out. Between 40 and 70 percent of area migrants are between the ages of 21 and 30, most are married and with about three economically dependent family members; there are few women in the flow.

Because of long-standing tradition, these migrants make intensive use of migratory networks. They generally stay in the United States for approximately one year and, in some cases, permanently. In most cases they are seeking to improve income, although some need to find work not available at home (see Table 5). In some cases this migration is the second alternative for coping with the deterioration stemming from the economic crisis, the first being that more family members should find work. About 25 percent of families interviewed expected to send one of their members to the United States. In these regions, as in the five others, remittances are spent on current household expenses, housing and, to a much lesser extent, investment in agricultural machinery and small businesses.

In the 1980s, small-scale industry increased in some urban areas of these regions, in part because of investment of remittances and the return of migrants who became small-scale entrepreneurs. A few others have

TABLE 5

REASONS FOR FIRST TRIP TO THE UNITED STATES ACCORDING TO REGION OF ORIGIN, JALISCO, 1989

Reasons	Lagos	Tepatitlan	Ocotlán	Ciudad Guzmán	Guadalajara (percentages)	Autlán	Vallarta	Ameca	Colotlan
Unemployment in Mexico	27.2	19.3	25.6	23.5	21.9	9.1	–	18.3	14.6
Better wages	13.0	16.9	20.5	11.8	34.4	20.0	17.6	4.2	4.
Could not support oneself	18.5	7.2	12.8	7.6	–	1.8	5.9	16.9	7.3
Travel and Adventure	1.9	14.5	2.6	8.4	12.5	10.9	5.9	11.3	12.2
Business in Mexico	5.6	1.2	–	2.5	3.1	–	–	2.8	4.9
Other	0.0	0.0	0.0	0.8	3.1	0.0	29.4(a)	2.8	2.4
Didn't know (b)	38.8	40.9	38.5	45.4	25.0	58.1	41.2	43.7	53.7

Source: Family Sample Survey, 1989.

Note: (a) This percentage was to obtain documents.
(b) In most cases, the person interviewed was not the migrant himself.
Total of temporary migrants: 511

sent machinery to start small-scale clothing workshops. In Villa Hidalgo, Encarnación and Lagos de Moreno, this industry has flourished through small family-type enterprises. The geographical location with proximity to Aguascalientes, where the clothing industry receives its main supplies of raw materials (thread, cloth, etc.) and León and Guanajuato, where machinery and parts can be obtained, has fostered the development of this industry.

Ciudad Guzmán is an interesting example where urban development and concentrated economic growth are fostered by nonagricultural activities and the economic integration of the region. Moreover, the city has export-oriented economic activities. This development may attract population that would otherwise migrate to the United States or to the Guadalajara metropolitan area, which is why we analyze the Guzmán region as a case study below.

The rest of those regions (those with no present potential for sustainable economic growth)—Colotlán, Ameca and Autlán—show an absence of activities capable of creating nonagricultural jobs. Therefore, migration is motivated mainly by lack of employment and is a survival strategy. Remittances are spent in the large urban centers and do not encourage the development of nonagricultural activities in these areas.

These regions are characterized by an agricultural base where modern and traditional agriculture exist in variable proportions around a hub-type urbanization with little dynamism. There are, however, a larger number of small urban centers than in other regions. The volume of migration from these regions to the United States is significant. It begins at an early age and continues for some time; only 5 percent are women. Remittances are important for the economic base of the regions and are usually spent on household expenses and housing. There appears to be little interest in investing in productive activities, given the structural difficulties for agricultural development, and even less interest in nonagricultural activities. We believe that migration from these areas is largely determined by the decline in traditional agriculture and the displacement of labor in modern agriculture. Therefore, migration is a means of survival. In these regions there is little prospect of influencing the migration phenomenon, except by modernizing agriculture which, over the long term, would lead to a revitalization of the urban base and nonagricultural activities.

In all regions remittances from temporary international migrants (sent or brought back by them) reported in our survey are low when compared with the potential income from employment in regional dynamic cities (see Table 6), if such employment can be created in sufficient quantities. This appears even more likely when one takes into account the costs of international and regional migration.

TABLE 6

AVERAGE REMITTANCES PER TEMPORARY WORKER IN THE UNITED STATES
ACCORDING TO REGION OF ORIGIN, JALISCO, 1989

Region	First Trip[2]	Last Trip[3]	Average Hourly Wage (Dollars)
Colotlán	1,199	2,240	4.45
Lagos	643	861	4.59
Tepatitlán	1,563	2,122	5.15
Ameca	1,409	1,540	4.91
Guadalajara	514	582	4.69
Vallarta	1,010	1,100	5.55
Ocotlán	1,068	1,707	5.69
Autlán	1,124	1,524	4.50
Guzmán	838	990	4.61

Source: Family Sample Survey, 1989.

Note: [1]Including money sent and saved.
       [2]Average length of stay 15.34 months.
       [3]Average length of stay 10.88 months.

VI. CASE STUDY: THE GUZMAN REGION

The Guzmán region is of particular interest in this study of the relationship between international migration and regional development. The
Ciudad Guzmán region is located in the southern part of the state and
includes municipalities with substantial agricultural and forestry production, as well as the beginnings of an industrial base in Ciudad Guzmán,
where there are some important manufacturing plants and a number of
small shops. The federal and state governments and entrepreneurs from
Guadalajara are interested in developing a manufacturing base in the
city, particularly in export-oriented industries, because of the region's
strategic geographic location in relation to Pacific Rim countries. Ciudad
Guzmán is only 80 miles from Manzanillo, a major Pacific coast port with
modern harbor facilities. Moreover, Ciudad Guzmán, the biggest urban
hub in the region, is the main regional center of trade (see Table 7). In the
context of Mexico's decentralization policy, it is seen as an alternative to
the Guadalajara metropolitan area for fostering industrial growth in
Jalisco.

The Guzmán region as a whole has a higher push index to the United
States than the other regions, although there are internal differences, for
example, Ciudad Guzmán itself which has a comparatively low push
rate.[33] The city has experienced a slight growth in population, less than

TABLE 7

POPULATION OF CIUDAD GUZMAN*

Year	Total	Rural	Rural (percentages)	Average Annual Growth Over the Decade
1940	23,100	974	4.22	
1950	25,223	1,593	6.32	0.9
1960	32,170	1,220	3.79	2.46
1970	49,417	1,251	2.53	4.55
1980	62,457	1,451	2.31	2.27

Source: General Population and Housing Censuses, Directorate General of Statistics, Secretariat of Industry and Commerce and Secretariat of Planning and Budget.

Note: *This refers to the municipality of Ciudad Guzmán. In 1970, 99.6 percent of the population of the municipality lived in the urban areas as defined by Arroyo, et al. (1986).

the natural growth of the population of the country as a whole, with the exception of the 1960s when the net rate of emigration for the economically active population was zero. In the 1950s and 1970s, Ciudad Guzmán was an area of labor outmigration (see Table 8). This may be due in large part to the population's high educational and cultural levels, the opportunities offered by Guadalajara (where many people from Guzmán have migrated) and the few opportunities offered by Ciudad Guzmán for a more educated and skilled population.

In spite of this, a study carried out in 1976 showed that the city does attract population from its area of influence and its growth stems largely from such migration (see Table 9). Furthermore, it was found that the im-

TABLE 8

CIUDAD GUZMAN: NET BALANCE FOR MIGRATION AND NET MIGRATION RATES*
FOR AGE GROUP 20–39**

Years	Net Balance for Migration	Net Migration Rate
1950–1960	− 824.0	− 87
1960–1970	− 1.0	0
1970–1980	−3 205.0	−184

Source: Arroyo Alejandre, Jesús. "Emigración Rural de Fuerza de Trabajo en el Occidente-Centro de México: Una Contribución de Información Básica para su Análisis." University of Guadalajara. Cuadernos de Divulgación, Guadalajara, Jalisco, 1986.

Note: *Per thousand inhabitants of the 15–39 age group in 1960, 1970 and 1980 respectively.
**This group contains the greater part of the work force.

TABLE 9

CIUDAD GUZMAN: IMMIGRANTS DURING 1954–1975 BY LAST PLACE OF
RESIDENCE, 1976

Last Place of Residence	Immigrants	Percentage
Total, 1964–1975	9,766	100.0
Local area	4,731	48.4
Other places of origin	5,035	51.6
Other Place of Origin	5,035	100.0
Guadalajara (Metropolitan area)	1,387	27.5
Other parts of Jalisco	1,235	24.5
Other parts of the West	1,140	22.6
Other areas of the country	1,216	24.2
Not reported	57	1.1

Source: Arroyo Alejandre, Jesús, William W. Winnie and Luis A. Velázquez Gutiérrez.
"Migración a Centros Urbanos en una Región de Fuerte Emigración: el caso del
Occidente de México" Center for Social and Economic Research, Faculty of Eco-
nomics, University of Guadalajara, 1986.

migrants employed in the urban economy had almost the same job structure as the native-born. This supports the hypothesis that migrants to the
cities are normally the youngest, the most ambitious and those with the
greatest initiative in their communities of origin (particularly true when it
is a question of rural communities).[34]

Economic activity in the Guzmán region is somewhat diversified, although agriculture predominates. The economy is strongly linked to
agroindustry; the main crops are hybrid corn, sorghum, tomatoes, chickpeas for animal fodder, alfalfa and sugar cane. Manufacturing has also
played an active part in the economy, the most important sections being
paper and cellulose, cement, limestone, furniture, chemicals and plastic
products.

Ciudad Guzmán is the center for the supply of goods and services to
the region; the main economic functions, especially commercial and almost all kinds of service activities, are concentrated there.

According to Table 10, in 1975, small and microindustries predominated
in almost all sectors of the city's industrial structure except the chemical,
rubber, plastic, textiles and shoe and leather industries. In these industries the average number of workers and the average productivity per
worker are higher than in the other sectors. The food processing industry
is outstanding due to the number of firms and the work force employed.
However, it appears to consist of small firms of comparatively low
productivity.

Insofar as the figures in Table 10 are acceptable, we can say that the city's
medium- and small industries are dynamic (a deduction based on the increase in average productivity). If to this we add a potentially large num-

TABLE 10

CIUDAD GUZMAN: INDUSTRIAL STRUCTURE

Sector	Number of Firms	Number of People	Average No. of People	Gross Output (Thousands of Pesos in 1975)	Value Added	Gross Output X No. of Workers
1975						
Total	87	273	3	18,471	8,153	67.7
Food Processing	43	119	3	6,366	2,317	53.5
a) Industries 23, 25 and 26	3	16	5	2,052	1,195	128.3
Publishing, printing, etc.	3	15	5	670	414	44.6
b) Industries 30 and 32	3	50	16	6,942	2,794	138.8
Other industrial sectors	35	73	2	2,441	1,433	33.4
1985						
Total	393(103)	11,629(748)	29(7)	2,484,618	970,544	83.5
Food Processing	155(41)	4,825(203)	31(5)	824,794	305,967	63.4
a) Industries 23, 25 and 26	26(23)	1,648(358)	63(16)	448,891	145,729	88.4
Publishing, printing, etc.	7(3)	56(16)	8(5)	10,948	4,639	82.8
b) Industries 30 and 32	17(4)	1,198(74)	70(18)	379,025	168,757	140.8
Other industrial sectors	188(32)	7,727(97)	41(3)	820,960	345,452	44.7

Source: Estimates from the Government of Jalisco's Planning and Development Department, based on Industrial Census for 1975 and the State Government Treasury's taxpayers' rolls. The numbers in brackets are from the 1985 Economic Census. Data from the state taxpayers' roll may include firms enumerated in the Census and others no longer active but still on the rolls.

Note: a) Includes: textile industry; shoe and leather manufacturers; wood and cork industries and products (except for furniture making).
  b) Chemical industry and manufacturing of rubber and plastic products.

ber of skilled laborers and potential linkages between industrial firms and services, then the city would offer potential for new enterprises, and the urban area would become attractive for carefully selected industries. There is also the possibility for the development of export-oriented manufacturing to take advantage of the new Guadalajara-Ciudad Guzmán-Colima-Manzanillo superhighway and the port infrastructure of Manzanillo.

Surprisingly, the portion of the economically active population from the Guzmán region working in the United States must be large relative to other regions, as an average of three members of each surveyed family with migrants are now or had been in the United States in the last decade. In addition, 45.9 percent of family income came from international migration. However, this is not the principal source of income, as only 19.1 percent of those interviewed so stated; it was the second source of income for 16 percent. It therefore appears that international migration is complementary to family income. Moreover, it continued to be the most common strategy (23.7 percent of the families) used to cope with the economic crisis in Mexico. Furthermore, families expect to incorporate more members into the migratory flow; 23 percent of the families, most with a history of migration, have members who are thinking of migrating soon to the United States.

In general, the profiles of the migrants are similar to those in other regions. The urban areas of the state of California are the main destination for about 90 percent of both first-time migrants and those who have been to the United States before. The next most common destinations are Illinois and Texas.

It seems that the type of work carried out in the United States has become more diversified, since earlier studies showed a large percentage of migrants working in agriculture. This study found that only 39.1 percent were doing agricultural work while the remainder was employed in urban areas, where manufacturing and construction (32 percent each), restaurants (15 percent) and domestic service were among the most important jobs. Moreover, the wages that migrants earn are relatively low, approximately 4.61 dollars per hour, on average, which is only a few cents above the minimum wage in California. In spite of this, the U.S.-Mexico wage differential is one of the main reasons for migrating. On the whole, migration is motivated by economic stress (83.3 percent)—particularly unemployment (47 percent), search for better income (30.3 percent) and inability to support the family when working in Mexico (6 percent). These motives persist among those on their first trip as well as with return migrants. Once they have entered the migratory stream, it is difficult to reenter an unchanged local labor market. Few (29.4 percent) of the migrants are self-employed in their home regions after their return. Slightly more than half of these are self-employed in agriculture or as small shop owners.

The traditional economic dynamism of the Guzmán area, and particularly of Ciudad Guzmán itself, has undergone some recent changes that add a new element in considering the linkage between migration and the region's economic development. Most important are the new options for regional integration that have arisen from the construction of the Guadalajara-Ciudad Guzmán-Colima-Manzanillo superhighway; the new possibilities for industrialization in the area; and the urban reconstruction policy carried out in Ciudad Guzmán after the September 1985 earthquake. The location of Ciudad Guzmán and the new superhighway—as well as the comparatively ample agricultural resources of the surrounding region—suggest that it may be a good choice for the development of an export industry aimed at the West Coast of the United States and some of the Asian countries.

VII. CENTRAL LOCATIONS OR REGIONAL CITIES AS COMPETITIVE ALTERNATIVES TO MIGRATION TO THE UNITED STATES

As an empirical test of the main hypothesis of this paper, we built a simple multiple regression model from a cross-section analysis that relates variations in migration to the United States at the municipal level to the degree of interaction between each municipality and Guadalajara, as well as between each municipality and its regional center. It also relates them to the importance of urban activities in each municipality and their comparative level of socioeconomic development. That is:

$$PR = -(II_{GMA})(II_{RC}) - UI - DI$$

PR is the push rate obtained from CONAPO data (1986). II_{GMA} is the index of interaction between the municipality in question and Guadalajara. II_{RC} is the index of interaction between the municipality in question and that which is the local center for the region (practically speaking, the regional hub city). UI is the index of importance of urban activities in relation to its region. DI is the index for the level of the municipality's comparative socioeconomic development.

According to our hypothesis, the greater the socioeconomic interaction with the region's urban center and with the Guadalajara metropolitan area, the less migration we would expect—thus, the negative multiplier for both interaction indices. The greater the level of the municipality's urbanization, the less migration we would assume over the geographic long term (stage of self-sustaining economic development), hence the negative sign. Finally, we assume another negative relationship with the comparative socioeconomic index, also in the context of the geographic long term.

The values of the variables and the method of calculating them are presented in the methodological appendix. The estimate of the model that accounts for the better fit between it and the data (converted into logarithms) is the following:

$$PR = .6018 - .2692(\text{II}_{\text{GMA}})\,(\text{II}_{\text{RC}}) - .0720\text{UI} + .0312\text{DI}$$
$$\qquad\quad (2.37)\quad (-3.4263)\qquad\qquad\qquad (-1.3029)\ (0.4321)$$

Degree of
Statistical
significance: 0.02   0.002   0.20   0.66
(2-tail sig)

$R^2 = 0.42$; Durbin-Watson $= 1.79$; and the F. parameter $= 8.37$.

For the calculation we took into account the 38 municipalities with the highest push factor indices to the United States. We excluded Ameca, Ciudad Guzmán and Puerto Vallarta, because each is the regional center of its particular area.

By applying the model, we deduce that, as expected, there is a statistically significant inverse relationship between the migration rate to the United States and the degree of interaction with the Guadalajara Metropolitan Area (GMA) and the regional center. This test is substantial evidence of the appeal of the urban centers and the GMA as destinations for migrants.

The inverse relationship between UI—which is in reality an index of "deurbanization" or the gap between the importance of the municipality's urban activities and those of the regional center—and the migration rate to the United States has a lower statistical significance. This demonstrates that when regional centers are excluded, precarious urbanization does not necessarily have an effect on bringing down migration. Not every type of urbanization influences the magnitude of volume to the United States. This may mean that most municipalities with a high push factor have not yet achieved the geographic long term, as we have defined it.

We see a direct relationship between the development index and migration, although at a low level of statistical significance. This is understandable in terms of our proposition: that socioeconomic development does not necessarily explain the reduction in the flow of migration. Rather, changes in migration depend on the type of activities that this development encourages and on the locality's position in the regional economic system. Moreover, this finding also supports the assumption that most of the municipalities in question have not yet reached the stage in which increases in economic development would decrease migration.

Thus, we can conclude that the estimated model corroborates the central implication of our hypothesis: it is possible to influence the magnitude of the migratory flow to the United States through the development of regional centers that serve as hubs after having defined their potential and identified their geographic integration with the regional economic system.

We recognize the limitations of this model, but we believe that the results obtained present interesting possibilities for broadening the hypothesis and, consequently, the model.

VIII. CONCLUSIONS AND POLICY IMPLICATIONS

Some population hub centers in the regions studied may attract migrants from their area of influence and compete with the United States as destinations for migration. The existence of an economic base for self-sustaining growth is an indispensable condition for these urban centers to attract migrants and incorporate them into productive activities. In Jalisco, the potential for the development of this base is different in each of the nine regions studied.

In general, remittances do not necessarily foster greater development in the communities of origin due to certain obstacles to development. These obstacles can be of a general economic nature, be related to the degree of regional integration or generally affect investment and marketing.

Obstacles of an Economic Nature

a) National macroeconomic policy in Mexico has stimulated the outflow of capital from rural and semiurban environments. This has placed the regions in an unfavorable situation vis-à-vis the country's large urban centers. At the local level, families are faced with a difficult economic situation and, if they already have experience with international migration, their expectations for bettering their standard of living are oriented in that direction. There is still a contrast between the conditions of production and subsistence in rural areas and the industrial bases of large cities which have had a privileged position for many years.

Rural Jalisco benefitted very little from the agricultural modernization policy which accompanied Mexico's industrial growth policy for a period of time. The trade-off between already developed and stagnating areas favored the former and gave rise to a process of extracting capital that deprived small communities of a good portion of their development potential.

b) Income generated by migration is cyclical, uncertain and too low to transform the structure of production. In the sending communities, income obtained from work in the United States generates a certain dependence on such income and alters spending and consumption patterns. However, we found that none of the remittances were very large; 17.54 percent of families received up to U.S.$300 from the last trip made by each temporary migrant; but another group of 11.19 percent received between U.S.$501 and U.S.$1,000,[35] and 10.07 percent received between U.S.$1,001 and U.S.$2,000. The irregularity of remittances results in spending on current consumer goods rather than productive economic investment; 65.13 percent of temporary migrants devoted their earnings in the United States to spending on current consumer goods.

c) A cyclical increase in income accelerates the flight of local capital. When income increases, relative luxury consumption may increase as well, which can generate a rapid flight of accumulated capital.[36] Receipt of legal status under IRCA facilitated the importation of cars into the country. This had an effect on local consumption patterns in smaller communities, as increased mobility fostered increased consumption outside the community and region.

Other evidence of capital flight is the families' tendency to improve their homes or to buy a new one. Investment in construction contributes to capital flight because of the materials and techniques used. Local building materials are abandoned in favor of materials imported from other regions, and modern homes are built which resemble those in American suburbs.

Due to the fact that a large percentage of the remittances are destined for current consumption, little remains to invest in productive enterprises. People who do manage to invest usually do so in small businesses[37] and, in some cases, in agricultural land.

In fact, income stemming from international migration hardly reaches third place as a source of financing for the establishment of new businesses. It is interesting to note that no enterprises of any kind have resulted from new investments generated from an original entity financed exclusively by remittances. Furthermore, it should be stressed that new businesses that are established are oriented toward the local economy: they trade in or manufacture products and services for the consumption of low-income groups.

We can say that families with migrants are relatively more prosperous than those without. For the former, income from the United States is the second most important source of income. Those families without migrants have to survive by taking advantage of local opportunities for employment, the variable outcomes of each season and, to a lesser extent, agriculture and small businesses. The relative prosperity of migrants' families is a common fact in all the communities visited. However, productive investments capable of retaining people tend to be made by non-migrant families. Perhaps this explains why they have not migrated.

Obstacles to Regional Economic Integration

a) The integration of the rural communities into wider urban systems is difficult. The socioeconomic relations between the small centers of population in our study and more developed urban areas are characterized by inequality. For example, urban products have become more expensive; manufactured goods and other imports are sold on the rural market at higher prices than in the big cities, and the extra charge is paid by the rural consumer. On the other hand, agricultural products sold in urban areas are subject to transportation costs usually covered by the producer, either directly or through a middleman. Although these are not the only market factors, 53.2 percent of the families with migrants and 40 percent of the families without sell their agricultural products in the nearest municipality itself and only one-tenth is sold outside. This type of trade is not only due to the nature of the mostly small producers, but also to the lack of adequate communication and transportation networks.

b) The increase in migration causes a more acute distortion in the community's integration into the regional economy. In general, it can be said that when migration increases, the integration of communities is affected by a marked reduction in local production activities. It seems that a vicious cycle is generated in which the initial local conditions encourage migration, and migration discourages the local economy. One must take into account the fact that an increase in the flow has immediate effects on the existence and consolidation of migrant networks which, in turn, tend to perpetuate the migratory flow.

General Problems for Fostering Investment and Marketing

a) The country's general economic conditions do not encourage the investment of savings in production. There are certainly some exceptions, but in view of the low indices of comparative socioeconomic development, a region with strong outmigration is hardly in a position to offer investment opportunities. Large-scale enterprises would not find sufficient market or inputs for their products. Agroindustries require a constant inflow of basic raw materials that local production cannot provide due to a whole range of external factors. A business that requires semi-skilled workers will probably not be able to find them in a rural municipality and sometimes not even in the region. Moreover, as means of communication are not adequate in rural areas, the possible locations for a new business are reduced to a few urban centers. These are the ones with potential for economic sustainability.

b) There is a lack of experience in the organizing, financing and administration of businesses in the municipalities. This makes it difficult to organize and finance rural and semiurban projects suited to local conditions. Operating a small firm in a region such as those studied here would require the coordination of the interests of various isolated producers in order to obtain minimal economies of scale that would make the firm competitive, at least in the local region. Another requirement is access to financing which could come from local investment and/or remittances. It appears that it is not unusual for customary work, like planting corn, to be supported by remittances; but this method of financing has little effect on the level of production. We found no cases of businesses that had been set up by a combination of remittances and additional loans so as to achieve a medium-sized investment; yet there were large savings in banking institutions.

IX. POLICY IMPLICATIONS

We argue in this paper that migration to the United States from rural and semiurban areas can be reoriented and/or retained by implementing policies to promote the rapid growth of nonagricultural employment, especially in those medium-sized cities that have a potential base for self-sustaining growth.

With that in mind, we suggest the following policy proposals:

1) The establishment of credit unions as an alternative savings and loan system. Remittances are often turned into savings, deposited in the formal banking system and transferred to other regions, especially to metropolitan areas. Local inhabitants normally have no access to soft loans to set up a business or build or improve their homes; these are important reasons for joining the ranks of potential migrants to the United States. Credit unions charge interest rates far lower than commercial banks; they work with reduced costs and credit is granted equally to all savers. There are at least 26 credit unions in Jalisco, eight of which are in the Guadalajara metropolitan area, and the rest are in the south of the state. The aim of the credit unions located in small cities should be to support agricultural and livestock activities. These institutions can function as regional banks for remittances and loans, as Rogers and Pastor suggest.[38] The advantages of credit unions are: savers manage their own resources; there are no risks of bureaucratic or governmental mishandling of funds; external funds can be handled at low cost and loaned to those who have savings accounts at the banks. In fact, in Mexico the savings in credit unions doubled from 1987 to 1988.[39]

2) The substantial improvement of the communications infrastructure to facilitate interaction between the regional centers, municipal centers and Guadalajara, by means of geographic decentralization of public expenditures in this regard.

3) The transformation of traditional agriculture into a modern, commercial one, concentrating resources and promoting agroindustry in the regional centers to obtain multiplier effects.

4) The promotion of urban development in the regional centers through the creation and expansion of activities related to agroindustry, manufacturing and services.
5) The expansion of urban areas through construction of infrastructure buildings and houses. As construction is labor-intensive, such projects would generate jobs for skilled and unskilled workers in the medium-sized cities which have good economic potential.
6) The creation of nonagricultural employment that enables migrants from rural and semiurban areas to use skills they already possess.
7) Education can also serve as a policy of reducing migration, so long as educated people can be absorbed into dynamic activities in medium-sized cities which are related directly or indirectly to the economic base of sustained growth. This implies promoting the diversification of the economy and with it the labor market.
8) The promotion of a widely diffused program of public information on opportunities for investing, marketing, financing and taking advantage of infrastructure in cities with a strong economic base in order to attract both national and foreign firms.
9) The establishment of a system to provide information about opportunities for employment, both within the region and in the United States. The latter should include information on wages, fringe benefits, living and working conditions, travel costs, costs of supporting oneself in the United States and possible social costs. This recommendation is particularly important because, according to our analysis, average net income from migration turns out not to be very different from that which could be obtained in a stable job in Mexico that provides health benefits and the possibility of acquiring housing. This net income from migration may be further reduced if we consider the psychological costs for the migrant and his family.

The viability of these proposals has to be analyzed in a macroeconomic context of decentralization of economic and political life in Mexico that encourages the participation of the private sector in the process of economic growth, as well as the development of export-oriented industry. Based on our analysis, we believe that these policies, if implemented in regions with economic growth and potential, could influence the prevailing patterns of migration in rural and semiurban environments in the state of Jalisco and particularly the migration to the United States.

These patterns, together with the changes taking place in Mexico, are now in the process of transformation. Alternatives for the migrants have also been created. Their communities and regions might benefit from policies which, as indicated in this paper, influence the magnitude of rural and semiurban emigration through regional development.

METHODOLOGICAL APPENDIX
METHOD FOR SELECTING REGIONS OF JALISCO WITH STRONG "PUSH" TOWARD THE UNITED STATES

Method for drawing up the Municipal Index on undocumented migration to the United States:

Municipality of Residence	No. of Persons Detained or Deported (1) 1984	% of Jalisco Total (2)	Economically Active Population 1980	% of Total Jalisco EAP 1980	Index (2)/(3) × 100
Acatic	2	.21	3,957	.28	74.99
Acatlán	2	.21	4,063	.29	73.03
Ahualulco	0	0.00	5,359	.38	0.00
Amacueca	8	.84	1,818	.13	652.84
Amatitán	3	.31	2,637	.19	168.78
Ameca	12	1.26	15,317	1.08	116.23
Antonio Escobedo	1	.10	2,563	.18	57.88
Arandas	14	1.47	13,428	.95	154.68
Arenal	2	.21	3,017	.21	98.35
Atemajac	0	0.00	1,991	.14	0.00
Atengo	0	0.00	1,913	.14	0.00
Atenguillo	0	0.00	1,621	.11	0.00
Atotonilco el Alto	10	1.05	11,953	.85	124.12
Atoyac	3	.31	3,292	.23	135.20
Autlán	10	1.05	13,630	.96	108.85
Ayo el Chico	1	.10	8,460	.60	17.54
Ayutla	3	.31	4,808	.34	92.57
Barca, La	7	.73	14,531	1.03	71.47
Bolaños	5	.52	2,052	.15	361.50
Cabo Corrientes	1	.10	2,334	.17	63.56
Casimiro Castillo	3	.31	5,819 °	.41	76.49
Cihuatlán	2	.21	6,554	.46	45.27
Cd. Guzmán	18	1.89	19,562	1.38	136.51
Cocula	10	1.05	7,488	.53	198.13
Colotlán	2	.21	4,123	.29	71.97
Concepción de Buenos A.	0	0.00	2,170	.15	0.00
Cuautitlán	0	0.00	4,035	.29	0.00
Cuautla	0	0.00	1,072	.08	0.00
Cuquio	2	.21	4,876	.34	60.85
Chapala	15	1.57	9,709	.69	229.21
Chimaltitán	1	.10	1,064	.08	139.43
Chiquilistlán	0	0.00	1,677	.12	0.00
Degollado	0	0.00	4,894	.35	0.00
Ejutla	0	0.00	779	.06	0.00
Encarnación de Díaz	8	.84	11,638	.82	101.98
Etzatlán	2	.21	5,381	.38	55.14
Grullo, El	5	.52	6,070	.43	122.21
Guauchinango	1	.10	1,469	.10	100.99
Guadalajara	484	50.79	550,194	38.91	130.51
Hostotipaquillo	3	.31	2,665	.19	167.01
Huejucar	9	.94	1,887	.13	707.59
Huejuquillo el Alto	3	.31	2,448	.17	181.81
Huerta La	5	.52	6,315	.45	117.46
Ixtlahucán de los M.	2	.21	4,134	.29	71.77
Ixtlahucán del Río	1	.10	5,665	.40	26.19

Municipality of Residence	No. of Persons Detained or Deported (1) 1984	% of Jalisco Total (2)	Economically Active Population 1980	% of Total Jalisco EAP 1980	Index (2)/(3) × 100
Jalostotitlán	1	.10	6,076	.43	24.42
Jamay	0	0.00	4,918	.35	0.00
Jesús María	1	.10	5,116	.36	29.00
Jilotlán de los Dolores	2	.21	2,949	.21	100.62
Jocotepec	2	.21	8,214	.58	36.12
Juanacatlán	0	0.00	2,317	.16	0.00
Juchitlán	0	0.00	2,023	.14	0.00
Lagos de Moreno	9	.94	27,189	1.92	49.11
Limón, el	4	.42	2,342	.17	253.39
Magadalena	11	1.15	4,426	.31	368.72
Manuel M. Diéguez	0	0.00	1,356	.10	0.00
Manzanillo de la Paz	1	.10	1,397	.10	106.20
Mascota	2	.21	4,732	.33	62.70
Mazamitla	2	.21	2,492	.18	119.07
Mexticacán	2	.21	2,104	.15	141.02
Mexquitic	1	.10	5,103	.36	29.07
Mixtlán	0	0.00	1,341	.09	0.00
Ocotlán	11	1.15	17,515	1.24	93.17
Ojuelos	2	.21	6,497	.46	45.67
Pihuamo	5	.52	5,294	.37	140.12
Poncitlán	9	.94	8,470	.60	157.64
Puerto Vallarta	17	1.78	20,738	1.47	121.62
Purificación	0	0.00	3,316	.23	0.00
Quitupan	7	.73	4,782	.34	217.17
Salto, El	0	0.00	5,928	.42	0.00
San Cristobal de la B.	0	0.00	1,513	.11	0.00
San Diego de Alejandría	5	.52	2,029	.14	365.59
San Juan de los Lagos	17	1.78	11,110	.79	227.01
San Julián	3	.31	3,105	.22	143.34
San Marcos	0	0.00	966	.07	0.00
San Martín de Bolaños	3	.31	1,438	.10	309.51
San Martín Hidalgo	2	.21	6,503	.46	45.63
San Miguel el Alto	7	.73	7,606	.54	136.54
San Sebastián Ex 90	2	.21	3,493	.25	84.95
San Sebastián Ex 10.	0	0.00	2,993	.21	0.00
Sta. María de los A.	2	.21	1,726	.12	171.91
Sayula	2	.21	7,695	.54	38.56
Tala	7	.73	12,052	.85	86.17
Talpa de Allende	2	.21	4,025	.28	73.72
Tamazula	4	.42	11,926	.84	49.76
Tapalpa	1	.10	3,802	.27	39.02
Tecalitlán	10	1.05	5,573	.39	266.21
Tecolotlán	4	.42	4,875	.34	121.73
Techaluta	0	0.00	982	.07	0.00
Tenamaxtlán	0	0.00	2,540	.18	0.00
Teocaltiche	7	.73	9,671	.68	107.38
Teocuitatlán de Corona	6	.63	4,100	.29	217.11
Tepatitlán	12	1.26	23,804	1.68	74.79
Tequila	13	1.36	7,471	.53	258.15
Teuchitlán	0	0.00	2,330	.16	0.00
Tizapán el Alto	0	0.00	5,584	.39	0.00
Tlajomulco	1	.10	16,616	1.18	8.93
Tlaquepaque	6	.63	56,252	3.98	15.82

Municipality of Residence	No. of Persons Detained or Deported (1) 1984	% of Jalisco Total (2)	Economically Active Population 1980	% of Total Jalisco EAP 1980	Index (2)/(3) × 100
Tolimán	2	.21	2,823	.20	105.11
Tomatlán	5	.52	7,886	.56	94.06
Tonalá	2	.21	16,621	1.18	17.85
Tonaya	0	0.00	2,376	.17	0.00
Tonila	0	0.00	2,188	.15	0.00
Totatiche	3	.31	2,109	.15	211.04
Tototlán	8	.84	4,852	.34	244.61
Tuxcacuesco	1	.10	1,380	.10	107.51
Tuxcueca	1	.10	1,635	.12	90.74
Tuxpan	4	.42	8,871	.63	66.90
Unión de San Antonio	0	0.00	3,855	.27	0.00
Unión de Tula	5	.52	4,380	.31	169.36
Valle de Guadalupe	1	.10	1,731	.12	85.71
Valle de Juárez	0	0.00	1,843	.13	0.00
Venustiano Carranza	1	.10	4,961	.35	29.90
Villa Corona	4	.42	4,736	.33	125.30
Villa Guerrero	3	.31	2,274	.16	195.72
Villa Hidalgo	11	1.15	3,403	.24	479.56
Villa Obregón	0	0.00	1,820	.13	0.00
Yahualica de González G.	5	.52	6,947	.49	106.78
Zacoalco de Torres	5	.52	7,628	.54	97.25
Zapopan	13	1.36	125,777	8.90	15.33
Zapotiltic	5	.52	7,453	.53	99.53
Zapotitlán de Vadillo	3	.31	2,481	.18	179.39
Zapotlán del Rey	3	.31	4,028	.28	110.50
Zapotlanejo	3	.31	11,049	.78	40.28

Source: CONAPO Survey 1984, in CONAPO (1986) and Census of Population, 1980.

Note: From the above list of municipalities, we selected 42 with the highest indexes and they constituted the region for our field study.

METHODOLOGY FOR THE SAMPLE OF FAMILIES IN THE REGIONS OF JALISCO WITH STRONG "PUSH" TOWARD THE UNITED STATES

Definitions

Universe studied

The population, or universe, under consideration is composed of family units settled in rural or semiurban areas of the state of Jalisco which have been identified as being regions where there is a strong push for people to migrate as undocumented workers to the United States.

Units of analysis

The basic unit for the sample was the family. We studied analysis their housing characteristics, the family economy, the composition of the family and, in particular, the type of work they did, the migratory status of the members of the family unit who were active migrants at the moment and those who had been migrants at some time or another over the last 10 years. Thus, we considered at one and the same time two units of analysis: the individual and the family, grouping them by region and according to their migratory status as migrants or nonmigrants. It should be explained that, although the information about each family generally referred to more than one of its members, usually only one member of the family acted as the informer, usually the housewife.

Aim of
the sample

The aim was to obtain a statistically representative sample of families living in the regions of Jalisco with a strong push toward undocumented migration to the United States, so as to enable us to characterize the profiles of behavior and development of each of the nine economic regions of the state and of the state as a whole.

Representativity
of information

The study was oriented toward drawing up profiles of families and individuals according to the categories a) current migrants; b) migrants at other times over the last ten years but not at present; and c) nonmigrants. To this end, we designed a sampling plan to make it possible to estimate statistically the distinctive characteristics of each of the six resulting profiles at the level of the strong push areas in both the state's economic regions and the whole. Quantifying the migratory flows was not considered to be a central part of the sample survey.

Sampling Plan

The sampling design applied in the study is a combination of conglomerate and stratified sampling divided into three geographic levels: the economic region, the municipality and the community. In each of the nine regions, we selected a representative sample of municipalities catalogued as having strong push factors. In the municipalities thus chosen, we selected a sample of communities; and within the communities we selected the families. A basic principle in our selection of sampling units was to capture the diversity and the intensity of the phenomenon under study.

Levels of Sampling

REGION

We considered the nine regions established by CONAPO-INESER based on criteria of population and socioeconomic interrelationships (see CONAPO-INESER, 1988). The universe of study in each region was composed of the subset of families that live in those municipalities of between 500 and 5,000 inhabitants which have strong push factors. The variable used for determining the number of families to be interviewed throughout the State and their regional distribution was the aggregated push rate for each region. The number of surveys assigned to each region was proportional to the push rate in each region.

MUNICIPALITY   Each municipality identified as having a strong push factor, according to our indicator, was considered statistically as a conglomerate composed of communities and, within them, of families who are the units of analysis for the study. In each region we selected a certain number of municipalities following the scheme of sampling according to conglomerates, for which we once again used the push rate as the selection criterion variable.

COMMUNITY   Each community was defined as a conglomerate of families. We only took into account rural and semiurban communities (with a total population of no more than 5,001 inhabitants, nor less than 500 according to the 1980 Census) in the municipalities chosen. The communities in these municipalities were stratified according to the size of their total population as follows:

501 to 1,000 inhabitants
1,001 to 1,500 inhabitants
1,501 to 2,501 inhabitants
2,501 to 5,000 inhabitants

In carrying out the survey, we considered only the communities with more than 500 inhabitants for reasons of homogeneity among the families belonging to the first two brackets, as well as for reasons of time, cost and other limited resources. This constraint did not affect the overall quality of the study and it did produce sizeable economies. The surveys assigned to each municipality selected were distributed proportionally to the population comprising this municipality in each of the above five categories.

Criteria for Assigning the Sample in the Municipalities Chosen

1) We determined the number of communities to be surveyed in each municipality based on the size of the sample assigned to each. A mini-

mum of two communities were surveyed within each municipality chosen and a minimum of three questionnaires were assigned to each community chosen.

2) From our analysis of the distribution of communities by size of population, we determined analytically the number of communities to survey in each category. We applied the principle that smaller conglomerates are generally the most homogeneous.

3) We determined the number of questionnaires to be assigned within each community previously selected according to the total population of the community and limiting interviews to a maximum of ten and a minimum of three per community chosen.

4) The families surveyed in each community were selected at random with the constraint that in each community selected, at least a third of the families chosen would have members who are international migrants at present. A six month time limit was imposed from the date the questionnaire was assigned.

METHODOLOGY FOR CALCULATING

PR
: "Push" rate of population to the United States, derived from data from the 1984 CONAPO survey, CONAP (1986).

II_{GMA}
: Index of interaction between the municipality and the GMA; calculated according to the following equation:

$$II_{GMA} = K^* (P_I^* P_{GMA})/D^{2i}, \text{ in which:}$$

P_i
: Number of inhabitants in the community "i" in 1980.

P_{GMA}
: Number of inhabitants in the GMA in 1980.

d
: Geographic distance between the communities.

K
: Constant factor = $1^* 10^{-4}$.

IIRC
: Index of interaction between the municipality "i" and its regional center, according to the above equation.

$$II_{RC} : K^* (Pi^* P_{RC})/d^2_i, \text{ in which}$$

P_{RC}
: Number of inhabitants in the regional center enclosing municipality "i".

Pi, d, k
: same as above.

UI
: Urbanization index. Value calculated from a ranking of urban activities (share of population employed in secondary and tertiary activities) in the municipality "i", with top rank assigned to the regional center.

DI
: Development index, according to Arroyo-Velázquez (1988) based on Census variables, based on the factorial analysis method.

VALUES OF THE VARIABLES USED IN REGIONAL DEVELOPMENT
AND THE MODEL OF MIGRATION TO THE UNITED STATES

Municipality	"Push" Rate (PR)	Index of Interaction Between Municipality & GMA (II_{GMA})	Index of Urbanization Rank (DI)	Index of Interaction Between Municipality & Its Regional Center (II_{RC})	Development Index* (DI)
Amacueca	652.84	58.29	15	9.11	0.837
Arandas	154.68	244.3	2	26.45	1.716
Atotonilco	124.12	477.59	3	40.03	1.917
Atoyac	135.2	122.56	11	20.8	0.883
Bolaños	361.5	11.75	4	0.09	0.635
Chimaltitan	139.43	0.89	8	0.07	0.
Cocula	198.13	507.81	3	24.88	1.575
El Grullo	122.21	112.46	3	74.15	2.584
Hostotipaquillo	167.01	41.1	11	0.5	1.156
Huejucar	707.59	4.21	5	4.34	0.815
Huejuquilla	181.81	2.07	2	0.09	0.796
Huerta la	117.46	18.62	5	4.09	1.085
El Limon	253.39	18.89	11	9.46	1.328
Magadalena	368.72	372.25	7	2.38	2.209
Mazamitla	119.07	13.27	12	2.39	1.042
Mexticacan	141.02	59.6	5	1.54	0.943
Pihuamo	140.12	36.23	6	6.83	1.53
Poncitlan	157.64	510.15	4	130.15	1.665
Quitupan	217.17	14.3	16	2.06	0.051
San Julian	143.34	50.37	4	3.3	1.512
San Miguel El A.	136.54	148.93	3	11.25	1.637
San Diego De Ale.	365.59	15.57	7	1.26	0.512
San Juan De Los L.	227.01	261.42	2	72.43	2.682
San Martin de Bolaños	3,409.51	1.25	6	0.08	0.678
Sta. Maria De Los A.	171.91	22.63	7	8	0.445

Tecalitlan	266.21	68.08	6	35.33	1.902
Tecolotlan	121.73	117.94	6	2.81	1.428
Teocuitatlan	217.11	87.43	14	4.22	1.004
Tequila	258.15	877.41	2	5.57	2.209
Totatiche	211.04	3.74	3	1.64	0.575
Tototlan	244.61	398.92	8	61.24	1.158
Union De Tula	169.36	62.48	7	16.53	1.537
Villa Guerrero	195.72	3.27	4	0.74	2.253
Villa Hidalgo	479.56	21.36	6	1.28	0.728
Zapotitlan De Bad.	179.39	18.37	18	6.46	0.885

*Ranked using as base the municipality with the least development (in this case Chimaltitán with −1.479).

COVARIANCE MATRIX

	C	II	UI	DI
C	.064009			
II	−.013443	.006176		
UI	−.008604	.000206	.003058	
DI	−.013439	.003552	.000512	.005220

NOTES

1. For an extensive bibliography on these studies, see Wayne A. Cornelius, "Los Migrantes de la Crisis: The Changing Profile of Mexican Labor Migration to California in the 1980s," prepared for the Conference on Population and Work in Regional Settings, El Colegio de Michoacán, 28–30 November 1988, Zamora, Michoacán, Mexico 1988 (unpublished); Douglas S. Massey, Rafael Alarcón, Jorge Durand and Humberto González, *Return to Aztlán: the Social Process of International Migration from Western Mexico* (Berkeley: University of California Press, 1987).

2. For a detailed report on the results of research, see Jesús Arroyo Alejandre, Adrián de León Arias and Basilia Valenzuela Varela, *Migración rural y semiurbana de Jalisco y el Desarrollo regional,* (Guadalajara, Jalisco: Institute for Economic and Regional Studies at the University of Guadalajara, 1990).

3. In western Mexico, we considered the states of Aguscalientes, Colima, Guanajuato, Jalisco, Michoacán, Nayarit, Sinaloa and Zacatecas. Migratory flows have been constant throughout their history (see J. Gómez and David Maciel, *Al Norte del Río Bravo (pasado lejano) (1600–1930),* ed. Siglo Veintiuno, Colección COHM, 16, Mexico City, 1981). During the 1930s, due to the Depression, it was considered a problem (see Carrera de Velasco, Mercedes, *Los mexicanos que devolvió la crisis, 1929–1932.* Secretariat of Foreign Relations, Mexico City 1984). This view changed during the period of the *bracero* program, when the migration phenomenon entailed no great problems (see Howard Lloyd Campbell, "Bracero Migration and the Mexican Economy, 1951–1964," Ph.D. dissertation, The American University, 1972, University Microfilms, Ann Arbor, Michigan, 1972).

4. See report by the Commission on the Future of Mexican-U.S. Relations, *El desafío de la interdependencia: México y Estados Unidos,* F.C.E., Mexico City, 1988. For the West there is material that pinpoints migration since the end of the 19th century. For a synthesis, see Humberto González, "Las migraciones a los Estados Unidos en el Occidente de México 1880–1935," in Alcántara, Sergio and Enrique Sánchez (eds.), *Desarrollo rural en Jalisco: contradicciones y perspectivas* (Mexico City: Colegio de Jalisco-CONACYT, 1985); other references are in Helen D'Arc Rivière, *Guadalajara y su Región* (Setentas, Mexico City: 1973); Jorge A. Bustamante and J. Martínez, "Undocumented Migration from Mexico: Beyond Borders but Within Systems," in *Journal of International Affairs,* vol. 33, no. 2, 1979, pp. 23–67; J. Gómez and Maciel, 1981; Mercedes Carrera de Velasco, 1974; AGN (Archivo General de la Nación), *Boletín del archivo general de la nación,* tomo 4, no. 14, 1988; David Maciel, *Al norte del Río Bravo (pasado inmediato) (1930–1981),* ed. Siglo Veintiuno (Mexico City: Colección COHM, 1981; J. Diez-Canedo, *La migración indocumentada de México a los Estados Unidos, un nuevo enfoque,* (F.C.E., Mexico City: 1984); Gamboa Erasmo, "Braceros in the Pacific Northwest: Laborers on the Domestic Front, 1942–1947" in *Pacific Historical Review,* 1987; Massey, Alarcón, Durand and González, 1987: Cornelius, 1988; López Castro, Gustavo (ed.), *Migración en el occidente de Mexico,* (Zamora, Mich., Mexico: El Colegio de Michoacán, 1988).

5. See table on indicators of origins of Mexican migration to the United States by region and state: 1926, 1973, 1978, 1984 in Jesús Arroyo Alejandre, *El abandono rural* (Guadalajara: University of Guadalajara, 1989), p. 161.

6. See Harry A. Cross and James A. Sandos, *Across the Border: Rural Development*

11. Douglas S. Massey, "Economic Development and International Migration in Comparative Perspective" in *Population and Development Review*, vol. 14, no. 3, September 1988; J. Edward Taylor, "U.S. Immigration Policy and the Mexican Economy" in *Impacts of Immigration in California*, Policy Discussion Paper (Washington, D.C.: The Urban Institute, 1988); Jorge Durand, *"Los migradólares:cien años de inversión en el medio rural,"* unpublished, 1988; Diez-Canedo, 1984.

12. Massey, Alarcón, Durand and González, 1987; Richard Mines, *Developing a Community Tradition of Migration: a Field Study in Rural Zacatecas, Mexico and California Settlement Areas*, Monographs in U.S.-Mexican Studies (San Diego: University of California at San Diego, 1981); Mines, 1984.

13. It has been found that many U.S. industries, especially restaurants, electronics, clothing, etc., have been able to meet outside competition thanks to their increasing use of foreign labor which, in the final analysis, has created a considerable dependency on this type of worker. See Cornelius, 1988 and Council of Economic Advisors on United States Immigration in *Population and Development Review*, vol. 12, no. 2, 1986, pp. 361–374.

14. For a follow-up on this evaluation, see the results published in *El Correo Fronterizo*, by the Colegio de la Frontera. During 1987, the review Foro International published a series of articles with this end in mind. Other efforts carried out in the Colegio de México can be found in the volumes of the Mexico-United States collection corresponding to the years 1984–1987. Jesús Arroyo Alejandre, "Algunos Impactos de la Ley de Reforma y Control de Inmigración (IRCA) en una Región de Jalisco de Fuerte Emigración Hacia Estados Unidos de Norteamérica", to be published by the Rand Corporation, 1989; supports these statements with information from case studies.

15. International Labour Office, *World Labour Report*, 1–2, Oxford University Press, Oxford, England, 1987. Bustamante's work is an important step forward. With photographic techniques and surveys taken at the main points on the Northern border, he constantly monitors the behavior of the flow. As a result, considerable progress has been made in defining its seasonal nature and the way it has been adapting to the new conditions.

16. See Jorge A. Bustamante, "Migración indocumentada México-Estados Unidos; hallazgos preliminares del proyecto Cañón Zapata," Paper presented at the 1st International Conference on the Effects of the Immigration Reform and Control Act (IRCA), Guadalajara, Mexico, 1989. For a detailed analysis, see Cornelius, 1988, who holds that in the last decade the state of California—particularly its urban areas—has been the main migrant-receiving area in the country. This is due in part to the maturing of the migration networks and the dynamism of the California economy.

17. Massey, 1988, pp. 383–402.

18. Philip L. Martin, *Labor Migration and Economic Development*, Commission for the Study of International Migration and Cooperative Economic Development, Working Paper No. 3, February 1989, Washington D.C., p. 11.

19. Peter Gregory, *The Determinants of International Migration and Policy Options for Influencing the Size of Population Flows*, Commission for the Study of International

Migration and Cooperative Economic Development, Working Paper No. 2, February 1989, Washington, D.C.

20. Richard E. Rhoda, "Development Activities and Rural-Urban Migration: Is it Possible to Keep them Down on the Farm?," Office of Urban Development, Bureau for Development Support, Agency for International Development, Washington, 1979.

21. Rhoda, 1979, pp. 65.

22. Arroyo, 1989.

23. Wayne A. Cornelius, "Presentation to the Ninth Annual Briefing Session for Journalists," Center for U.S.-Mexican Studies and Foundation for American Communications, 22 June 1989, La Jolla, Ca. (not published).

24. Jesús Arroyo Alejandre, and Luis Arturo Velázquez, "Las ciudades menores de Jalisco y la migración interna" in *Investigación demográfica en México-1980*, (Mexico City: Consejo Nacional de Ciencia y Tecnología (CONACYT), 1982, pp. 391–406 study this type of migration (through sample surveys) in six cities of Jalisco that attract a relatively large number of people from their "immediate area of influence or local attraction." They found that the population of these cities on average is 45 percent immigrant, the majority of whom stem from their area of influence. In addition, the more consolidated the city's economic base is for self-sustaining growth, the more rural population it attracts from its area or from further afield.

25. In our field work we found cases of people who even had a master's degree who had migrated to the United States because of a lack of expectations in Mexico.

26. See J. Turner and R. Fitcher (eds.), *Libertad para construir*, ed. Siglo XXI, 1976, 1976; Duo Dickinson, "The Architect and the House: Building Relationships," *Cornell Architecture Art and Planning*," (Ithaca, N.Y.: Cornell University, Ithaca, 1989).

27. In December 1988, we made a survey of 67 migrants who were visiting their home towns and who had in some way or another been affected by IRCA. This survey is not claimed to have any statistical representativity. However, we did manage to gather information in 19 of the places with the strongest "push" factor.

28. Jalisco is the state that contributes the most migration to California. In 1973, it was 26.2 percent (Jones, 1984); this coincides with our information from the survey of key informers.

29. This index is built on the basis of socioeconomic variables from the Census (1980) for all the municipalities of Jalisco, using the factorial analysis method.

30. CONAPO-INESER, "Estudio del subsistema de ciudades Guadalajara-Ciudad Guzmán-Colima-Manzanillo," University of Guadalajara-CONAPO (being revised for publication), Guadalajara, Mexico, 1988.

31. See Arroyo, De León and Valenzuela, 1990.

32. Cornelius, 1978, also reported that migrants invest the income earned in the United States in productive activities in his study on rural communities in the Lagos de Moreno area of influence, carried out in 1976.

33. Jesús Arroyo Alejandre, "Emigración rural de la fuerza de trabajo en el occi-dente-centro de México: una contribución de información básica para su análisis," *Cuadernos de Divulgación*, University of Guadalajara, Guadalajara, Mexico, 1986.

34. Arroyo, et al., 1986.

35. In other studies, it has been found that there is nothing typical about remit-tances, for example, Diez-Canedo, 1984.

36. This fact has been widely pointed out by Taylor, 1988, who holds that if there is a positive relationship between the sum of family income and the goods pro-duced locally, it is to be assumed that the families' marginal propensity to con-sume these goods goes down as their income increases; therefore one can assume that there is a strong association between income earned and the demand for im-ported consumer goods.

37. The creation of wage-jobs in this type of business is almost nil. 3.20 percent of the migrant families and 1.96 of the nonmigrant ones create one job. Other studies have found that the average for jobs created is around 2 family workers and hired labor is less than 1 (see Massey, Alarcón, Durand and González, 1987).

38. Robert A. Pastor, *Migration and Development in the Caribbean Basin: Implication and Recommendations for Policy,* Commission for the Study of International Migra-tion and Cooperative Economic Development, Working Paper No. 7, November 1989, Washington, D.C.

39. Curiel Gutiérrez, Federico and Victor Aguilar Peña. "El financiamiento popu-lar ante la crisis de los ochenta" in *Carta Económica Regional*, vol. 2, no. 9, (Guadalajara, Mexico: Instituto de Estudios Economicos y Regionales at the Uni-versity of Guadalajara, 1989). This article is a partial result of a broader project on popular financing in Jalisco.

3

Labor Migration to the United States: Development Outcomes and Alternatives in Mexican Sending Communities

Wayne A. Cornelius

I. RESEARCH DESIGN AND METHODOLOGY

Site Selection

The universe for this study is defined as all households maintaining a residence in three purposely selected rural communities in west-central Mexico. To be included in the sampling frame, a household need not occupy a dwelling in the community on a year-round basis. Indeed, in all three communities, numerous dwelling units are occupied for only a few weeks each year—usually in December, January and early February, when migrant families traditionally return from the United States—or are occupied for most of the year by renters or house sitters (14.4 percent of all houses in the three communities).

All three research communities were studied in depth by members of our research team in the late 1970s and early 1980s, prior to enactment of the U.S. Immigration Reform and Control Act of 1986.[1] The availability for these communities of detailed historical, ethnographic and sample survey data on pre-IRCA emigration patterns were some of the principal criteria determining their selection. The earlier studies done in these communities established a base line against which changes in migration behavior that may have resulted from the new U.S. immigration law can be measured. Accordingly, an effort was made to make portions of the primary questionnaire administered in our 1988–1989 field study as comparable as possible with survey items administered in the previous studies of these communities. In addition, our personal familiarity with these communities and many of their residents gave us better access than we would have had in any other appropriate research sites in Mexico.

Since our research sites were selected purposely, we make no claim that our findings are statistically representative of the entire universe of Mexican communities—now including large cities as well as rural localities—that send migrants to the United States. Our research sites are, however, typical of the small rural communities of west-central Mexico that have contributed heavily to the U.S.-bound migratory flow since the 1920s.[2] That our research communities are representative of their region is also suggested by the striking similarities between our findings on the impacts of IRCA and those of researchers who have conducted recent survey studies of other traditional labor-exporting communities in the same region of Mexico.[3]

Sampling Procedures

The first step in the field research was to map the communities and do complete censuses of the dwelling units within them so that random samples of their populations could be drawn. These tasks were completed in May 1988. According to our census, the research communities contained 299, 400 and 691 households, respectively. When unoccupied dwellings were encountered, information about their owners (who were invariably working in the United States) was obtained from neighbors. In most cases, we asked how long the family had been absent, whether they normally return home for the year-end holidays and whether they were expected back in December–January of 1988–1989. New maps of the three communities, showing all dwelling units, were prepared during the household census. The three questionnaires developed for the study were also pretested in the research communities during the census period.

A simple random sample of 200 households was drawn in each community. To prevent underrepresentation of residents who spend most of the year working in the United States, we took several steps. The field interviewing was divided into two principal periods: July–August of 1988 and December–January of 1988–1989. The latter period was timed to coincide with the habitual return of migrants from the United States for the Christmas holidays and the annual community fiestas.[4] Some interviewing was also conducted in the interim months, as families returned from the United States. The following procedure for sample replacements was adopted: If an entire household was found to be absent both in July–August of 1988 and in December–January of 1988–1989, it was replaced with a household that was also absent in July–August of 1988, but had returned to the community by December–January of 1988–89.[5] Finally, nine interviews with heads of household (1.5 percent of the total) were conducted in various California cities, where they were located during the fall of 1988.

The primary interview in each household was conducted with the person identified by its members as the head of household, unless that person was absent during the fieldwork period. In the latter circumstance, interviewers were free to choose any other adult member of the household as the respondent. A total of 586 of these household interviews lasting an average of two hours each were completed. Migration histories and other socioeconomic data were gathered on all members of the household, which totaled 3,471 people.

In addition to the head of household or substitute respondent, we attempted to interview in each household a post-January 1, 1982 migrant to the United States and a would-be, first-time migrant to the United States. Special questionnaires were developed for each of these types of interviews.[6] They were intended to yield detailed information on migratory and employment history; knowledge, attitudes and perceptions relating to migratory behavior; evaluations of the local community; and other areas not covered in depth in our head of household interviews. Thus, the number of interviews conducted per household could range from one to three. We completed 233 interviews with recent migrants to the United

States and 126 interviews with prospective first-time migrants. The recent-migrant interviews averaged 1.5 hours in duration; interviews with prospective migrants lasted about one hour. Thirteen of the recent-migrant interviews (5.6 percent of the total) were conducted at various sites in California, the remainder in the research communities.

For the recent-migrant interview, interviewers were free to choose any available person in the household, aged 15 through 68, who had a history of post-January 1, 1982 migration to the United States. For the prospective migrant interview, interviewers were instructed to select as the respondent a household member, aged 14 or older, who had no history of work in the United States but who identified himself or herself as likely to migrate in the future. In the event that several household members met this description, the person who claimed to be the most likely to migrate to the United States for the first time was interviewed.

We found that most of the people who qualified for the prospective migrant interview were teenagers (both boys and girls) and women in their 20s. This reflects traditional patterns of U.S.-bound migration from the research communities. Most people—especially males—who are going to migrate to the United States do so by their early 20s. Generally speaking, women have been much less likely than males to migrate to the United States. Our field research suggests that, unless they migrated as members of family units, U.S.-bound emigration by teenage girls and young women has been strongly constrained by parental authority.[7] Since 1987, the legalization programs mandated by IRCA have permitted more women to migrate, both individually and as members of family groups.

Our selection of the nonmigrant household member deemed most likely to migrate to the United States in the near future necessarily was based on the judgment of the interviewer. Nevertheless, the subsequent behavior of these interviewees suggests that we succeeded in tapping a highly migration-prone stratum of the nonmigrant population. A follow-up study of residents of one of the three research communities who had been interviewed in July–August of 1988 as prospective first-time migrants to the United States found that about 15 percent had actually migrated between 1 August and 1 December 1988. This rate of emigration is particularly impressive, since these were first trips, occurring during a season when very few people normally leave for the United States. Indeed, migration during the August–December period traditionally runs in the opposite direction, as migrants return to their home communities for end-of-year holidays.

Field Interviewing

A total of 945 interviews were conducted with 798 persons. In 147 cases, the people interviewed as household heads were also interviewed as recent migrants to the United States or as prospective first-time migrants. In these cases, the respondent was interviewed on two different occasions, using two separate questionnaires. This strategy was employed due to the length of the questionnaires and our desire to minimize respondent fatigue. The 798 respondents were distributed among the three research communities as follows: Tlacuitapa, 321; Gómez Farías, 227; Las Animas, 250.

The field research team consisted of 24 interviewers, including 14 females and 10 males. Fourteen of the interviewers were citizens of Mexico, nine were U.S. citizens, and one was a citizen of Colombia. All interviewers were completely bilingual, had advanced training in social science or cognitive science from the B.A. to the Ph.D. level and most were experienced in field studies of this type. Eleven of the interviewers resided in towns within a few kilometers of the research sites; the remainder came from Mexico City and southern California. The interviewers were trained and supervised by the principal investigator and by an experienced field supervisor in each of the research communities.

Interviewee cooperation was quite high. For example, the refusal rate (the proportion of contacted eligible respondents who declined to participate in the study) for the household interviews in the three communities ranged from 2.5 to 4.0 percent. The most difficult people to interview were long-term *norteños*—migrants who had lived in the United States for many years and were acculturated to U.S. norms. They were more suspicious of the researchers' intentions and more likely to resent having to take the time to answer questions than people based primarily in the research communities. These *norteños* considered themselves "on vacation" during their stay in the research communities.[8] The most sensitive interview questions, especially for heads of households based mainly in the research communities, related to remittances of money earned in the United States. Some respondents apparently feared that they would be taxed on this income by the Mexican government.

In addition to the sample survey of households, we conducted a census of all businesses operating in the research communities during the July–January of 1988–89 fieldwork period. The only types of economic activity excluded from this census were agriculture and home work, such as knitting of garments for sale by women working in their own homes. Basic descriptive information about the nature, operation and sources of capitalization for each enterprise was collected through the business census.

Finally, in an effort to better assess the social and economic linkages between sending communities in Mexico and receiving areas in the United States, two members of our research team conducted unstructured interviewing and ethnographic observation among a "snowball" sample of U.S.-based emigrants from one of the communities we studied in Mexico over a period of 18 months in 1988 and 1989.[9] These informants reside, more-or-less permanently, in northern California, primarily the San Francisco Bay area, the Sacramento area and the city of Watsonville.[10]

Sample Structure

In the quantitative analysis that follows, we will make use of six different samples derived from our 1988–89 household survey in the three Mexican research communities. They include:

1. Household heads sample: 586 cases.
2. Recent (post-1 January 1982) migrants to U.S. sample: 233 cases.
3. Prospective first-time migrants to U.S. sample: 126 cases.
4. All respondents sample: 798 cases (586 household heads + 233 recent migrants to the U.S. + 126 prospective first-time migrants to the United States −147 cases in which the same person was interviewed both as a head of household and as a recent migrant or prospective migrant.)[11]
5. All U.S. migrants sample: 1,123 cases (all members of the 586 sampled households, aged 15–64, who have migrated to the U.S. at least once).
6. All household members sample: 3,471 cases (all members of the sampled households).

II. THE RESEARCH COMMUNITIES

Our research sites are located in west-central Mexico, a region with a 100-year tradition of sending workers to the United States.[12] U.S.-bound migration from all three communities began in the first decades of this century, was briefly interrupted in the 1930s by the Great Depression and became a mass movement in the 1940s and 1950s, when many residents participated in the *bracero* program of contract labor importation. In numerous families having homes in these communities, members of three different generations have worked in the United States.

Tlacuitapa, Jalisco

Located on the site of a pre-Columbian Indian settlement, Tlacuitapa reemerged in the 19th Century as a settlement of peons and sharecroppers who worked on nearby haciendas. The community received *ejido* land in 1937, during the most active phase of Mexico's agrarian reform program. By 1970, government statistics showed the community with 2,474 hectares of *ejido* land (1,939 hectares of which was deemed cultivable), being worked by 127 *ejidatarios*.[13] By the mid-1970s, the average size of an ejidal parcel was just 11 hectares. By 1988, according to government statistics, the community had a total of 157 agricultural producers, including private landowners as well as ejidatarios, whose landholdings averaged 14.3 hectares. Only 5 percent of the land was irrigated.[14]

Given the poor quality of the soil and lack of water for irrigation, cattle raising for milk production has always been more important than crop cultivation as a source of income for Tlacuitapeños. Since 1943, the milk has been sold to large processing plants in the city of Lagos de Moreno—one operated by the multinational Nestlé corporation and a large ice cream factory that supplies a national chain of retail outlets. With their small landholdings, most Tlacuitapeños can produce only small quantities of milk. About one hectare of grazing land is needed for each head of cattle. Some corn, beans, sorghum and alfalfa are raised, but scant and erratic rainfall makes agriculture a precarious enterprise. Most of the agricultural product is self-consumed or fed to dairy cattle. Despite the presence of an *ejido*, land tenure is more diversified in Tlacuitapa than in the other two research communities. In addition to *ejidatarios*, the local agricultural labor force contains substantial numbers of sharecroppers (*medieros*), small private landholders (*pequeños propietarios*) and landless laborers (*jornaleros*). Most land is owned by residents of the community, or by long-term *norteños*—persons born in Tlacuitapa whose primary residence is now in the United States.

Apart from retail commerce and a few specialty shops producing metalwork, the only nonagricultural economic activity in the community is garment making—specifically, the knitting of baby clothing and blankets by women in their homes. The handmade garments are sold for a relative pittance to merchants in nearby cities or to intermediaries living in Tlacuitapa itself. Beginning in the 1950s, the majority of Tlacuitapa women have taken up garment making in the home as a modest source of supplemental income, as in other communities in the region.[15]

Tlacuitapeños have easy access to major urban centers in Jalisco and points north. The community is located a few miles off the main highway linking Guadalajara to Lagos de Moreno, an industrial city of more than 100,000. San Juan de los Lagos, another major commercial and religious pilgrimage center, is also within a half hour's drive. An all-weather feeder road connecting Tlacuitapa to the highway was built in the mid-1960s and paved in 1981. It is also linked by unpaved road to the municipal seat, Unión de San Antonio.

By comparison with most rural Mexican communities of its size, Tlacuitapa has long enjoyed a relatively high level of public services and urban infrastructure. The town has had electricity since 1970, telephone service since 1972 and potable drinking water since 1976. A primary school has operated in the community since 1958 and a secondary school since 1967, although the poor quality of these schools is loudly lamented by community residents. Public health services were available in the community only sporadically in the 1960s and 1970s, but a resident private physician as well as a government clinic staffed by a doctor and several nurses now function year-round. Most streets are paved with cobblestones and the state government recently built a handsome central plaza that is the focal point for social and commercial activity.

Tlacuitapa serves as a marketing and service center for residents of smaller localities (*rancherías*) in the surrounding area, and the plaza is surrounded by general stores and other retail businesses. The availability of nonagricultural employment opportunities is reflected in the community's occupational distribution: only 44 percent of the economically active population whose primary residence in 1988–1989 was in Tlacuitapa (versus the United States) worked in agriculture, while 14 percent were employed in services, 8 percent in retail commerce, 8 percent in construction and 26 percent in light manufacturing, mostly in-home garment making.

Like many other communities in the Los Altos de Jalisco region, Tlacuitapa began sending migrant workers to the United States in the first decade of this century.[16] The pioneer migrants went to work in the mines of Arizona and Utah, on the railroads throughout the western United States and in the foundries of Chicago and Canadian border cities. Many more traveled as *braceros* in the 1940s, 1950s and 1960s for agricultural work in Texas and California. Later, some Tlacuitapeños found employment in heavy construction in Oklahoma. The work—mostly bridge building and highway construction—is highly dangerous, and at least four Tlacuitapeños have been killed and several others seriously injured in Oklahoma construction accidents.

The most recent generation of Tlacuitapeño migrants has headed overwhelmingly for California's urban areas, seeking work in the residential construction and service industries. Smaller numbers of Tlacuitapeños have migrated in recent years to Oregon for agricultural work and Nevada for work in Las Vegas hotels and restaurants. In general, Tlacuitapa exhibits a considerably more diversified pattern of U.S.-bound migration than the other two communities included in our study, in terms of destinations and sectors of employment in the United States. Nearly half (47.7 percent) of all Tlacuitapeños aged 15 or older at the time of our household survey had migrated to the United States on at least one occasion.

Over the years, and especially since the mid-1970s, Tlacuitapa's economic and social links with the United States have become very strong. One telling indicator of the community's closer ties with U.S. society is the increased frequency of marriage of young Tlacuitapeños to U.S.-born women—a rarity as recently as 1976, but fairly common by the late 1980s. This phenomenon is related to longer stays in the United States by Tlacuitapeño males in recent years. There are many other signs of pervasive U.S. cultural influence and dollars earned in the United States, including the proliferation of VCRs (24 percent of all Tlacuitapeño households own one), parabolic television antennas sprouting from roof tops (6 percent of all households have them), and pickup trucks bearing U.S. license plates (49 percent of all households own a pickup truck).

Despite substantial permanent emigration to the United States in the last fifteen years, Tlacuitapa's population continues to grow slowly, due primarily to the in-migration of extremely poor families from smaller localities in the surrounding countryside. Our 1988 census counted 400 households, and we estimate the community's total 1988 population at 2,322, up from 1,536 in 1976.[17]

Las Animas, Zacatecas

Las Animas (also known as Daniel Camarena) is located in the southernmost portion of the state of Zacatecas, a region more integrated culturally and economically with the Los Altos region of Jalisco than with the rest of Zacatecas. The community formerly was part of a large hacienda that was subdivided and sold off by the owners over a period of many years. The last hacienda parcels were sold off in the early 1960s. Thus, the community was bypassed by Mexico's agrarian reform program in its most active phase, and there is no ejidal land in Las Animas today. It is a community of small private landowners, sharecroppers, and landless day laborers, with a large absentee landlord class comprised of long-term permanent emigrants living in the United States.

Las Animas' most striking physical characteristic is its poorly developed urban infrastructure. Houses are scattered haphazardly over a large area, with no street grid and no central plaza. Most homes have electricity (introduced in 1973) and the community has a large primary school and a "tele"-secondary school;[18] but as of the time of our field interviewing, there was no potable water service, no functioning sewage system, no health care facilities and no telephone service. The only access to the community was a badly deteriorated, unpaved road leading to Nochistlán, the county seat, five kilometers away. Streams crossing the road at several points make it frequently impassable during the rainy season.

Virtually all agriculture in Las Animas is rainfall-dependent and uses only the most traditional, unmechanized technologies. Corn is the main crop and virtually all of it is self-consumed or used as cattle feed. Much of the cultivable land is now used for cattle raising and numerous parcels lie idle, with their owners employed more or less year-round in the United States.

As in Tlacuitapa, the only nonagricultural activity of any significance in Las Animas is garment making by women. A sewing cooperative was formed in the 1970s, at the encouragement of a local priest, and it continues to produce embroidered goods for sale in nearby markets. The cooperative provides full-time employment for about a dozen young, unmarried women. In contrast to Tlacuitapa, there is very little retail commerce in Las Animas; residents make most of their purchases in Nochistlán. The closest large cities are Aguascalientes and Guadalajara, both of which are more than two hours away.

The economy of Las Animas, like that of the entire *municipio* of Nochistlán, depends fundamentally on dollars earned in the United States. Since 1940, there has been some emigration of Animeños to Guadalajara and Tijuana, but by far the majority of migration—both temporary and permanent—has been to California. The first major wave of Animeño migrants to the United States came during the period of the *bracero* program (1942–1964). Increasingly since the late 1960s, Animeños have sought work in the construction industry (specifically, construction site cleanup) of Orange County, the apparel industry of Los Angeles and the restaurant industry of south San Francisco. Approximately 150 Animeños are employed in the United States by a single Las Animas family, whose members now operate residential construction cleanup firms in Los Angeles, Orange and San Bernadino counties. A small minority of Animeño migrants continue to work in California agriculture, sharecropping on strawberry farms near Watsonville or harvesting melons in the Central Valley. Among all residents of Las Animas who were 15 years of age or older at the time of our household survey, 47.4 percent had migrated to the United States at least once.

Las Animas today is growing only through natural population increase; there is no appreciable in-migration from surrounding areas. In our 1988 household census of the community, 299 households were identified. We estimate the total 1988 population at 1,938, up from 1,333 people counted in the 1979 census.[19] As in the other two communities included in our study, the elderly, children under 15 years of age and women, including many young, single women, are the largest components of Las Animas' population during most of the year, due to the absence of so many working-age males employed in the United States.

Gómez Farías, Michoacán

Formerly called Puentecillas, the community of Gómez Farías is situated in the Valley of Zamora, one of the most fertile and productive agricultural zones of the state of Michoacán. It was established in the 19th century as a settlement of day laborers employed on the hacienda de Guarucha. With the expropriation and redistribution of the hacienda's land in 1935–1936, it became an *ejido* community. The *ejido* plots were extremely small, however, averaging only 2 hectares. Even with fertile soil and ample access to irrigation water from a government irrigation district or by pumping from a nearby river (at least 60 percent of the cultivable land can be irrigated), plots of this size are inadequate to support an average-sized family. With the passage of time much of the original notation of *ejido* land was sold or rented to large, absentee private landholders living in the nearby cities of Zamora and Tangancícuaro, who use it to produce strawberries, mostly for export to the United States. As a result, the vast majority of Gomeños today are landless laborers. The community has very little nonagricultural economic activity; 77 percent of the economically active population whose primary residence in 1988–1989 was still in Gómez Farías (rather than the United States) was employed in agriculture.

With the exception of telephone service, which was not functioning at the time of our fieldwork and the absence of paved streets within the community, Gómez Farías possesses a more highly developed urban infrastructure than the other two research communities. For example, 95 percent of the sampled households had potable water service, and 84 percent had connections to a functioning sewerage system. Community residents have easy access, via a recently paved four-kilometer road, to the main Zamora-to-Morelia highway.

Gomeños have been migrating, mainly to the United States, for four generations. The first group of U.S.-bound emigrants left in 1909 to work in railroad construction in various southwestern states.[20] Subsequent waves of emigrants have worked mainly in agriculture, almost entirely in California. While the most recent generation of Gomeño migrants has increasingly sought employment in the U.S. service sector, Gomeños as a whole remain remarkably specialized in migrating seasonally from March through October each year, to a single place—Watsonville, California, to engage in a single activity—strawberry cultivation and harvesting.

While in the United States, virtually all Gomeños with legal-immigrant status live in the same state government-operated migrant labor camp on the outskirts of Watsonville. The camp, which Gomeños have dominated numerically for the past 15 years, provides one- or two-bedroom bungalows at a cost of $92–102 per month, including all utilities and free child care. This highly advantageous housing arrangement, which is limited to legal agricultural workers, is a strong incentive for Gomeños to maintain their pattern of seasonal migration for agricultural labor in Watsonville rather than to diversify destinations and types of employment, as residents of the other two research communities have done.[21] The availability of guaranteed, low-cost housing also encourages whole-family migration. This is reflected in the low level of educational attainment among Gomeños with a mean of 3.4 years of schooling, according to our household survey, versus 4.4 years among Tlacuitapeños and 4.7 among Animeños. Gómez Farías also has by far the highest illiteracy rate (15.5 percent) among the three research communities. Despite efforts by school authorities in Watsonville to facilitate enrollment of Gomeño children in local elementary schools, it is evident that many Gomeños have spent most of their school-age years picking strawberries in Watsonville.

Among our three research communities, Gómez Farías has by far the highest proportion of migrants to the United States—57 percent of all persons 15 years or older in the community had migrated to the United States at least once—and of legal migrants—people with legal permanent U.S. residency and those who were legalizing their status under the amnesty programs created by the 1986 U.S. immigration law. The large amount of time spent by Gomeño families in the United States each year is reflected in the relatively high proportion of household members who were born in the United States (8.5 percent, as compared with 5.7 percent of Tlacuitapeños and 5.0 percent of Animeños).

The most impressive physical feature of Gómez Farías is the large number of spacious, two-story, brick and concrete houses with modern, U.S.-style architecture. Most of these houses reportedly have been built within the last 15 years. Many (6 percent in our household survey) are equipped with large, parabolic television antennas. Equally striking is the fact that most of these elaborately built and equipped houses are completely vacant for most of each year or are occupied by house sitters. Indeed, 15 percent of the heads of households interviewed in our survey were house sitters for *norteño* families. They return to Gómez Farías for only a few weeks each year, usually in the November–January period, coinciding with the local fiestas. Gómez Farías' population therefore oscillates widely, from a low of about 2,000 in July to double or triple that number in December and January. Based on our household census (which identified 691 households) and subsequent sample survey, we estimate the average, year-round population at 3,767 in 1988.

III. IMPACTS OF EMIGRATION TO THE UNITED STATES ON SENDING COMMUNITIES

Migrant Remittances and Their Utilization

On a day-to-day, year-to-year basis, the economic impact of labor migration to the United States is felt most strongly in the form of cash remittances by migrants to their relatives in the home community. Among our sample of post-1982 migrants to the United States, 73.4 percent sent money to relatives in Mexico during their latest sojourn in the United States. Most of those who did not were legal immigrants whose dependents accompanied them to the United States. Spouses and children were the primary recipients in 55 percent of the cases; parents and siblings were the second most common recipients (40.4 percent). Most migrants remitted on a monthly basis (70.8 percent), using money orders sent through the mail (85.3 percent).[22]

According to our household survey, the average amount remitted by a household member from the United States during the 12 months preceding the interview was $150 per month. Remittances varied significantly by community, ranging from $118 per month per remitting household member among Tlacuitapeños to $168 among Gomeños. Those who were in the United States as unauthorized migrants remitted significantly less at $128 per month than legal immigrants at $164 per month. This is not surprising, considering the younger age, shorter length of total U.S. labor market experience and lesser job seniority of the unauthorized migrants, in addition to their legal status. Short-term migrants tend to remit considerably more money than long-term or permanent emigrants. Among those whose principal residence is now primarily in the United States, remittances to relatives remaining in the community of origin tend to diminish and become more irregular as time passes.

Family maintenance—food, clothing, rent, medicines and other everyday needs—is by far the most important way in which U.S. earnings are utilized in the research communities (see Table 1). Among our sample of recent (post-1982) migrants to the United States, 82.8 percent reported that most of the money they had sent during their latest trip to the United States had been used for this purpose.[23] House construction was the second most frequently cited principal utilization.

According to our survey, three-quarters of the households in the research communities had been adversely affected by the economic crisis of the 1980s and government austerity measures taken to deal with it.[24] The crisis also caused over 30 percent of the households in the research communities to change their way of using migrant remittances. These families now found it necessary to use remittance income exclusively for subsistence in order to offset the sharp decline in their purchasing power. Despite the strength of the dollar in relation to the Mexican peso, skyrocketing local inflation increasingly eroded their advantage.[25]

Most recent migrants (65.7 percent) brought consumer goods to their families when they returned from their latest U.S. sojourn. The gifts most commonly brought were clothes and toys (63.3 percent), television sets (12.7 percent), other consumer electronics (cassette tape-recorders, stereos, VCRs—13.3 percent) and cars and trucks (3.3 percent).

Two-thirds of our sample of recent migrants also managed to save some money during their last trip to the United States, which they brought back to their home community in a lump sum. Among those who had saved something, the mean amount brought back was $2,718 and the median was $2,000. How were these impressively large sums utilized? As shown in Table 2, the bulk of the money was used for expenses incurred while the migrant and his family were visiting their home community. These vacation expenses include travel from the United States, general

TABLE 1

PRINCIPAL UTILIZATION OF MONEY REMITTED DURING MOST RECENT U.S.
SOJOURN, AMONG RECENT MIGRANTS

Utilization	% of Cases
Family maintenance	82.8
House construction or improvement	5.3
Pay debts	2.4
Deposited in bank savings account	2.4
Medical expenses	1.8
Purchase livestock	1.2
Other	4.2

Source: Center for U.S.-Mexican Studies survey of three rural communities, 1988–1989.
The sample for this table consists of persons who had migrated to the United
States at least once since January 1, 1982. Missing data cases are excluded. There
are 169 valid cases.

TABLE 2

PRINCIPAL UTILIZATION OF MONEY SAVED IN THE UNITED STATES AND
RETURNED TO HOME COMMUNITY IN LUMP SUM, AMONG RECENT MIGRANTS*

Utilization	% of Cases
Visiting home community (travel, living expenses; social activities)	26.9
Purchase, construction, or improvement of house	16.4
Family maintenance (*not* while on vacation)	11.2
Deposited in bank to earn interest	9.9
Productive investment started a new business, invested in an existing business, purchased agricultural equipment, purchased livestock)	7.9
Purchased car or truck	6.6
Purchased household appliances or furniture	5.9
Medical expenses	5.3
Nothing—being kept in house	2.6
Other	7.3

Source: Center for U.S.-Mexican Studies survey of three rural communities, 1988–1989.
The sample for this table consists of persons who had migrated to the United
States at least once since 1 January 1982. Missing data cases excluded. There are
152 valid cases.

living expenses while in the home community and money spent on social activities (religious celebrations, gambling, etc.) during the year-end fiestas. Sixteen percent of the migrants used their savings from the U.S. mainly to purchase, build or improve a house. One out of ten deposited his U.S. savings in an interest-earning bank account. Only 7.9 percent invested their U.S. savings in directly productive ways (starting or expanding a small business, acquiring agricultural equipment or livestock).

Nevertheless, over the years a relatively large number of small businesses in the research communities have been capitalized with U.S. earnings. Of the 250 nonagricultural businesses identified in a complete census of such enterprises in the three communities which we surveyed from December–January of 1988–89, 63.1 percent were owned by present or former migrants to the United States, of whom over half had migrated at least once since 1982.[26] Of these businesses, 61 percent had been started with dollars earned in the United States, and 44 percent continue to be sustained at least partly by income earned in the United States, which is used to buy merchandise, livestock or other inputs. Among the owners who have migrated most recently (1986–1989) to the United States, 74 percent continue to draw upon dollars earned in the United States to sustain their business.

Most of the businesses established by migrants to the United States in our research communities are truly small enterprises—grocery stores, butcher shops, restaurants, shops of metal workers, auto repairmen, etc.—that require relatively little capital to start. They represent a fairly wide array of products and services (see Table 3). At the time of our census, the average U.S. migrant business had been operating for 12 years (see Table 4). Most (78 percent) are open throughout the year. The remainder normally function only in the fall and winter months to serve returning migrants from the United States (businesses owned by non-migrants are more likely to stay open year-round).

One of the ironies of U.S.-bound emigration from these communities is that it has probably done more to fuel entrepreneurship in nearby Mexican urban centers, and perhaps even in the United States, than in the source communities themselves. For example, Animeños prefer to invest in small businesses in the county seat of Nochistlán—a city of about 50,000 inhabitants 5 kilometers away—because the return on investments there is much higher than in Las Animas. Similarly, Tlacuitapeños view their home town as a poor place in which to invest, since a large part of the population is absent in the United States for most of the year. Nor is it possible to sell clothing or electrical appliances there, since such items normally are brought from the United States by returning migrants. Just 20 minutes' drive up the highway, Lagos de Moreno, a bustling industrial city and regional marketing center with more than 100,000 inhabitants, offers much better prospects for would-be small businessmen.

TABLE 3

TYPES OF BUSINESSES OWNED BY MIGRANTS TO THE UNITED STATES

Type of Business	% of Cases
Retail grocery store	25.2
Butcher shop	8.2
Street vendor of food, other consumer goods	8.2
Restaurant or cantina	6.8
Buying/selling of agricultural products	6.8
Skilled craftsman shop	6.1
Transportation of cargo or passengers	5.5
Buying/selling of livestock	5.4
Wholesaler of groceries	4.8
Tortilla manufacturing and sale	4.1
Mechanical repair shop (vehicles, etc.)	4.1
Ice cream/popsicle/fruit juice shop	2.7
Buying/selling of agricultural inputs	2.7
Tailor shop	2.1
Billiards/other games	2.0
Bakery	1.4
Barber shop	0.7
Other	3.4

Source: Center for U.S.-Mexican Studies census of nonagricultural businesses in three communities, 1988–1989. Missing data cases excluded. There are 216 valid cases.

TABLE 4

PROFILE OF BUSINESS OWNED BY MIGRANTS TO THE UNITED STATES

Attribute	Frequency
Year established	1976 (mean)
U.S. dollars used to start business	61.0%
U.S. dollars still used to sustain business	43.5%
Open throughout year	78.1%
Number of family members employed	1.97 (mean)
Number of nonfamily members employed	0.46 (mean)
Migration history of owner:	
Most recent trip to U.S. before 1982:	46.3%
Most recent trip to U.S. 1982–1985:	14.3
Most recent trip to U.S. since 1986:	39.5

Source: Center for U.S.-Mexican Studies census of nonagricultural businesses in three communities, 1988–1989. Missing data cases excluded. There are 147 valid cases.

On the U.S. side of the border, Animeños belonging to a single extended family have established several highly successful construction site cleanup firms that operate throughout Los Angeles, San Bernadino and Orange counties. These firms together employ hundreds of workers, including about 150 migrants from Las Animas. This seems to be an exceptional case, however. We are not aware of any other large-scale businesses that have been formed in the United States by emigrants from the research communities.

Consumption Patterns

A minority of *norteños* in the research communities use their dollars to engage in various kinds of what is, by Mexican standards, conspicuous consumption. Perhaps the most notable example is the increasingly ubiquitous parabolic television antenna. In 1988–1989, *parabólicas* were owned by just 23 households in our sample (4 percent), but their numbers were increasing rapidly, despite an average cost of about (US) $1,000. These technological marvels are especially popular among long-term migrants to the United States, who use them to watch their favorite soap operas and sports attractions while they are visiting their home towns.

A total of 78 percent of households in the three communities had television sets in 1988–1989. Using them with video-cassette recorders purchased in the United States to watch U.S.-made movies has become a common form of entertainment in these communities in recent years. More than 13 percent of the households owned a VCR in 1988–1989, and video rental stores in the research communities and nearby towns were doing a brisk business.

The vast majority of motor vehicles operating in these communities have been purchased with U.S. earnings. A total of 15 percent of all households in the research communities owned a car and 30 percent had at least one pickup truck. These individually owned vehicles have become the most common means of transport to the United States. When migrants return for Christmas and the annual town fiestas, traffic jams are produced in the narrow streets by the large numbers of cars, trucks and campers bearing California, Illinois, Oklahoma, Oregon, Texas and Nevada license plates.

The majority of houses in the research communities have been built, at least in part, with income earned in the United States. The houses of long-term *norteños* are immediately recognizable, with their modern U.S.-style architecture, two-story construction, use of modern construction materials and small front yards rather than the traditional central patio. The largest of the *norteño* houses in our research communities reportedly cost about (US) $20,000 to build. Elaborate *norteño* houses are most prevalent in Gómez Farías, where migrants seem to have competed among themselves to build the largest and most ostentatious houses. Gomeños prefer to invest in housing in their home town rather than in the United States, where most of them stay in a migrant-labor camp.

Unfortunately, most of the multiplier effect of consumption by migrants to the United States is not experienced by the migrants' home communities. Most consumer goods as well as inputs for home construction are purchased outside of the home community, usually in a nearby city that serves as a regional marketing center and offers lower prices. Nevertheless, most small businesses in the research communities could not survive without the consumer spending that is fueled by the constant influx of remittances by U.S.-based migrants to their relatives or the extensive recreational spending by returned migrants during their winter vacations.

Impacts on Agriculture

Only a handful of persons in the research communities have used their U.S. earnings to become agricultural entrepreneurs. This is not surprising, since the poor local climatic and soil conditions for agriculture in Tlacuitapa and Las Animas, coupled with national economic policies that have squeezed profits for most agricultural producers, make it necessary to invest large sums of money to have a chance at success. Even the individual in Tlacuitapa who has made the most substantial investments in agriculture since 1970—buying more land for cultivation or grazing, drilling wells, installing watering systems, etc.—continues to spend most of each year working in California; he and his family are not dependent on local agriculture for their disposable income. Local conditions are much more favorable in Gómez Farías; agriculture can be profitable there if one spends enough money for inputs, machinery and labor from nearby towns. Even there, however, very few *norteños* have chosen to become agribusinessmen, while absentee landlords based in nearby cities have gained control over local agriculture.

A more modest form of investment in agriculture, occurring far more often in the research communities, is the purchase of a few heads of livestock. Acquiring dairy cattle is also a form of saving: people buy cows with their U.S. earnings, then sell them when they are ready to make another trip to the United States. They also sell them in order to finance house construction and other major expenditures.

The most generalized impact of U.S.-bound migration on agriculture in the research communities operates through migrant remittances. In most cases, it is only the supplemental income from the United States that enables agricultural units in these communities to stay in production. Otherwise, farmers could not afford to purchase the necessary inputs. As a government extension agent described the ejido of Tlacuitapa, "In

Tlacuitapa, people don't live from their *parcelas;* the *parcelas* live from *El Norte.*"

Nevertheless, in all three research communities, U.S.-bound migrants increasingly are abandoning land that was formerly cropped, as the financial incentives for keeping it in production continue to diminish.[27] Our 1988–1989 household survey shows that even now, most of the land owned by migrants is not left idle when its owners go north; wives, children, brothers, in-laws or sharecroppers typically manage it. But the proportion of land completely out of production is rising. With low prices for agricultural products and high costs, more and more small, private landholders and *ejidatarios* are concluding that it is not worth it even to have their land sharecropped while they are away in *El Norte.*

Impacts on Employment

The employment-multiplier effects of small-business investments by migrants in the research communities have been modest. As shown in Table 4, the average U.S. migrant business employs just 2.43 people, 1.97 of whom are members of the owner's family. The largest such businesses in Tlacuitapa, for example, are a ceramic tile factory and a dairy farm, each of which employs four people. Nevertheless, small businesses established by migrants to the U.S. provide work for a total of nearly 400 people in the three communities—a nontrivial portion of the economically active population.

The most striking effect of migration to the United States on the employment situation in the research communities has been the creation of labor shortages. Large landowners in all three communities routinely complain that they cannot find day laborers because the *norteños*—who comprise the vast majority of young, able-bodied workers in these communities, when they are there—refuse to work for prevailing wages in the region. In Gómez Farías, for example, landowners must go to the nearby cities of Tangancícuaro and Zamora to find willing workers. In Tlacuitapa, the *norteños* generally refuse to work as cow milkers or agricultural day laborers while they are in town; so destitute families from nearby small villages have moved into Tlacuitapa to provide this labor. In Las Animas, Richard Mines observed that "even those present in the village at peak harvest season chose not to work. Those with decent jobs in the United States saw no reason to work at less than a dollar an hour when they were earning several times as much in the United States."[28]

Conclusion

The sending communities that we have studied have not escaped the economic distortions frequently associated with large-scale labor emigration from the Third World to advanced industrial countries. These include consumption of nonessential durables; inflated land, housing and food prices; income polarization, culminating in the emergence of absentee landlord and vacationer elites; low levels of investment in productive activities because income earned in the United States goes mostly to finance personal consumption and housing construction; declining agricultural production; and even labor shortages as local wages become increasingly unacceptable to returning migrants.

These processes are cumulative. Out-migration breeds more out-migration, as economic incentives to remain there continue to weaken, and residents increasingly view their community as a temporary refuge from labor in the United States rather than an environment for work and investment. With each passing year, there is less investment in productive activities. Dependence on *El Norte* as the principal source of disposable income in the community deepens.

There is another side to the ledger, however, which is often overlooked by social scientists and public policymakers. For example, income inequality undoubtedly has been increased by migration to the United States, but absolute poverty in the research communities has been ameliorated by remitted income. A significant portion of the capital returned by migrants who have worked in the United States continues to be dispersed through their home communities, in the form of at least some consumer spending that benefits local commerce, loans made by returned migrants to other community residents and employment opportunities created by the small business investments of *norteños*. Permanent emigration from the community to cities within Mexico as well as to the United States has been lower than it would have been in the absence of large-scale temporary migration to the United States. More land probably has been kept in agricultural production than has fallen out of production because of U.S.-bound migration.

All this is reflected in the attitudes of community residents toward the migratory process. When asked whether they thought that the emigration of many people from their community had benefited or harmed the community, nearly 56 percent of those expressing an opinion perceived an overall beneficial impact and an additional 18 percent saw some benefits and some detrimental effects (see Table 5).[29] When asked to explain their response, most of those who viewed emigration positively cited the large sums of money remitted or brought back by the migrants; the ability of at least some community residents to improve their economic situation and living standards through migration (mentioned especially in Gómez Farías, whose population includes relatively more legal, higher-wage-earning immigrants than the other two communities); and the absence of alternative local employment opportunities (see Table 6). Those who believed that migration had harmed their community mentioned such problems as the long or permanent absence of relatives, idle farm lands, espe-

TABLE 5

EVALUATION OF EMIGRATION IMPACTS ON COMMUNITY OF RESIDENCE
BY COMMUNITY
(percentages)

Response	Tlacuitapa (N = 310)	Gómez Farías (N = 212)	Las Animas (N = 237)	All (N = 759)
Has benefited community	53.2	60.4	54.0	55.5
Has harmed community	22.9	13.7	15.2	17.9
Neither benefited nor harmed	11.0	6.6	7.6	8.7
Benefited in some ways, harmed in others	12.9	19.3	23.2	17.9

Source: Center for U.S.-Mexican Studies household survey of three communities, 1988–1989. The question was: "It can be seen that many people have left the community to live somewhere else. Do you believe that the departure of people from this community has benefited or harmed the community?" The sample for this table consists of all respondents in the research communities. "Don't know" cases have been excluded. There are 759 valid cases. Chi-square = 25.01; significance: $p < .0015$.

TABLE 6

REASON FOR PERCEIVED BENEFICIAL IMPACT OF EMIGRATION ON
COMMUNITY OF RESIDENCE, BY COMMUNITY
(percentages)

Response	Tlacuitapa (N = 165)	Gómez Farías (N = 127)	Las Animas (N = 127)	All (N = 419)
Money remitted or brought by migrants	74.6	50.4	57.5	62.1
Lack of local employment alternatives	21.8	11.0	20.5	18.1
Economic mobility of some people in community	1.8	28.3	18.9	15.0
Other	1.8	10.2	3.1	4.5

Source: Center for U.S.-Mexican Studies household survey of three communities, 1988–1989. The question was: "It can be seen that many people have left this community to live somewhere else. Do you believe that the departure of people from this community has benefited or harmed the community?" The sample for this table consists of all respondents in the research communities. "Don't know" cases excluded. There are 419 valid cases. Chi-square = 62.21; significance: $p < .0000$.

cially in Tlacuitapa, drug addiction and delinquency among young returned migrants and socioeconomic inequalities (Table 7).

What mass migration to the United States has not done here nor in most other labor-exporting communities in Mexico is to provide a basis

TABLE 7

REASON FOR PERCEIVED HARMFUL IMPACT OF EMIGRATION ON
COMMUNITY OF RESIDENCE, BY COMMUNITY
(percentages)

Response	Tlacuitapa (N = 48)	Gómez Farías (N = 25)	Las Animas (N = 29)	All (N = 102)
Relatives absent from community too long	33.3	52.0	48.3	42.2
Much land no longer cultivated	39.6	8.0	20.7	26.5
Drug use, juvenile delinquency	6.3	8.0	3.4	5.9
Social/economic differences among residents are greater	4.2	4.0	3.4	3.9
Other	14.6	24.0	24.1	19.6

Source: Center for U.S.-Mexican Studies household survey of three communities, 1988–
1989. The question was: "It can be seen that many people have left the community
to live somewhere else. Do you believe that the departure of people from this
community has benefited or harmed the community?" The sample for this table
consists of all respondents in the research communities. "Don't know" cases excluded. There are 102 valid cases. Chi-square = 14.32; significance: p<.2810.

for sustained local economic development. It remains to be seen whether
the very substantial resources generated by the migratory process can be
channeled in such a way as to alter this outcome. It is to this challenge that
we now turn.

IV. COMMUNITY DEVELOPMENT AND MIGRATION: OBSTACLES AND POSSIBILITIES

What are the possibilities for reorienting the economic and social life of
traditional labor-exporting communities, at this point in time, so as to create viable alternatives to international migration? In this chapter, we attempt to address this broad question by evaluating several of the most
commonly prescribed remedies for mass out-migration, in light of our
findings from the three sending communities that we have studied. We
begin by describing perhaps the most fundamental obstacle to the success of any of these remedial schemes—i.e., the *culture of out-migration.*

The Culture of Out-migration

The economic and demographic forces promoting emigration from the
research communities are powerful and obvious, but in many cases they

are insufficient to explain the intensity of migratory behavior. In communities with a multigenerational history of migration to the United States, new and repeat migration is also impelled by a very pronounced culture of out-migration. We refer to a set of interrelated perceptions, attitudinal orientations, socialization processes and social structures, including transnational social networks, growing out of the international migratory experience, which constantly encourage, validate and facilitate participation in this movement.[30]

In the culture of out-migration, men in their 20s and early 30s readily come to see themselves as professional migrants, whose lifetime vocation is to specialize in *El Norte*. Girls grow up expecting that, after they marry, they will spend a large part of their lives either apart from their husbands or, more recently, shuttling with them between the United States and the home community. Migration to the United States becomes a complete substitute for local economic activity—a solution to one's economic problems that is considerably easier and less risky than starting a business in the home community, or investing in agricultural infrastructure or organizing a production cooperative. It is also difficult to become concerned about the lack of public services, unpaved roads or other deficiencies of the home community when one spends most of his time in the United States; so there is little civic spirit and no collective efforts to secure public goods.[31] Some of those who migrate to the United States have no apparent economic necessity for going, like the skilled metal craftsman in Tlacuitapa who owns his own shop and gets plenty of orders for his wrought iron grillwork from customers in Lagos de Moreno, León, Guadalajara and other cities. Despite his gainful employment, in July 1988 he was preparing to leave for California to pick fruit out of sheer boredom with life in his home community.

A central element of this culture of out-migration is a view of the local opportunity structure as being extremely restricted. When we asked our interviewees whether it was possible for a person born in their community to get ahead in life without leaving the town, 76.6 percent responded "No, one must leave."[32] In Tlacuitapa, 79.5 percent felt that getting ahead required emigration—up from 69.6 percent in 1976, when we asked the same question among Tlacuitapeños. Interviewees in all three communities in the 1988–1989 survey were asked to explain their response to this question: why can't someone progress without emigrating? Most cited lack of jobs in their home community (39.3 percent); some mentioned the lack of advanced educational opportunities there (9.5 percent) and low prevailing wages (5.1 percent). But nearly one out of three respondents simply explained, "here, there is *nothing*."

When we asked whether a person could get ahead in life by migrating to some other place in Mexico, rather than to the United States, 56 percent of the total sample answered "yes"; but only 47.8 percent of the heads of household saw any possibility of getting ahead through internal migration. Moreover, there were significant differences according to migratory history. Those who had never migrated to the United States were most optimistic about opportunities elsewhere in Mexico; experienced migrants to the United States, especially legal or legalizing ones, were more pessimistic. Even among those who believed that opportunities for upward mobility still existed in Mexico, only a tiny minority were themselves considering a move to a Mexican destination.

Changing the Local Opportunity Structure

How would conditions in traditional sending communities have to change in order to alter such perceptions? We asked our interviewees in the research communities: "What are the things that are most lacking in this community?" They were then asked to specify the three most important deficiencies, in order of importance. Finally, the respondents were asked, with respect to the three most important community problems, "How do you think the lack of each of these things could be solved?

The responses to this series of questions are summarized in Tables 8, 9, and 10. Jobs—more and better ones, especially factory jobs—are a major concern for more than half of the residents of our research communities. Tlacuitapeños are particularly eager to have factories as a means of improving employment opportunities in their community. By comparison, Gomeños seem unconcerned about the lack of jobs at home. This is not surprising, since so few residents of Gómez Farías try to retain an economic base in Mexico.

Overall, two-thirds of our respondents see a need for improvements in basic urban services and physical infrastructure, although there are very large cross-community differences that reflect the actual services/infrastructure deficiencies of the three towns. For example, Animeños are nearly twice as likely to be concerned about such needs as Tlacuitapeños. Similarly, health care facilities are a major concern where they do not exist, as in Las Animas.

It is striking that only about one in ten residents of these three predominantly agricultural communities sees a high-priority need for improvements that would benefit agricultural producers, like irrigation, land redistribution or credit. This finding suggests the extent to which residents of these communities have, in effect, given up on agriculture, at least as an engine for local development. Again, the extreme case is Gómez Farías, where people see their community's agricultural sector as a source of employment primarily for nonlocal peons and sharecroppers and as a source of wealth for nonlocal landlords.

Table 9 reveals some interesting variations by immigration status. In

TABLE 8

PERCEIVED MOST IMPORTANT COMMUNITY NEEDS, BY COMMUNITY
(percentages)

Type of need	Tlacuitapa (N = 321)	Gómez Farías (N = 227)	Las Animas (N = 250)	All (N = 798)
Jobs (more jobs and better-paying jobs)	54.2	12.3	37.2	37.0
Factories of any type	44.5	1.8	24.0	25.9
Either jobs or factories	77.1	14.2	49.8	50.8
Schools (more or better; all levels)	43.0	55.9	8.0	35.7
Health care facilities (clinics, physicians, pharmacies)	13.7	14.1	52.8	26.1
Basic urban services (sewerage, electricity, telephones, potable water)	44.2	79.3	81.6	65.9
Paved streets and/or access roads	19.6	69.2	38.8	39.7
Agricultural improvements of all types	15.0	1.3	17.6	11.9
Irrigation works	10.9	0.4	16.4	9.6
Land redistribution	1.9	0.4	0.0	0.9
Church (church building or priests)	1.2	0.0	3.2	1.5
Retail stores/supermarkets	5.0	13.7	2.8	6.8
Parks/recreational centers	11.5	6.6	2.4	7.3

Source: Center for U.S.-Mexican Studies survey in three communities, 1988–1989. The sample for this table consists of all respondents in the communities. Table entries represent the proportion of all respondents who mentioned this need as one of the three most important needs of all their community.

general, unauthorized migrants to the United States and nonmigrants are more concerned about the local employment base than legal immigrants to the United States and those in process of legalization. The "legals" and "Rodinos"[33] seem more concerned about amenities such as paved streets and urban services. These variations suggest the difference in perspective that long-term experience in the United States brings. Those having permanent U.S. legal resident status and those striving to achieve it are more interested in their home towns as vacation and possibly retirement spots, not as places where they must or may have to earn a living. However, a PROBIT analysis of the responses concerning each type of community need, with immigration status, community of residence, age, gender and education as independent variables, shows that the net impact of immi-

TABLE 9

PERCEIVED MOST IMPORTANT COMMUNITY NEEDS
BY IMMIGRATION STATUS
(*percentages*)

Type of Need	Legal Immigrants (N = 143)	"Rodinos" (N = 83)	Unauthorized Migrants (N = 225)	Nonmigrants[a] (N = 331)
Jobs or factories	39.9	42.2	52.0	56.8
Factories	18.7	14.9	30.7	28.9
Schools	42.0	41.0	28.0	38.7
Health care facilities	17.5	26.5	29.3	28.7
Basic urban services	78.3	69.9	67.1	61.9
Paved streets/access roads	60.1	53.0	36.0	32.0
Agricultural improvements	13.3	9.6	18.2	8.2
Retail stores/supermarkets	7.0	8.4	7.1	6.3
Parks/recreational centers	5.6	10.8	2.7	10.6

Source: Center for U.S.-Mexican Studies survey in three communities, 1988–1989. The sample for this table consists of all respondents in the communities. Table entries represent the proportion of all respondents within a given immigration status group who mentioned this need as one of the three most important needs of their community.

[a]People who have never migrated to the United States.

TABLE 10

PREFERRED SOLUTION FOR MOST IMPORTANT COMMUNITY NEED

(percentages)

Type of Need	PREFERRED SOLUTION				
	Governmental action[a]	Nonlocal private sector action[b]	Foreign assistance[c]	Community residents[d]	Other
Jobs or factories	54.8	24.7	3.5	16.3	0.8
Basic urban services/streets/ health care	59.9	3.4	0.0	36.6	0.0
Agricultural improvements	60.5	7.9	2.6	29.0	0.0

Source: Center for U.S.-Mexican Studies survey in three communities, 1988–1989. The sample for this table consists of all respondents in the communities. Missing data cases excluded. There are 259 valid cases for jobs or factories; 262 for urban services/streets/health care; 38 for agriculture. Table entries represent the proportion of respondents who identified this need as their community's single most important and prefer a given solution to this problem.

[a]Governmental action at any level (local, state, or federal); also action by the ruling party (P.R.I.).

[b]Action by private investors, businessmen, and other nonlocal economic actors.

[c]Foreign aid (unspecified); aid from international agencies, non-Mexican banks, and U.S. Government.

[d]Self-help residents of the community, including migrants to the United States.

gration status is weak, especially compared with that of community of residence. The principal exceptions are basic urban services, paved streets and access roads, where immigration status does seem to have an independent effect that approaches minimum levels of statistical significance.[34]

The residents of our research communities see the Mexican government as the principal source of solutions for all of these problems (see Table 10). Nonlocal, private-sector actors are viewed as a source of job-creating investments—more so than the community's own residents. Self-help efforts are most likely to be seen as the preferred way of solving urban service/infrastructure problems, usually in combination with government financing.

To more precisely identify the kinds of changes that might be needed in order to deter future migration from the research communities, we asked our interviewees the following question: "In your opinion, what would be necessary in order for fewer people to leave this town?" The responses are presented in Table 11. They reveal an even more pronounced fixation on job creation than the responses to the previous and more general question about community needs: 79.4 percent of all respondents gave an employment-related answer. Once again, the perceived need is to create jobs in nonagricultural industries; very few residents of these communities are interested in improving agriculture. And again, residents of Gómez Farías display their relative lack of concern about the local employment base.

The employment-related responses to this question and others in our survey must be interpreted with care. Nearly 40 percent of the respondents simply mentioned *trabajo* (jobs or work) in general, with no qualifications. Another 12 percent called for creation of more jobs. But 13 percent specified that better jobs—jobs paying higher wages, or more stable, year-round jobs—were needed. And another 16 percent felt that it would be necessary to create factory jobs to reduce future emigration. Among the types of manufacturing enterprises mentioned were shoe factories, garment and textile factories and factories for processing cattle fodder and milk products. A few thought that enterprises that would employ primarily women or youths were needed. In short, many residents of our research communities apparently believed that mere job creation was not enough to deter out-migration. Rather, it would be necessary to create jobs whose characteristics would make them an acceptable alternative to international migration. If they had been pressed sufficiently, many of the interviewees who gave an undifferentiated jobs response probably would have made the same kind of distinction.

TABLE 11

TYPE OF CHANGE NECESSARY IN ORDER TO REDUCE EMIGRATION
BY COMMUNITY

Type of Change	Tlacuitapa (N = 317)	Gómez Farías (N = 221)	Las Animas (N = 248)	All (N = 786)
Unspecified jobs	47.3	19.5	48.8	39.9
More jobs	13.9	14.5	6.0	11.6
Better-paying jobs	7.6	20.4	11.7	12.5
More stable jobs	0.6	0.0	1.2	0.6
More jobs for women or youths	1.5	0.0	0.4	0.8
Factories	19.1	2.3	22.6	15.5
Schools	0.6	0.0	0.8	0.6
Agricultural improvements	6.3	3.2	5.2	5.2
Better government	0.0	1.9	0.4	0.7
Other	0.9	24.9	1.6	7.6
Don't know, or nothing can be done	0.9	12.2	0.4	3.9

Source: Center for U.S.-Mexican Studies survey of three communities, 1988–1989. The sample for this table includes all respondents in the communities. Missing data cases excluded. There are 786 valid cases.

Implications for Public Policy

Clearly, what the residents of the labor-exporting communities that we have studied are seeking is the creation of permanent, nonagricultural employment opportunities, preferably in small-scale manufacturing enterprises. Our studies of the three communities and of the regional economies in which they are situated suggest that fostering the development of such nonagricultural microenterprises may be the *only* strategy to appreciably reduce future migration flows from them.

Due in large part to their U.S. experience in nonagricultural jobs (construction, light manufacturing, urban services, restaurants, etc.), the younger generation of workers in these communities is not disposed to taking agricultural jobs in their home towns. Not even higher than prevailing local wages in year-round activities like irrigation projects that would permit multiple cropping were appealing. It is entirely possible, if not probable, that any new jobs created in local agriculture would be taken by in-migrants from surrounding villages who are not yet part of the U.S.-bound migratory stream. Moreover, prospects are bleak for the creation of a new generation of self-employed agricultural entrepreneurs in these communities. Altering the present allocation of fundamental resources for agriculture, especially land and water, in these places would be extremely difficult and costly.[35] Land prices have risen so high over the years that acquiring enough of it for reasonably efficient farming or live-stock raising requires large sums of money, to say nothing of the substantial investments that would have to be made in irrigation facilities, machinery and other inputs. Without major investments in irrigation, any additional jobs created in agriculture would be seasonal in nature and therefore unattractive to would-be migrants. The employment insecurity and underemployment suffered by agricultural wage laborers in communities like those we have studied is a major contributor to U.S.-bound migration today. Moreover, especially under present and foreseeable market conditions for Mexican agriculture, new agricultural entrepreneurs would have every incentive to use labor-saving technologies; so the employment-generating impacts of new investments in agriculture are likely to be more limited than those of investments in nonagricultural enterprises.[36]

But what kinds of nonagricultural enterprises? There are severe limits on the number of retail businesses that can be supported by the populations of traditional labor-exporting communities in Mexico. In the communities that we have studied, those limits probably have already been reached. Moreover, as our data suggest, the employment-multiplier effects of investments in small retail businesses are modest. A more viable approach to creating significant numbers of the types of jobs that might retain workers in these communities is that of rural industrialization.

It has been demonstrated that under certain conditions, labor-intensive, small-scale manufacturing enterprises can flourish in such places, if their commercialization problems can be solved. The family-owned garment *maquiladora* (factory) has become quite common throughout the Los Altos region of Jalisco, for example, in the last 15–20 years.[37] Moreover, case studies have also shown that small-scale, rural industries can be important in reducing out-migration. For example, the town of Villa Hidalgo, Jalisco, lost population through out-migration at an average annual rate of 9.9 percent per year during the 1950s and 1960s, but gained population through in-migration at a rate of 4.8 percent per year during the 1970s. The major change in this case was the creation of a large number of jobs in approximately 200 small, family-owned textile and garment factories established within the town since 1967.[38] The industrialization of Villa Hidalgo began in that year, when a migrant returning from several years of employment in the United States invested his savings in two manually operated cloth weaving machines. Producing a variety of carefully finished garments for women and children that were successfully marketed in Mexico City and adding motorized machinery and workers as his profits increased, this initial entrepreneur set an example that was quickly emulated by many of his neighbors. Villa Hidalgo became a supplier of clothing to major department stores in Aguascalientes, Mexico City, Monterrey and other cities.

The industrialization effort in Villa Hidalgo began with no government assistance, other than the introduction of electricity, which came after the first textile-garment factories in the town. Even the single feeder road leading to the town was unpaved when industrialization began. Later, financial help was provided to factory owners by the state government in the form of tax exemptions. Virtually all of the initial investment capital came from savings accumulated through employment in the United States. Later, as the local manufacturers became better credit risks, commercial bank credit became available for expansion. But factory jobs could have been created faster and in larger numbers with Mexican government or international agency support. Such support might take the form of low-interest loans, training programs for local entrepreneurs and assistance in developing domestic and export markets.

The rarity of cases like Villa Hidalgo suggests the need for caution in generalizing from its experience. The town of Nochistlán, Zacatecas, only a short distance from Villa Hidalgo, used to have numerous small clothing and shoe factories, but new technologies and mass production have wiped them out; local entrepreneurs were unable to compete with large producers in Guadalajara and León. Nor does Villa Hidalgo-style industrialization guarantee that out-migration will cease permanently. In the town of Moroleón, Guanajuato, for example, returned migrants from the United States also invested their savings in some 900 small garment firms. Multiple currency devaluations since 1982 have forced an estimated 30 percent of the small family firms to incorporate themselves into larger firms, which had access to sufficient credit to buy the raw materials necessary to survive the devaluations. Another 20 percent have gone out of business. Simultaneously, the introduction of fabric purchased from large, computerized factories in Mexico City has diminished the role of male members of the families involved in this industry. Rather than making the fabric to be transformed into garments, they are now carriers of finished goods to market—a role neither as significant nor as profitable as they had in the industry when it began in Moroleón. Many men can now be expected to resume migrating to the United States.[39]

Indeed, a frequently heard criticism of rural industries in Mexico is that they do not provide enough employment opportunities attractive to the most migration-prone segment of the population, such as young males. In Las Animas, key informants told us that a nonagricultural industry in that community would mainly reduce female emigration. Males would continue to migrate to the United States, they argued, unless the wages offered by such an industry began to approximate U.S. levels. We suspect that such concerns are overdrawn and that some nontrivial portion of the would-be, first-time migrants to the United States in today's labor-exporting communities could be induced to take jobs in small-scale, non-agricultural industries that pay well below U.S. levels.

Nevertheless, we must be concerned about the evident fragility of microenterprises in rural communities. The available evidence from case studies shows that some of these firms can succeed in weathering the storms of devaluations, basic technological changes and other threats to their survival; but many do not. A 1990 census of businesses throughout the state of Jalisco has encountered a high incidence of small-business failures in the state's rural communities and small towns, attributable to the economic crisis of the 1980s, which wiped out much of the local market for their goods. The same census has found numerous cases of non-agricultural small businesses being moved out of rural communities into large cities where consumer markets are more promising.[40]

These patterns suggest the need for programs to assist small, rural industries to deal more effectively with their marketing problems. They need greater access to credit, not only for start-up but to finance necessary adjustments and expansion. The formation of production cooperatives may be necessary to improve the commercialization of non-agricultural products. Production cooperatives started by priests have functioned with moderate to high levels of success in several towns in the region where our fieldwork was conducted. In the town of Dolores, Jalisco, a successful dairy products cooperative reportedly has sharply reduced short-term labor migration to the United States.[41] A smaller production cooperative for apparel that was formed in Las Animas in 1978 (subsequently assisted by a grant from the Inter-American Foundation) seems to have had less success in enlarging the market for its goods. It has had little impact on emigration from the community.

How is the establishment of nonagricultural small businesses to be financed? Most discussions of this problem, in the context of international migration, stress the need for mechanisms to pool or channel migrant remittances. It is assumed that in the absence of some organized effort to collectively invest the capital accumulated by migrant workers abroad, their earnings will simply go to finance personal consumption and will never stimulate sustained economic development in the place of origin.[42] As the Villa Hidalgo case demonstrates, such pooling schemes, whether presided over by governments or private agencies, are not always necessary to insure productive investment of migrants' earnings. However, in the sending communities that we studied in 1988–1989, there was a clear need for better mechanisms to harness the capital being generated by migrants to the United States. In this conservative, strongly antistatist region, and in many other parts of rural Mexico, any efforts by official agencies to channel migrant remittances through taxation or other means would probably be resisted by most migrants. They would be much more likely to cooperate with pooling mechanisms based on local, private *asociaciones civiles* rather than vertically organized government programs.

Why encourage the formation of microindustries in rural communities instead of larger-scale enterprises either in rural communities or in regional growth-pole cities? Indeed, some members of the local elites in our research communities questioned the wisdom and efficacy of a microenterprise strategy. They argued that what is needed to retain people in their community is not more small, family-owned businesses, but a larger, more formal enterprise that would offer higher wages and employ more people. This argument is open to challenge on at least two grounds. First, the kinds of financial incentives and infrastructure investments that would probably be necessary to induce large firms to locate manufacturing plants in communities of this size, thus foregoing the enormous locational advantages of cities like Guadalajara, León and Mexico City, would be extremely costly. Such investments are not likely to materialize. Second, owning and managing one's own business, however small, is a more powerful deterrent to emigration than being a wage worker in a medium- or large-sized industrial plant.[43]

As for industrialization based on a regional growth pole, the evidence supporting its efficacy in reducing out-migration is thin. Indeed, as Rafael Alarcón has pointed out, this notion is directly contradicted by the experience of the region surrounding Lagos de Moreno, where Tlacuitapa is located.[44] The rapid growth of industrial employment in Lagos de Moreno during the last 15 years has had no impact on emigration from Tlacuitapa, just 30 kilometers away. Indeed, as a potential source of employment, Lagos de Moreno barely registers in the consciousness of Tlacuitapeños. When asked where in Mexico one might be able to get ahead economically, only 9.4 percent of Tlacuitapeños mentioned Lagos de Moreno. Such facts inspire little confidence that increasing industrial or other nonagricultural employment in medium-sized cities located within high-emigration regions will constrain U.S.-bound migration from rural communities within the same regions.

Conclusion: The Need for Realism

There is a need for realism in gauging the capacity of any sending community-based development scheme to retain would-be migrants to the United States. As narrowly economic motivations for migration recede in importance and social processes like family reunification and network formation become the driving forces behind the migration phenomenon, it will be increasingly difficult to stem the outflow using the kinds of incentives created by most development projects and programs. Moreover, development initiatives themselves, while deterring the out-migration of some workers, may promote the movement of others. A recent study of high-emigration *municipios* in the state of Jalisco, for example, found that commercialization of agriculture and nonagricultural development in relatively underdeveloped areas of the state where demographic pressure on land and other local resources remains strong tends to stimulate the out-migration of labor.[45]

Clearly, the outlook for retaining the majority of workers in such areas is bleak, whatever governments choose to do. With regard to mature migrating communities like the ones we have studied, the only realistic objective of government intervention can be to reduce somewhat—rather than eliminate—their present high level of dependence on income-earning opportunities in the United States. In particular, the goal should be to create viable alternatives to international migration for would-be, first-time migrants to the United States, rather than try to persuade already experienced individuals and families to abandon this source of income. Achieving this more limited goal will be difficult but not impossible, even in the context of traditional labor-exporting communities.

Douglas Massey has argued recently that Mexico, as a sending country, should not be the focus of policymakers' concerns, because "it is much too late in the process to have any realistic expectation of markedly affecting the level of Mexican emigration to the United States," and because "the pool of potential migrants [in Mexico] will gradually decline" over the next two decades, as the rural population from which emigrants are drawn continues to dwindle.[46] By extension, it could be argued that within Mexico, traditional sending communities and their regions should be overlooked in order to channel scarce resources for promoting development to places not yet integrated into the U.S.-bound migratory stream to prevent the formation of new transnational migrant networks.

Massey's broader argument is undercut by fragmentary but growing evidence that Mexico's largest urban centers, including Mexico City and Guadalajara, have become important exporters of labor to the United States in recent years.[47] Over half of the Mexican population now lives in large-scale urban areas, and as Victor Urquidi has pointed out, labor force growth rates in these new sending areas remain quite high. Thus, migration from the urban sector may offset future reductions in migration from the traditional, rural source areas.[48] The traditional source areas show little evidence of dropping out of the flow. What seems to be occurring is that U.S.-bound migration is involving ever larger and more diverse segments of the Mexican population.

The derivative argument about bypassing mature sending communities in favor of nonmigrating ones is also fraught with difficulties. Both fertility and labor force growth rates in our research communities remain high and the places of permanent emigrants to the United States are often taken by new in-migrants from nearby villages. While total population in these communities is not growing appreciably, neither is it shrinking in absolute terms. Traditional sending communities like these will contain a large reservoir of potential first-time migrants to the United States for at least another generation. And our data suggest that the majority of them will not be deterred from migrating to the United States—with or without legal-entry papers—by actions on the U.S. side aimed at reducing the demand for immigrant labor.[49]

In short, if U.S. policymakers seek to have any major influence on future rates of emigration from Mexico, even in the short- to medium-term, they must help to create alternatives to international migration in what have long been, and will continue to be in the foreseeable future, the principal source areas within Mexico.

NOTES

This study has been a binational, collaborative research enterprise involving graduate students, faculty and staff researchers from the University of California-San Diego, El Colegio de México, El Colegio de Michoacán, the Universidad Autónoma de Zacatecas, El Colegio de Jalisco, the Universidad Nacional Autónoma de México, El Colegio de la Frontera Norte, Cornell University, the University of California-San Francisco and the U.S. Department of Labor.

Funding for the study was provided by the Commission for the Study of International Migration and Cooperative Economic Development (Washington, D.C.), the Ford Foundation (Mexico City office), the Pacific Rim Research Program of the University of California and the Program for Research on Immigration Policy of The RAND Corporation and The Urban Institute.

This paper was prepared with the technical assistance of Manuel García y Griego, Jeffrey Weldon, Delfina Duarte, Steven Dubb, Amparo Astorga and Dolores Tello. The members of our extremely dedicated field research team included Rafael Alarcón, Macrina Cárdenas, Angelina Casillas, Blanca Chaidez, Delfina Duarte, Cristina Escobar, Guillermo Fernández, Rosie Fregoso, Anna García, Luin Goldring, Francisca Isabel Gutiérrez, Gilberto Gutiérrez, María Asunción Gutiérrez, Paul Kersey, Gustavo López Castro, Holly Mines, Richard Mines, Alejandro Murillo, Adrián Ortiz, Jeffrey Ring, Ethelvina Rivas, María Torres Hernández, Socorro Torres Hernández, Germán Vega and Jeffrey Weldon.

I am deeply grateful for the contributions of all these collaborators, none of whom bears responsibility for the contents of this report. Wayne A. Cornelius

1. The pre-IRCA fieldwork in these communities has been reported in Gustavo López, *La casa dividida: Un estudio de caso sobre la migración a Estados Unidos en un pueblo michoacano* [Gómez Farías] (Zamora, Michoacán: El Colegio de Michoacán, 1986); Richard Mines, *Developing a Community Tradition of Migration: A Field Study in Rural Zacatecas, Mexico (Las Animas) and California Settlement Areas* (La Jolla, Calif.: Center for U.S.-Mexican Studies, University of California-San Diego, Monograph No. 3, 1981); and Wayne A. Cornelius, "Outmigration from Rural Mexican Communities [Tlacuitapa, Jalisco, and eight others]," in *The Dynamics of Migration: International Migration* (Washington, D.C.: Interdisciplinary Communications Program, Smithsonian Institution, Occasional Monograph Series, vol. 2, no. 5, 1976), pp. 1–40.

2. See, for example, Douglas Massey, Rafael Alarcón, Jorge Durand and Humberto González, *Return to Aztlán: The Social Process of International Migration from Western Mexico* (Berkeley, Calif.: University of California Press, 1987); Thomas Calvo and Gustavo López (eds.), *Movimientos de población en el occidente de México* (México, D.F. and Zamora, Michoacán: Centre d'Etudes Mexicaines et Centramericaines and El Colegio de Michoacán, 1988); and Roger C. Rouse, "Mexican Migration to the United States: Family Relations in the Development of a Transnational Migrant Circuit," unpublished Ph.D. dissertation, Stanford University, 1989.

3. See, for example, Mercedes González de la Rocha and Agustín Escobar Latapí, "Migratory Patterns and Legislation: The Impact of the Simpson-Rodino Immigration Act on the Village of Altos de Jalisco," report submitted to the Commission on the Study of International Migration and Cooperative Economic Development, Washington, D.C., November 1989; Douglas Massey, Katherine M. Donato and

Liang, "Effects of the Immigration Reform and Control Act of 1988: Preliminary Data from Mexico," unpublished paper, Population Research Center, NORC/University of Chicago, October 13, 1989; and Jesús Arroyo Alejandre, "Algunos impactos de la Ley de Reforma y Control de Inmigración (IRCA) en una región de Jalisco de fuerte emigración hacia Estados Unidos de Norteamérica," paper presented at the conference on "International Effects of the Immigration Reform and Control Act of 1986," The Rand Corporation and Urban Institute, Guadalajara, Mexico, 3–5 May 1989.

4. In two of the three research communities, the annual town fiesta is held in January; the third occurs during the first ten days of February. Almost immediately after the fiestas end, migrants begin returning to the United States.

5. The highest sample replacement rate was recorded in the community of Gómez Farías, Michoacán, which also has the highest frequency of emigration to the United States among the three research sites. In that community, 26.5 percent of the originally sampled households had to be replaced. In 83 percent of those cases, replacement was necessary because the originally sampled household failed to return from the United States during the July–January 1988–1989 fieldwork period. Most of the other replacements were made, in this and the other two communities, because the household head was discovered to be older than 68 years of age.

6. Copies of all three questionnaires administered in this study can be obtained from Wayne Cornelius, Center for U.S.-Mexican Studies (D-010), University of California-San Diego, La Jolla, Calif. 92093.

7. For example, when interviewees in our research communities who said they were considering emigration were asked why they had not yet left, 32 percent of the females mentioned family constraints (usually, parental opposition), while only 12 percent of the males cited such reasons.

8. Other researchers have also noted higher noncooperation rates among foreign-born Hispanics who have lived longer in the United States and who had greater command of English. See Gerardo Marín and Barbara VanOss Marín, "A Comparison of Three Interviewing Approaches for Studying Sensitive Topics with Hispanics," *Hispanic Journal of Behavioral Sciences*, vol. 11, no. 4 (November 1989), p. 334.

9. For a description of the snowball sampling technique as it has been applied in studies of Mexican immigrants in the United States, see Wayne A. Cornelius, "Interviewing Undocumented Immigrants: Methodological Reflections Based on Fieldwork in Mexico and the United States," *International Migration Review*, vol. 16, no. 2 (Summer 1982), pp. 378–411.

10. This fieldwork was done by Rafael Alarcón and Macrina Cárdenas, based in the San Francisco Bay Area. Their findings are reported in several unpublished papers, the most detailed of which is "Migratory Tradition, the Simpson-Rodino Law and Economic Crisis in the Mexican Region," prepared for the Commission on the Study of International Migration and Cooperative Economic Development, Washington, D.C., February, 1990.

11. This all-respondents sample is made possible because, despite the use of three different questionnaires, the recent U.S. migrants and prospective first-time migrants answered most of the same questions asked of heads of household as well as several series of more detailed questions about migration. Our purpose in constructing this pooled sample was to increase the representation of people with post-1982 migratory experience and of nonmigrants (people who haven't migrated to the United States) in the sample under analysis, and thus to expand the range of variance on key variables relating to migratory behavior.

12. See, for example, Richard C. Jones, "Macro-Patterns of Undocumented Migration between Mexico and the United States," in *Patterns of Undocumented Migration: Mexico and the United States,* (ed.) R.C. Jones (Totowa, N.J.: Rowman and Allanheld, 1984), pp. 33–57; W. Tim Dagodag, "Illegal Mexican Immigration to California from Western Mexico," in *Patterns of Undocumented Migration,* (ed.) Jones, pp. 61–73; Rafael Alarcón, Macrina Cárdenas and Germán Vega, "Los procesos migratorios en los Altos de Jalisco," *Encuentro: Estudios Sociales y Humanidades* (El Colegio de Jalisco, Guadalajara, Jalisco), No. 16, forthcoming, 1990; and Jesús Tamayo, "La emigración laboral zacatecana a los Estados Unidos," paper presented at the Annual Meeting of the Association of Borderlands Scholars, Tijuana, Baja Calif., 21–24 February 1990.

13. Secretaría de Industria y Comercio, Directorio de ejidos y comunidades agrarias: V Censo Ejidal, 1970 (México, D.F.: Dirección General de Estadística, 1972). Figures supplied to the author in 1975 by local leaders differed considerably. They claimed that fewer than 1,000 hectares of land remained in the hands of the town's ejidatarios. Presumably much of the original dotation had been transferred, illegally, over the years to private landowners through sale or rental agreements. Such practices are widespread in Mexico's ejidal sector.

14. Calculated from data reported in Alarcón, "Tradiciones migratorias," footnote 27.

15. See Patricia Arias, "Maquila, pequeña industria, y trabajo a domicilio en Los Altos de Jalisco," *Relaciones* (El Colegio de Michoacán), vol. 28, (1986).

16. The Los Altos region consists of 19 municipios (counties), forming the northeastern portion of the state of Jalisco. Since the 1880s, this region has been one of the principal contributors to the flow of Mexican migrants to the United States, as well as a zone of exceptionally heavy emigration to urban centers within Mexico. See Paul S. Taylor, *A Spanish-Mexican Peasant Community: Arandas in Jalisco, Mexico* (Berkeley, Calif.: University of California Press, Iberoamericana Series, 4, 1933); William W. Winnie, Jr., *La movilidad demográfica y su incidencia en una región de fuerte emigración* (Guadalajara, Jalisco: Universidad de Guadalajara, 1984), especially pp. 76–77; Andrés Fábregas, *La formación histórica de una región: Los Altos de Jalisco* (México, D.F.: Ediciones de la Casa Chata, 1986); Jesús Arroyo Alejandre, et al., *Migración a centros urbanos en una region de fuerte emigración: el caso del occidente de México* (Guadalajara, Jalisco: Universidad de Guadalajara, 1986). The region's total population in 1980 was 491,167, according to the official census of that year.

17. The 1976 census data were collected by the author and his research team in the month of January. The 1988 household census was conducted by the author and several research associates in May. The estimate of total 1988 population is derived

from the household census result combined with more detailed data on household size gathered in our sample survey of 201 Tlacuitapeño households, conducted in 1988–1989. The same procedure was used in estimating total 1988 population size for the other two research communities.

18. Animeños are significantly better educated than residents of the other two research communities. The median years of schooling completed among Animeños in 1988–1989 was five years, compared with three years in Gómez Farías and four years in Tlacuitapa.

19. The 1979 population census of Las Animas was conducted by Richard Mines and a research assistant in January. Mines found a very high birth rate among the women of child-bearing age still living in the community. His census results are reported in Mines, *Developing a Community Tradition*, p. 65. Another census, conducted by a federal government rural development agency (Programa Integral para el Desarrollo Rural, Secretaría de Programación y Presupuesto) in 1983, counted 1,351 persons living in 211 households.

20. Gustavo López Castro, "La migración a Estados Unidos en Gómez Farías, Michoacán," in *Migración en el occidente de México*, (eds.) Gustavo López Castro and Sergio Pardo Galván (Zamora, Mich.: El Colegio de Michoacán, 1988), p. 128.

21. Unauthorized migrants from Gómez Farías must seek housing in central Watsonville, where whole families can be found living in garages, basements, single rooms in multifamily apartments and improvised shacks in backyards.

22. The sheer volume of mail from the United States—most of it bearing money orders or checks—that is received in the research communities is impressive. In Gómez Farías, for example, nearly 900 letters are received each month from the United States by the local post office. (López Castro, "La migración a Estados Unidos," p. 130.)

23. Most previous studies have also shown that, at least since the 1960s, two-thirds or more of the money remitted by Mexican migrants from the United States typically has been used for family maintenance purposes. See, for example, Robert M. Brown, "The Impact of U.S. Work Experience on Mexican Agricultural Workers: A Case Study in the Village of Jacona, Michoacán, Mexico," unpublished Ph.D. dissertation, University of Colorado, 1975, p. 262; and Ina R. Dinerman, "Patterns of Adaptation Among Households of U.S.-Bound Migrants from Michoacán, Mexico," *International Migration Review*, vol. 12, no. 4 (Winter, 1978), pp. 485–501.

24. The survey question was: "How has the economic situation of the country in the last few years affected you and your family?" There were 758 valid responses to this question.

25. Merilee Grindle has detected a similar change in the use of remittance income in the rural municipio of Tepoztlán, Morelos, where "prior to 1982, remittances were often used to purchase construction materials for housing. Many also used this money to pay for their children's education or to invest in small businesses. Increasingly in the 1980s, however, remittances were needed to ensure mere subsistence and fewer investments in the long-term sustainability of the household

were made." See Merilee S. Grindle, "The Response to Austerity: Political and Economic Strategies of Mexico's Rural Poor," in *Lost Promises: Debt, Austerity, and Development in Latin America*, (ed.) William L. Canak (Boulder, CO: Westview Press, 1989), p. 201. Similar problems were observed by another researcher in a rural community in Michoacán during the 1980s; see Rouse, "Mexican Migration to the United States," pp. 200–201.

26. Our census excluded small-scale agricultural enterprises as well as home work, most commonly, knitting of garments by women working individually in their homes.

27. In addition to the reduced profitability of agriculture in recent years, Richard Mines has observed another causal mechanism at work in the community of Las Animas. He notes a tendency for land in Las Animas to fall increasingly into the hands of an absentee landlord class made up of long-term, permanent emigrants to the United States. These people hold land not to generate income from agriculture but for prestige, security and food for their parents. He attributes much of the recent decline in agricultural production in the community to this change in land tenure. See Mines, *Developing a Community Tradition*, pp. 133–35. Similar problems have been observed in the town of Acuitzio, Michoacán; see Raymond E. Wiest, "Implications of International Labor Migration for Mexican Rural Development," in *Migration Across Frontiers: Mexico and the United States*, (eds.) Fernando Cámara and Robert Van Kemper (Albany, N.Y.: Institute for Mesoamerican Studies, State University of New York at Albany, 1979), pp. 85–100.

28. Mines, *Developing a Community Tradition*, p. 127.

29. Note that the wording of the questionnaire item seems to emphasize long-term or permanent emigration rather than temporary wage-labor migration. Nevertheless, the responses indicate that many interviewees interpreted it as a question about emigration in general. It is possible that the proportion of favorable evaluations would have been higher, if the question had specified short-term migration as the phenomenon to be evaluated.

30. Other researchers have used different terms to denote essentially the same phenomenon. Rafael Alarcón refers to the "process of nortenización," R. Alarcón, "El proceso de 'nortenización: impacto de la migración internacional en Chavinda, Michoacán," in *Movimientos de población en el occidente de México*, (eds.) Thomas Calvo and Gustavo López (México, D.F. and Zamora, Michoacán: Centre d'Etudes Mexicaines et Centramericaines and El Colegio de Michoacán, 1988), pp. 337–58. Joshua Reichert has described it as "the migrant syndrome," J. Reichert, "The Migrant Syndrome: Seasonal U.S. Wage Labor and Rural Development in Central Mexico," *Human Organization*, vol. 40 (1981), pp. 56–66.

31. The most striking example of this neglect of community needs that we encountered in our fieldwork was in Las Animas. Ten years after a project to supply potable water to the Las Animas community was begun, and five years after a water pipe system had been installed throughout the community and a well had been dug to supply it, the system was still not operative because the well had not yet been connected with the distribution network. And because there was no functioning water system, the town's sewage system—also completed years before—was still disconnected from the dwellings. Trying to explain this situation

to us, one nonmigrating Animeño complained that "if the norteños spent more of their time here rather than there, perhaps they would be more concerned" about such problems. The head of the municipal government in nearby Nochistlán was somewhat more diplomatic in his explanation: "the returning migrants know that there are better living conditions elsewhere; they have broader horizons. But their presence is too brief to get things in motion."

32. The survey item was: "Some people say that a young person born here in this town can progress in life without leaving the town. Other people say that to get ahead in life, a young person born here has to move somewhere else in order to get ahead. What do you think?" There were 753 valid responses to this question.

33. "Rodino" is the term popularly used in the research communities to identify an applicant for legalization under the U.S. Immigration Reform and Control Act of 1986 (the "Simpson-Rodino Act").

34. The standard used was a t-statistic with an absolute value of at least 1.96, indicating a confidence interval of 95 percent.

35. For an elaboration of this argument, based in part on data collected in the Los Altos de Jalisco region, see Merilee S. Grindle, *Searching for Rural Development in Mexico* (Ithaca, N.Y.: Cornell University Press, 1988).

36. The same conclusion has been reached with respect to the possible expansion of export-oriented tomato production in northwestern Mexico. See Gary Thompson, Ricardo Amon and Philip L. Martin, "Agricultural Development and Emigration: Rhetoric and Reality," *International Migration Review*, vol. 20, no. 3 (Fall 1986), pp. 575–97. It does not necessarily hold for all regions of Mexico, however. For example, Los Altos de Morelos is one of the few central plateau regions that has virtually stopped exporting labor to the United States. In the 1960s, braceros returning from the United States introduced new production techniques for tomato growing, which stimulated the local economy and stabilized the work force. See Guillermo de la Peña, "Social Change and International Labor Migration: An Overview of Four Agrarian Regions in Mexico," in *Migration and Narcotics: Background Papers Prepared for the Bilateral Commission on the Future of U.S.-Mexican Relations* (Mexico City and La Jolla, Calif., Spring, 1988), pp. 21–24.

37. Such enterprises have become a particularly important source of employment for women in rural communities. See Arias, "Maquila."

38. The following account is based on fieldwork conducted by the author in Villa Hidalgo in the late 1970s. The town was revisited briefly in January 1989.

39. Robert C. Smith, "Migration, Development, and the Effects of IRCA: A Comparative Study of Two Mexican Sending Communities and Their Receiving Communities in the United States," unpublished paper, Immigration Research Project, Institute for Latin American and Iberian Studies, Columbia University, November 1988, p. 22.

40. Preliminary findings from a business census in Jalisco being conducted by the Mexican Center, Institute of Latin American Studies, University of Texas-Austin, in collaboration with El Colegio de Jalisco and El Colegio de México, as reported

by Bryan R. Roberts at the Executive Seminar on "Mexico Under Salinas: The First Year," Center for U.S.-Mexican Studies, University of California-San Diego, La Jolla, Calif., 19 January 1990.

41. Juan Luis Orozco, unpublished Ph.D. thesis, cited in Rafael Alarcón, "Tradiciones migratorias," pp. 27–28.

42. See, for example, Philip L. Martin, "Labor Migration and Economic Development," Working Paper No. 3, Commission for the Study of International Migration and Cooperative Economic Development (February 1989), p. 19.

43. Self-proprietorship does not necessarily end migration by the proprietor or other members of his family. Indeed, 68 percent of the post-1982 migrants who owned nonagricultural businesses in our research communities continued to use dollars earned in the United States to sustain their business. Also, a lower proportion of migrant-owned businesses (78 percent) than businesses owned by nonmigrants (89 percent) were open throughout the year.

44. Alarcón, "Tradiciones migratorias," p. 15.

45. See Jesús Arroyo Alejandre, El abandono rural: un modelo explicativo de la emigración de trabajadores rurales en el occidente de México (Guadalajara, Jalisco: Universidad de Guadalajara, 1989).

46. Douglas S. Massey, "Economic Development and International Migration in Comparative Perspective," *Population and Development Review*, vol. 14, no. 3, (September 1988), pp. 408–409.

47. The available evidence bearing on this point, from several different field studies, is summarized in Wayne A. Cornelius, "Los Migrantes de la Crisis: The Changing Profile of Mexican Labor Migration to California in the 1980s," in *Labor Market Interdependence between the United States and Mexico*, (eds.) Jorge Bustamante, Raul Hinojosa and Clark Reynolds, (Stanford, Calif.: Stanford University Press, forthcoming).

48. Victor Urquidi, "Critique," in "Proceedings of the Workshop on the Relationship Between Migration and Development, 24, February 1989," Working Paper No. 10, Commission for the Study of International Migration and Cooperative Economic Development, (November 1989), p. 25.

49. Among prospective first-time migrants to the United States interviewed in our research communities, 71 percent believed that unauthorized migrants could still get jobs in the United States, despite the employer sanctions provision of the 1986 U.S. immigration law; and only 40 percent thought that it was more difficult to cross the border clandestinely now than before passage of the 1986 law. A total of 47 percent had considered migrating to the United States during the 12 months preceding the interview. For further data concerning the impact of IRCA on perceptions of the U.S. job opportunity structure and propensity to migrate in our research communities, see Wayne A. Cornelius, "Impacts of the 1986 U.S. Immigration Law on Emigration from Rural Mexican Sending Communities," *Population and Development Review*, vol. 15, no. 4 (December 1989), pp. 689–705.

4

Mexican Provision of Health and Human Services to American Citizens: Barriers and Opportunities

David C. Warner

I. INTRODUCTION

Because of the juxtaposition of very different demographic and economic profiles, it would appear many potentially mutually beneficial opportunities exist for trade between the United States and Mexico. To date, these exchanges have primarily consisted of migration of labor from Mexico to the United States and the development of the *maquiladora* industry in Mexico, although trade in a number of other areas is escalating. In the areas of health and human services, constraints upon U.S. entitlement programs may have significantly reduced a number of potentially mutually beneficial arrangements.

To put current arrangements between the two nations in context, I will initially examine cross-border usage of services on the U.S.-Mexico border. The second part of the paper examines the potential market for Mexican provision of services to U.S. citizens in retirement living facilities and arrangements for the elderly. The third section examines the size of the U.S. market and levels of both current and prospective government expenditures in a number of areas such as nursing homes, veterans' health care, and programs for the mentally retarded, the chronically mentally ill, and other severely ill patients such as the head injured and AIDS sufferers. Several proposals are made regarding possible changes in U.S. policy regarding Medicare, Medicaid and Veterans Administration reimbursement, so as to increase the choices available to U.S. citizens in a way that would be cost effective from the perspective of the U.S. taxpayer.

The final section discusses some of the licensing and certification issues that are likely to arise, as well as some other areas, such as prisons, in which contracting between nations might be feasible. The main focus of this paper is this: if less expensive options for residential care could be developed in Mexico—options that persons in need of care or their agents might choose as being more appropriate—it could be possible to slightly mitigate some of the wrenching decisions most policy analysts foresee in the United States in the decades ahead.

II. UTILIZATION OF SERVICES ACROSS THE BORDER

There is extensive utilization of health services on the Mexican side of the border by U.S. residents and on the U.S. side by Mexican residents. To the extent that Mexican residents can be induced to stay in Mexico for services, it will in effect be import substitution, and when U.S. residents increase their usage of services in Mexico it is export expansion from the perspective of Mexico.

Use of U.S. Services by Mexican Residents

On the Mexican side there is a two- or even three-tiered system of care. The highest income persons have access to private facilities and practitioners throughout the United States as well as in Mexico. The broad middle class—which includes government workers, employees of larger private firms, members of unions and other selected workers groups— generally have access to social security or government employee clinics and hospitals, such as Instituto Mexicano de Segura Social (IMSS) and Instituto de Seguridad y Servicios Sociales para los Trabajadores del Estado (ISSSTE). The balance of the population (perhaps 50 percent) may have access to a government clinic, such as the Social Security Administration, often staffed by fresh medical graduates doing their required year of service, and relatively inadequately staffed and equipped hospitals run by local governments.[1]

Those Mexican residents who make use of U.S. health resources can be broken into three distinct groups—those who shop for very high quality care, those who choose to give birth in the United States for nonmedical reasons, and those who live on the border and pick and choose the services they care to use. Prior to the slump in oil prices in 1982, upper-class Mexican patients sought care in Houston, Los Angeles, Boston, New York and the Mayo clinic in Cleveland with great regularity. Although the volume of demand has abated somewhat, there are still a number of wealthy Mexican citizens who seek care abroad.

The development of higher quality facilities in Mexico would certainly retain a number of these persons. But attempting to duplicate several of these world-class referral facilities in Mexico would be very uneconomical and perhaps difficult to achieve. At the same time, a significant upgrading of facilities should be a reasonable endeavor, not only to retain foreign exchange but also to enhance the treatment of persons who would remain in Mexico in any case. Improved training facilities would also be provided.

Access to the United States for childbirth by Mexican border residents is much easier in Texas where there are fewer restrictions on who can deliver a baby. In 1980, roughly 4,000 persons identified as Mexican residents gave birth in Texas border counties. The Mexican residents tended to have higher numbers of prior fetal deaths than U.S. residents and were far more likely to deliver outside the hospital.[2] It would appear that the motivation for delivering in the United States by Mexican border residents is primarily to achieve U.S. citizenship status for their children and to have the citizenship option in the future for themselves.

A stratified random sample of 660 households in Tijuana in 1987 found that 40.3 percent of the subjects had used health services in Mexico in the prior six-month period, while 2.8 percent had used services in the United States during that period. Of those who sought care in the United States, 11.1 percent were covered by Medicaid (possibly inappropriately because of limitations on nonresidents) and 4.9 percent by Medicare. Much of this coverage was earned due to either prior residence in the United States or to U.S. citizenship. About 25 percent of the U.S. users belonged to a Health Maintenance Organization (HMO) or had private insurance. The balance of those surveyed either paid out of pocket (47.3 percent), received free care (8.6 percent) or did not respond adequately (5.4 percent). Although this does not represent a significant percentage of health service use, it does show the complexity of conditions under which Mexican border residents seek care in this country.[3]

The issue of U.S. health services use by undocumented Mexican citizens has a literature of its own, and in light of the Immigration Reform and Control Act legislation and related programs, the nature of this usage and its impact upon U.S. facilities has certainly undergone a change. It is ironic that the U.S. government has decided that only public hospitals will be eligible for reimbursement for uncompensated care given to newly legalized immigrants. With the exception of El Paso, the U.S. border area has very little in the way of true public hospitals. In neither the lower Rio Grande area nor Laredo is there a general hospital that would be eligible for reimbursement under the State Legalization Impact Assistance Grant (SLIAG) program.

The Use of Mexican Services by U.S. Border Citizens and Residents

Users of Mexican services who reside in the United States usually seem to do so because the Mexican services are less expensive or they are seen as being more appropriate. A recent survey of low income residents in the Lower Rio Grande Valley found that more than one-fourth of low income respondents go to Mexico for pharmaceuticals at least once a year, 15 percent go to receive medical care, and 10 percent to receive dental services in a year.[4] Some insurance companies do seem to be willing to cover services for U.S. residents on the Mexican side since they are generally less expensive.

In some cases, physicians on the U.S. side refer patients to Mexican labs where an ultrasound may cost $20.00 as opposed to $150.00 on the U.S. side. These tests are also of comparably high quality.[5] The Brownsville Community Health Center has developed a binational program called PROFAX to provide sterilizations in Mexico for U.S. residents who cannot afford them. The cost is $3.00 to $5.00 in Mexico. The program is used by persons who can't afford a hospital or clinic on the U.S. side and who don't qualify for Planned Parenthood programs.[6]

A fundamental difficulty with developing many services on the Mexican side of the border for U.S. citizens is that, in general, the government entitlement programs for medical care (Medicare and Medicaid) will not reimburse for care given in another country. Medicare can help pay for care in a qualified Canadian or Mexican hospital under three conditions:

(1) You are in the United States when an emergency occurs and a Canadian or Mexican hospital is closer than the nearest U.S. hospital that can provide the emergency care services you need;

(2) You live in the United States and a Canadian or Mexican hospital is closer to your home than the nearest U.S. hospital that can provide the care you need, regardless of whether or not an emergency exists; and

(3) You are in Canada traveling by the most direct route to or from Alaska and another state and an emergency occurs that requires that you be admitted to a Canadian hospital.[7]

Clearly, most residents on the U.S. side of the border would *not* be eligible to receive Medicare coverage for most care in Mexico. Further, residents of Mexico, even if they are covered by Medicare, are not likely to have it pay for any care received in Mexico.

Medicaid is a joint state-federal entitlement administered by the states. It will not generally cover services in Mexico for U.S. citizens. In South Texas, which has very limited Medicaid coverage and no public hospitals, it appears that many poor and near poor persons choose to go to Mexico for services because they have neither the means nor the entitlements to cover care in South Texas.

The development of hospital and physician services on the Mexican side for U.S. border residents will probably have to be cost effective in order to attract patients. Since the U.S. border areas are often winter homes or even permanent retirement areas, the lack of Medicare coverage is a real obstacle. Also, the lack of neonatal and other high tech care means that, often, it is not possible for Mexican nationals in the United States who need such specialized care to be transferred to facilities on the Mexican side of the border.

III. THE POTENTIAL MARKET FOR HEALTH AND HUMAN SERVICES FOR RETIREES IN MEXICO

The comparative economics of living in Mexico has attracted a large and increasing number of retirees. Europe is the current home of 50 percent of the American retirees living abroad but is declining in relative importance. The largest growth in the U.S. expatriate retiree population has been in Mexico. In 1966, only four percent of U.S. retirees living abroad lived in Mexico. Today, 12 percent of social security recipients abroad live there.[8] Although Medicare won't cover medical care in Mexico and there may be problems with sanitation, the climate and low cost of living appear to offset these disadvantages for those who choose to retire there.[9]

In the last decade, the number of elderly persons in the United States choosing to move into organized living communities has also increased dramatically. Residents of these communities usually live in apartments ranging from efficiencies to four-bedroom living units. Residents also pay for at least one meal a day in the dining room, and there is usually a busy social schedule at the facility that includes trips and excursions to shop or to sightsee. Facilities often provide transportation to town, to recreational or community activities, since many of the residents lack the mobility or the eyesight to drive themselves.

Nearly all these communities provide a continuum of health care. Nurses are often employed. Part of the reason persons are encouraged to eat at least one meal a day communally in the dining room is so that the staff can informally monitor their health status. Generally, personal care facilities are available in which 24-hour supportive care and some nursing care is provided, and most facilities have skilled and intermediate care nursing facilities to which residents are given priority.

Traditionally, most such facilities have been of the endowment variety—run by a nonprofit entity that persons buy into with a large initial payment and a relatively modest monthly fee thereafter. Increasingly, however, for-profit chains have entered this sector. Due in part to the more stringent regulation of endowment programs and also due to the preferences of prospective residents, the facilities they develop tend to be of the rental variety requiring little or no upfront commitment of capital. With the increase in size and corporatization of these facilities, a trade organization, the National Association of Senior Living Industries (NASLI), has developed; NASLI sponsors an annual convention and a variety of services.

Those persons who choose to live in retirement living facilities in the United States are persons who are no longer terribly active. Most couples or individuals who decide to move into these facilities are in their mid- to late seventies. This population has risen steadily and will continue to do so (primarily through increased longevity) until around 2020, at which time the "baby boom" population will be reflected in an explosion of persons in the 75+ and, ultimately, the 85+ population. By 2050, it is estimated that 68 million persons, or 22 percent of the population in the United States, will be over 65 years of age, while the population over 85 will increase eight times to account for five percent of the total population.[10]

Along with this rapid increase in the retirement age population, there has been a rapid escalation in the number of persons above 65 and above 75 years of age with substantial incomes. Of the 27 million persons above 65 in 1985, 35 percent had incomes between $10,000 and $15,000 annually; 28.4 percent had incomes between $15,000 and $25,000; and 21.3 percent had incomes above $25,000.[11] Not only are there a number of retired persons with family incomes above $25,000 a year, there are also many in the $15–25,000 per year level. For many of these, retirement in Mexico can mean a substantially higher standard of living.[12]

Typically a facility is chosen that is close to children or to the community in which the individual or couple has retired. Accordingly, it would appear that retirement living facilities will be most viable if they are located near a large enough late middle-aged population whose parents might also be appropriate for such a facility. Indeed, when persons retire in their late fifties and their sixties, their parents are often alive and in need of such facilities. Since visits to Mexico may require some adventurousness, there may be a market for residential facilities that also rent some apartments or beds on a weekly or monthly basis to reduce concerns about backup services. On a parallel track, the Japanese government has discussed developing retirement communities around the world because of the high cost of land and living in Japan. It should also be noted that the aging of the Japanese population is about 20 years ahead of the United States since the Japanese did not have a comparable baby boom in the late 1940s and 1950s.[13] There may be hope in Mexico for the development of retirement communities focused on serving both the European and the Japanese markets, as well as the United States.

IV. U.S. GOVERNMENT PAYMENT FOR HEALTH AND SOCIAL SERVICES IN MEXICO

There is a range of services in the United States that are funded in whole or in part by government agencies on behalf of citizens as an entitlement or as a governmental function. These include: medical, hospital and skilled nursing services to the elderly; medical, hospital and nursing care for veterans; nursing home care for the indigent and disabled; care for the mentally retarded and the chronically mentally ill; care for those addicted to drugs or alcohol; care for the terminally ill; and prisons. Altogether, these government funded services absorb well over $200 billion annually, and most of the services are performed by relatively low-skilled workers whose availability will be diminished in the years ahead under current demographics and immigration policy. In many—if not most cases—it would be illegal and inappropriate to provide these services in Mexico without the agreement of the person receiving the services, and in most cases, the U.S. government funding would not be available. However, through the development of options in Mexico for the delivery of these services with some U.S. state or federal governmental assistance, it may be that there are a number of persons who would choose to receive services in Mexico at a significant savings to the governmental entities of the United States. If only half of one percent of these services were provided in Mexico, over $1 billion would be added to the current Mexican GNP of $150 billion. In addition, there would be an increase in living expenditures by those who would choose to move to Mexico if they were not tied to the United States by Medicare or other limitations on services outside this country.

Nursing Home Care for the Elderly

In 1985, U.S. expenditures for long term care were estimated at $45 billion,[14] while by 1998 it is estimated that these costs will reach $80 billion.[15] Private resources accounted for about 48 percent of expenditures in 1985, and public resources (primarily Medicaid but also including Medicare and VA payments) accounted for the balance. It should be possible for Mexican alternatives to be less expensive in many cases.

Most persons who pay for nursing home care from their own resources exhaust these resources within the first six months. This is because private pay rates for 24 hour care in a U.S. nursing home currently range from $30 to $150 a day. Even at $30 a day, which may pay for unskilled care in a semi-private room in a right-to-work state, this amounts to more than $10,000 a year. This is beyond the resources of many retired persons, and has left the remaining spouse of many retired couples with minimal resources to meet living expenses. As of 1 January 1990, regulations will increase the amount of funds reserved for the member of the couple living *outside* the nursing home will be increased to $800.00 per month—a level that would support a more comfortable life in Mexico. With the increase of the minimum wage in the United States in April 1990, the cost of nursing home care in many states will increase as well.

About four percent of the more than 27 million persons over 65 in the United States are living in nursing homes at any one time. Only about one percent of those from 65–74 are typically in a nursing home, while about ten percent of those from 75–84 are so placed. The rate of institutionalization increases rapidly at ages above 85.[16] Accordingly, there will be an extremely rapid increase in the number institutionalized from 2010 on. Between 1930 and 1945, the depression and the war moderated births and immigration so that most of the growth in the elderly population from 1995 to 2010 will come from increased longevity. The later anticipated explosion has a number of analysts and social commentators concerned about the capacity of the United States to care for the disabled elderly[17] or to afford to grow old.[18]

As with retirement living facilities, Mexico would appear to offer less expensive options with regard to nursing care for retirees. It is certainly far cheaper to have help in the home in Mexico on a 24-hour-a-day basis. What does not yet seem to have developed in Mexico are fully staffed 24-hour care nursing homes with the involvement of registered nurses and physical, speech and other therapists. In part, this is because the third-party reimbursement that pays for this care in the United States is not in place there, and partly because these are not professions and modes of organization that are well-established in Mexico. In 1976, for example, there were 12,935 medical students in the six northern states of Mexico while there were only 4,902 nursing students.[19]

In the United States, wages for dieticians, occupational therapists, physical therapists and head nurses working full-time in long-term care facilities in 1985 averaged from $10.69 to $13.25 per hour.[20] Today these levels are probably about 25 percent higher. Clearly, Mexican wage scales would allow for less expensive nursing home care.

It seems that there would be a ready interest in developing such facilities in Mexican retirement communities. It may be that the push for this is somewhat attenuated by the low cost of help in an individual household in Mexico; in the United States, 24-hour help would be at least $50 to $100 a day. Nonetheless, when one compares the cost of retirement areas in southern Florida to retirement areas in Mexico—both areas where individuals are quite isolated from traditional friends and family, the Mexican alternative is clearly less expensive. The difference is that the U.S. and state governments subsidize or can entirely pay for the nursing and medical costs of their citizens in the United States while individuals with the same problems and the same eligibilities would receive nothing if they reside in Mexico.

With the expansion of the Medicare program in 1989—to cover up to 150 days of care in a skilled nursing facility for persons on social security who require 24-hour skilled care and who are able to be rehabilitated—this subsidy for care received in the United States as opposed to Mexico becomes even more significant. The future of this expansion will depend on the extent to which the legislation is repealed in the fall of 1989. Since Medicare reimburses at cost and covers its share of capital costs as well as a number of therapies, the average cost to Medicare for a day's care in a skilled nursing facility (SNF) in the United States is at least $80.00. This is a federal expenditure that comes out of Part A of Medicare, which is funded by the social security tax. One solution to the strong fiscal disincentive for disabled retirees to stay in or locate to Mexico would be to offer to pay $15–25 a day for skilled nursing care given to qualified individuals in Mexico. If there were some way to certify that a beneficiary needed this

24-hour care, it would be possible to agree to pay for such care at home or in a certified facility for the fixed "Mexican" rate. This would provide savings to the Health Care Financing Administration (HCFA) and to the social security system funds, as well as provide more choices to people who wish to retire in Mexico. Of course, it would also provide a benefit to persons living there already who would not have come back to the United States for care. And, if available in Mexico, it would raise the question of whether or not such money would then be available to retirees and other beneficiaries in other countries like Poland, England or Ireland. These countries also have significant numbers of U.S. retirees.

Traditionally, however, the largest payer for nursing home care has not been Medicare—skilled care only accounts for about 15 percent of patient days, and until 1989, the number of days and access to facilities under Medicare was quite limited. Rather, it has been Medicaid that covers most government supported care. Medicaid is a program that is subject to federally mandated basic benefits and eligible groups but which then gives the individual state the option to extend coverage to additional groups and to offer expanded benefits. The states administer the program but receive matching federal funds, ranging from 50 to 80 percent of the costs.

Only low income individuals are eligible for Medicaid. Individuals must also meet an asset test by selling all but a homestead, a car in which there is little equity and some personal belongings. Once in the nursing home, the person's income goes to pay the bills, and Medicaid only picks up the difference.

There may be two ways in which Medicaid could fund nursing home care in Mexico. The first, which is consistent with our discussion of Medicare, would be for the federal government unilaterally to say that persons who meet the income eligibility guidelines and are certified to be in need of nursing home care could receive a federal payment per day as long as they resided in a nursing home abroad. There would not necessarily be an unreasonable requirement for asset disposition, and the couple's income would not be exhausted. An incentive to shop for cost effective alternatives could be given, and state governments would not have to contribute anything. This policy would also enhance the individual's choices and be cost effective for the federal and state governments. This, along with the Medicare option, would also be consistent with emerging U.S. policy related to the elderly.[21]

The second possible use of Medicaid to pay for nursing home care would be for state governments to contract directly with private vendors in Mexico to provide nursing home services to their residents. Here the incentive would be the savings to state government. Since the cost of individual nursing home care to Medicaid ranges from an average of $35.00 to $70.00 per day in various states, the state net cost when the person has no income ranges from $15.00 to $35.00 a day. The state could save one-half to two-thirds of its cost if it could obtain discounts of that size from the Mexican vendors. There have been precedents; states have controlled new nursing home beds through the certificate of need program and then contracted with neighboring states for beds.

There are two potential problems with permitting states to contract directly with vendors in Mexico: quality control and the preferences of patients and their families. These are both important issues that should be addressed before the federal government grants such permission.

Care for Veterans and Retired Military

Entitlement to Veterans Administration benefits will become increasingly significant as the proportion of the elderly eligible for these benefits increases. The Veterans Administration had a health care budget of $9.7 billion in fiscal year 1987, and cared for 1.3 million inpatients and 18.5 million outpatient visits. The Veterans Administration operates 172 medical centers and cares primarily for aging male veterans, many of whom have chronic conditions. Military retirees can alternate between the VA and military facilities because most have dual eligibility.[22] Because of the aging of World War II and Korean War veterans, the number of veterans over the age of 65 is anticipated to increase from 5.5 million in 1986 to 8.9 million by the year 2000. By that time, two-thirds of all males over age 65 will be veterans. Projections by the VA estimate the number of veterans with dementia will have increased to 550,000—up from about 200,000 in 1983.[23] In a 1983 study, the VA estimated that by the year 2000, the VA could need up to $24 billion for annual medical costs. In addition, the VA estimates that it might need as much as $25 billion for hospital and nursing home construction through 2000.[24]

Since 1 July 1986, veterans with nonservice related ailments and incomes above $15,000 for singles and $18,000 for those with one dependent have been subject to a copayment averaging $500.[25] Because most elderly veterans have Medicare coverage and many veterans of all ages have private health insurance, users of the VA system have increasingly been lower income persons. However, because of limited coverage for nursing home care under Medicare and private health insurance, the demand for such care at VA facilities should increase substantially in the future.[26]

While the VA rarely contracts for care in non-VA hospitals, it frequently contracts for nursing home care. About 40 percent of the care paid for by the VA is in community nursing homes, while another 30 percent is in facilities operated by state governments.[27]

The problems faced by the VA are exacerbated by the migration of elderly veterans to the sunbelt where there are relatively fewer facilities.

Veterans with anticipated medical problems who are likely to be dependent on the VA may also tend to locate close to one of their facilities. Clearly, it would be more difficult for a veteran who is likely to be dependent on VA care to retire to Mexico. Here again, however, the VA could potentially find a more economical alternative while enhancing the choices available to retired and dependent veterans. If, instead of the $80–100 a day the VA is likely to spend currently on nursing home care, or even $300–400 a day on hospital care, it might be possible to pay for care in one of three or four hospitals in Mexico and to provide $15–20 a day for persons who otherwise would be in VA-paid nursing care in the U.S..

Champus, a government program for military retirees and dependents, pays for private facilities in the United States if a military hospital is more than 50 miles away or if the patient can be issued a certificate of non-availability which attests that the needed services are not available at the military hospital. If Champus also paid for services in Mexico, that would certainly be a potential benefit for military retirees covered by Champus.

Payment for Physician and Hospital Care

For persons who are of retirement age but not in need of nursing or retirement living care, the major difficulty in Mexico is that they do not receive their VA or Medicare coverage for physician and hospital care. In the case of specialized medical care requirements or hospital care, they have to return to the United States to receive the coverage to which they are entitled. One solution might be to develop, with the consent and co-operation of the Mexican government, four or five hospitals and clinics that would be certified by Medicare and the VA, at which persons could receive care without having to leave Mexico.

Such facilities could also serve to provide some specialty care to Mexican citizens and help to provide training programs. The alternative—to certify many hospitals and physicians in Mexico—could be administratively complex and would likely be more expensive. Whether this entitlement would save money is unclear. If the reimbursement rates were set at one-fourth or less of U.S. rates, it is possible that savings could be realized.

Care for the Mentally Retarded and Head Injured Persons

Although a number of mentally retarded persons live with their parents or other relatives or in group settings, about 250,000 mentally retarded and developmentally disabled persons resided in long term care facilities in 1985.[28] These included Medicaid-certified Intermediate Care Facilities for the Mentally Retarded (ICF-MRs), Skilled Nursing Facilities

(SNFs) and intermediate care nursing homes, foster homes, and board and care facilities.

Federal and state governments pay for the bulk of this care. Medicaid payments to ICF-MRs were $4.7 billion in fiscal 1985.[29] ICF-MR recently has been the fastest growing Medicaid expense category, rising 28.7 percent annually from 1975 to 1985.[30] At this rate, expenditures double in just under three years. Many groups and individuals wish to develop community placement and in-home facilities, and Medicaid permits states to develop home and community waiver programs if they will cost the government less. These programs can spend funds on alternative and not normally approved services on designated clients, as long as keeping the client out of the hospital or intermediate care facility reduces the cost.

The difficulty of hiring persons in the United States makes in-home arrangements very arduous for families. Increasingly, families are paid to provide foster care or give home care to their family member who would otherwise be in an institution. If such payments could continue to be made to a family member, that person could then afford to hire help and live with the disabled relative in Mexico. For many families, an extra $10–15 a day in Mexico would adequately cover the cost of the help and other services needed and would save state and federal governments $50–100 a day.

In addition, as with nursing homes, there is the possibility that state governments would contract with facilities in Mexico for placement of their residents. The same remarks with regard to quality and appropriateness apply in this case as well.

At least one mental retardation facility in Austin, Texas maintains a facility in Guadalajara where the residents spend the months of January, June, July and August. The facility is an institution serving mentally retarded children and does receive funds for the students who are wards of the state.[31]

A related and rapidly growing population is that of persons with severe head injuries who, because of more rapid emergency response, now survive in long-term dependence. The National Head Injury Foundation estimates the lifetime costs of treating and maintaining an individual with severe head injuries at $4.567 million, of which probably $4.162 million is for long-term residential programs of 30 to 60 years duration. The mean cost of such programs is $92,000 annually.[32] One study found that roughly six persons per 100,000 survive a severe brain injury annually.[33] This would imply an annual incidence of 15,000 persons surviving with severe brain injuries. If indeed these individuals require $4.2 million for care in a lifetime, this would imply a lifetime cost for each year's injured group of $60 billion. This figure clearly includes a number of future expenses that should be more aggressively discounted to the patient. In any case, as the numbers of such persons grow this could be a significant problem. Once again, it may be that less expensive rehabilitative facilities might be developed in Mexico that would be both cost effective and chosen by some patients, their families and insurers.

The Chronically Mentally Ill

It is estimated that there are roughly two million persons in the United States who are seriously mentally ill and who require some kind of protected environment.[34] There is an emerging consensus that many persons with schizophrenia and other serious long-term mental health problems can, with drug therapy and a supportive environment, be maintained for some time outside institutions. The census of U.S. state mental hospitals has dropped rapidly from 552,150 patients in 1953 to 118,647 patients in 1984.[35]

Although no one knows definitely where the seriously mentally ill live, estimates for those with schizophrenia at any one time are that 40 percent live with their families; 21 percent are in foster homes, board and care homes, halfway houses or county homes; eight percent are hospitalized (in private, public general, and state mental hospitals); 14 percent are in nursing homes; eight percent live by themselves, often in boarding houses or single room occupancy hotels; seven percent are living in public shelters, abandoned buildings or in the streets; and three percent are in jails or prisons. The breakdown for those with other serious mental illnesses is not as well-known.[36]

The public expenditure on those with serious mental illness has been estimated at $17 billion a year.[37] In Texas alone, it appears that annual public expenditures on behalf of the seriously mentally ill totalled more than $400 million in 1987, and Texas is not a high spending state as compared to others in the field of mental health.[38] These expenditures come from a variety of state and federal sources. Federal sources include food stamps, Social Security Income (SSI), Social Security Disability Income (SSDI) and rehabilitation payments; and most persons with these diagnoses qualify for one of these disability programs as well as Medicare or Medicaid coverage, Housing and Urban Development (HUD) Section 8 housing vouchers, Veterans Administration programs, and block grants to the states for community level services. All but the last are federal entitlement programs that go to the individual either as a cash payment, receipt of voucher to pay for food or housing, or entitlement to medical care subject to the limitations of the various programs. It is probable that federal expenditures on those who are on SSI, SSDI or veterans benefits and have a diagnosis of being seriously mentally ill average at least $12–15,000 annually and possibly much more.

State expenditures include direct funding for state mental hospitals, the state share of Medicaid payments for nursing homes, hospitals and medical care, part of the funding for community mental health centers, the state share of rehabilitation programs, and supported work and subsidized contracts.

Of all this, the only funds available to a person with these disabilities living in Mexico would be the SSDI payments.

One would think that very high quality therapeutic communities could be developed in Mexico for a cost of $5–10,000 annually that many persons who now cost the system much more would then choose. The problem with the currently very fractionalized funding system is that no one level of government accurately understands the *total* cost of these entitlements, and so none is motivated to take full responsibility for the clients, nor to fully seek the best and most effective level of care. Accordingly, many of these people end up on the streets receiving little or no supportive care.

Care for AIDS and ARC Patients

Current estimates of the cost of caring for patients with Acquired Immune Deficiency Syndrome (AIDS) in their final 18 months to two years of life are at least $50,000. Because of the length of time it takes to become eligible under social security disability for Medicare, most AIDS sufferers' medical and habilitation costs are covered either by Medicaid [Andrulus] or by local governments and their public hospitals and welfare agencies.

Fred Hellinger has estimated that 64,000 cases of AIDS would be diagnosed in 1989; 71,000 in 1990; and 114,000 in 1992. He estimates that costs are approximately $60,000 for lifetime treatment of an AIDS case. Using this estimate, the 71,000 persons diagnosed in 1990 would have lifetime costs of roughly $4.2 billion.[39] In addition, newer estimates by the Government Accounting Office allege that the earlier estimates for 1991 of the numbers of AIDS and AIDS Related Complex (ARC) patients are about one-third too low.

In many ways, the ideal living arrangement for AIDS sufferers is not unlike the retirement living arrangements discussed above. A continuum of living arrangements is appropriate. Some of the time an apartment is adequate, sometimes personal care is necessary, and sometimes hospitalization and skilled nursing care is required. In New York City, several such projects are being developed with the use of HUD Section 8 funds and Medicaid. Also, large numbers of persons are in public hospitals at a cost of $400 to $800 per day. It would be interesting to see whether Mexico might not encourage the development of several AIDS treatment and residential facilities; persons with AIDS who have the resources could choose to live there, and public agencies from the United States could contract to pay for persons who chose this option.

Such therapeutic facilities could combine nursing care, residential and medical facilities. Since a person suffering from full-blown AIDS is in need of care, and with any reasonable precautions should not be considered a public health risk, these facilities or communities could be very valuable. They would provide choices for AIDS sufferers and additional jobs and revenues for Mexico.

V. CONTRACTING WITH THE U.S. AND STATE GOVERNMENTS FOR OTHER SERVICES

Federal, state and city governments contract with a broad variety of private agencies for health and human services. In many cases, rather than persons having an entitlement to a service or a voucher that they can use in limited circumstances, the government entity *mandates* that the service be received. This occurs, for example, when the human service agency becomes the foster guardian of children who are removed from their homes. The ultimate case, of course, is when a person is incarcerated for a period of time.

In the juvenile correctional system, contracting out to long-term private correctional facilities has become much more common. Between 1970 and 1983, the percentage of juveniles held in nonprofit and proprietary private long-term correctional facilities in the United States increased from 13 percent to 48 percent.[40] There are a variety of arrangements that have been developed for adolescents, ranging from camps to fairly high security locked units. In addition to normal concerns about security, developing services for those adolescents in Mexico would raise a number of issues with regard to the state's duty to provide for them and to develop ways for them to be integrated into society. Increasingly, experts in the field have advocated developing ways to continue involvement of the family in their rehabilitation.

With adult prisoners the situation is different. There is considerable precedent for states to contract with one another to care for each other's prisoners. Minnesota has leased its prisons to neighboring states for a number of years; with the development of private prisons, the arrangements have become even more interstate. Washington D.C., in lieu of building new prisons, contracts with a private prison in Zavalla County, Texas, as well as with facilities in other locations to house their prisoners. Limestone County, Texas recently adopted a bond issue for the purpose of building a prison that it intends to lease to New York State.

Contracting with facilities in Mexico would quite clearly have to be undertaken with due cognizance of the Constitutional rights that prisoners have: due process of law in the fifth and fourteenth amendments, and the eighth amendment's prohibition against cruel and unusual punishment.[41] If Mexican prisons were to house U.S. citizens, there obviously would be a number of possibly insurmountable issues of international law and sovereignty to be confronted. Criteria for parole, personal due process with regard to punishment, and extradition arrangements between countries might all be requirements that would be insuperable. Nonetheless, if the conditions in the Mexican prison alternatives were made completely explicit and if potential prisoners were given the option of choosing, many of the problems could be mitigated. However, state governments and state officials probably would remain liable and could be sued for conditions and actions in the contracted prison.

There is no doubt that if current trends continue, the cost of incarcerating increasing numbers of persons will be a progressively more expensive proposition. The number of prison beds in the United States has increased rapidly, and severe overcrowding in many states has only been held in check by very aggressive—even arbitrary—parole and release policies. Between 1980 and 1984, the population in U.S. federal and state prisons grew by 134,000 inmates to 463,866 persons. In addition, in late 1984 there were an estimated 130,000 persons in jails.[42] The total, roughly 600,000 persons incarcerated, has continued to increase.

VI. CONCLUSIONS AND ISSUES TO BE RESOLVED

This survey of health care utilization on the United States-Mexico border and the potential benefits to be derived from Mexican provision of health and human services to U.S. citizens has been designed to identify a number of targets of opportunity where policy changes on the part of the U.S. government could serve to enhance the choices of U.S. citizens, generate employment in Mexico and be cost effective from the perspective of the U.S. taxpayer. Many details, of course, will have to be worked out.

From the Mexican perspective, determining which of these populations it would be appropriate to serve and under what conditions, establishing conditions under which persons with U.S. licenses might be permitted to practice in these facilities, and determining who could own these facilities would all be issues that would need to be resolved. It might be that joint Mexican-U.S. operation of certain facilities would be appropriate. Issues faced by any project—such as zoning, adequate infrastructure (including water and sewage services), and licensure—would have to be resolved in Mexico as much as they would have to be in the United States. In many cases, it would seem that some kind of U.S. certification and inspection with a relatively laissez faire attitude on the part of Mexican officials would be most likely to elicit a satisfactory supply response.

From the perspective of the U.S. government, conditions of participation by providers and facilities in Mexico, staffing requirements and determination of eligibility of U.S. beneficiaries are issues which also would need to be addressed and could require quite detailed negotiations. If a number of facilities were established in Mexico, teams of accreditors and medical examiners would possibly have to tour or be stationed in Mexico.

There are, of course, potential downsides to many of these proposals. From the perspective of Mexico, there might be concern that a two-tiered level of care is being developed or that the United States is exporting those who are impaired. But when one examines the increased competition in the United States between communities that want prisons, mental hospitals and other such facilities, it should be clear that the employment effect would outweigh other effects.

With regard to the U.S. government, there may be the perception that the proposal is not cost effective because many persons will request services who have not done so before. There also may be a concern that this will cost U.S. jobs and will be difficult to monitor or to assure quality. These are legitimate considerations, but probably are outweighed by the potential cost savings, the increased equity of treatment of those who live abroad and the increased choice afforded to U.S. citizens. In some of these areas, perhaps the United States should initiate short-term demonstration projects to assess their efficacy and replicability.

In spite of potential obstacles and difficulties, the benefits that would accrue from many of these changes would seem to outweigh the costs. Not only will general welfare be enhanced by any benefits that accrue from freer trade, but also productive interdependence and understanding will be enhanced.

NOTES

1. Linda Chan, Roy McCandless, Bernard Portnoy, Chandler Stolp and David Warner, *Maternal and Child Health on the U.S.-Mexico Border* (Austin: LBJ School of Public Affairs, 1988), Ch. 7.

2. Eve Powell-Griner, *Characteristics of Births in Two Areas of Texas: 1980*, Working Paper No. 21 (Austin: LBJ School of Public Affairs, 1983).

3. Sylvia Gundelman and Monica Jasis Silber, "Crossing the Border for Health Care: The Binational Use of Services by Mexican Residents of Tijuana," 1988.

4. Indigent Health Care Review Committee, *Valley Primary Health Care Review* (Houston: University of Texas School of Public Health, U.T. Health Services Center, 1988).

5. Virginia Fowkes, W. Fowkes and E.G. Walters, *Assessment of Factors Which Impede Development of Area Health Education Centers in Medically Underserved Areas Along the U.S./Mexico Border in Texas* (United Management Systems of Arizona and Division of Family and Community Medicine, Stanford University, 1989), p. 24.

6. Amber Lawrence, "Health Issues on the Texas Mexico Border," Senior Paper, Plan II (University of Texas, 1989).

7. DHHS, *The Medicare Handbook*, p. 10.

8. Scott Cambell Brown, "Retiring to Mexico," *American Demographer* (March 1987), p. 14.

9. John Moody, "Paradise Down Mexico Way," *Time*, 24 August 1987, p. 63.

10. U.S. Senate Special Committee on Aging, *Aging America: Trends and Projections*, SSA Publication No. 13-11727, 1984.

11. U.S. Bureau of the Census, "Health Care Availability in the Texas-Mexico Border Area," *Current Population Reports*, Series P. 60, No. 156 U.S. General Accounting Office, 1988.

12. John Howells and Don Merwin, *Retire on $400 a Month: Choose Mexico* (San Francisco, CA: Gateway Books, 1988). See also Peter A. Dickinson, "Travel and Retirement Edens Abroad," *AARP Book* (Glenview, IL: Scott, Foresman and Company, 1989).

13. Linda Martin, *The Graying of Japan* (Washington, DC: Population Reference Bureau, 1989).

14. House Health Task Force and Committee on the Budget, Statement by Nancy Gordon, 1987.

15. Charles Culhane, "Long Term Care Costs Seen Doubling by Next Decade," *American Medical News*, 1988, p. 9.

16. National Center for Health Statistics, "The 1986 Inventory of Long-Term Care Places: An Overview of Facilities for the Mentally Retarded," Advance Data Number 143, DHS Publication No. DHS-87-1250, 1987.

17. Alice Rivlin and Joshua Weiner, *Caring for the Disabled Elderly: Who Will Pay?* (Washington, DC: The Brookings Institution, 1988).

18. Henry Aaron, Barry Bosworth and Gary Burtless, *Can America Afford to Grow Old?* (Washington, DC: The Brookings Institution, 1989).

19. Daniel Lopez-Acuna, *La Salud Desigual en Mexico* (Mexico, DF: Siglo Veintiuno Editores, 1980).

20. Institute of Medicine, *Allied Health Services: Avoiding Crises* (Washington, DC: National Academy Press, 1989).

21. John Melcher, "Keeping the Elderly Out of Institutions by Putting Them Back in Their Homes," *American Psychologist*, vol. 43, no. 8 (1988), p. 643–647.

22. James Simmons, "Integrating Federal Health Care Resources at the Local Level," *Hospital and Health Services Administration*, vol. 34, no. 1 (Spring 1989), pp. 113–122.

23. Lynn Wagner, "VA Hospitals Struggling to Keep Pace with Patient Demands, Staff Shortages," *Modern Healthcare*, vol. 17, (5 June 1987), p. 162.

24. Veterans Administration, *Caring for the Older Veteran*.

25. Maria Rudensky, "Eligibility Test May Force Some Veterans to Community Hospitals," *Modern Health Care*, vol. 16 (1986), p. 170.

26. Constance Horgan, Amy Taylor and Gail Wilensky, "Aging Veterans: Will They Overwhelm the VA Medical Care System?" *Health Affairs*, vol. 2, no. 3 (1983), p.84.

27. Mark Schlesinger and Terrie Wetle, "Care of the Elder Veteran: New Directions for Change," *Health Affairs*, vol. 5, no. 2 (1986), pp. 65–66.

28. National Center for Health Statistics, 1987.

29. National Conference of State Legislators, *A Legislator's Guide to Long-Term Care*, 1987.

30. B. Burwell, S. Clausen, M. Hall and J. Simon, "Medicaid Recipients in Intermediate Care Facilities for the Mentally Retarded," *Health Care Financing Review* (Spring 1987), pp. 1–12.

31. Denise Gamino, "Unlicensed in Mexico," *Austin American Statesman*, 28 August 1989, pp. A1, A4.

32. National Head Injury Foundation, "Average of Total Lifetime Costs for an Individual with Severe Head Injury in Appropriate Settings," and addendum to

"The Need for Coverage for Persons with Traumatic Brain Injuries by Catastrophic Insurance Legislation," (Southborough, MA, 1987).

33. Jeff Kraus, Mary Ann Black, Nancy Hersol, Pacita Ley, William Rokaw, Constance Sullivan, Sharon Bowers, Sharon Knowlton and Lawrence Marshall, "The Incidence of Acute Brain Injury and Serious Impairment in a Defined Population," *American Journal of Epidemiology*, vol. 119, no. 2, pp. 186–201.

34. E. Fuller Torrey, Sidney Wolfe and Laurie M. Flynn, *Care of the Seriously Mentally Ill: A Rating of State Programs* (Washington, DC: Public Citizen Health Research Group and the National Alliance for the Mentally Ill, 1988).

35. Torrey, et al., 1988.

36. Torrey, et al., 1988.

37. E. Fuller Torrey, *Nowhere to Go: The Tragic Odyssey of the Homeless Mentally Ill* (New York City, NY: Harper and Row, 1988).

38. David Warner, Laurie Crumpton and Gary Watts, "The Cost of Care for the Chronically Mentally Ill in Texas in 1987," in *Community Care for the Mentally Ill* (Austin, TX: Hogg Foundation for Mental Health, University of Texas, 1989).

39. Fred J. Hellinger, "National Forecasts of the Medical Care Costs of AIDS: 1988–1992," *Inquiry* vol. 25, (1987), p. 470.

40. Daniel J. Curran, "Destructuring, Privatization and the Promise of Juvenile Diversion: Compromising Community-Based Corrections," *Crime and Delinquency*, vol. 34, no. 4 (October 1988), pp. 363–378.

41. Douglas Dunham, "Inmates Rights and the Privatization of Prisons," *Columbia Law Review* (November 1986), pp. 1475–1504.

42. Gilbert Geis, "The Privatization of Prisons: Panacea or Placebo?" in *Private-Means Public Ends*, (eds.) Caroll B., Convant R. and Easton T. (New York: Praeger, 1986).

5

The *Maquiladora* Industry in Mexico:
Its Transitional Role

Sidney Weintraub

I. INTRODUCTION

My purpose is to provide some perspective on the role of the *maquiladora* industry in Mexico's economic development. In doing so, I will seek to strike a balance between the benefits *maquiladora* bring to Mexico and the uncertainties inherent in this mode of production.

Each of us brings the biases of our discipline to the examination of the *maquiladora*. Economists see the industry as an example of the international division of labor.[1] Sociologists and anthropologists tend to focus on the family and societal consequences of employment in assembly operations.[2] Industry based in the United States (and Japan, South Korea, and Taiwan, to name just a few countries) votes with its feet by annually increasing the number of plants and workers in the Mexican *maquiladora*.[3] The U.S. industrial labor movement, as exemplified by the American Federation of Labor/Congress of Industrial Organizations (AFL/CIO), deplores the lack of union organization in most of Mexico's *maquiladora*. Students of international migration debate whether the *maquiladoras* on the Mexican-U.S. frontier stimulate movement of persons, first to the border and then clandestinely to the United States.[4] Political scientists concern themselves with how a border population intimately linked economically with the United States reacts to initiatives from Mexico City.

The listing could easily be extended. There can be no one analysis of the *maquiladora* (or export processing zone) phenomenon since each dissection depends on the approach taken. While I cannot escape the perspective of my own discipline (economics), I will seek to broaden this outlook to provide a balanced picture. At any rate, that is my intent.

II. WHAT WE KNOW

There has been an explosion of research on the *maquiladora* and export processing zone phenomenon in recent years. Scholars have examined the industry from virtually every angle. Governments have involved themselves in the examination as they increasingly build up export processing zones.[5] Consequently, we know a good deal about the factual side of the industry.

Personnel employed in Mexican *maquiladora* at the end of 1989 came to about 450,000.[6] Total *maquiladora* exports in 1988 were $10.1 billion, imported inputs $7.8 billion, for a value added figure in Mexico that year of $2.3 billion.[7] This was one-third of the value added for all of Mexico's manufactured exports.[8] The value added in Mexican *maquiladora* was about $3 billion in 1989.

The principal benefits of the *maquiladora* are thus clear. To the direct employment of 450,000, one must add a similar amount of indirect employment. If average family size is five, *maquiladora* employment thus contributes to the income of more than four million people. This is significant and no responsible government can ignore this reality. For a country in which foreign exchange is perennially in short supply (a situation aggravated in recent years by the external debt burden), the net exports generated by *maquiladora* operations are crucial to development.

We can quantify other variables. The most important industries in which Mexican *maquiladora* are engaged are electrical and electronic equipment and transportation. The cities with the greatest number of establishments are Tijuana, Ciudad Juarez and Mexicali.[9] We know that *maquiladora* plants in Mexico started with predominantly female employees, quite young and many not previously employed. This is the pattern in export assembly operations in much of the world. But we also know that the female proportion is not static. It has come down from more than 80 percent in Mexican *maquiladora* some ten years ago to about 65 percent today. This tendency toward hiring more males has coincided with the increasing sophistication of *maquiladora* production. It results also from labor shortages at Mexico's northern border. Most *maquiladora* jobs are simple, repetitive tasks. Increasingly, however, Mexicans hold managerial positions in the *maquiladora* plants and many Mexicans work as advisors, lawyers, accountants and technicians.

About half the value added in Mexico from the *maquiladora* comes from wages and salaries and another 45 percent from utility and other business expenses. Only about 6 percent of the value added in Mexico comes from national material inputs and packaging.[10] However, this proportion has been increasing; as few as three years ago, it was less than 4 percent. Mexican inputs tend to be used more in locations where supplier industries have been established, such as Guadalajara and Monterrey, than at the border, where supplier industries are still scarce.

The *maquiladora* plants are established essentially as export industries. They burgeoned after the Mexican peso was devalued in the early 1980s. The decline in the value of the peso coincided with growing competition in the U.S. market from Japan, Western Europe and many advanced developing countries. This is a manifestation of the economist's international division of labor approach. U.S. industries had to reduce costs to compete and turned to Mexico, and other low-wage countries, for labor-intensive aspects of production.[11] Mexico has certain advantages in addition to low wages, particularly location. This explains the reluctance of many *maquiladoras* to move away from the border.

However, the stereotype of *maquiladora* plants as being simple, labor intensive operations is no longer fully accurate. Many have sophisticated technology, where wages comprise only 10 to 25 percent of total costs. These are likely to be durable establishments, even if wages in Mexico increase more than in other locations where export processing industries have been established.

The market for the products of *maquiladora* is mostly the United States. U.S. tariff items 806.30 and especially 807.00, which permit payment of U.S. import duties only on the value added outside the United States, has encouraged production for the U.S. market.[12] But this is not the only reason. Many of the *maquiladora* are captive plants, established precisely to provide intra-firm inputs; and since most investors in *maquiladora* are U.S. companies, this makes the U.S. market the natural one for the output. *Maquiladora* established by non-U.S. firms are also predicated on exporting to the U.S. market, again largely as part of a single firm's production operations.[13]

Mexico permits a proportion of *maquiladora* (or export processing zone) production to be sold internally. However, the *maquiladora* were conceived as export enclaves with little expected forward linkages with national industry. This was not the pattern for the assembly operations in the Asian countries, where assembly gave way to production linkages with national industry in both directions, forward and backward. These national connections are still relatively primitive in Mexico compared with Asia, but not absent.

There are, thus, facts—quantifiable data—that we know about the Mexican *maquiladora*. The facts make clear why the Mexican government —every national government in Mexico City since the border industrialization program began in the 1960s—encourages investment in the *maquiladora*. They create many jobs, support many people, and provide export earnings. Each of these aspects is essential to the maintenance of tranquility in Mexico.

There are other aspects of the *maquiladora* about which we know much, but which are less quantifiable. Perhaps the most important of these is the degree to which the *maquiladora* bring new technology to Mexico. No Mexican wants the country to be attractive to foreign investors only because wages are low; successful development means higher wages and higher incomes for the general population. This will be possible only if Mexico develops its informational and manufacturing sectors sufficiently to move from being a less–to a more-developed country. What we are learning is that *maquiladora* plants are increasingly becoming more automated, more sophisticated in production techniques and greater users of microelectronic technology.[14]

We know, also, that most *maquiladora* are a part of a total firm strategy, a way to obtain inputs for a conglomerate's comprehensive production program. The *maquiladora* are thus part of a growing worldwide tendency of increasing trade across national boundaries by individual firms. This ten-

dency is not limited to *maquiladora* (if we define *maquiladora* as plants established to take advantage of a particular way that the United States
levies its import duties). Viewed more broadly, the *maquiladora* plants
are but one manifestation of growing intra-firm and intra-industry trade
—trade in parts as well as in finished goods. Intra-firm trade between
Mexico and the United States is not confined to *maquiladora*, but is part of
a general configuration of industrial integration of the two economies.
Similar developments are occurring in Asia between Japan and other
countries.

What we know, therefore, but lack the information to make quantifiably
precise, is that the *maquiladora* are a particular aspect of a broader tendency of Mexican-U.S. economic integration. This less quantifiable aspect—the combination of technology acquisition and becoming part of a
transnational productive network—is apt to be more important for Mexico and its development and for Mexican-U.S. relations, than the precise
quantifiable information we have about *maquiladora*.

III. THE UNEASE OVER *MAQUILADORA*

While the Mexican authorities have no viable choice but to foster the
further development of *maquiladora* because the jobs and the foreign exchange are needed, they do have some control over the form this development takes. Encouragement can be given to establishing *maquiladora* away
from the border; efforts can be made to integrate the *maquiladora* into the
total Mexican industrial structure; training can be provided so that more
Mexicans are able to operate the changing technologies and manage the
operations. All of these steps have been taken, to some degree.

Yet, if the *maquiladora* remain but one subset of total Mexican-U.S. industrial integration, this means that Mexico will be the minor partner for
some years to come. This must be disconcerting to Mexicans. However,
the point should not be pushed too far. All countries are somewhat captive to others as the global economy becomes integrated; and with time,
the positions of major and minor partners change.

The *maquiladora*, because they prospered at a time when Mexican wages
were extremely low, especially when calculated by foreign investors in
their dollar equivalents, smack of exploitation. This sense of manipulation
by giant foreign firms was exacerbated by the predominance of young
women in the *maquiladora* plants. The issue is not that women do not need
to earn a living, but rather the concern that young women were being
used in dead-end jobs because of their docility and then dumped as new
cohorts were hired. The growing male proportion of workers and employees in the *maquiladora* is serving to reduce the tension, but the problem has not disappeared.

Perhaps the deepest source of unease is that the *maquiladora* are in Mexico but not part of Mexico, other than to take advantage of the low-wage employees. There is a nagging fear that the boom of the *maquiladora* buildup can give way under certain circumstances to the shock of build-down. These conditions may originate outside of Mexico and, therefore, not be amenable to Mexican control. A prolonged U.S. recession is but one such scenario. Mexican authorities must concern themselves about growing protectionism in the United States. Organized labor in the United States regularly petitions for an end to the 806.30/807.00 system (levying import duties only on the value added outside the United States) on the grounds that this takes jobs away from Americans in favor of low-wage foreign labor. U.S. labor has regularly lost this battle, but the war seems eternal.

If Mexican wages (Mexican unit costs) rise more rapidly than in other locations suitable for export processing operations, many plants, the less sophisticated of the *maquiladora*, may just pick up and move. This lack of assurance of continued employment is unsettling. The purpose of development is to raise incomes; but if this is accomplished, the source of this income may disappear. What this means is that the *maquiladora* are best seen as a transitional phenomenon, as a source of wages and employment in the process of moving to a higher level of development, when other, more secure jobs will be available.

There is also discomfort that the *maquiladora* structure has an anti-Mexico City political and cultural influence and that the growing border integration with the United States may lead to increasing estrangement between *norteños* (Mexican border residents) and *chilangos* (Mexico City residents). This is rarely stated in precisely this form, but is reflected in writings from the center about the mercenary mentality being developed by people in the north.

IV. SIGNIFICANCE OF THE *MAQUILADORA*

Maquiladora plants represent a stage in international industrial production. They are a means of carrying out co-production between firms in advanced industrial societies and subsidiaries in developing countries. The main difference between *maquiladora* operations and the more traditional establishment of overseas subsidiaries is that the latter were undertaken in the first instance to capture the internal market in the host country, whereas *maquiladora* production is for export. *Maquiladora* are captive plants producing intermediate goods or finishing the processing of previously assembled products. The traditional establishment of overseas subsidiaries was to produce either finished or intermediate products for local sale. The production cycle theory of international trade, under which production of products, as they become standardized, moves from the innovating country to other places, fits the traditional pattern of foreign investment. It is not applicable to *maquiladora*, at least not until these plants cease to become captives and transform themselves into producers and not just assemblers.

The more appropriate theoretical model for *maquiladora* is Heckscher-Ohlin, under which trade is explained by national differences in factor proportions. Companies in high-wage, developed societies move labor-intensive operations to locations where wages are lower, thereby setting up a co-production rather than a production transference relationship. Thus *maquiladora*, or other export-processing zones, are a feature of production in developing societies, whereas traditional foreign direct investment is more significant among industrial countries. The United States has no *maquiladora* operations to speak of in Japan, Western Europe or Canada; it does in Mexico, Central America and the Caribbean.

These differences have implications for the industrial development of countries where *maquiladora* or export-assembly operations are located. Foreign manufacturing production, motivated by sales in the host country, is by its very nature integrated into the industrial structure of these countries. Developing host countries took steps to assure this outcome by establishing domestic-content regulations. Production of an automobile or a computer in Mexico entails using a high proportion of nationally produced material inputs, a process intended to have spread effects within Mexico itself. While these domestic-content provisions may have reduced the competitiveness of Mexico's national industrial structure, it did insure against the establishment of a foreign enclave activity.

Maquiladora production, whether in Mexico or export-processing zones elsewhere, are archetypical and enclave operations. They use few local material inputs. Their purpose is to take advantage of cheap labor. Their operations, at least in Mexico, have few production spread effects. They are generators of employment and sources of foreign-exchange earnings. They are in the country where they produce but are not part of the country's total industrial structure. They are thus not a long-term solution to development because their existence is completely dependent on the health of the parent firm and on continued low wages in order to make the products of the parent firm competitive.

However, it is not foreordained that *maquiladora* plants remain an enclave, at least not in Mexico. This is an important difference between the export-processing zones elsewhere in Latin America and the Caribbean and the *maquiladora* in Mexico. Mexico does have an industrial structure. After first limiting *maquiladora* production to the export market, the authorities have since permitted sales within Mexico itself for a proportion of total output. Producers in Mexico are able to shift the status of plants from *maquiladora*—with a focus on the export market—to another legal regime which permits easier sale in the domestic market. Co-production, in other words, need not be between foreign parent and a Mexican *maquiladora* captive, but can be between firms within Mexico itself. As occurred in Asia, South Korea and Taiwan, assembly can give way to manufacturing in which the critical element is not necessarily low wages but efficient production to bring down unit costs.

This possibility hardly exists in the Caribbean or Central America. It is an important distinction between Mexico and other hemispheric locations. One can talk generically of co-production or of export-processing zones, but then a distinction must be made between the co-production that exists and that which can develop—and in this respect, the Mexican *maquiladora* must be differentiated from the Dominican or Jamaican plants that produce largely textile products for the foreign market. Mexican *maquiladora* plants do this, but they also produce sophisticated machinery, automotive parts and electronic equipment for the U.S. market; and the producing firms often have a mixture of *maquiladora* and traditional plants integrated into a total process, integrating Mexican and U.S. production.

V. WHAT'S NEXT?

The *maquiladora* are best viewed as a stage in the development process. They are based on low-wage labor, while the objective of economic development is to raise real wages. They were originally predicated on simple, repetitive tasks—Adam Smith's division of labor in its most simplistic form—and manufacturing is increasingly demanding more skilled personnel. Women were used because they tend to demand low wages and demonstrate little militancy, but docility ceases to become a virtue as production becomes more flexible, technically complex and automated.

The *maquiladora* phenomenon is therefore best viewed dynamically, from the perspective of what it is a transition to. How effectively will the *maquiladora* encourage Mexico's industrial and economic development? If the social and political aspects of the *maquiladora* generate unease in Mexico, the proper question to ask is how to reduce this concern.

I will give one point of view. My own vision, now that Mexico has entered into the world economy more thoroughly than at any time in its modern history, is that this global immersion will accelerate. To paraphrase Malthus, economic globalism will grow exponentially and looking inward only arithmetically. If Mexico's global involvement does not increase, then the cost will be inadequate economic development.

For Mexico, the outside world is overwhelmingly the United States. The United States takes between 60 and 70 percent of Mexico's exports, including oil. For manufactures, the United States is the market for 80 percent of Mexico's exports. Two-thirds of all private direct investment in

Mexico is by U.S. firms. Increasingly, Mexico's non-oil foreign commerce—its imports and exports—is intra-firm trade; and these firms are largely American, but with much Mexican ownership. The two economies are becoming integrated, and further economic development in Mexico will only deepen this integration.

Viewed from this perspective, the *maquiladora* should be seen as a stage in the global integration process, a way to move from one mode of industrial production to another—from looking inward to involving the nation's industries in the global competitive challenge. This requires that assembly continue to give way to manufacturing, that the linkages of the *maquiladora* be not just with affiliated firms in the United States and other foreign countries, but, much more crucially, with firms in Mexico itself. These, in turn, will have their own links with related firms in the United States and elsewhere. The export processing zone must increasingly become a productive operation fully part of Mexico's industrial and technical structure. Failing this, the great long-term opportunity of the *maquiladora* will be lost.

I have no easy answers on how the transition from export processing to national industrial integration is best achieved. Some policy steps are self-evident. Mexico must invest heavily to augment the skills of its workers. The country should not try to keep the *maquiladora* production from entering into the national economy, but rather should encourage it. Much of the *maquiladora* production is now based on tariff advantages for sales into the U.S. market, but over time this should be a less compelling feature of production than national industrial integration.

This last point requires elaboration. Based on data from the U.S. Department of Commerce, the value added by Mexico for U.S. imports under tariff item 807 was 49 percent in 1987. But this overall average masks differences among products. For transportation items, value added in Mexico was 58 percent; for furniture it was 73 percent; for clothing it was only 27 percent; and for fabricated metals, 25 percent.[15] To the extent that *maquiladora* production is more thoroughly integrated into the Mexican productive structure, value added in Mexico will increase; and, therefore, duties levied when the goods are imported into the United States will cover a large proportion of total value. This structure of substantial domestic value added is typical of U.S. 807 imports from more developed countries. For example, the duty free proportion on imports from Japan in 1987 was only 3 percent; this means that of $14 billion of U.S. 807 imports, Japan used only $379 million of U.S. imports. Other proportions of U.S. inputs for 807 imports in 1987 were 2 percent for West Germany, 4 percent for the United Kingdom, 15 percent for France and 15 percent for South Korea.[16] These low proportions reveal that the more industrially developed countries do not have merely export processing or export production zones, but rather integrated industries. This is the direction in which Mexico must move.

My overall conclusion is that, despite the justifiable unease they generate, the *maquiladora* industries are serving a valuable function in Mexico at the present time. I close by emphasizing the time dimension because I believe the way to examine the *maquiladora* industry is as a transition from enclave to an integral part of the national industrial structure.

NOTES

An earlier version of this paper was prepared for the seminar on *La Industria Maquiladora en México*, sponsored by the Centro de Estudios Económicos de El Colegio de México, El Colegio de la Frontera Norte, and the Fundación Friedrich Ebert, in Mexico City, June 5–7, 1989.

1. See Mario Carillo Huerta and Victor Urquidi, "Trade Deriving from the International Division of Production: Maquila and Postmaquila in Mexico," *Journal of the Flagstaff Institute*, Vol. 13, No. 1 (April 1989), pp. 14–47; and Joseph Grunwald and Kenneth Flamm, *The Global Factory: Foreign Assembly in International Trade* (Washington, D.C.: Brookings Institution, 1985).

2. A good example of this is Maria Patricia Fernandez-Kelly, *For We Are Sold. I and My People: Women and Industry in Mexico's Frontier* (Albany: State University of New York Press, 1983).

3. *El Mercado de Valores*, "La industria maquiladora de exportación," año 49, num. 9 (1 May 1989), pp. 19–25, gives the annual growth between 1982 and 1987 as 14 percent in number of establishments, 19.2 percent in employment, and 16.1 percent in Mexican value added.

4. The issue is analyzed in Mitchell A. Seligson and Edward J. Williams, *Maquiladoras and Migration: A Study of Workers in the Mexican-United States Border Industrialization Program* (Austin: Mexico-United States Border Research Program, University of Texas, 1981).

5. Gregory K. Schoepfle and Jorge F. Perez-Lopez, "Employment Implications of Export Assembly Operations in Mexico and the Caribbean Area," Working Paper No. 16, Commission for the Study of International Migration and Cooperative Economic Development, 1990, provides excellent background on export processing zones in Mexico, the Dominican Republic, Haiti, Costa Rica, Jamaica, El Salvador, Honduras and Barbados. One of my doctoral students at the University of Texas at Austin is doing his dissertation on a comparison of Mexican and Taiwanese export processing industries.

6. Banco de México, *Indicadores económicos*.

7. Banco de México, *Indicadores económicos*.

8. The one-third figure assumes that imported inputs constitute one-third of the value of Mexico's non-maquila manufactured exports, so that in 1988, value added in Mexico was roughly $7 billion ($10.5 billion total manufactured exports, less $3.5 billion of imported inputs). A further assumption is that all maquiladora exports were manufactures. This is an exaggeration; the proportion of value added of maquiladora to total manufactured exports may be about 30 percent, instead of 33 percent.

9. "La industria maquiladora de exportación," *El Mercado de Valores*, año 49, num. 9 (1 May 1989), p. 23. While figures are for 1987, the same ranking persists in 1990.

10. "La industria maquiladora de exportación, p.22.

11. In the textile and clothing industry, the choice of locations was also determined by the availability of quotas for entering the U.S. market.

12. Under the harmonized system introduced in the United States on January 1, 1989, these tariff items are now 9802.00.60 and 9802.00.80.

13. Elsie Echeverri-Carroll, *Maquilas: Economic Impacts and Foreign Investment Opportunities: Japanese Maquilas—A Special Case* (Austin: Bureau of Business Research, The University of Texas, 1988) is an examination of the Japanese maquiladora strategy.

14. Flor Brown y Lilia Dominguez, "Nuevas tecnologías en la industria maquiladora de exportación," *Comercio Exterior,* Vol. 39, Num. 3 (March 1989, pp. 215–223).

15. Data are from Scheopfle and Perez-Lopez, "Employment Implications of Export Assembly Operations in Mexico and the Caribbean Basin.

16. U.S. Census tapes prepared for the U.S. International Trade Commission.

6

Maquiladoras and Local Linkages:
Building Transaction Networks
in Guadalajara

Patricia A. Wilson

I. INTRODUCTION

For Mexico's assembly industry to be more than a source of foreign exchange and low paying jobs, the *maquiladora* plants must create linkages with the local economy. These linkages occur through the network of transactions that the plant undertakes with local firms, such as the purchase of locally manufactured inputs and local services, subcontracting to local firms, the sale of products as inputs to local manufacturers and the creation of spinoff firms. Each transaction serves as a possible conduit for technology transfer and an impetus to more diversified job opportunities. This chapter examines the *maquiladora* industry in the large interior city of Guadalajara to see where the local linkages are strong, where they are tenuous and how the public sector could increase the local linkages. The analysis is based on in-plant surveys of all 26 of Guadalajara's *maquiladoras*. The case of Guadalajara is contrasted with Monterrey and the northern border, to show that public sector efforts to encourage local transactions network of the *maquiladora* industry would have to be tailored to the particular city or region. Fifteen plants were surveyed in Monterrey and 30 along the border (ten each in Tijuana, Juarez and Nuevo Laredo).

In Guadalajara, there are two large clusters of *maquiladoras*, each with its own pattern of local networks. One is the sector of mostly small, home-grown, craft-based *maquiladoras* in apparel, footwear, furniture, jewelry and toys. These *maquiladoras* represent the tip of a long standing craft sector in Guadalajara. The other large cluster of *maquiladoras* is the electronics sector: foreign subsidiaries, many quite large, producing electronics components and subassemblies. The electronics *maquiladoras* form a part of Guadalajara's much larger electronics industry, which includes foreign plants that are not *maquiladoras* but do export, joint ventures between foreign and Mexican capital and locally owned start-ups. In addition to the crafts cluster and the electronics cluster, there is a small cluster of auto part *maquiladoras*, primarily U.S. branch plants, attracted in the late 1970s and early 1980s to Guadalajara by the local metal mechanics industry.

The policy recommendations in the final section are based on the notion that the public sector can play a role in augmenting these local transaction networks. The recommendations draw upon the experience of export-oriented local craft networks in north-central Italy and Denmark, as well as the experience of electronics networks in France.

Conceptual Framework

Mexico has opted for an export-led development strategy. One of the pitfalls of such a strategy is the reliance on foreign capital, technology, raw materials and markets. The result can be an isolated enclave of export-oriented manufacturing that does not create a broad-based internal industrialization. This risk is particularly high with foreign assembly industry, such as Mexico's *maquiladora* industry. By their very nature, foreign assembly plants tend to be industrial enclaves. They are rewarded with tax exonerations for bringing in inputs and machinery from abroad and exporting the output. In fact, records of the *Instituto Nacional de Estadísticas, Geografía y Informática* show that after 25 years, the *maquiladoras* in general source less than 2 percent of their inputs domestically. Yet the government of Mexico continues to vigorously promote the *maquiladora* industry as part of its overall export-led industrialization strategy, encouraging plants to locate in the interior where they have shown a greater tendency to source domestically.

The changing global economy points to a possible new opportunity for creating greater local linkages from the maquiladora industry: the rise of flexible production.[1] As a corporate strategy aimed at meeting Japanese competition, flexible production emphasizes quality competition over cost competition and adaptability to changing market opportunities over production for a standardized mass market. Economies of scope overshadow economies of scale as flexibility becomes the hallmark of the competitive edge. Vertical disintegration replaces vertical integration as large producers unburden themselves of all but their most productive or technologically sensitive endeavors in the pursuit of flexibility. What replaces the vertically integrated global complexes of mass production is a series of tightly integrated multifirm networks of buyers, suppliers and subcontractors. Some authors refer to this change in corporate strategy as the rise of post-Fordist flexibility and the decline of Fordist mass production.[2]

These new flexible inter-firm networks have a spatial dimension to them. The need for just-in-time deliveries, the careful sharing of technology, and the supervising of quality control between firms create the need for geographical clustering of these networks that telecommunications cannot totally obviate. While many observers have predicted that the rise of flexible production will bring the far-flung corporate empires back home,[3] others admit the possibility of clustering in Third World locations.[4] The Mexican government needs to foster local networking among these clusters. The electronics cluster in Guadalajara, which already has been dubbed Mexico's Silicon Valley by some of the international business press, holds particular potential.

The rise of flexible production also creates a new opportunity for small-scale producers to enter the international market without an inherent disadvantage from the lack of economies of scale. In fact, the economic development literature has formalized a craft paradigm modeled after the successful entry of north-central Italy's locally owned craft shops, particularly in textiles and clothing, into the international market.[5] The basis of their success has been networking and cooperation among the local small firms. The Mexican government should seek ways to promote local networking for export among Guadalajara's craft industries.

II. ECONOMIC DEVELOPMENT IN GUADALAJARA

Until the 1930s, Guadalajara was a commercial center serving the large landowners in the surrounding agricultural region. Trade was dominated by a few powerful merchants. Beginning in the 1930s, the merchants diversified into the production of consumer articles for the regional market, primarily by subcontracting to small workshops of craft producers using temporary, family and largely female home workers. By the mid-1960s, other urban centers in the region had grown up and begun to take over some of the region-serving commercial functions of Guadalajara. The Guadalajaran oligarchy entered manufacturing on a larger scale, often employing craft workers in formal factories, such as that of the nationally known shoe manufacturer, Canada.[6] At the same time, both domestic and foreign capital from outside the region began to set up factories in Guadalajara. Outside manufacturers were attracted, in part, by the growing regional market and industrial infrastructure, but also by the cooperative, trained labor force.

The first U.S. owned *maquiladoras* arrived in Guadalajara in the late 1960s. The presence of a female industrial labor force stemming from the craft industries was particularly attractive to them.[7] Burroughs (now Unisys), arriving in 1968, employs 80 percent (about 640) women line workers. Motorola, arriving in 1969, employs 70 percent (about 1,750) women line workers. General Instruments and TRW (since bought out by Shizuki), arriving in 1973/1974, employ 80 to 90 percent women line workers (450 to 500 each). Foreign auto part *maquiladoras* started showing up in the late 1970s. They use a predominantly male labor force. Attracted by the existing metal mechanics industry and its labor force, Borg Warner opened up two auto parts plants, one in 1978 and one in 1980. Another U.S. auto parts producer, Reliance Electric, and a Spanish auto parts manufacturer both established *maquiladoras* in 1981.

A total of 15 of the 24 *maquiladoras* in Guadalajara have been established since the crisis of 1982, largely in crafts (8 plants) and electronics (3), with one each in home appliances, auto parts, plastics and chemicals. The 1980s have also witnessed the growth of non-*maquiladora* manufacturing plants, especially in electronics. The state of Jalisco, reflecting Guadalajara's growth, more than doubled its share in total foreign investment in Mexico from 1.7 percent in 1982 to 3.8 percent in 1987. The *maquiladora* growth rate for Jalisco, which also reflects the Guadalajara metropolitan area, exceeded both that of the border and the interior for these years in terms of number of plants, but not in terms of number of employees (see Appendix 1).

Methodology

While INEGI records the amount of domestic inputs used by each *maquiladora*, the published data allows only a broad sectoral or geographic analysis of the plants by average percent of national inputs used. The Mexican government does not gather data on local inputs—those inputs manufactured in the local metropolitan area. Thus, information on local inputs purchased by *maquiladoras* has been purely anecdotal.

For this analysis, managers from all 26 *maquiladora* plants in Guadalajara were interviewed, providing 100 percent coverage. Two responses, both from small plants, were thrown out because of inconsistent answers. Plant managers were asked to specify the degree and nature of four kinds of local linkages: (1) local productive inputs purchased, such as inputs used in the production process that are manufactured in the local metropolitan area; (2) local productive services purchased (specific questions were asked about tool and die, metal stamping and plastic molding),[8] (3) sales made locally and (4) local spinoff companies started. Follow-up questions were asked about the names of local manufacturers, service providers and spinoff firms in order to subsequently survey a selection of local suppliers and spinoffs about their sourcing patterns. Questions were also asked about the degree and nature of non-local domestic inputs. Finally, respondents were asked to rank location factors to determine in which cases access to local goods and services was considered important.

III. CRAFTS NETWORK

Maquilization of Crafts. Most craft industries responded to the fall of the internal market in 1982 in one of two ways. Some began to deformalize the work process again by increasing home work and temporary work, not paying taxes and scaling back to family-sized operations. The lack of operating capital made others decide to return to subcontracting for larger companies in Guadalajara.[9] However, there was another strategy followed that has not been noted in the literature: the *maquilization* of the crafts industries. Faced with a falling internal market and capital shortages, a number of craft manufacturers sought *maquiladora* status in order to produce for the export market and find a U.S. client who would provide most of the inputs. Some did not like either the red tape or the vagaries of the foreign client's demands and subsequently stopped using their special legal status. In visiting craft manufacturers registered as *maquiladoras*, we found several who were no longer operating as such. Ten craft producers, however, were actively operating as registered *maquiladoras* at the time of the survey in 1988/1989.

The crafts sector of *maquiladoras* largely accounts for Guadalajara's relatively high percent of local inputs (see Table 1). A total of 16 percent of the inputs used by the ten firms, on average, are made in the Guadalajara metropolitan area. Most are small, locally owned companies in footwear, furniture, clothing, jewelry and toys. Unlike *maquiladoras* in these sectors along the border, the ones in Guadalajara have emerged from a strong local tradition of craft manufacturing for the domestic market. In fact, seven of the ten craft manufacturers operating as *maquiladoras* in Guadalajara sell also on the domestic market, four of them a minor portion of their output and three of them the majority of their output. The latter use *maquiladora* status primarily as excess capacity warrants. One of the clothing manufacturers existed as a factory for the domestic market before recently restructuring as a *maquiladora* exporting all of its output. Almost all have started operations as *maquiladoras* since the 1982 crisis, and most since 1987.

Technology. Unlike the craft *maquiladoras* along the border, most of these maquiladoras offer more than contract labor services to assemble inputs brought in by a North American client firm. The plant managers in fully 70 percent of them characterized their *maquiladora* production process as being largely manufacturing as opposed to assembly.[10] Many of the craft-based firms in Guadalajara add value to the product by cutting, forming, molding, dying and painting, in addition to the more traditional labor-intensive assembly of stitching and joining. On the other hand, none of them goes beyond the Fordist mass production model to adopt the techniques of post-Fordist flexible manufacturing. Almost all of them reported no use of computer controlled machinery or just-in-time inventorying, nor had any plans to introduce them in the future (see Appendix 3).

Local Inputs. Guadalajara's craft-based *maquiladoras* use more local inputs on average than do any other cluster (Table 1). The toy firm, which manufactures mylar (metallic) balloons, uses locally made photopolymer engravings for each design and adds locally manufactured plastic sticks and connectors. Nevertheless, it imports most of its major raw material—nylon. The footwear producers get their main inputs largely from their U.S. clients, both for leather and synthetic shoes. However, they do buy locally manufactured tacks, nails, glue, thread and dyes. The furniture manufacturers, whose inputs come largely from the United States, also

TABLE 1

CHARACTERISTICS OF GUADALAJARA'S MAQUILADORAS BY SECTOR, 1988–89

Sector	No. of Plants	Average % Local Inputs	Average % Natl. Inputs	% Foreign-Owned	Year Established (average)	Average No. of Workers	Average % Female
I. Crafts	10	16	23	0	1984	45	65
Toys	1	40	70	0	1984	70	60
Furniture	2	25	43	0	1987	28	43
Footwear	4	10	15	0	1983	65	54
Textiles & clothing	2	8	8	0	1983	21	100
Jewelry	1	10	10	0	1985	28	86
II. Electronics	6	2	6	100	1978	749	72
III. Auto Parts	5	4	37	100	1982	59	38
IV. Other	3	10	45	100	1987	90	85
Appliances	1	30	35	100	1988	24	95
Plastics	1	0	96	100	1985	97	80
Chemicals	1	0	0	100	1987	150	80

buy locally manufactured rivets, tacks, solder, screws, wood, glues, nails and staples. Of the two apparel plants, one buys no local inputs and the other buys thread and glues from local manufacturers. The manufacturer of fine jewelry buys locally produced industrial gases. While this use of local inputs is unusually high for *maquiladoras*, it is not for domestic industry. According to plant managers (often owners) who produce for the internal market, in addition to their *maquiladora* operations, their export production uses fewer local inputs than does their domestic-oriented production. The difference is due primarily to the fact that their U.S. clients provide most of the inputs.

National Inputs. Several of the craft-based *maquiladoras* also use significant inputs from elsewhere in Mexico (see national inputs in Table 1, which are a sum of local and non-local domestic inputs). The balloon manufacturer gets a part of its major input—nylon—and some of its dyes from both Mexico City and Monterrey. One of the furniture makers, which makes water beds, gets some of its wood, paint and varnish from elsewhere in Mexico. However, its principal input, plastic cloth, comes from the United States. Other furniture makers buy metal stampings from the states of Mexico and Monterrey. The shoe manufacturers buy some of their chemicals and plastics for synthetic shoes from Mexico City and Puebla. A small portion of the leather comes from Leon. The jewelry maker gets a small portion of its gold from Mexico City.

Other transactions. While the craft *maquiladoras* use a comparatively high amount of local inputs compared to the other *maquiladoras*, they use few local manufacturing services and have created no spinoffs that we could identify. In terms of local manufacturing services, only two of the ten use local tool and die and two use local plastic molding. None uses local metal stamping. Most get their plastic molding from their principal U.S. client and have their metal stamping done in either Mexico City or the United States.

Unlike the domestic craft producers in Guadalajara, which subcontract much of their work and employ a high proportion of temporary workers,[11] only one footwear firm among the *maquiladora* craft factories does a large amount of subcontracting and none relies on temporary employees. While the *maquiladoras* provide jobs that are more protected and regulated than in most of the smaller craft plants, they do not experience the fluid interaction among firms that the domestic craft producers are known for.

IV. ELECTRONICS NETWORK

Maquiladoras

The six electronics *maquiladoras* use a very small percentage of local inputs, varying from none to 6 percent. Neither do they use substantial

Mexican inputs from elsewhere in the country. Nevertheless, a substantial proportion of them do use local productive services and have created some important spinoffs. Moreover, the sheer size of some of them means that while the percentage of local inputs is small the volume is important.

The six electronics *maquiladoras* are all fully owned subsidiaries of foreign firms, five by U.S. companies and one by a Japanese firm. Unlike the crafts *maquiladoras*, these plants are an outgrowth of foreign industry, having been established from the beginning as complete *maquiladoras* exporting nearly all their outputs. They include the three oldest *maquiladoras* of Guadalajara: Unisys (formerly Burroughs), General Instruments and Motorola. These large plants were all established in the late 1960s and early 1970s and employ between 500 and 2,500 line workers each. The other three were established since 1985: Tulon (Easterline), Digital Power and Shizuki.[12] The newer plants are smaller, ranging from less than 50 production workers to 650 in the case of Shizuki. The older plants produce electric cable assemblies and wiring harnesses for computers, power supplies, semiconductors, electronic voltage surge supressors and relays. The newer plants make power supplies, circuit board drills and capacitors.

Technology. Only three *maquiladora* plants in Guadalajara make substantial use of computer controlled production machines, a key element of flexible technology. Two of them are electronics firms—the two largest and oldest electronics *maquiladoras* in Guadalajara: Unisys and Motorola. Unlike General Instruments, Unisys and Motorola significantly updated their technology and shop floor methods in the 1980s to incorporate some flexible production capabilities. While these two do use more local productive inputs than the other electronics *maquiladoras* (4 percent on average compared to .5 percent for the other electronics *maquiladoras*), this may reflect the time they have had to develop some local suppliers rather than some inherent tendency of the technology. Certainly, the use of just-in-time inventorying is not associated with greater local inputs (see Appendix 3). While all but one of the six electronics *maquiladoras* use just-in-time inventorying or are in the process of implementing it, they reported that they do so with inputs coming from the United States.

Local and national inputs. Unisys, which makes electronic cables, harnesses and power supplies for Unisys equipment, gets most of its inputs from Unisys in Dallas. It buys only metal chassis made in Guadalajara and terminals and connectors made in Mexico City. The Motorola semiconductor plant, which manufactures wafers, brings in all the chip parts from the United States and Europe. Some chemicals are purchased in Monterrey. The only local productive inputs are industrial gases from the Union Carbide plant in Guadalajara. The plant also purchases local packing material. General Instruments has been unable to find good local suppliers but is talking to IBM about their local suppliers, such as U.S. owned

ADTEC for double-sided, high-density printed circuit boards and U.S. owned Cherokee for power supplies. Taking all the electronics maquiladoras together, the main local productive inputs are industrial gases, metal chasis, varnish, wire, screws and tools. Nonproductive local materials include packaging materials such as cartons, dry ice, styrofoam, rubber boots and uniforms for workers.

As to national inputs from elsewhere in Mexico, a few of the electronics *maquiladoras* get gases and chemicals from Monterrey (Motorola helped to set up some of these suppliers); machine parts, lubricants, screws, tools and coolants from Mexico City; and solvents, solder and casting agents from both Mexico City and San Luis Potosí. The Unisys general manager said that the plant currently buys cables and connectors that are assembled in Mexico City but are in the process of setting up suppliers in San Luis Potosí and San Juan Del Rio to manufacture cables and connectors using 50 percent domestic content.

Spinoffs. The older electronics *maquiladoras* have generated three local spinoffs. Burroughs was responsible for two of them. Before it became Unisys, Burroughs created Compubur, a joint venture between Burroughs and Mexican capital that manufactures computers for the Mexican market. Compubur, in turn, sources 25 percent of its inputs from Guadalajara, including connectors from a Canadian-owned manufacturer that also supplies the local IBM plant, but which, at the time of the interview, had not yet qualified to supply local plants of other blue chip electronics firms. In 1985, a former Burroughs general manager founded Electrónica Pantera as a joint venture with a Mexican partner. With 210 production workers, it builds cables and harnesses for the growing Guadalajara computer industry (Hewlett Packard, IBM, Compubur, Wang, Cherokee) and exports a small part (2 percent) to the United States.

General Instruments generated a spinoff in 1983 when the plant manager left to start Sistemas Delfi, a joint venture with Telmex, the national telephone company of Mexico. With 100 production workers, the plant makes computer keyboards, keys and printed circuit boards, primarily for Telmex (60 percent of output), but it also does special orders of PCBs and computer keys for Hewlett Packard, IBM and Unisys. Sistemas Delfi, whose machines were brought from the United States under the *maquiladora* regimen, exports as a *maquiladora* when there is excess capacity but was not doing so at the time of the interview. This spinoff uses 80 percent national inputs for its Telmex products, with 50 percent from Guadalajara, including metal and plastic parts, along with gas tubing from General Instruments. Its other clients provide their own inputs. Productive services, such as metal stamping, plastic molding, and tool and die are done in-house.

Services. Four of the six electronics *maquiladoras* use local tool and die to some degree, covering some or all of their needs. Two of the six use local metal stamping, and only one uses local plastic molding. Much of the latter two services still come from the parent company or are done in-house. One of the local metal stamping firms used by the foreign electronics plants was started by a former Hewlett Packard engineer. A frequently cited tool and die supplier of the foreign electronics plants, TROMOL Troquelas y Moldes, is a local company with totally Mexican capital.

The two oldest electronics *maquiladoras*, which are also the two post-Fordist or flexible producers, use local productive services more heavily than the others. Motorola uses several local productive services: tool and die, metal stamping, plastic molding and metal plating. The U.S. company helped create some of these local service providers. It brought in a very high tech Japanese metal plating shop. It developed a high quality local tool and die shop, which eventually stopped supplying Motorola and the other *maquiladoras* because of fluctuations in demand. The tool and die shop now supplies the local internal market. Motorola created some locally owned packaging companies to make dry ice and styrofoam. It also developed a chemical plant and electric capacitors plant in Monterrey to supply the Guadalajara plant. As the manager of the Motorola wafer fabrication plant said, the plant came here from Nogales to be an integrated manufacturer instead of an assembler.

Foreign Non-Maquiladora Exports

Unlike the border cities, the electronics industry in Guadalajara is composed of more than just foreign owned *maquiladoras* producing for their parent company. There is a sector of large, foreign owned electronics plants that do not operate as *maquiladoras* but do export the majority of their output, which is primarily computer related. IBM initiated the trend in 1981 with a plant that was originally oriented toward the domestic market. As the Mexican market collapsed, however, IBM began exporting more of its output. By 1988, the IBM plant was exporting about four-fifths of the personal computers and memory boards assembled there to 44 countries in the Pacific Rim. Hewlett Packard (1982), Cherokee, Wang (1985), Tandem (1988) and Siemans (Encitel) followed with their own plants. Also in 1988, the existing Kodak plant opened up a new line with 1,000 additional employees producing floppy disks and magnetic heads, primarily for export and was due to open an automated production line of high density printed circuit boards in 1989.[13]

There is very little buying and selling of products among these wholly owned foreign subsidiaries, whether *maquiladora* or not, for several reasons. They may not be set up as profit centers and can sell only to their parent company; they may have to send products back to their parent company for testing before they can be sold. In the case of *maquiladoras*, they may not want to deal with the red tape in getting permission to sell locally or they may not need local sales to complement their parent company's demand. The only examples of transactions among the foreign owned electronics firms we found were Cherokee supplying power supplies to IBM and the Siemans plant (Encitel) providing inputs to Hewlett Packard.

Two of the spinoffs from the electronics *maquiladoras* have become suppliers to the foreign electronics firms: Electrónica Pantera, which supplies Hewlett Packard, IBM, Compubur, Wang, Cherokee and Sistemas Delfi, which supplies Hewlett Packard and IBM. Similar to Sistemas Delfi, Mitel de Mexico, a joint venture between the Canadian Company and Telmex, supplies electronic parts not only to Telmex but also to other electronics firms in Guadalajara.

Both to satisfy local content requirements and have greater just-in-time supplier capabilities, IBM brought in two captive suppliers from the United States and Hewlett Packard brought in one. IBM brought in Space Craft Inc. (SCI), which formed a joint venture with the Juarez-based Mexican group ELAMEX to produce high density printed circuit boards with wholly imported inputs. Called Adelantos Tecnológicos (ADTEC), the joint venture with 51 percent Mexican capital wanted to supply IBM from Juarez, but IBM insisted it needed a supplier of sophisticated two-sided PCBs close at hand. ADTEC applied for *maquiladora* status in order to sell to U.S. buyers in addition to the local IBM plant. However, after landing a contract to supply the local Hewlett Packard plant, ADTEC decided that local demand by the foreign electronics firms was sufficient. Instead, it registered under PITEX, a recent alternative to the *maquiladora* regimen that requires less red tape, in order to keep open the export option. IBM also brought in another U.S. supplier, Molex, which set up as a wholly owned subsidiary of its U.S. parent company. Hewlett Packard has brought in Matsa, which organized as a joint venture, similar to ADTEC.

Endogenous Firms[14]

We identified six endogenous, or locally owned electronics producers. Only one of these firms, Instrumentos Electrónicos Profesionales (IEP), has worked itself into the supplier network of the local multinational electronics firms. IEP sells manually assembled printed circuit boards, not only to its Mexican parent company, Mexel, but also to Tandem and Wang. Lack of capital keeps them from expanding into sophisticated surface mount technology as ADTEC and Kodak have. The remaining endogenous electronics producers, which sell only to domestic firms, include Logix, which was started by a local employee of IBM; Kitron, which is most like a Silicon Valley garage start-up firm; Infor Espacio, which designs and builds computer printers; and Wind, which builds its own brand of computers for the Mexican market. These firms do their own product design, buy almost totally foreign made parts and assemble them.

Kitron, for example, started up in 1980 with six local partners, four of whom work in the firm. The firm is a member of the Cámara Nacional de La Industria Eléctrica y Electrónica (CANIECE). It has nearly 30 employees, 9 engineers in research and development, 10 production workers, 4 supervisors and 4 clerical staff in operations. It designs and assembles digital control instruments. Ten percent of its inputs are domestically manufactured metal housings in Mexico City. A total of 60 percent of its inputs are directly imported integrated circuits and switches. Another 30 percent—resistors and connectors—are bought through local distributors, although they are manufactured abroad. All the engineers were educated in Guadalajara, read English and follow the industry journals.

Microton, another local electronics start-up, was established in 1979 to design and assemble computer products. The firm imported 80 percent of its inputs directly and bought the remaining 20 percent through local distributors of foreign-made components. It was not a member of any industry association. In 1982, Microton tried to establish its own line of computers, but government red tape for importing equipment proved to be too complicated. The firm subsequently developed an inexpensive way to build a buffer multiplexor, which allows a computer to be used while its printer works. By December 1988, the owners were unable to find a firm willing to market their buffer in Mexico, and decided to close up the design and production activities altogether to become simply a computer service and software firm.

While the foreign-based electronics industry in Guadalajara is gradually networking within its own ranks through spinoffs, captive suppliers and joint ventures, there is a growing endogenous electronics industry that continues to source almost all inputs from abroad. It is almost totally unlinked to the foreign based electronics industry in Guadalajara.

V. AUTO PARTS NETWORK

Four of the five auto part *maquiladoras* were established between 1978 and 1981 to manufacture engine, transmission and brake parts. Three are U.S. subsidiaries and one is a Spanish subsidiary. The only automotive *maquiladora* built in Guadalajara after the 1982 economic crisis is a Honda plant, established in 1988, which assembles motorcycles. Two of the three U.S. plants are partial *maquiladoras*, producing primarily for the Mexican market and exporting to the United States as excess capacity warrants. The Spanish plant, which sells exclusively to Europe, is applying for permission to sell a portion to the domestic market. Honda has permission to sell 10 percent of its output in the domestic market. The rest goes to the U.S. market. These plants are small, ranging from 25 to 125 production workers. The use of female workers varies considerably, from only 2 percent in the Honda plant, to 75 percent in one of the U.S. plants. Only the Borg Warner plant reported a 25 percent use of temporary workers. This plant uses 60 percent women line workers.

The auto parts *maquiladoras* cite the existence of the local metal mechanics industry as an important location factor for both inputs and experienced labor force. In fact, the local productive inputs they use come mainly from this sector: metal casting boxes, metal ball bearings and pellets, brass, nails, cutting tools, solvents and paints. Nevertheless, the plants do not use much of these inputs. The use of local inputs, which varies from none to 10 percent for the five plants, averages only slightly higher than that for the electronics plants (see Table 1). Two out of the five use local tool and die services, and two use local metal stamping. Only one of the firms, Honda, reports any significant use of local subcontracting, and just to a moderate degree.[15]

Unlike the electronics plants, the auto parts *maquiladoras* use substantial inputs from elsewhere in Mexico, averaging 37 percent of total inputs (see Table 1). Far from its parent company, the Spanish plant gets a major part of its solvents and paints from Mexico City, Puebla and Monterrey. One of the U.S. plants that is a partial *maquiladora* gets its main input, steel, from Monterrey and Mexico City. Other domestic inputs from outside Guadalajara include rivets, ball bearings, steel bars and plates from Monterrey and Mexico City.

Borg Warner opened its first plant in Guadalajara in 1978, called Industria de Repuestos. It produces rings for car engines and pillow blocks for transmissions using a substantial degree of computer controlled production machines. It is the third post-Fordist plant identified among the *maquiladoras* in Guadalajara, along with Motorola and Unisys. Industria de Repuestos is a partial *maquiladora*, exporting 15 percent of its output, primarily rings, to the United States. In 1980, Borg Warner opened another branch plant, BW Componentes. This one is a *maquiladora* producing time chains for car engines for its parent company in the United States.

The Spanish plant, Renza (Elementos de Freno), currently gets its metal stamping from Italy and Spain but is planning to open a metal stamping factory in Guadalajara for easier access. Renza has also applied to sell 5 percent to 10 percent of its output domestically, primarily in Guadalajara.

Other

The appliance firm is of note (see Table 1) because of its high percent of local inputs. Belonging to Krups, the German home appliance manufacturer, this plant is the exception for foreign owned *maquiladoras* in terms of its high degree of local sourcing. Opened in December 1988, the plant uses plastic inputs from Guadalajara, glass from Monterrey, metal from the United States and electric motors from Germany. Labor represents only 10 percent of their total costs, and access to inputs is cited as a major location factor in coming to Guadalajara, along with low turnover rates and skilled labor. The Krups firm, which in 1989 employed only 24 skilled workers, plans to be at capacity in 1991.

The U.S. plastics firm is of note because it uses 96 percent national inputs. The plant, which manufactures plastic tablecloths, gets its major input, plastic resin, from Mexico City and Puebla (coming originally from the petrochemical complex in Tampico).

VI. A COMPARISON WITH MONTERREY

Monterrey is a city of heavier industry and more conflictive labor relations than Guadalajara. It is Mexico's second largest industrial city and the leading producer of metal and glass for the internal market. Monterrey's leading *grupos*, or locally owned industrial conglomerates, were greatly affected by the crisis of 1982, the dismantling of tariff protections accompanying Mexico's membership in GATT, and the decline of the internal market. By 1983, the unemployment rate for Monterrey had reached 11.5 percent, more than twice the 1980 rate of 5.5 percent. In 1986, the state of Nuevo Leon began to promote *maquiladoras* to absorb the unemployed labor created by the decline in Monterrey's domestic industry. There were three *maquiladoras* registered in Nuevo Leon in 1986, 18 in 1987, 58 in 1988 and 73 in 1989. About 60 percent were located in Monterrey. Nevertheless, the unemployment rate in February 1989, was down only to 10 percent. As a point of comparison with the Guadalajara findings, 15 *maquiladoras* were surveyed in Monterrey.[16]

The high local content in Monterrey's *maquiladora* products (see Table 2) does not mean that new local manufacturing capacity is supplying foreign initiated export activity. Rather, the high local content reflects, in great part, the successful efforts of some of Monterrey's local grupos to adapt to the new milieu by using excess capacity for the export market. Thus, the *maquiladoras* associated with a local grupo average 32 percent of local content, while the independent foreign subsidiaries average only 5 percent.

For greater detail Appendix 4 ranks the *maquiladoras* by degree of local content. Five of the top six *maquiladoras* in terms of local content are associated with a local grupo. Two of the five are majority owned by long-standing local grupos who were restructuring towards the export market by adding *maquiladora* operations. One is operated by a local grupo who re-

TABLE 2

CHARACTERISTICS OF MONTERREY'S MAQUILADORAS

Sector	No. of Plants	Average % Local Inputs	Average % Natl. Inputs	% Foreign-Owned	Year Established (average)	Average No. of Workers	Average % Female	Average Training (wks.)
I. Associated with a local "grupo"	8	32	39	75	1985	181	41	7
Glass	1	100	100	100	1987	60	0	8
Metal	3	34	53	100	1984	286	0	5
Food	2	25	25	0	1983	100	85	12
Electric/ electronics	2	0	0	100	1986	167	78	3
II. Independent	7	5	6	100	1987	202	76	4
Electronics	2	0	0	100	1988	249	93	4
Auto Parts	1	10	20	100	1986	60	50	8
Other	4	6	6	100	1986	216	75	3

structured by seeking a foreign buy out. The remaining two are joint ventures with the local grupo holding the minority share. One of these joint ventures existed before becoming a *maquiladora* in 1986.[17]

Besides being associated with a local grupo, the top firms in terms of local content are manufacturers as opposed to pure assembly plants. All seven of the firms surveyed that reported some local content are classified Fordist manufacturers (see Appendix 4). These seven *maquiladoras*, therefore, show high degrees of manufacturing versus assembly and little or no use of computer controlled production machinery. Because of the high value added in these top seven manufacturing firms, four of them do not receive 806/807 tariff exemptions in entering the goods into the United States. Three of these plants enter the goods duty-free into the United States under GSP, which requires 35 percent domestic content. Another plant uses 806/807 only for some of its product lines. Reflecting the high value-added manufacturing, labor costs represent less than 14 percent of total costs for these firms, compared to the remaining maquiladoras surveyed in Monterrey, whose labor costs average 47 percent of total costs.

The high usage of temporary workers in these plants reflects the striking difference in labor relations between Guadalajara and Monterrey. The heightened industrial working class consciousness and unionization in Monterrey as compared to Guadalajara, led the local grupos to restructure, not only by looking for export markets but also by reducing labor costs through the hiring of temporary workers with little job security and low benefits.

Sectorally, most of the seven plants with local content represent Monterrey's leading industrial sectors—three metal plants, one glass plant and one citrus processing plant. One of these seven firms sources all of its inputs locally: a joint venture with a local grupo, it manufactures glass table tops using local glass, chemicals and packaging material, all for export to the United States, but it avoids paying duty on its imported machinery by retaining *maquiladora* status.

The main locally manufactured productive inputs that these seven firms buy are glass, laminated steel, galvanized steel, aluminum finishing stock, iron castings, copper wire, paint, chemicals, insulation material and orange juice. Several also get packaging material, including cardboard cartons and plastic bags and wooden pallets. One firm, however, said it no longer sources laminated steel bearings, steel bars or copper wire locally because the exchange rate with the dollar has made them too expensive. It now sources these items from the United States.

The use of local services among the *maquiladoras* is surprisingly limited, compared to Guadalajara. Of the seven plants with local content only four of them use local producer services, mainly tool and die. One uses some local plastic molding, although most of their plastic molding is done in the United States. One uses local painting and metal stamping. Several said that the exchange rate now makes local services and some components too expensive.

The eight plants with no local or national content use even fewer local productive services. The three post-Fordist plants, two of which are in electronics, use no local productive services, have created no spinoffs and utilize no local inputs other than packaging material, such as boxes and plastic bags. Of the remaining five plants with no local productive inputs, only one uses local tool and die, one uses local plastic molding, and two use local packaging materials. None uses any national productive inputs.

The motivation for *maquiladoras* unassociated with local grupos to locate in Monterrey does not hinge on the availability of local inputs. One electronics plant relocated to Monterrey because of higher labor turnover rates at the border. Mattel, which has a plant in Tijuana, opened one in Monterrey because of better schooling and work ethic, availability of technical personnel and a labor cost that the company found to be 13 percent lower than at the border—an important consideration for their very labor-intensive production process.

Local spinoffs are not happening in Monterrey to the degree that they are happening in Guadalajara. Of the 15 plants surveyed, we identified only one case in which one Carrier plant (Elizondo #1) created another plant (Elizondo #3) for low volume, short batch production of air conditioning parts for both export and the internal market. We did discover two unusual spinoffs to the Texas border: two of the plants created their own U.S. parent companies, although wholly with Mexican capital, locating headquarters in a warehouse in Laredo in one case and McAllen in the other case.

There are fewer local sales, sales among *maquiladoras* and partial *maquiladoras* in Monterrey than in Guadalajara. Only two are partial *maquiladoras*. One, S&P Metals (Maquilas Metálicas), sells 10 percent of its steel profiles as a non-*maquiladora* directly to a local manufacturer of trailers. S&P sells 50 percent of its output as a *maquiladora* to another firm in its own "grupo" which then exports it. The other plant, Oranjugos, sells only 20 percent of its fruit concentrate on average as a *maquiladora*. At any given moment it may be operating totally as a *maquiladora* if the internal market is not there. At other times it may not be using its *maquiladora* status at all. ·

Two of the Monterrey *maquiladoras*, American Electric and Rogers Electronics, both subsidiaries of U.S. firms, have applied for and been approved to sell up to 20 percent of their product on the internal market. Rogers Electronics wants to integrate into the growing network of trade among foreign owned electronics firms in Mexico and is starting to sell to IBM and Hewlett Packard in Guadalajara.

Three firms—all Fordist manufacturers with high local inputs—report a sizably higher amount of national inputs than local. One gets its steel from Altos Hornos in Monclova, Coahuila. Another gets 50 percent of its iron castings from Torreon, Aguascalientes, Mexico City and Saltillo. A third gets wire and insulating tape from elsewhere in Mexico.

VII. A COMPARISON WITH THE BORDER

A total of 30 border plants—ten each from Tijuana, Juarez and Nuevo Laredo—were interviewed, representing 2.7 percent of all border plants.

The border *maquiladoras* generate very few local linkages. Only one *maquiladora* out of the 30 surveyed reported any local inputs. Located in Tijuana, it is a sporting goods plant manufacturing wooden oars for its parent company in Los Angeles. It uses sand paper and varnish made in Tijuana. Five of the 30 border plants interviewed indicate some use of non-local national inputs. Three are in Tijuana and two in Nuevo Laredo. The Japanese home appliance manufacturer, Sanyo, which manufacturers and assembles vacuum cleaners in Tijuana, buys resins and motor ventilators manufactured in Mexico City and the state of Mexico. While it has the greatest use of national inputs among the border *maquiladoras* interviewed, it is not a pure *maquiladora*. Sanyo sells 40 percent of its output on the internal market. Another Japanese company in Tijuana with national inputs manufactures and assembles electric transformers and coils. It brings in its main inputs—laminated steel and copper wire—from the United States, but buys Mexican-made alcohol, glue, tools and argon gas from distributors in Tijuana. The third company in Tijuana with national inputs is the sporting goods manufacturer, which uses unspecified minor inputs from Guadalajara and Monterrey. One of the two plants with non-local domestic content in Nuevo Laredo repairs, laminates and converts cars. Owned by a Mexican American from Laredo, the company buys Mexican-made paints from a distributor in Nuevo Laredo and cleaners made in Monterrey. However, its principal inputs of wood and resin come from the United States. A U.S. owned shoe plant that assembles moccasins in Nuevo Laredo sources a small percentage of its leather from Leon, Guanajuato.

Unlike in Guadalajara, there are fewer partial *maquiladoras* along the border. In fact, the only one in our sample is the Sanyo plant in Tijuana, which produces 40 percent of its output for the Mexican market. Of the *maquiladora* production, 55 percent goes to the United States and 45 percent to other countries, including Canada, Panama and Asia (Japan, Hong Kong and Malaysia).

Very few border *maquiladoras* use productive services from the Mexican side or from the U.S. twin city, except in Tijuana. The most frequently used local productive service is tool and die, with four of the ten Tijuana plants using occasional local tool and die services, one of ten Nuevo Laredo firms and none of the Juarez firms. Most of the plants needing tool and die services get it done in the interior of the United States. Of the 13 plants reporting the use of metal stamping services, almost all source this service in the United States as well, including the Japanese firms. One Japanese firm sources it in Japan and another Japanese plant does some of it in-house as well as sourcing from both the United States and Japan. Only one firm, a U.S. assembler of switches for automobiles in Juarez, reported sourcing metal stamping in their twin city of El Paso.

Plastic molding, both extrusions and injection molding, are used by 16 (over half) of the *maquiladoras* surveyed along the border. All the U.S.owned plants reported getting their plastic molding from the U.S. interior except two: the automobile switch assembly plant in Juarez that gets its plastic molding along with metal stamping in El Paso, and an electronics plant in Tijuana that gets it from Singapore.

Among the Japanese plants in Tijuana, there is an interesting trend in plastic molding. Some *maquiladoras* continue to source plastic molding from Japan, while some have substituted those imports with their own in-house plastic molding, and others have brought captive suppliers over from Japan, who then diversify their *maquiladora* clients. In our sample of five Japanese *maquiladoras* in Tijuana,[18] two still bring their plastic molding from Japan and one does it in-house. Another, Sanyo, does part of it in-house and gets part from a Japanese supplier, Mutsutech, which Sanyo brought over as a captive supplier from Japan. Mutsutech set up as a *maquiladora* that sells all of its output in the foreign trade zone in Tijuana to other *maquiladoras*, not only Sanyo now, but also Matsuchita and Hitachi. Mutsutech, in turn, imports all of its inputs from Japan and the United States. Another Japanese plant has developed a local supplier relationship with a plastic molding company in Otay, California.[19] In 1988, the Sony plant in Nuevo Laredo[20] began to manufacture its own plastic cassette holders with robotic machines brought from Japan, after having imported cassette holders manufactured in Japan by Sanyo.

The role of the twin cities in the border *maquiladoras'* transactions networks is quite limited, primarily to non-productive services. In terms of productive inputs produced in the twin cities, the survey found one Tijuana *maquiladora* buying tools made in the San Diego area, another Tijuana plant buying resin from the San Diego area and a Juarez company buying tools and oil from El Paso. In terms of twin city productive services, the survey found the one Japanese company in Tijuana sourcing plastic molding in Otay and one Juarez company sourcing plastic extrusion and metal stamping in El Paso.

None of the 30 border respondents reported any local spinoffs from their plants.

VIII. CONCLUSIONS

The relatively high percent of both local and national Mexican input used by the *maquiladoras* of the interior is not a result of foreign investment creating enough demand to stimulate a local supplier industry. Rather, it is the result primarily of local capital seeking to survive by looking for export markets through *maquiladora* status. Local producers, as they become *maquiladoras*, continue to use some of their local supplier networks for inputs. In contrast, foreign-owned and initiated *maquiladoras*, like those that typify the border region, continue on the whole to rely almost exclusively on imported inputs.

In the case of Guadalajara, the *maquiladoras* with greatest local inputs are part of the endogenous crafts sector, mainly small, locally owned plants producing shoes, clothing, furniture, jewelry and toys. Most continue to sell on the internal market but export to U.S. clients as excess capacity warrants. In Monterrey, the *maquiladoras* with greatest local inputs were initiated primarily by the leading local industrial conglomerates, or grupos, in an attempt to survive the decline of the domestic market by seeking U.S. clients, joint ventures or even buy outs. In both locations, local content in these *maquiladora* operations still consists of minor inputs and is less than in their counterpart domestic operations.

The foreign owned and initiated *maquiladoras* remain largely integrated to their U.S. supplier networks, despite the interior location. Even in Guadalajara, the plant managers claim they maintain just-in-time inventories with U.S.-based providers. Despite the few local or national inputs used by the foreign owned *maquiladoras* in Guadalajara, there is nonetheless a developing local transactional network involving the foreign-owned electronics firms. The older ones especially have established joint ventures, created spinoffs, brought in outside suppliers and worked with a few local service providers. There is now a nationally recognized electronics market in Guadalajara. The emerging network, however, excludes almost all the small endogenous electronics firms.

In Monterrey, the foreign initiated *maquiladoras* that are unassociated with local grupos have located there to escape the high labor turnover rates of the border and have access to an industrial milieu along with urban amenities, but not because of access to local inputs. They have established very few local linkages in terms of inputs, services or spinoff firms.

In the interior, as well as the border, the post-Fordist *maquiladoras* use fewer domestic inputs than average (see Appendix 2). In Guadalajara, nevertheless, the three post-Fordist *maquiladoras* use somewhat more domestic inputs than do the other foreign *maquiladoras*. This fact could be explained by the age of the *maquiladoras* in two of the cases: they are both over 20 years old. In the other case, it could be explained by the sector. Auto parts *maquiladoras* in Guadalajara use locally manufactured metal mechanic inputs as well as significant national inputs from both Mexico City and Monterrey. In Monterrey, most of the domestic content is accounted for by Fordist manufacturers. In Guadalajara, the use of domestic inputs is split more evenly between Fordist manufacturers and labor-intensive assembly plants (with emphasis on the Fordists), reflecting the mixed classifications of the craft-producing maquiladoras.

The border plants are still largely appendages of the U.S. firms without much local networking. The main exception is the Japanese plants in Tijuana, which are bringing in captive suppliers as a local source of some inputs and manufacturing other inputs themselves. The heralded anecdotes about U.S. border *maquiladoras* bringing in captive suppliers did not show up in this survey.

IX. POLICY IMPLICATIONS

While it is true that foreign assembly industry tends to be an enclave, this analysis of *maquiladora* transaction patterns shows that the lack of linkages is not due to some inherent structural characteristic that transcends policy intervention. Although the new wave of post-Fordist investment in *maquiladoras* generates fewer linkages than ever, the analysis shows that the post-Fordist plants in Guadalajara still generate some important linkages that can be encouraged and replicated. While it is true that national Mexican policy, especially in computers and technology transfer, has helped create some local linkages, this analysis makes it apparent that most of the obstacles and opportunities are rather specific to both place and sector. These obstacles and opportunities should be identified and treated at the local level with finely tuned efforts aimed at making each sectoral cluster of firms into an effective transactional network.

The transactional analysis identifies a set of existing linkages that could be replicated or strengthened. For example, if one electronics *maquiladora* is using local tool and die services, it is possible that another one with the right information and contacts would do so, too. Or if one apparel plant is able to sell abroad with local thread, dyes and glues, then quite likely others could. Their U.S. clients may not be aware of the availability of these inputs, or perhaps the producers need bridge loans to finance their acquisition until revenues start coming in.

The transactional analysis also identifies a set of missing linkages that could be established. If one electronics firm is manufacturing a component needed by another that currently sources the item abroad, a new local linkage could be created. Or, if there is sufficient local demand for a specialized input that is currently imported, an opportunity for a new provider to fill the need locally could be pointed out.

In broader terms, the transactional analysis can also lay the basis for turning clusters of related businesses into effective networks, as has been done elsewhere. The following sections describe some cases of effective networking with both craft producers and electronics manufacturers.

Building Networks Among Crafts Producers

With a supportive local public sector, leadership from the trade association of craft producers and active sectoral organizations for the different networks of craft firms, the Emilia Romagna region in north-central Italy was able to transform itself from a branch plant economy to one of independent small producers.[21] The transformation began as the large firms restructured, laid off their strongly unionized employees and began to subcontract much of their work. Some of the unemployed workers began to establish small craft shops that were at first little more than sweatshops of cheap labor subcontracting on terms set by the large firms.

Gradually, however, the small producers built linkages among themselves to counterbalance their dependence on the large factories.[22] Supported by their own networks, the small firms learned to use their comparative advantage of flexibility. They combined the production lines of different small producers to produce finished or nearly finished products and larger outputs. They took advantage of market niches in which a small scale was not a technological disadvantage.

The craft manufacturers gradually increased the technological level of the machines used. "I began with a simple sewing machine, the kind you see at home," explained one woman owner of a small specialty sewing company for the knitwear industry in Carpi interviewed by Hatch. "Then step by step I got real sewing machines and now I have electronic ones." The firms began to do more of their own work rather than subcontracting and began to export their own products as they found market niches abroad. In the case of textiles, they were able to diversify their client base away from Germany. The economy of north-central Italy now consists of growing industrial districts of small producers in textiles and apparel, shoes, machine tools, agricultural equipment and a few others. Wages have risen to 175 percent of the national average and half of the craft workers are now unionized.[23]

One of the central ingredients to the region's success was the development of transactional clusters into effective organizations or networks aimed at helping member firms. The local municipal and regional governments have played a catalyst role in helping to establish networks, although the initiative and development have largely been private, by the companies themselves.

In Emilia Romagna, Hatch has identified four trade associations that serve craft manufacturers.[24] They provide a wide range of business services such as payroll, billing, inventory control, general accounting and legal services. They offer management training and group insurance; gather and disseminate market information; represent member firms in trade shows in Italy and abroad; help create consortia or joint ventures among member firms so that they can respond to large contract opportunities and negotiate industry-wide union contracts for the small producers on a national and regional basis.

Some of the trade associations help member firms gain access to financing, not subsidized government loans, but market rate private sector loans. An individual small craft manufacturer typically has difficult access to traditional bank financing at any interest rate because of the high risk and high transaction cost associated with lending to a small firm. The National Confederation of Artisans (CNA) has established loan guarantee consortia in Emilia Romagna. A consortium reduces the risk to the lending institution by guaranteeing the loan and thus also reduces the transaction cost because the bank does not have to investigate the particular borrower's credit worthiness. The loan guarantee consortium, meanwhile, can evaluate at a very low cost the credit worthiness of the loan applicant because the CNA has probably been keeping her books for years and she is known in the local chapter.[25]

The trade associations have also provided special management assistance for new firm start ups. For example, ECIPAR, the training arm of the CNA, teaches administrative skills to fledgling entrepreneurs, assists them in preparing business plans, handles legal procedures required to open an enterprise, helps to organize financing and uses network contacts to help set up initial contracts.[26] Gaining access to affordable space with a design that facilitates frequent face-to-face interaction is another area in which the trade unions, in cooperation with local government, have assisted member firms. In Bologna, the largest city of Emilia Romagna, the municipal government has contracted with the CNA to form consortia of firms in need of space. The municipality builds the infrastructure, then gives a long-term lease to the consortium to develop the land according to its members' needs. In some cases, publicly assisted housing has been built nearby to minimize commuting and facilitate the entry of women into the labor force. In the small city of Modena, the CNA has organized groups of users to buy completed developments of artisan villages planned and built by the municipality. By 1987, 500 small businesses employing 7,000 workers had been accommodated in these urban villages.[27]

Beyond the general assistance of the CNA and other broad trade associations for small manufacturers, there are six sector-specific organizations in Emilia Romagna that have been created since 1980 through the cooperation of local government, trade associations and labor unions. Called Sectoral Service Centers, they are organized as membership corporations to promote marketing and technology transfer geared to the special needs of the particular craft sector. Small as well as large firms in the sector may join. CITER, the textile industry's center, was founded in 1980 with primarily public funding. By 1987, however, it was almost totally supported by its 500 member companies. With a permanent staff of ten, CITER provides current information on world markets, suppliers and technological change in fibers and production machinery. CITER is helping to develop an affordable CAD system for knitwear design. It sponsors technology demonstrations and group meetings to stimulate peer pressure to modernize.[28]

The Italian case is not the only example of craft industry restructuring as a flexible network able to compete in the export market. In Denmark, the domestic textile and apparel industry of mainly small producers was declining sharply in the 1970s. During the 1980s, it restructured by putting a new emphasis on designing for specialized market niches, maintaining reliable delivery schedules, offering good service and enhancing quality through worker-management collaboration. By 1987, the Danish textile industry was exporting more than 80 percent of their production.[29]

Networking among firms was a key to their successful restructuring. The director of the Danish Federation of Textile Industries points out that the trade association no longer deals only with the traditional issues of collective bargaining, political lobbying and "export assistance at the so-called embassy level." She says that "today we offer both small and large member firms comprehensive service in labor law, social law, commercial law, export and sales, technology, international and external environment, education, political lobbying activity, and special services (on a fee-for-service basis) in the fields of credit rating information, national and international bill collection, translation, telex and the like."[30]

The Federation of Danish Textile Industries has also emphasized worker training and technology upgrading. To overcome the image of being a low-skill industry, the association has introduced vocational training at all levels and started recruiting campaigns in the schools. The association also has a technology institute that helps develop and disseminate suitable new technologies to the members. "Our member companies are now using our services extensively. Usually we are in contact with about half of our 310 members every day".[31]

Building Networks in the Electronics Industry

There are similar experiences in the case of electronics. Niles Hansen examines the region of Montpellier in Mediterranean France.[32] In the late 1960s, IBM established a major manufacturing plant in Montpellier that spawned a cluster of related small and medium-sized enterprises in data processing, robotics and artificial intelligence. Drawing on this existing cluster, along with some others in which Montpellier already had a competitive advantage, a local network composed of "managers and directors from local universities, research laboratories, corporations, banks, local government and regional advisory organizations created a regional program designed to facilitate the introduction of new technologies into existing companies, to assist newly arriving companies, and to promote the creation of small and medium-sized enterprises."[33]

In discussing the emergence of Ile de France South, another emerging "technopole," Allen Scott[34] describes how public planning and policy intervention were necessary to bring the ingredients of the growth complex into full functional interrelationship. The Scientific City Association, founded in 1983 with the support of the French government, local planning agencies and several corporations, provided a collective identity to the area and facilitated contacts and information exchange among the local planning agencies, educational institutions, research laboratories and private firms. It is planning to offer venture capital services for local entrepreneurs in order to circumvent the conservative attitudes of the established local banking system.[35]

Also, the French government began a program in 1982 to establish regional centers for technology innovation and exchange known as CRITTs. Four CRITTS serve the needs of particular sectoral clusters in the Ile de France. They encourage the development of small innovative firms by bringing together researchers and entrepreneurs. The CRITTS help to break the barriers between large-scale national technology agendas and the specific "relational practices involving incremental problem-solving in a context of continual mutual readjustment between firms."[36]

Building Transactional Networks in Guadalajara

Drawing on these and similar success stories of building effective local business networks, a strategy emerges that could be tailored to the case of Guadalajara and perhaps elsewhere in Mexico: mobilize local businesses, cluster by cluster, whether in traditional crafts, electronics, heavy manufacturing or services, to network among themselves and directly with the exterior. The public sector can play a catalyst role at the local or regional level, although implementation should be pursued by the firms themselves.

The basic steps are as follows:

1. Analyze transaction networks, looking at who produces what, how, and for whom, what inputs and services are used and who supplies them.
2. Identify gaps in supplier chains—i.e., inputs and services for which there is sufficient local demand, but no local production.
3. Create communication networks among the firms. Trade associations are a vital communications link.

4. Help trade and industry associations provide member firms with management assistance, new firm start-up assistance, group procurement, worker training, financial assistance, such as loan guarantees, sector-specific marketing and technology assistance and physical facilities that promote interaction.

Of course, public policy and planning intervention will probably not be enough to turn clusters of related businesses into effective transactional networks in some places like the border area, and in others it may not be necessary to achieve the same result. Yet, Guadalajara, with its long-standing crafts sector embedded[37] in the local economy and its endogenous, as well as foreign electronics sector, seems a propitious candidate for effective public sector efforts to create local transactional networks around the *maquiladora* industry.

Some additional considerations specific to Guadalajara are necessary. The craft sector is the main contributor to the high percentage of local inputs in Guadalajara's *maquiladora* industry. Yet, there is probably a ceiling to local integration of *maquiladora* craft production that is far below the degree of local integration of domestic craft producers because of the use of client-supplied inputs by the *maquiladoras*. As a conduit for technology transfer and a solution to capital shortages, *maquiladora* status provides an easy short-term solution. To increase local linkages, however, it would be necessary to develop more independent conduits to the export market that would not require such extensive use of imported inputs. The networking strategy suggested above could be used to create new conduits.[39]

The foreign electronics firms in Guadalajara have established a small local transactions network through generating spinoffs, bringing in captive suppliers, encouraging joint ventures and using some local productive services. But the network has not extended to endogenous electronics manufacturers, except for one. Public sector efforts to encourage networking in the electronics sector should focus on integrating the endogenous electronics firms among themselves, with the *maquiladoras* and other foreign electronics firms and directly to the exterior.[40] The analysis of the *maquiladoras'* transaction patterns in Guadalajara points to the need to assist local business development not on a firm-by-firm basis, but in the context of turning sectoral clusters into effective collaborative networks of firms. By building on existing clusters that are embedded in the local economy, local linkages are more likely to be forged. Only in this way could the foreign assembly industry gradually be transformed into a catalyst for integrated local development. In this light, *maquiladoras* should be seen as a transient measure—by choice and necessity—in an export-led strategy that can lead to a comparative advantage beyond that of cheap labor.

APPENDIX 1

ANNUAL GROWTH RATES OF MAQUILADORA PLANTS BY REGION, 1982–87[1]

Year	Border	Region Interior	Jalisco
1982	−3.3	−3.6	18.2
1983	2.6	3.7	0.0
1984	12.0	11.6	0.0
1985	13.1	12.9	7.7
1986	17.1	14.6	14.3
1987[2]	25.1	18.8	56.3
Average 82–87	11.1	9.7	16.1

ANNUAL GROWTH RATES OF MAQUILADORA EMPLOYMENT BY REGION, 1982–1987[1]

Year	Border	Region Interior	Jalisco
1982	−3.0	−2.2	−4.7
1983	18.7	19.2	16.5
1984	32.3	32.1	25.0
1985	6.2	6.5	−17.3
1986	17.9	17.2	2.1
1987[2]	21.5	20.4	13.7
Average 82–87	15.6	15.5	5.9

Source: INEGI, Tables 13 and 14.
[1]Monthly averages per year.
[2]Monthly averages from January to November.

APPENDIX 2

A. AVERAGE PERCENT OF LOCAL INPUTS USED IN MAQUILADORAS BY TYPE OF PLANT AND LOCATION, 1988/89

Type of Plant	Sample	Border	Guadalajara	Monterrey	Nation[2]
Post-Fordist Producers[1]	1.7	0.0	6.0	0.7	0.5
Fordist Manufacturers	14.5	2.6	10.5	31.9	6.2
Labor-Intensive Assembly	3.1	0.0	9.2	3.3	1.1
Average	8.1	0.7	9.6	19.9	3.4

B. AVERAGE PERCENT OF NATIONAL INPUTS USED IN MAQUILADORAS BY TYPE OF PLANT AND LOCATION, 1988/89

Type of Plant	Sample	Border	Guadalajara	Monterrey	Nation
Post-Fordist Producers	2.6	0.0	9.7	0.7	0.8
Fordist Manufacturers	31.0	17.1	31.0	43.3	20.9
Labor-Intensive Assembly	7.0	3.6	13.3	6.7	4.7
Average	17.4	6.3	23.9	27.5	9.9

[1]Post-Fordist, or flexible, producer; measured as those plants that have substantial use of computer-controlled production machinery. They also exhibit a high degree of other post-Fordist characteristics (see Wilson 1990).

Fordist manufacturer; measured as those plants with low or no use of computer-controlled machinery, but a substantial degree of manufacturing.

Labor-intensive assembly plant; measured as those plants with low or no use of computer-controlled machinery and little or no manufacturing.

[2]Weighted average to reflect performance of border region.

Source: Wilson survey 1988/89.

APPENDIX 3

CHARACTERISTICS OF GUADALAJARA'S MAQUILADORAS BY LOCAL INPUTS

% Local Inputs	Type[1]	Parent Company[2]	Sector	No. of Workers[3]	Plant Age[4]	Computer Use[5]	Just-in-Time Inventorying[6]	% Nat'l Inputs	% Fem[7]
40	F	Local	Toys	70	5	F	F	70	60
30	F	Local	Furniture	43	2	F	F	50	25
30	F	Krups (G)	Appliances	24	1	F	F	35	95
20	A	Local	Footwear	120	1	F	F	20	60
20	F	Local	Footwear	15	2	F	F	20	15
20	A	Local	Furniture	12	2	F	F	20	60
15	F	Local	Textiles	8	1	F	F	15	100
10	F	Local	Jewelry	28	4	F	F	10	86
10	PF	Borg Warner	Auto Parts	25	11	B	D	13	60
6	PF	Unisys	Electronics	790	21	A	B	12	80
5	F	Renza (SP)	Auto Parts	47	8	F	F	50	33
5	F	Borg Warner	Auto Parts	125	9	C	D	10	75
2	PF	Motorola	Electronics	2440	20	B	D	4	70
2	F	Easterline	Electronics	100	4	F	F	4	15
1	A	Honda (Jap.)	Auto Parts	40	1	E	B	15	2
0	F	Efka Plastics	Plastics	97	4	C	F	96	80
0	F	Reliance Elec.	Auto Parts	57	8	F	D	95	20
0	A	Digital Power	Electronics	16	2	F	B	15	95
0	F	(Mexican-DF)	Footwear	68	12	D	E	10	70
0	A	Local	Footwear	55	7	D	E	10	70
0	F	Local	Textiles	34	11	F	F	0	100
0	F	Shizuki (Jap.)	Electronics	650	2	F	A	0	80
0	A	Gen. Instrum.	Electronics	500	15	C	E	0	90
0	F	(US)	Chemicals	150	2	C	F	0	80

[1]PF: Post-Fordist, or flexible, producer; measured as those plants that have substantial use of computer-controlled production machinery. They also exhibit a high degree of other post-Fordist characteristics (see Wilson, 1990).

F: Fordist manufacturer; measured as those plants with low or no use of computer-controlled machinery, but a substantial degree of manufacturing.

A: Labor-intensive assembly plant; measured as those plants with low or no use of computer-controlled machinery and little or no manufacturing.

[2]If foreign, name of parent company and abbreviation of national origin of company are given (except in case of one US parent company whose name could not be determined). Locally owned Mexican firms whose parent company is in Guadalajara are indicated by 'local.' The one Mexican plant whose headquarters are in Mexico City is indicated by "Mexico—DF."

[3]Line workers.

[4]Age in years since date operations began.

[5]A,B: Substantial use of computer-controlled production machinery.

C-E: Little or no use of computer-controlled production machinery, but with plans to use more in the near future.

F: No use of computer-controlled production machinery and no plans to introduce it in the future.

[6]Use of just-in-time inventorying, following same scale, A-F, as for computer-controlled production machinery.

[7]Percent of line workers that are female.

Source: Wilson survey, 1988/89.

APPENDIX 4

CHARACTERISTICS OF MONTERREY'S MAQUILADORAS
BY PERCENT OF LOCAL INPUTS

% Local Inputs	% Natl Inputs	Type[1]	Parent Company[2]	Local "Grupo"[3]	Sector	Plant Age[4]	No. of Workers[5]	% Fem[6]	Use of Temps[7]	Training Weeks[8]
100	100	F	Sentek	Yes	Glass	2	60	0	High	8
50	90	F	(McAllen)	Yes	Metal	8	50	0	Low	6
50	50	F	Local	Yes	Food	2	100	90	High	12
34	35	F	Carrier	Yes	Metal	3	320	0	Med	4
25	25	F	Am. Electric		Electric eq.	3	400	65	Med	4
18	35	F	Emerson El.	Yes	Metal	3	488	0	Low	6
10	20	F	(McAllen)		Auto Parts	3	60	50	High	8
0	0	A	Mattel		Toys	4	200	90	High	1
0	0	PF	Calmar Inc.		Plastics	3	200	95	Med	4
0	0	F	Local	Yes	Food	9	100	80	High	12
0	0	PF	(McAllen)	Yes	Electronics	2	70	95	Low	4
0	0	F	Lasting		Ceramics	0	65	50	Low	4
0	0	PF	James El.		Electronics	1	48	90	Low	4
0	0	A	Emerson El.	Yes	Electric eq.	3	263	60	Low	1
0	0	A	Rogers El.		Electronics	1	450	95	Low	4

[1]PF: Post-Fordist, or flexible, producer; measured as those plants that have substantial use of computer-controlled production machinery. They also exhibit a high degree of other post-Fordist characteristics (see Wilson, 1990).

F: Fordist manufacturer; measured as those plants with low or no use of computer-controlled machinery, but a substantial degree of manu-facturing.

A: Labor-intensive assembly plant; measured as those plants with low or no use of computer-controlled machinery and little or no manufacturing.

[2]If foreign, name of parent company is given (all US in this case). Locally owned Mexican firms whose parent company is in Monterrey are indicated by 'local.' Three locally owned firms have set up nominal company headquarters just across the border in McAllen, Texas. They are indicated by '(McAllen).'

[3]'Yes' indicates the plant is associated with a local industrial conglomerate.

[4]Plant age given in years since date operation began.

[5]Line workers.

[6]Percent of line workers that are female.

[7]Use of temporary workers— Low: less than 25% of line workers; Med: 25% to 50%; High: greater than 50%.

[8]Average number of weeks of on-the-job training a line worker receives.

APPENDIX 5

MAQUILADORA PLANTS BY TYPE
1988/89

	Total in Sample		Border		Guadalajara		Monterrey		Nation[e]
	n	%	n	%	n	%	n	%	%
I. Post-Fordist producers[a]	12	18%	6	22%	3	12%	3	20%	21%
II. Fordist manufacturers[b]	32	47%	8	30%	15	58%	9	60%	35%
III. Labor-intensive assembly plants[c]	24	35%	13	48%	8	31%	3	20%	44%
	68	100%	27[d]	100%	26	100%	15	100%	100%

Source: Wilson survey of 71 maquiladora plants, 1988/89.

a. Those plants that have substantial (responding "a" or "b") use of computer-controlled production machinery. They also exhibit a high degree of other post-Fordist characteristics.

b. Those plants with low or no use of computer-controlled machinery ("c"–"f"), but a substantial degree of manufacturing ("a" or "b").

c. Those plants with low or no use of computer-controlled machinery ("c"–"f") and little or no manufacturing ("c"–"f").

d. Only 27 of the 30 border plants surveyed are used here. Two border plants surveyed were eliminated because they did not respond to the question on the degree of manufacturing (although neither used any computer-controlled machinery) and one was eliminated because it was a service provider (coupon counting), rather than a manufacturer or assembler.

e. Weighted by regional plant population sizes to reflect importance of border.

APPENDIX 6

CHARACTERISTICS OF MAQUILADORA PLANTS BY TYPE

	I Post- Fordist	II Fordist Mfrs.	III Labor Intensive Assembly	Total[9]
	n = 12*	n = 32*	n = 24*	n = 68*
I. Production technology				
A. Computer-controlled machinery[1]	100%	0%	0%	18% ±9
B. Manufacturing-oriented[1]	33%	100%	0%	53% ±12
C. Capital-intensive[1]	33%	28%	17%	25% ±10
D. Labor costs as % of total operating costs[2]	53%	34%	56%	46% ±8
II. Inter-firm relations				
A. JIT[1]	42%[7]	9%	25%	19% ±9
B. Subcontracting[1]	0%	13%	3%	6% ±6
III. Shop floor practices				
A. Multi-skilling[1,8]	50%	39%	21%	34% ±12
B. Worker participation[1]	75%	29%	46%	42% ±12
IV. Management practices				
A. Continuous quality control[1]	92%	81%	88%	85% ±8
B. SPC[3]	75%	28%	58%	53% ±12
V. Labor force characteristics				
A. Percent female	66%	51%	63%	59% ±7
B. Percent temporaries	11%	21%	13%	17% ±7
C. On-the-job training[4]	4.0 wks	7.1 wks	1.6 wks	5.1 ±1.7
VI. Other				
A. Ownership: Percent US[5]	75%	53%	67%	62% ±12
Percent Mexican[6]	8%	31%	25%	25% ±10
B. Size (no. line workers)	556	143	222	270 ±94
C. Year established (av.)	1981	1984	1983	1983 ±1
a. Percent since 1982	50%	75%	75%	71% ±11
b. Percent since 1986	33%	56%	46%	46% ±12

*except where indicated

[1]Percent with substantial use (i.e., responding "a" or "b")

[2]n = 5, 20, and 13, respectively

[3]Percent with some use (i.e., responding "a," "b," or "c")

[4]n = 3, 9, and 4, respectively

[5]Percent of plants with at least 40 percent US capital

[6]Percent of plants with at least 60 percent Mexican capital

[7]Another 33% said they were currently in the process of implementing JIT (compared to 16% of Fordist manufacturers and 0% of the labor-intensive assemblers).

[8]n = 10, 28, and 24, respectively

[9]Approximate 95 percent confidence limits shown.

NOTES

The author wishes to thank the Commission for the Study of International Migration and Cooperative Economic Development, Washington D.C., for their financial support of this project and Mario Carrillo Huerta, Umberto Lona, Paul Castillo, and Juan Jose Palacios for their collaboration in the field research.

1. Erik A. Swyngedouw, "Social Innovation, Production Organization and Spatial Development: The Case of Japanese Style Manufacturing," *Revue d'Economie Regionale et Urbaine*, Vol. 3, 1987, pp. 91–113; Erica Schoenberger, "Technological and Organizational Change in Automobile Production: Spatial Implications," *Regional Studies*, Vol. 21, No. 3, 1987, pp. 199–214; Meric S. Gertler, "The Limits to Flexibility: Comments on the Post-Fordist Vision of Production and Its Geography," *Trans. Institute of British Geography*, Vol. 13, No. 4, 1988, pp. 419–32.

2. See review of literature in Patricia A. Wilson, "The New Maquiladoras: Flexible Production in Low Wage Regions," *Maquiladoras: Economic Problem or Solution?*, ed. Khosrow Fatemi (New York: Praeger, 1990).

3. Susan W. Sanderson, "Automated Manufacturing and Offshore Assembly in Mexico," in *The United States and Mexico: Face to Face with New Technology*, ed. Cathryn L. Thorup (New Brunswick: Transaction Books, 1987), pp. 127–148; and Schoenberger, 1987.

4. Allen J. Scott, *New Industrial Spaces* (London: Pion Limited, 1989); Wilson, 1990.

5. Michael J. Piore and Charles F. Sabel, *The Second Industrial Divide* (New York: Basic Books, 1984); Scott, 1989; C. Richard Hatch, "Learning from Italy's Industrial Renaissance," *The Entrepreneurial Economy*, Vol. 6, No. 1, 1987, pp. 4–10.

6. Agustin Escobar, "The Manufacturing Workshops of Guadalajara and their labor Force: Crisis and Reorganization (1982–1985)," Texas Papers on Mexico, No. 88-05, Institute of Latin American Studies, University of Texas at Austin, 1988, pp. 7–8.

7. Luisa Gabayet, *Regional Development, Industry and Workforce: The Case of Guadalajara and its Region.* University of Durham, Ph.D. Thesis, 1983.

8. Pre-testing of the survey instrument along the border showed these three productive services to be the most sought after by the maquiladoras.

9. Escobar, 1988, p. 10.

10. Among craft-related sectors in the border sample, only three plants were identified, two in footwear and one in apparel. Only one of the footwear plants identified itself as primarily a manufacturer as opposed to assembly plant. All three are large, ranging from 240 line workers to 1,300. None of the three reported any local inputs.

11. Escobar, 1988.

12. Shizuki bought out the old TRW *maquiladora* in 1987, closed it, then con-

structed a new plant in 1988.

13. The Kodak plant had been established in Guadalajara in 1966 to make film for the Latin American market, including Mexico. (Source: interview with plant manager, December 1988).

14. Paul Castillo, master's candidate in community and regional planning at the University of Texas, identified most of the endogenous electronics firms and conducted interviews with them as part of his master's thesis on technology transfer in the Guadalajara computer industry (forthcoming).

15. Very few *maquiladoras* anywhere in the sample subcontract. Only one other *maquiladora* in Guadalajara—a footwear plant—subcontracts as much as Honda does. It seems that the maquiladoras are at the end of the international subcontracting line.

16. The total number of *maquiladora* plants in Monterrey is difficult to pinpoint. The list provided by the local Association of *Maquiladoras* in February 1989, had 58 plants listed, but included many that were not yet built and many that had registered in Monterrey, because of the particular bureaucratic ease of registering there, but were located along the border or elsewhere. Also, in 1988 some of the *maquiladoras* changed to PITEX, which allows more national inputs and national sales than *maquiladora* registration, and involves less red tape. The Association itself had only 25 local members at the time of the survey, some of which were not *maquiladoras*, but simply wanted to stay informed. I used the government figure of 34 plants as the base (data for June, 1988, from INEGI, *Secretaría de Programación y Presupuesto*), and interviewed 15, or 44 percent, of them.

17. We found two *maquiladoras* that were created by the same local grupo as part of their restructuring process using foreign capital: USEM, using Emerson Electric, created a manufacturing *maquiladora* and an assembly plant *maquiladora* in 1986, the former making metal castings for electric motors, the latter assembling electric motors. Both export all their production to the United States, the former using GSP and the latter 806/807. There are no supplier relations between the two plants.

18. There were 19 Japanese *maquiladoras* in Tijuana in 1989 according to Echeverri. (Elsie Echeverri-Carroll, *Maquilas: Economic Impacts and Foreign Investment Opportunities, Japanese Maquilas—A Special Case* (Austin: Bureau of Business Research Monograph No.1988-1, 1989).

19. We were unable to determine the national origin of this supplier.

20. While not included in this survey, the Sony plant in Nuevo Laredo was one of the plants I visited during the pretest of the survey instrument.

21. Robert E. Friedman, "Flexible Manufacturing Networks," *The Entrepreneurial Economy*, Vol. 6, No. 1, 1987, pp. 2–4; and Hatch, 1987, pp. 4–10.

22. Hatch, 1987, p. 5.

23. Hatch, 1987.

24. Italian law defines craft manufacturers, or artisan firms, as businesses with up to twenty two workers and a full-time owner/operator. (Hatch, 1987, p. 7).

25. Sebastiano Brusco and Ezio Righi, "The Loan Guarantee Consortia," *The Entrepreneurial Economy*, Vol. 6, No. 1, 1987, pp. 11–13.

26. Hatch, 1987.

27. Hatch, 1987, p. 8.

28. Hatch, 1987.

29. Anne B. Lundholt, "Flexible Networks in the Danish Textile Industry," *The Entrepreneurial Economy*, Vol. 6, No. 1, 1987, pp. 13–15.

30. Lundholt, 1987, p. 15.

31. Lundholt, 1987.

32. Niles Hansen, "Innovative Regional Milieux, Small Firms, and Regional Development: Evidence from Mediterranean France," unpublished paper, Department of Economics, University of Texas, 1989.

33. Hansen, 1989, p. 14.

34. Scott, 1989.

35. Scott, 1989, p. 75.

36. Scott, 1989, p. 77.

37. Hansen, 1989, p. 17.

38. Why even bother with small craft firms as a source of employment? Young small firms have a high failure rate. They produce low-wage, low-quality jobs. Their existence is dependent on demand by large firms who subcontract out to them. Escobar points out that in Guadalajara many of the local large firms are former small-craft shops, that until the crisis of 1982 the craft producers were regularizing employment conditions, and that the craft sector has been a long-term source of vitality, including a channel of upward mobility for workers from employee to owner. Gabayet adds that they also present a flexible source of income for female workers.

39. Monterrey presents a different set of circumstances. Since much of the large-scale *maquiladora* industry in Monterrey is not foreign initiated, its phenomenal growth should be seen largely as a short-term strategy by local economic groups to survive, restructure and enter the export market. To increase local sourcing in the long run will require, as for the Guadalajara craft producers, a more autonomous conduit to the exterior.

7

The Development of Mexico's Living Marine Resources

Alejandro Nadal Egea

I. INTRODUCTION

Mexico has an important potential for exploiting marine resources. With a total coastline of 11,592 kilometers and an exclusive economic zone (EEZ) of more than 2,946,825 square kilometers, marine resources could play an important role in Mexico's development. This paper examines three critical aspects of the growth potential of the fishing sector in Mexico. First, trends in the world catch (world landings) are analyzed and compared with estimates of available fish stock, (biomass) for different species. Second, the main features of the regulatory system of fisheries are examined to identify the areas in which changes could promote new investments and prevent misallocation of resources. This part of the analysis covers the standard regulations used in marine fisheries management, as well as price controls affecting the industrial processing of fish products. Third, direct and indirect employment generation in the fishing sector is examined through statistics and standard input-output techniques.[1]

Total Landings and the Structure of Mexican Fisheries[2]

The Food and Agriculture Organization (FAO) projections of world fisheries production have been rather conservative over the past years. This stems from recognition of the fact that production growth is subjected to rather strict limits. In the recent past, growth of world production has come from selectively increasing fishing of the most desirable species, and increases in total world landings, during the 1960s created the impression that increasing returns in the fishing industry were inexhaustible. However, during the 1970s and early 1980s, the world catch did not rise spectacularly. The annual growth rate between 1977 and 1986 was 3.3 percent. Finally, between 1983 and 1986, the world catch grew again at a rate of 4 percent.[3]

In the case of Mexico, the annual growth rate of total catch for the period 1979 through 1987 was 4.84 percent. The annual growth rate for the 1981–1987 period, according to data from the Ministry of Fisheries, SEPESCA, was −1.1 percent.[4] This can be explained primarily by the dynamics of the entire economy. As Table 1 indicates, the years 1980–1981 show spectacular increases in the Mexican catch. This can be explained by increased fishing and the overall impact of the oil boom years. On the other hand, the negative rate of change between 1982 and 1983 and the modest recuperation in 1984 are related to the economic crisis and rising operational costs for the entire fishing fleet.

One of the most important features of the Mexican fishing sector is the intense concentration of fishing in a few species. Whether measured in

TABLE 1

MEXICO'S FISHING SECTOR: EVOLUTION OF TOTAL LANDINGS

Year	Tons (Fresh Weight)	Change (Percentage)
1979	1,002,925	25.3
1980	1,257,148	24.5
1981	1,565,465	−13.3
1982	1,356,305	−20.7
1983	1,075,547	5.5
1984	1,134,592	10.6
1985	1,255,888	8.0
1986	1,357,000	
1987	1,464,841	12.1
	Annual growth rate 1979–1987: 4.84%	
	Annual growth rate 1981–1987: −1.10%	

Source: Anuario Estadistico de Pesca, México: Secretaría de Pesca. Several years.

terms of nominal capture, identifiable species fished, or in dollar value, the production of Mexican fisheries is concentrated in a small number of key species (tuna, shrimp, sardines, anchovies). This means that the potential of other species (oysters, abalone, octopus, squid), some of high commercial value, has not been developed.[5]

The specialization trends in Mexican fisheries that have been observed in the past are not necessarily associated with more competition, either in the domestic market or in the more contested international markets. Specialization is associated with geographical concentration of resources in fisheries that have reached their limits of sustainable yields. Table 2 shows the relative importance of the 20 most important species in Mexican fisheries in 1981 and 1986. The four main species chosen for this study—sardines, anchoveta, tuna and shrimp—accounted for more than 58 percent of the total nominal catch in 1986, which was up from 55.3 percent in 1981.

As Table 2 indicates, the concentration ratio for 20 species increased from 91.05 percent in 1981 to 94.05 percent in 1986. The composition of the top ten species changed, primarily because of the dramatic drop in the north Pacific anchovy (Engraulis mordax), from 23.89 percent to 8.97 percent.[6] If only the five top species are considered, the degree of concentration increased between 1981 and 1986 from 55.3 percent to 58.3 percent respectively. The main contributor to this increment was the nominal catch of yellowfin tuna related to the expansion of the Mexican fleet of purse seiners.

A few species are worth mentioning because of their newly acquired importance among the top 20 species. The rapid development of cichlids and carps is the result of important government-supported programs in rural areas. In particular, the popular tilapias have expanded rapidly; to-

TABLE 2

STRUCTURE OF MEXICO'S FISHERIES
20 MOST IMPORTANT SPECIES IN NOMINAL CATCH
(Metric Tons)

Common name	Species	1981	Percent	1986	Percent
Common carp	Cyprinus carpio	1,732	0.11	18,817	1.44
Cichlids nei	Cichlidae	421	0.03	55,500	4.26
Freshwater fishes nei	Osteichthyes	14,072	0.92	10,457	0.80
Groupers nei	Epinephelus spp	9,950	0.65	13,004	1.00
Ponyfishes	Leiognathidae	58,948	3.84	11,546	0.89
Flathead grey mullet	Mugil cephalus	2,893	0.19	5,224	0.40
Jacks, crevalles, nei	Caranm spp	4,549	0.3	5,252	0.40
California pilchard	Sardinops caeruleus	344,433	22.42	466,799	35.81
North Pacific anchovy	Engraulis mordax	366,969	23.89	116,906	8.97
Atlantic Spanish mackerel	Scomberomorus maculatus	5,908	0.38	5,892	0.45
Skipjack tuna	Katsumonus pelamis	22,486	1.46	6,006	0.46
Yellowfin tuna	Thunnus albacares	43,838	2.85	98,277	7.54
Chub mackerel	Scomber japonicus	3,832	0.25	7,946	0.61
Requiem sharks	Carcharhinidae	14,683	0.96	9,837	0.75
Sharks, rays, skates	Elasmobranchii	20,641	1.34	15,315	1.17
Marine fishes nei	Osteichthyes	355,728	23.16	248,131	19.03
Panaeus shrimps nei	Penaeus spp	72,010	4.69	72,996	5.6
American cupped oyster	Crassostrea virginica	37,706	2.45	40,633	3.12
Venus clams	Veneridae	10,965	0.71	8,684	0.67
Common octopus	Octopus vulgaris	6,868	0.45	8,975	0.69
SUB-TOTAL 20 SPECIES		1,398,632	91.05	1,226,197	94.05
TOTAL ALL SPECIES		1,536,188	100	1,303,720	100

Source: FAO, *Yearbook of Fisheries Statistics, 1986.*

tal production figures show a 1984 peak of 63,567 metric tons. This species is particularly relevant to employment generation potential and diet improvements for peasant populations. However, these factors must be balanced against capital requirements, both in terms of infrastructure and variable inputs, particularly of fresh water catches.

In monetary terms, the relative importance of the main species changes significantly. Table 3 describes in value terms the structure of Mexican fisheries for 1986. In contrast to its value in the nominal catch, shrimp accounts for more than 37 percent of the total catch value. Sardines and anchovies, which are under price controls, represent a very low percentage of total value and are not included among the top ten.

Finally, the importance of finfish should be emphasized. The species

TABLE 3

VALUE COMPOSITION OF MEXICAN FISHERIES
Marine Fish and Organisms 1986

Scientific Name	Common name	Value (thousands of pesos)	Percent
FRESHWATER FISHES		43,898	10.13
Gerreidae	Freshwater mojarra*	22,247	5.13
Cyprinus carpio	Common carp	8,158	1.88
Chirostoma chapalae	Charal	3,280	0.76
Ictalurus punctatus	Catfish	1,838	0.42
Micropterus salmoides	Black bass	923	0.21
	Other species	7,452	1.72
MARINE FISHES		109,315	25.23
Sardinops caerulea	California pilchard	5,542	1.28
Engraulis mordam	Anchoveta	1,058	0.24
Thunidae spp	Tuna & related species	27,577	6.37
Carcharhinidae	Sharks	6,874	1.59
Gerreidae	Seawater mojarra	4,465	1.03
Carcharhinus porosus	Small tail shark	4,244	0.98
Mugil cephalus	Stripped mullet	4,165	0.96
Scomberomorus maculatus	Atlant. spanish mackerel	4,235	0.98
Epinephelus morio	Red grouper	3,848	0.89
Katsumonus pelamis	Skipjack tuna	1,746	0.40
Lutjanus campechanus	Red snapper	7,128	1.65
Centropomus	Snook	4,162	0.96
Bardiella chrysoura	Silver perch	2,203	0.51
Caranx hippos	Common jack	1,218	0.28
Lutjanidae nei	Snappers	2,329	0.54
Bagre marinus	Sea catfish	679	0.16
Euthynnus alleteratus	Bonito	202	0.05
	Other species	27,640	6.38
CRUSTACEANS		178,809	41.27
Penaeus spp	Shrimp	161,434	37.26
Callinectus sapidus	Bluecrab	3,480	0.80
Palaemonidae	Prawns	5,126	1.18
Palinuridae	Lobster	8,679	2.00
	Other species	90	0.02
MOLLUSCS		21,396	4.94
Ostreidae	Oysters	3,906	0.90
Veneridae	Venus clams	2,472	0.57
Octopodidae	Common octopus	7,783	1.80
Strombidae	Conch	1,962	0.45
	Other species	5,273	1.22
AQUATIC ANIMALS		3,852	0.89
Echinoidae	Sea urchins	2,280	0.53
Chelonidae	Turtles	578	0.13
	Other species	994	0.23
AQUATIC PLANTS		1,919	0.44
	Sargassum	636	0.15
	Algae	1,247	0.29
UNREGISTERED CATCH		74,071	17.10
TOTAL		433,260	100

*Includes the popular Tilapia melanopleura (African mojarra).

Source: Secretaria de Pesca, *Anuario Estadístico, 1986.*

involved (red snapper, grouper, mackerel, snook, sea bass, etc.) have a high commercial value and are very important resources. Data from SEPESCA reveal that in 1986 the commercial fishing fleet concentrating on these species landed 150,000 metric tons and small local fishermen landed 190,000 metric tons. Local fishermen produce for waterfront markets, while the large fishing fleets produce for the domestic market. There is some exporting, but at present it is still rather modest.

Estimates of Fish Stock Availability

Research on the availability of fish stock in Mexico is incomplete, and the information that is available concentrates on a few species.[7] Data from this research should be treated with caution because in some cases it does not provide a good base for policy recommendations.[1] SEPESCA stopped publishing data on the availability of fish stocks in 1984. Table 4 shows the complete data for that year, with a total of more than 6.3 million metric tons that can be produced from marine waters, coastal lagoons and other inshore fisheries. If total available stock for all species is considered, the potential for Mexican fisheries appears to be enormous. In 1986, the total catch represented 21 percent of available stock. However, commercially exploitable species are estimated at not more than 3 million metric tons. If these estimates are accurate, current levels of exploitation allow little room for expansion. Total landings for 1986 amounted to more than 1.46 million tons; therefore, even at modest growth rates, the limits to sustainable yields would soon be surpassed. Besides, certain elements suggest

TABLE 4

MEXICO: AVAILABILITY OF MAIN SPECIES 1984
(thousands of tons)

Species	Pacific	Gulf	Total
Minor Pelagic (a)	1475	201	1676
Major Pelagic (b)	235	71	306
Coastal (c)	92	101	193
Crustaceans (d)	392	80	472
Molluscs (e)	206	104	311
TOTAL	5081	1306	6388

Source: Secretaria de Pesca, *Anuario Estadistico, 1984.*

(a) Essentially sardines and anchoveta.
(b) Tuna and related species.
(c) Various species: mullet, grouper, snapper, etc.
(d) All crustaceans.
(e) All molluscs, including abalone.
(f) Includes other species not listed.

that the picture is more serious for individual species. Sardines and anchovies represent more than 26 percent of total available stock estimated for 1984; crustaceans, of which shrimp is the most important, repesent 7.3 percent; and tuna and related species accounty for 4.7 percent. Therefore, according to official estimates, a few species make up more than 38 percent of available stocks.[9]

Table 5 shows the relation between actual landings for 1986 and SEPESCA's estimates of available stock in 1984 for each of the four main species in total catch. Even if estimates of available stocks are overly optimistic, the 1986 figure showing that 72 percent of the catch was in high-value species such as shrimp is alarmingly close to total available stock. This fact suggests that the limits of exploitation are not far away.[10]

Anchovy. Researchers recognize that estimates of this resource are difficult to make because the species is influenced by a complex set of climatic and oceanic factors. Anchoveta spawns along the western coast of the Baja peninsula where it has been traditionally caught by Mexican trawlers. However, since the early 1970s, the nominal catch of anchoveta has steadily declined. There may be multiple causes, ranging from the changes of ocean temperature caused by El Niño to the competition between sardines and anchovies. However, excessive exploitation and lack of good resource management cannot be excluded as negative factors.

The analysis of the available anchovy stock off the western coast of Baja California is not very reliable. In 1977, a study of larval density[11] concluded that total spawning stock covering the entire peninsula was between 1 million tons in 1976 and 2.5 million tons in 1977. However, spawning stock estimates through larval density analyses are not a critical indicator for policy recommendations, because studies using this analytical tool are

TABLE 5

MEXICO: AVAILABLE STOCKS AND ACTUAL LANDINGS
(thousands of tons)

Species	Available Stocks (1984)	Actual Landings (1986)	Actual Landings to Actual Stock
Sardines/anchoveta	1,676,000	639,237	38
Tuna & rlted. species	306,000	112,484	36
Demersal*	1,074,000	166,647	15
Crustaceans	472,000	98,657	20
Of which: Shrimp	116,000	83,882	72
Molluscs	311,000	80,549	25

*Actual landings for demersal species are not presented by official data. Author's estimates include landings for species such as red snapper, sea bass, snook, grouper and others.

Source: Secretaría de Pesca, *Anuarios Estadisticos,* 1984 and 1986.

limited. Other research results have led marine biologists to conclude that excessive exploitation of this species has not been followed by rational stock management programs.[12]

According to FAO data, the total anchovy catch dropped from 366,969 metric tons in 1981 to 116,906 in 1986. Total catch has averaged 140,000 tons per year during the last four years, but it is very difficult to estimate the maximum sustainable yield from total catch statistics. The FAO/World Bank (1988) Mission Report assumes that "the fishery could safely sustain a production of about 110,000 tons to 120,000 tons." Thus, little space exists for increases of nominal catch.

Sardines. The Baja California peninsula and the Gulf of California are essential in the biological and migratory development of the species known as California pilchard (Sardinops caerulea). The spawning areas are located off the coast of Baja California and the Gulf of California. Total catch has expanded significantly during the 1981–1986 period. According to FAO's data, total catch was 344,433 metric tons in 1981 and 466,799 tons in 1986, but most analysts consider the levels over the last three years to be exceptionally high and a poor indicator of future catches.[13] In the long run, the maximum potential sardine catch will level off at approximately 220,000 metric tons per year.[14]

Tuna and related species. The most important species for Mexico is yellowfin tuna and catches for this species are strongly concentrated in the Pacific Ocean. FAO's statistics show a most remarkable performance by Mexican purse seiners in the Eastern Central Pacific, with a nominal catch exceeding 90,000 metric tons—more than 33 percent of total nominal catch. During the same period, the U.S. fleet saw its share reduced from 51 percent to 32 percent; the Japanese fleet's share dropped from 12 percent to 7 percent. It is clear that Mexican purse seiners, equipped with state-of-the-art seeking and capture technologies, have managed to exploit the comparative advantages at its reach.[15]

Shrimp. Because of a constant level of fishing in Mexico during the last decade, all analysts agree that the supply is already exploited almost to the point of maximum sustainable yield. Total nominal catch has leveled off at an average of 80,000 metric tons. Both the Pacific fleet and its counterpart in the Gulf of Mexico operate in a high-value fishing fleet with excellent comparative advantages over other countries. However, any important increases in shrimp production will have to come from aquaculture fish farming.

Aquaculture of Crustaceans. Recent studies estimate the aquaculture potential of Mexico at 300,000 hectares.[16] The special fund for the development of fisheries, FONDEPESCA, calculates that more than 335,000 hectares can be utilized for aquaculture. SEPESCA's estimate is even higher: 470,000 hectares. This compared quite favorably with the surface that can be used for aquaculture in Ecuador: 175,000 hectares.

The annual yield ranges between .55 tons per hectare in Ecuador and Panama and .40 tons per hectare in Thailand. However, these estimates have yet to be validated by rigorous and detailed studies. Even if these studies overestimate the potential, an average yield of .4 tons per hectare annually would produce 120,000 tons every year. As much as 90 percent of Mexico's shrimp production comes from sea catch. Competition in Mexico will get even stronger as leaders in aquaculture consolidate their positions and newcomers start production.

Other Species. In a self-reinforcing mechanism, concentration in a few species has promoted research of fish stock availability on these same species. Very few estimates of existing fish stock are compatible with notions of maximum sustainable yield for other species. Of the existing studies, the Grande Vidal study published in 1983 covered the Gulf of California between 1979 and 1980 and concentrated on coastal resources. The study indicated that the Gulf of California supports an exploitable quantity of coastal fish of approximately 1.37 million tons per year. Of this total figure, more than 60 percent are species of important commercial value and 39 percent are species with no commercial value but with potential use. The estimated maximum potential yield for commercial species, including some deep water fish, was 162,800 tons per year.[17] The 13 most important commercial species and their estimated exploitable stock appear in Table 6.

To sustain a healthy growth rate for the entire sector in the near future, a diversification strategy is needed. Finfish, small-scale fishing and aqua-

TABLE 6

EXPLOITABLE BIOMASS OF 13 COMMERCIAL
SPECIES IN THE GULF OF CALIFORNIA

Species	Exploitable Biomass (mt)
Menticirrhus litoralis (Shore whiting)	207,797
Diplectrum pacificum (Sea bass)	6,939
Menticirrhus undulatus (Corbina)	13,047
Bothidae spp (Halibuts)	13,066
Merluccius productus (Pacific hake)	64,112
Gerreidae spp (Mojarras)	24,876
Lutjanidae spp (Snappers)	16,081
Serranidae spp (Rock basses)	9,985
Lagocephalus laevigatus (Rabbitfish)	18,759
Carcharhinus porosus (Small tail shark)	166,289
Rajidae spp (Skates)	63,117
Carcharhynidae spp (Sharks)	20,148
Trachinotus falcatus (Ovate pompano)	37,019
TOTAL	661,235

Source: Grande Vidal, 1983, p. 119

culture may have an important part to play in this strategy, but have not yet received adequate attention.

II. THE REGULATORY SYSTEM IN MEXICO'S FISHERIES[18]

Most commercial fisheries are open-access fisheries, i.e., fisheries in which there is no individual ownership of fishing grounds. In these cases, it is not possible for individual fishermen to control the complete fishing effort. In general, the evolution of future fishing depends on population dynamics. But, because there are no definite property rights, it is impossible for individual fishermen to preserve fish stock. Thus, open-access fisheries require an institutional and regulatory framework as part of a good resource management strategy.[19]

Mexico's open-access fishing grounds, particularly of anchovy, sardine and shrimp, show signs of overfishing, a concentration of capital and labor, as well as important levels of idle capacity. To control the fishing effort, Mexico has resorted to systems of fishing licenses or permits, minimum-size regulations, controls of fishing gear, closed-seasons systems, production quotas, absolute prohibition of certain fishing operations and protection of endangered species. In some cases, there is more than one regulation in effect. For example, the anchovy and sardine fisheries have restrictions on fishing permits, on minimum size of fish (100 mm for Engraulis mordax, 150 mm for Sardinops sagax caerulea and 170 mm for Ophistonema spp), as well as fishing seasons. Closed seasons are observed voluntarily by boat owners in order to avoid the long fishing trips that barely allow the enterprise to reach the break-even point. Shrimp fishing is also subject to permits, minimum size and, in the case of lagoons and estuaries, fishing gear is strictly controlled. In some cases, an absolute prohibition of all fishing is enforced.

The objective of these regulations is to control fishing to guarantee reproduction of stock. Overall, these regulations seem to be adequate, although in some cases they may be insufficient. One important example is in the sardine and shrimp fleets, in which a concentration of vessels already exists. In addition to regulations on minimum size, a fleet rationalization program may be needed. Other regulations affecting the fishing effort have different objectives, such as protection of endangered species. In the case of dolphin-tuna threatened by tuna fishing techniques in the Eastern Pacific Ocean, restrictions on fishing gear are aimed at reducing incidental dolphin mortality.[20]

A different type of restriction applies to the commercial exploitation of certain species by cooperatives. Since the late 1930s, the following species can be commercially exploited by cooperatives: shrimp, lobster, clams, oysters, rock hind, Mexican sea bass and marine turtle. The system of protection of these species includes their cultivation through aquaculture, with extensive, semi-intensive or intensive technologies. Of these species, only shrimp is of strategic importance in Mexico's fisheries.[21]

In December 1989, the Salinas de Gortari administration proposed abolishing the system of reserved species, leaving fishing for specific kinds of fish as the only operation exclusive of cooperatives.[22] If the project is accepted by Congress, private investors will be able to compete with cooperatives in the production and processing of shrimp. This measure will be part of a vast effort to deregulate the economy and it may open the door to an important development of shrimp production through aquaculture. This line of production may be an important employment generator, but a note of caution is required. Although exports to the United States and European markets can be expanded, there is a real risk that the international price of shrimp may be drastically reduced, thereby affecting the profit margin, particularly in farms using intensive aquaculture technologies. Although the potential for aquaculture is important, there may be undesirable environmental effects that will also reduce yields, for example, if salinity is not carefully controlled. Thus, the deregulation of this branch of Mexico's fisheries should also be accompanied by good resource management schemes.

Price controls of fish products are an important part of the regulatory system in Mexico's fisheries. These price controls have been used as part of an anti-inflationary strategy, and they are designed to favor consumers. The two most important consumer goods subjected to price controls are canned sardines and canned tuna; the wholesale price of sardines and tuna for canneries is also controlled, as well as the base price of fish for fishmeal (anchovy, sardine and waste from canneries).

It is widely recognized that this combination of price controls has resulted in a gross misallocation of resources in the tuna and sardine processing industries. The comparative advantage of Mexico's fisheries has also been negatively affected by price controls. Tuna fishermen, for example, prefer to export the larger-sized whole frozen tuna because domestic canneries do not work at capacity. Even for an industry of sharp seasonal adjustments, lower yields are associated with the use of smaller whole tuna as raw material.

Canned sardines are considered part of the basic basket of wage goods and this has justified the decision to strictly control sardine prices. Today, canned sardines in tomato sauce are the cheapest protein source in Mexico, but the profitability of canneries has suffered considerably. The great comparative advantage of Mexico's sardine harvest (producing California pilchard of excellent quality) is not being capitalized. In 1987, more than 80 percent of total sardine landings end up in fishmeal plants! Since fishmeal plants evade official controls and pay a premium on sardines for raw material, and since most sardine purse seiners do not have the proper refrigerating equipment, sardines that could otherwise be preprocessed on board, canned and exported are reduced to fishmeal. Cannery equipment and machinery are usually old; most of it was bought in the international second-hand market. Modernizing these plants would require adequate profit levels. Canned sardines in tomato sauce would not disappear with modernization, because price liberalization would bring about a diversified and more flexible range of canned products. As a matter of fact, the domestic market could be expanded through the appropriate commercial campaigns, and as economies of scale were attained and equipment was modernized, a solid foothold could be gained in the U.S. market. A summary of the most common regulations in Mexico's fisheries is outlined in Table 7.

TABLE 7

REGULATORY MEASURES BY SPECIFIC FISHERIES IN MEXICO

Measure	Fisheries
Fishing permits	All commercial fisheries
NFI[a] approval	All commercial fisheries
Reserved species	Shrimp, pismo clam, lobster, oysters, rock hind, Mexican sea bass (Totoaba), marine turtle
Minimum Size	Anchovy, sardine, stripped mullet, abalone, pink conch, clams, lobster
Mesh Size	Anchovy, sardine, mullet, shrimp
Closed Season	Anchony,[b] sardine, shrimp,[c] prawns
Size of Hooks	None
Diving Equipment	Pink conch, clams
Restrictions for Commercial fishing as opposed to sportsfishing	Billfish (blue and stripped marlin, sailfish)
Quotas for Total Catch	Marine turtle
Special safety measures in fishing gear	Tuna (dolphin safety panel)
Price controls	Anchovy and other raw materials for fishmeal plants, canned sardine, canned and whole frozen tuna[d]

[a]National Fisheries Institute.

[b]The season is voluntarily observed by boat owners.

[c]The closed season regime for shrimp is applicable only to the Gulf of California. In the Gulf of Mexico the season encompasses the entire year.

[d]Almost all fish products are subject to price controls during Lent.

III. EMPLOYMENT GENERATION POTENTIAL IN THE MEXICAN FISHING SECTOR[23]

The objective of this section is to identify the current levels of employment, the structure of the labor force and the forward and backward linkages of the fishing sector with the rest of the economy. Direct and indirect employment generation is examined through the interdependencies of the Leontief matrix of the Mexican economy for 1980.

Aggregate Employment Data

In terms of overall employment, the fishing sector does not make a critical contribution to the rest of the economy. Table 8 shows that in 1988, total population employed directly and indirectly in fishing, aquaculture, processing, marketing, administration and infrastructure was 281,300. Overall employment in this sector maintained a 5 percent annual growth rate between 1979 and 1988. This rate is higher than the approximate 4.84 percent growth rate corresponding to nominal catch over the same period. However, the contribution of the fishing sector to overall employment in the economy is still quite modest; in 1988, official estimates show total employed labor force in the fishing sector to be approximately 1 percent of the total labor force. Approximately 100,000 jobs were created during the period—an average of 11,000 new jobs per year.[24]

More than 52 percent, or 147,100 people, are occupied in harvesting activities. This sector of the fishing industry maintained a growth rate of 5.3 percent. In contrast, total employment in processing and marketing de-

TABLE 8

EMPLOYMENT BY MAIN FISHING ACTIVITIES, 1979–1988
(thousands of persons)

Activity	1979	1980	1981	1982	1983	1984	1985	1986	1987	1988	Annual Growth Rate
Capture	91.9	100.1	106.3	101.3	117.1	124.1	131	137.6	143.9	147.1	5.3
Aquaculture	27.1	31.5	37.1	51.6	51.5	54	60.5	64	67.2	69.2	10.9
Processing	25.2	29.2	32	24.8	30.1	26.3	26.9	27.4	27.8	27.9	1.1
Marketing	23.1	24.1	26.3	21.2	24	23.7	23.9	23.4	23.7	23.9	0.3
Administration	4.4	5.3	5.9	6	6	6.6	6.3	6.8	6.8	5.4	2.3
Infrastructure	8.4	8.8	7.6	8.1	6.6	6.6	9.8	8.7	8.7	7.8	−0.8
TOTAL	180.1	199	215.2	212.9	235.3	241.3	258.4	267.9	278.1	281.3	5.0

ANNUAL GROWTH RATE (percentages)

	1979–1983	1984–1988	1979–1988
Aquaculture	17.4	6.3	10.9
All Fisheries	6.9	3.9	5.0

Source: SEPESCA, *Anuarios Estadisticos de Pesca*, several years.

creased; from 14 percent to 9 percent in processing and from 13 percent to 8 percent in marketing. The employment growth rate in each of these activities was extremely slow due to minimum investment in processing. In terms of absolute numbers, only 3,500 jobs were created during the entire decade in processing and marketing.

In contrast, aquaculture activities show a dynamic performance with an annual growth rate of 10.9 percent between 1979 and 1988. This is probably the most important element in the otherwise bleak employment panorama in the fishing sector. Aquaculture thus increased its participation in total employment in the fishing sector from 15 percent in 1979 to more than 24 percent in 1988. More than four out of every ten new jobs created in the fishing sector were in aquaculture activities. Rapid growth of employment in aquaculture is related to its labor-intensive techniques and the official promotion programs for the production of fresh water aquaculture.

Dividing the last decade in two halves shows that there is a declining trend in the annual growth rate of employment in all fisheries: 6.9 percent between 1979 and 1983 and 3.9 percent between 1984 and 1988. The annual growth rate for aquaculture also tended to decrease during the second half of this period. Between 1979 and 1983, the employment growth rate in this activity was 17.4 percent. During the period 1984–1988, the growth rate decreased to 6.3 percent, reflecting the effects of the general economic crisis affecting Mexico.

Employment Per Ton of Product

A standard measure of the employment generation capacity of the fishing sector is the employment per ton measure. Table 9 compares the employment per ton coefficient for the entire fishing sector with the coefficients for aquaculture and direct capture activities. The employment per ton of production (nominal catch) measure is an important indicator of employment generation potential. Between 1979 and 1988, the coefficient for all fisheries and all phases of production, covering direct capture, processing, marketing and support activities, went from 0.179 to 0.201. This is the result of differing growth rates. While the nominal catch grew 3.7 percent annually during the period, total employment grew 5 percent.

The employment per ton coefficient for direct capture activities in all fisheries except aquaculture is very low. It evolved from .122 to .121 at the end of the period. This trend is not enough to conclude that there are productivity gains in direct capture activities. The coefficient itself is very low and is an important indicator of the very small employment generating capability of this phase of fishing activities. The link between fixed capital investments and employment became stronger, probably as a result of the importance of tuna fishing.

TABLE 9

EMPLOYMENT PER TON OF FISH PRODUCTION, 1979–1988

	1979	1980	1981	1982	1983	1984	1985	1986	1987	1988[a]
Aquaculture production (Live weight: tons)	n.a.	n.a.	n.a.	n.a.	122,148	144,039	133,309	151,124	174,385	182,300
Employment (Thousands)	27.1	31.5	37.1	51.6	51.5	54	60.5	64	67.2	69.2
Employment per ton	—	—	—	—	0.421	0.374	0.453	0.423	0.385	0.379
Capture (other fisheries) (Tons)	—	—	—	—	953,399	990,553	1,122,579	1,205,876	1,290,456	1,217,874
Employment[b] (Thousands)	91.9	100.1	106.3	101.3	117.1	124.1	131	137.6	143.9	147.1
Employment per ton	—	—	—	—	0.122	0.125	0.116	0.114	0.111	0.121
All Fisheries (Tons)	1,002,925	1,257,148	1,565,465	1,356,305	1,075,547	1,134,592	1,255,888	1,357,000	1,464,841	1,400,174
Total Employment[c] (Thousands)	180.1	199	215.2	212.9	235.3	241.3	258.4	267.9	278.1	281.3
Employment per ton	0.179	0.158	0.137	0.156	0.218	0.212	0.205	0.197	0.189	0.201

NOTES: [a]Preliminary figures.
 [b]Employment in capture activities only.
 [c]Includes employment in all fisheries and all phases of production.

Source: SEPESCA, *Anuarios Estadísticos*, several years.

In the case of aquaculture activities, the coefficient shows that this is a very labor intensive industry. The coefficient in this activity evolved from .421 in 1983 to .379 in 1988. These coefficients are much higher than for direct capture or the coefficient for the entire fishing sector. A tendency towards a smaller coefficient could be the result of increments of yield in already established aquaculture units. On the other hand, more employment may be needed in developing new areas for aquaculture—opening canals and other infrastructure components for new production units.[25] These two opposing trends may contribute to maintaining a constant level of the employment per ton well into the next decade.[26]

The evolution of the employment per ton coefficient for all fisheries, including aquaculture, and all phases, including processing, marketing and support, cannot be interpreted in terms of a simple physical relation. It involves the employment composition of this sector, which can be divided into direct and indirect employment.[27] Total direct employment can be easily determined by adding direct employment in aquaculture production. Data from SEPESCA allow us to identify total direct employment, but not indirect employment. The technical coefficients of the input-output matrix (and estimates of direct labor coefficients for every sector) permits analysis of the linkages of direct and indirect employment. Analysis of the input-output matrix is the standard way to approach this problem.[28] However, it is also possible to examine the relation between direct employment figures in fishing and aquaculture and indirect employment in processing, marketing and administration.[30] Through the data in Table 10, we can compare employment in capture and aquaculture with employment in processing, marketing and administration. We can thus calculate an aggregate direct/indirect employment coefficient in the following manner: direct employment is employment in capture and aquaculture activities; indirect employment is employment in processing, marketing and administration.[30] The coefficient thus calculated went from 2.933 in 1982 to 3.614 in 1987. Direct employment in fishing and aquaculture accounted for 71 percent of total employment in 1982 and 75 percent in 1987. This is probably the result of the investment lag in the industrialization of fish products. The growth rate for direct employment in capture and aquaculture was 6.64 percent, versus a sluggish 2.28 percent for indirect employment in processing and marketing. Therefore, changes in employment composition in the fishing sector are not responsible for the behavior of the employment per ton coefficient for all fisheries and all phases of production. Perhaps a more plausible explanation is a negative growth rate in productivity per person for the sector.[31]

There are signs of excessive capital concentrations in some of the most important commercial fisheries. Fleets do not have the optimum size in some of these fisheries, and longer fishing trips are sometimes required to obtain yields just above a breakeven point.[32] This reduction in the effi-

TABLE 10

DIRECT AND INDIRECT EMPLOYMENT IN
THE MEXICAN FISHING SECTOR, 1981–1987

	1982	1987		
ALL PHASES	213,352	278,348		
State	29,545	35,008		
Other	183,807	243,340	DIRECT/INDIRECT EMPLOYMENT[a]	
CAPTURE	101,353	143,951	1982	1987
State	962	2,754	2.933	3.614
Other	100,391	141,197		
AQUACULTURE	51,699	67,214		
State	1,582	1,820		
Other	50,117	65,394		
PROCESSING	24,857	27,807		
State	11,797	12,991		
Other	13,060	14,816		
MARKETING	21,219	23,788		
State	980	1,855		
Other	20,239	21,933		
ADMINISTRATION	6,097	6,822		
INFRASTRUCTURE	8,127	8,766		

[a]Total employment in capture and aquaculture. Total employment in processing, marketing and administration.

NOTE: Data in this table covers the Pacific, Gulf and Caribbean coastlines, as well as landlocked states.

ciency levels of the fleet may also help explain a fall in the employment per ton coefficient, because employment is growing at a faster rate than nominal catch. Finally, deficiencies of infrastructure facilities, such as mooring and docking space and maintenance installations, may also contribute to lower productivity.[33]

Employment in Individual Fisheries

To calculate the employment per ton coefficient for the main large-scale commercial fishing operations in shrimp, tuna, small deep water species, finfish, etc. would require statistical information of these various activities. However, Mexican fishery statistics are not this detailed.[34] Aquaculture is, once again, an important exception. Since 1985, a special section on aquaculture has been presented in fishery statistics, allowing comparisons between all fisheries and aquaculture. Qualitative information is available for other fisheries, and it allows for some comparisons between different fisheries. Although it is difficult to base policy recommendations on these considerations, there are enough elements to assess the employment objective in policy-making for this sector.

Shrimp. The investment cost required for each direct job is very high. A typical trawler of the Pacific Ocean fleet (18 meters) or of the Gulf fleet (20 meters) is operated by a crew of only six. The fixed investment cost for a typical trawler in the Pacific Ocean may be as high as $350,000; in the Gulf Coast this cost is even higher, averaging $400,000. Thus, initial capital investment for the creation of one new direct job in shrimp fishing costs between $58,333 for the Pacific Ocean and $66,666 for the Gulf Coast.

Sardine-Anchovy. An examination of the sardine-anchovy fleet, which uses purse-seining techniques, reveals a higher capital intensity coefficient. The fleet is concentrated in the ports of Ensenada (anchovy) and Guaymas (sardine). In general terms, total investment in both classes of purse seiners for lengths between 25–30 meters is $2.3 million. On an average trip, the crew of a sardine and/or anchovy purse seiner is composed of 12 people. Thus, new capital investment needed per employed worker is $191,666.

Tuna. Tuna fishing involves the most capital-intensive operation. Total investment in a modern tuna purse seiner may reach between $10 million and $14 million for 750 ton and 1,200 ton capacity vessels, respectively. Thus, with a crew of 19 or 17 men, new capital investment needed to create one direct job in the tuna fishery is $526,315 to $736,842 dollars per person, depending on the size of vessel.[35]

Comparing the fixed capital investment-labor ratios for these three fisheries, we obtained the 1988 investment per unit of direct employment for several species. These include $58,000–$66,000 for shrimp, $191,000 for sardines/anchovies and $526,000–$736,000 for tuna. Direct employment generation in these activities is quite expensive. There is very little generation of indirect employment through backward linkages, such as in the manufacture of hull, machinery and equipment, electronics and nets, because most of these components are imported. Naval construction is not an important activity, and it has not received adequate attention in the past.

Finfish and Small Scale Fishing.[36] Finfish is exploited by a fleet of trawlers and small vessels using trawl nets, long lines and a wide variety of small nets. The size of a typical trawler for finfish implies a relatively important capital layout for each direct job. In 1987, there were 682 vessels of more than 5 meters in length operating in this fleet. Direct employment is low because the average crew of a typical finfish trawler is no more than seven members. Thus, approximately 4,774 fishermen are directly involved in the capture of finfish for all vessels. About 2,814 of these are in the Yucatán, Campeche and Veracruz.

In addition, small or local fishermen are engaged in this harvest, but the precise number of boats engaged in this operation is not known. It is, therefore, difficult to estimate the number of people employed. Official sources include data for vessels in small fisheries, usually related to waterfront markets. In 1987, there were 62,773 boats of less than 5 meters in length, usually equipped with a small outboard motor. A considerable proportion of these boats line for finfish and although individual statistics are not available, it is estimated that 30,000 boats are involved in these operations. The number of people working on each boat on a regular basis varies from one region to another, but there are indications that three people per boat is a plausible average. Thus, there may be up to 90,000 small or local fishermen involved in this industry. The number of direct fishermen in this operation could very well increase because the stock of finfish available does not seem to impose limitations. Indirect effects should also be carefully studied because the demand for small boats, with small outboard motors and standard fishing gear, can be quite important to the local industry.[37]

Aquaculture. In comparison with other facets of the fishing industry, aquaculture is a very labor-intensive process. The employment per ton coefficient is, on average, twice the coefficient of all fisheries—.411 versus .163 for the period 1983–1987—and physical yields per person in aquaculture are normally lower than in direct capture. On the other hand, live weight of catch per person is 8.96 tons, versus 2.59 tons per person in aquaculture. In addition to employment in actual production in both the extensive and intensive methods of aquaculture, labor requirements are also high for infrastructure building and for blocking flows of seawater during the different phases of production.

Thus, the employment potential may be very important. SEPESCA has estimated that no more than 3,000 hectares are currently being devoted to shrimp aquaculture. A total of 69,200 people are now employed in aquaculture, but only a fraction of them are devoted to shrimp aquaculture. Shrimp production through aquaculture is concentrated in four northwestern states and employs a total of 19,551 people in the production of 286 tons of shrimp. In Baja California, live weight production of 8 tons employs 1,951 people; in Sonora, 23 tons employs 1,327 people; in Sinaloa, 243 tons employs 10,309 people; and in Nayarit, 12 ton production employs 5,964 people.

Only a fraction of these 19,551 people are devoted to shrimp aquaculture. These states are also important contributors to the total production of aquaculture of freshwater species like carp, catfish, tilapia and mollusks.[38]

Employment in the aquaculture production of shrimp varies sharply between extensive, semi-intensive and intensive (industrially integrated) methods. The study by Margaret Miller et al.[39] concludes that semi-intensive methods employ 0.215 persons per hectare; extensive methods employ 0.13 persons per hectare. The FAO/World Bank Mission Report of 1988 said that employment is as high as 0.8 persons per hectare, but this appears to be too high even for semi-intensive methods.

Recently, the Mexican government launched the National Program for

Shrimp Aquaculture (Programa Nacional de Cultivo de Camarón), which estimated total potential land for this line of production at 470,000 hectares. Preliminary studies also revealed that only 42,723 hectares were used in 1988.[40] At an estimated rate of 0.13 persons per hectare in extensive and 0.215 in semi-intensive methods of shrimp aquaculture[41] the total estimate would be 5,553 and 9,185 respectively. These figures are more in line with data for the four states that represent total shrimp aquaculture production.

Several estimates exist for prospective employment scenarios. Considering a possibility of 300,000 hectares[42] the employment potential oscillates between 64,500 jobs with semi-intensive methods and 39,000 with extensive methods, utilizing the employment per hectare coefficients in the Miller study. With the potential of 470,000 hectares[43] and considering these coefficients, potential new employment ranges between 61,100 and 101,500 persons.

Data from other studies are more optimistic, because they include production projections for other species through aquaculture methods. For example, Andres Armenta González (1989)[44] estimated that the total surface of coastal lagoons, potentially useful for aquaculture production, is about 1,329,000 hectares. There are also 1,023 hectares of land that could be flooded and used for aquaculture of species such as tilapia, the families of common carp and mojarra, as well as shrimp. This study concludes that as many as 200,000 new direct and 80,000 indirect jobs can be generated by aquaculture production. Although these figures are overestimates, they do show that there is an interesting potential.[45]

Fishing Sector Employment and Production Linkages With the Mexican Economy

This section presents estimates of total employment and production linkages[46] for the Mexican fishing sector. The estimates correspond to the 1980 input-output matrix of the Mexican economy. The objective is to evaluate the degree of interdependence between the fishing sector and the rest of the economy. Employment and production linkages were calculated for all of the 72 sectors that are included in the input-output matrix in order to make inter-sectoral comparisons.[47]

Employment Linkages. Employment figures for each of the 72 sectors of the matrix reveal that the fishing sector employs 43,828 people. In absolute terms, the fishing sector is 43rd in employment levels.[48] Through the employment linkages with the rest of the economy, it is possible to calculate the total direct and indirect employment needed to produce one unit of output in each sector. Considering direct and indirect employment levels, the fishing sector occupies the 23rd position, behind such sectors as soft fiber spinning and weaving, leather, footwear, sawmills and clothing. The fishing sector's total employment linkage coefficient is higher than that of construction, which is traditionally considered a very important employment generator. However, that does not mean that the fishing sector should be considered as important as construction in an employment generation strategy, because in the case of the fishing sector, 75 percent of the total employment linkage corresponds to direct employment. The fishing sector occupies the 44th position, if sectors are classified in order of importance of indirect employment linkages alone. In strong contrast, the construction sector's total employment linkage has a very important indirect employment component, occupying 22nd position in indirect employment linkages.[49]

Production Linkages

One key indicator of the importance of production linkages is offered by the coefficient of direct and indirect inputs that the entire economy must produce to obtain one unit of net sectoral output for any given sector. For the fishing sector, an increase of one unit of output—one million pesos in 1980—requires 1.49 million pesos worth of direct and indirect inputs. This coefficient reveals that the impact of increases in the activity of the fishing sector on the rest of the economy, through the backward linkages, is not very important. If all economic sectors are listed by order of importance of their production linkages, the fishing sector (Sector 4) occupies the 49th position, together with the sugar industry.

The structure of the fishing sector's demands for inputs offers an overview of the production linkages with the rest of the economy. The vast majority of inputs appear to be of national origin, and imports account for only 0.02 percent of total input demand. However, retail purchases (Sector 62) account for 19.7 percent of total inputs, and it is clear that part of these purchases are of imported boats, hulls, motors, winches, cranes, electronic gear and nets. Next in order of importance are purchases of intermediate inputs from two sectors: oil and its products in 33rd place and other food industries in 19th place. Together, these two sectors account for 20 percent of total inputs and this shows the importance of these operating costs in the activities of the fishing sector.

Direct purchases of capital goods and intermediate inputs required by the fishing sector from the manufacturing sectors are as follows: transportation equipment (11.7 percent), nonelectric machinery and equipment (6.8 percent), plastic articles (5.2 percent), other textile industries (4.3 percent), other metallic products excluding machinery (4.2 percent), spinning and weaving of soft fibers (3.6 percent). Together, purchases from these sectors account for more than 31 percent of total inputs required by the fishing sector.[50]

Value Added Structure in the Fishing Sector

The value added structure in the fishing sector shows that 25.2 percent of the cost is for employees' compensation, including wages, while gross production surplus accounts for 73.3 percent of value added. In conventional sectors of the input-output matrix, this would indicate a very high level of profitability. However, an important part of fishing activities is carried out by independent fishermen. Therefore, in addition to employers' profits, production surplus includes payments to the nonwage labor force. Thus, it is not possible to estimate the profitability of the fishing sector from the input-output data.[51]

IV. CONCLUSION

Total landings statistics show that there is a high degree of concentration in four commercial species. This is a critical issue because the limits of maximum sustainable yield have already been attained in the cases of anchovies, sardines and shrimp. Tuna is a different case, but more controls of the fleet operations of purse seiners are required. Coastal species, mollusks and other crustaceans offer interesting possibilities, and an effort to diversify the fishing into these areas should be made. The finfish and small-scale fisheries should receive particular attention in this diversification strategy. In the case of small-scale fisheries, the specific problems of fishing for waterfront markets should be identified and tackled. Aquaculture is another important option, both for freshwater fish and for crustaceans (prawns and shrimp). In the case of shrimp produced through aquaculture methods, the regulatory system has to be revised in order to consider the possible entry of private firms into this line of production.

The fishing sector has not been an important employment generator. Official statistics, as well as data on capital investments per unit of employment, reveal that the sector cannot be relied upon as the backbone of an employment generating strategy.[52] Besides, concentration of fishing effort in four basic commercial species will continue to show a poor performance in employment generation. An interesting employment generation potential exists in the case of aquaculture (fish and crustaceans) and small local fishing efforts. Further research is required to determine the impact of changing the regulatory system for shrimp production through aquaculture techniques and to unravel the difficulties faced by small fishermen supplying waterfront markets as far as infrastructure, access to credit and price controls are concerned.

NOTES

The author wishes to express his gratitude to Carlos Salas Páez for his collaboration in the second part of this essay. His work on the input-output matrix was essential for the analysis of the direct and indirect employment coefficients of the fishing sector. Mr. Rodrigo Moya, editor of the fisheries journal *Técnica Pesquera*, also provided useful comments and insights on the particular problems of the fishing sector.

1. Consumption trends are an important indicator of production evolution. This aspect of the problem is not covered here. However, fish are not an important component of the regular diet in Mexico. In fact, consumption shows rather intense variations associated with the Christian calendar, with two high points in Lent and Christmas. This situation may have improved only marginally in the last 15 years. In 1987, annual per capita consumption of fish and fish products stood at an estimated 13 kilograms. This consumption level is very high, implying that Mexico ranks with countries like Spain that are traditionally big per capita consumers. This figure is, therefore, unreliable, and we conclude that consumption levels are low. Thus, with adequate commercialization policies, domestic consumption can probably be increased.

2. This section is based on Alejandro Nadal, "The Growth Potential of Mexican Fisheries," El Colegio de México, Centro de Estudios Económicos, 1989.

3. Against this background, it is clear that one of the key issues is stock management. The standard economic models for fisheries management show there is a need to regulate fishing effort to avoid misallocation of resources. But the sophisticated models proposed by Geoffrey Waugh in *Fisheries Management: Theoretical Developments and Contemporary Applications* (Boulder: Westview Press, 1984) require detailed information of population dynamics, which is far from being available in the case of most fisheries, particularly in developing countries. Therefore, no spectacular increases in landings should be expected in Mexican fisheries. Total catch in the four most important fisheries is stabilized, and evidence suggests that maximum sustainable yields have already been attained.

4. SEPESCA is the acronym for the Ministry of Fisheries. For the period 1981–1986, FAO's statistics revealed a slightly darker picture with a rate of -3.22 percent. The differences between FAO's figures and Mexican official fishery statistics can be explained by the adjustments made by FAO to assure international uniformity in fishery statistics.

5. Species concentration is a global phenomenon and is also present in the two fishing zones adjacent to Mexico: the western-central Atlantic Ocean and the eastern Pacific Ocean (FAO's fishing zones 31 and 77 respectively). This is part of a global trend toward excessive exploitation of species that have higher commercial values and have an acceptable fishing effort-to-yield ratio. Unfortunately, fishery management has systematically ignored the fact that yield rapidly collapses for species that are excessively exploited. In many cases, recovery can extend through decades; sometimes, previous levels of fish stock are never recovered.

6. This important decrease must be investigated further but, at this stage, one of the possible explanations that emerges is the climatic phenomenon of "El Niño."

The consequences of this phenomenon, which appears annually around December 24, hence its name, have been devastating for the Peruvian anchovy industry. Since 1972, the Peruvian fleet has not been able to recuperate from losses in nominal catches caused by the shifts in the patterns of anchoveta's trajectories. The effects of El Niño sometimes have an impact on Mexican fisheries, and it is possible that this explains why anchoveta has been gradually losing ground in total nominal catch. The trend for the first half of this decade can be appreciated if we consider the data on Mexican nominal catch for each year of the period 1981–1986. For Engraulis mordax (North Pacific anchovy) the nominal catch in metric tons was 366,969 in 1981, 318,070 in 1982, 97,917 in 1983, 126,892 in 1984, 147,116 in 1985, and 116,906 in 1986.

7. Observations usually come from experimental stations gathering egg or larval concentrations. The density of these concentrations is analyzed and, through standard statistical methods, estimates are made of adult reproductory population. Different estimates of fish stock and fishing yields can be made in this fashion. However, they do depend much on the frequency of observations and the geographical coverage of experimental stations. If there are few observations and the geographical coverage is small, the results will be limited; heroic assumptions regarding oceanographic and biotic parameters can be introduced in order to enlarge (somewhat artificially) the scope of a particular study, but the credibility of results is negatively affected.

8. The case of tuna is a good example of the problems with these estimates because this is a highly migratory species. As a recent study by J.M. Grande Vidal, C.A. Severino H., and A.J. Valdez G, "Evaluación tecnologia de las posibilidades de explotación comercial de atún en el Golfo de México," *Ciencia Pesquera,* 6 May 1988, p. 112, points out: "Highly migratory pelagic populations are very difficult to evaluate quantitatively, due precisely to their almost instantaneous horizontal movements that cover vast oceanic surfaces. In addition, their vertical movements in the ocean column are another factor that prevents determining their relative abundance from the point of view of time and space." (Our translation). For a country with a modern fleet of purse seiners that may fish in distant waters, estimates of available stock in the Pacific and Gulf Coasts are not very significant.

9. Important indicators cast a shadow on the realism of these estimates. First, these estimates reflect the same structure of actual landings, suggesting the necessity to revise the methodology and supporting studies behind availability estimates. In fact, this exercise may be more the result of projecting partial results of research on the most important species of Mexican fisheries. These estimates may simply reveal that there are very few studies on the species that are not within the top four or five. Needless to say, this is not the best way to encourage the diversification of Mexico's fisheries. The geographical or regional distribution of these estimates is closely related to actual landings. The Pacific coastline is responsible for almost 80 percent of available stocks. In 1984, it accounted for more than 66 percent of total landings.

10. The figures for sardines and anchoveta are not realistic. The table shows that 38 percent of total available stock is being exploited. However, most analysts share the view that both fisheries have stabilized at the limits of sustainable yield, and it will be difficult to see spectacular increases in landings of these two species.

232   *Alejandro Nadal Egea*

11. See R. M. Olvera, M. Escudero, S. de la Campa and M. Padilla, "Estimación de biomasa reproductora de anchoveta (Engrauliss mordax) en la costa occidental de Baja California, temporada 1976 y 1977," *Ciencia Pesquera*, 4 December, 1983, pp. 5–17.

12. See O. Tapia, C. E. Cotero and C. M. Garcla, "Determinación de madurez gonadal y fecundad en anchoveta (Engraulis mordax) de la subpoblación central," *Ciencia Pesquera*, 6 May, 1988, pp. 96–101.

13. This expansion is sustained by a catch of the one-to-two-year old population, in contrast with the two-to-five-year old catches of the early 1980s. The continuous exploitation of this species before individuals reach maturity will necessarily result in a reduction of the available resource.

14. A study undertaken in 1986 in the Gulf of California to determine the extent of the reproductive population of California pilchard and Japanese sardine (Etrumeus teres) established a total of 343,000 and 295,000 metric tons respectively. See R. M. Olvera and M. Padilla, "Evaluación de la población de sardinas japonesa (Etrumeus teres) y Monterrey (Sardinops caerulea) en el Golfo de California," *Ciencia Pesquera*, 5 March 1986, pp. 1–16. However, as the authors admit, these estimates are very rudimentary and have two main problems. First, in most cases very strong assumptions have to be introduced in relation to the number of eggs per station or size of the fish as a function of mesh size. Second, the success or failure of sardine fisheries in the Pacific is a consequence of anomalies in the dynamics of water masses. Abrupt changes in physio-chemical and biological parameters and these changes have not been well studied. Finally, another important point is the apparent competition between sardines and anchovies.

15. Most of the attention is concentrated on Pacific Ocean tunids. However, there are studies confirming the existence of tuna in commercial concentrations in the Gulf of Mexico. See J. M. Grande, C. A. Severino H. and A. J. Valdez G, "Evaluación tecnológica de las posibilidades de explotación comercial de atún en el Golfo de Mexico," *Ciencia Pesquera*, 6 May, 1988, pp. 104–118. These studies show that Atlantic blackfin tuna (Thunnus atlanticus) and other tuna related species have important spawning areas off the coasts of Campeche and southern Veracruz. The studies were carried out through longline fishing techniques and the catch per unit of fishing effort (CPUE) coefficients, as well as with other efficiency coefficients, seem encouraging. Other studies (see Olvera et al, 1986) reveal that not only the Gulf of Mexico, but also the Caribbean Sea, is an important spawning area for Blackfin, Skipjack, Bigeye and other species of tuna. The importance of these resources is difficult to evaluate because the stock estimates are based on sparse data. However, all figures are related to exploitable stock within Mexico's EEZ.

16. See Booz-Allen & Hamilton and INFOTEC, *Camarón de Aquacultura* (México, D.F.: Banco Nacional de Comercio Exterior and Secretaría de Comercio y Fomento Industrial, 1988).

17. To appreciate the importance of these resources, consider that this figure is more than 53 percent of total nominal catch for the 20 most important species in Mexico's fisheries in 1986 (see Table 2).

18. This section is based on Alejandro Nadal, "The Regulatory System of Fisherie Management in Mexico," El Colegio de México, Centro de Estudios Económicos, 1989.

19. These are also the results of the highly abstract, theoretical models used in fishery economics. Both the static version of surplus yield models and the dynamic pool with eumetric yield models reach the same general conclusion: because property rights are not defined, open-access fisheries require regulatory systems in order to prevent overfishing and the excessive concentration of capital and labor.

20. As of June 1987, Mexican purse seiners operating in the Eastern Pacific Ocean tuna fishery must employ a double-depth fine mesh dolphin safety panel which, during the backdown procedure, helps reduce dolphin mortality.

21. Sea bass and marine turtles are on the list of endangered species. An absolute prohibition forbids fishing sea bass, while turtles are subject to a system of strict quotas. Lobster, oysters and clams have a high commercial value, but together they represent 3.1 percent of total value of Mexican fisheries (data for 1987). Because of their habitat, the large scale commercial exploitation of rock hind is not possible.

22. According to the Fisheries Law of 1986, fishing cooperatives could launch investment projects as joint ventures. They could thus become partners with ejidos and other cooperatives formed by nonfishermen. The law recognized the possibility that the private sector might intervene, but such intervention had to come through the formation of new cooperatives. Too much bureaucratic red tape was still needed to launch and approve a project.

23. This section is based on Alejandro Nadal and C. Salas Páez, "Employment in the Mexican Fishing Sector," El Colegio de México, Centro de Estudios Económicos, 1989.

24. These figures correspond to SEPESCA's statistics. Other official sources of statistics in the case of Mexico suggest that these figures may overestimate the actual levels of employment. In particular, as will be shown in the section on production and employment linkages, the Ministry of Labor's 1982 estimates on direct employment in the fishing sector, and adjustments made by Teresa Rendón and Carlos Salas for the employment figures in the population census should be considered more reliable. Data from SEPESCA is 100 percent higher than these alternative figures. See Teresa Rendón and Carlos Salas, "La población económicamente activa en el Censo de Población de 1980. Comentarios críticos y una propuesta de ajuste," *Estudios Demográficos y Urbanos,* Vol. 2(2), 1986, pp. 291–309; and Comisión Consultiva del Empleo y la Productividad, "Proyecto para la planificación de recursos humanos. Necesidades de recursos humanos de México 1980–2000. Anexo Estadístico," (México, D.F.: 1982).

25. Infrastructure requirements in extensive methods of aquaculture frequently imply large earth-moving operations, which allow for the use of labor-intensive techniques.

26. Regulatory agencies are unable to control moonlighting and clandestine fishing off-season, or to control fishing in prohibited zones. Thus, an unspecified capture tonnage of high commercial value, such as shrimp and tuna, is simply not registered adequately. In this way, the employment per ton coefficient will appear lower than it would be otherwise.

27. Direct employment is the name given to the set of jobs directly related to capture, including search, capture, transportation to docks and discharge. Indirect employment is the name given to employment generated through forward and backward linkages—upstream and downstream economic activities. Official statistics from SEPESCA are presented with a classification between direct and indirect employment that has nothing to do with this standard nomenclature. For SEPESCA, direct employment refers to jobs generated by state-owned firms and indirect employment is generated by cooperatives and private firms.

28. This analysis is presented in Section Two of this report.

29. Indirect employment in this case is underestimated because only forward linkages are considered. There is no information outside the input-output matrix on indirect employment generated in industries that supply inputs to the fishing sector. The term indirect employment in the following comparisons would correspond to direct employment in the context of input-output analysis.

30. A few comments about these statistics are necessary. First, the inclusion of administration has a marginal effect on these calculations. Second, employment in infrastructure, essentially docking services, maintenance of ports, etc., can be set aside because employment in these activities is also related to other economic activities. Third, it is not possible to distinguish between processing and marketing activities exclusively associated with capture or with aquaculture production. Perhaps this is not a very important limitation for the objectives of this aggregated analysis. It should be noted, however, that aquaculture production has stronger links with indirect employment in marketing activities. The nature of its produce is such that little or no industrialization takes place. For example, common carp (Cyprinidae), tilapia (Cichlidae) and oysters, the most popular species, accounting for more than 87 percent of total aquaculture production, are taken to market, either as fresh fish or frozen product, but very little is processed industrially.

31. Productivity may decrease due to a series of factors. One of them is the possible effect of excessive exploiting of some of the existing resources. This would mean that as fishing grounds closer to the coast, or the most productive grounds, become overexploited, productivity decreases. Boats will tend to move to other fishing grounds, probably farther away from the coastline. An irrational exploitation of existing fish stock may also lead to increased numbers of juveniles in total catch, with the resulting decrease in yields in the medium and long term. This would reflect itself in the increase of fishing effort (for example, in terms of total fishing days) per unit of catch.

32. See Nadal and Salas Páez, 1989.

33. One final point warrants attention. Cooperatives have resorted to hired labor; this is a negative trend because it seriously distorts the spirit of truly cooperative structures. This artificial employment generation is not an encouraging trend be-

cause it is associated with contraband of reserved species and, thus, mismanagement of resources.

34. In many cases, population employed in fishing activities is occupied in multi-species fishing so that evaluating employment generation potential by individual fisheries is not possible. This is particularly true in the case of finfish and small-scale fishing activities that are not species discriminating.

35. Data on investment costs for direct and indirect employment for specific fisheries is not available, except for estimates of the tuna section of the National Chamber of the Fishing Industry (CANAINPES). According to this source, total capital investment in the tuna fleet, direct and indirect employment between 1982 and 1986 evolved as follows:

		EMPLOYMENT		
YEAR	INVESTMENT*	DIRECT	INDIRECT	TOTAL
1982	232.5	904	2,088	2,992
1986	533	1,500	3,750	5,250

*Millions of current US dollars.

Fixed capital investment per unit of direct employment went from $257,190 in 1982 to $355,333 in 1986. Although these figures are lower than those previously mentioned, they do confirm an increasing trend in fixed capital investment per unit of direct employment.

36. Finfish includes a group of coastal species, such as the high-value red snapper, groupers, snook, sea bass, flounders and other species. These species are very important for direct human consumption in Mexico's urban centers, and they may be the key to a more balanced development of Mexico's fisheries, breaking away from the extreme concentration in the sardine-anchovy-shrimp-tuna complex. Local fishing exploits these species, sometimes for autoconsumption, but also for waterfront markets.

37. On the other hand, the specific problems of waterfront markets must be examined because there are indications that infrastructure and institutional factors may constitute important obstacles in the development of this fishery. Those deserving particular attention include the lack of adequate freezing equipment, of middlemen and credit suited to the needs of small fishermen, who find it difficult to offer an acceptable collateral.

38. The total production of crustaceans by aquaculture was 3,510 tons in 1987, of which 3,224 was river prawns (Macrobrachium americanum and M. rosenbergi), and only 286 tons—not more than 8.1 percent of total aquaculture production of crustaceans—was of shrimp. However, studies to evaluate the potential of aquaculture for shrimp in Mexico have not differentiated between prawns and shrimp and have relied on this aggregate data to carry out their analysis. Two examples of this mistake are Francisco Gil Díaz, "El potencial del sector camaronero en Mexico," ITAM-CINDE seminar on Institutional Aspects of Economic Development in Mexico, 1988, and Booz-Allen & Hamilton and INFOTEC (1988). The production technology and inputs are not equivalent and careful analysis should treat these two items separately. But a point of critical importance in these two studies

236   *Alejandro Nadal Egea*

is that prawns are not a reserved species for exclusive exploitation by cooperatives in the so-called social sector. The conclusion of these studies—mainly that production is lagging behind because of regulations in the production of shrimp through aquaculture—is based on a high proportion of prawns (92 percent), and the exploitation of this species has always been open to private enterprise.

39. See Margaret Miller, Pablo Reyes Pruneda and Javier Morales, "The Development of Shrimp Aquaculture in Mexico: Implications for U.S.-Mexico Fishery Relations." Working Paper, Project on United States-Mexico Relations, Food Research Institute (Stanford: Stanford University, 1988).

40. See Secretaría de Pesca, Programa Nacional de Cultivo de Camarón (PRONACUCA), *Informe de Avance*, August 1988.

41. See Miller, et al., 1988.

42. See Booz-Allen, 1988.

43. See PRONACUCA, 1988.

44. See Andres Armenta González, *El potencial de la producción de acuacultura en México*, presented to SEPESCA by the National Chamber of Commercial Fishing (México, D.F.: 1989).

45. The figures are overestimates because, first, not all the surface considered potentially useful can be effectively used in production. Second, not all the surface that has been identified will be subjected to production with the labor intensive methods. There will be a combination of methods of production (extensive, semi-intensive and possibly intensive methods) used at any given moment in time.

46. See P. A. Yotopoulos and J. Nugent, "A Balanced-Growth Version of the Linkage Hypothesis: A Test," *Quarterly Journal of Economics*, May 1973.

47. The lack of adequate attention for the fishing sector is revealed by the fact that it appears together with hunting, which is not an important economic activity. For the purposes of our analysis, we will consider that figures for hunting are negligible and that data for Sector 4 correspond to the fishing sector.

48. The figure for absolute employment in the fishing sector does not correspond with SEPESCA's data. According to Table 1, employment in capture activities alone in 1980 was 100,100 people. This disparity is due to different criteria in defining "fishing population in direct capture activities." For example, SEPESCA's data include members of cooperatives involved in administration, transport of catch, maintenance and servicing of boats, in addition to vessel crews.

49. In addition, the total employment linkage coefficient should not be considered independently of the absolute employment generation capacity of each sector. In absolute terms, construction occupies one of the highest positions, with 1,191,028 people employed in this activity. The important point here is that the low indirect employment linkage coefficient for the fishing sector is explained by the weak technical linkages between the fishing sector and the rest of the economy.

50. An interesting feature of the fishing sector is the level of requirements from the transportation sector. Total purchases from this sector represent 3.7 percent of inputs. Transportation services are required to take catches to markets and the employment generated here is through a forward linkage of the fishing sector with processing and marketing activities.

51. This situation is similar to the case of commerce and the other services sectors, because a large part of total nonwaged labor is concentrated in them.

52. Technical interdependencies between the manufacturing sector and the fishing sector do not appear to be a solid base for employment generation. In the case of the fishing sector, direct employment is the most important component, accounting for two-thirds of the total employment linkage coefficient. It is possible that a higher level of integration with some of the manufacturing industries that furnish capital goods could translate into a slightly higher employment generation coefficient. Once again an exception must be made in the case of small artisanal fisheries. The production of small boats, nets, line-and-pole gear, etc., are mostly local. The development of small fishing may generate more employment through the production of these components. However, small outboard motors are not produced in Mexico and, at this stage, it is difficult to conclude that the size of domestic and foreign markets justifies investment in a modern competitive plant.

8

Mexican Foreign Trade of Agricultural and Livestock Products: Tendencies and Impacts of Alternative Policies

Antonio Yunez-Naude
and Ramón Blanno-Jasso

I. INTRODUCTION

The subject of this article is relevant in its own right and it is urgent due to the critical condition of the Mexican economy, which now, more than ever, needs to improve its balance of trade. The subject is even more timely because of the potential in the agricultural and livestock sector to provide remunerative employment to Mexico's population and thereby reduce its need to migrate.

Interpretation of the phenomena that explain the evolution of foreign trade in agricultural and livestock products varies according to the theoretical framework being used, (i.e., the variables being emphasized, the degree of detail and the time frame). To overcome the biases this implies, a relatively long period of time was chosen and divided according to changes that took place in economic policy. General trends as well as those specific to Mexico's more important agricultural and livestock products were studied; the impact of phenomena favored by different currents of interpretation was also considered.

Concerning the latter, the validity of two trends of thought was thoroughly examined: that which considers prices as the most important explanatory variable of economic performance and that which emphasizes conditions of supply and demand.

The narrative contains an evaluation and an analysis of the effects of alternative policies. The evaluation looks at the reasons for the deterioration of the agricultural and livestock balance of trade, the role of state policy and the effects of the stabilization measures, devaluations and commercial liberalization actions implemented by the Miguel de la Madrid administration. The analysis estimates the effects on agricultural and livestock production, employment of alternative paths of growth and evolution of foreign trade.

The evaluation covers the period 1965–1988 as a whole covering the last two presidential terms. It is drawn on three levels: that of the agricultural and livestock sector as a whole, by agricultural and livestock subsectors, and by product.[2] The time frame for the analysis of effects is broken down into five-year periods (1970 to 1985), and the projections are for 1989 to 1994.

II. TRENDS: 1965–1988

Notwithstanding the abrupt annual fluctuations in purchases and sales of agricultural and livestock products abroad, the sector's role as a net provider of foreign exchange to the Mexican economy has been reduced since the mid-1960s. This can be clearly observed by comparing the balances of its foreign trade by presidential terms.[3] In fact, the sector's trade surplus decreased from an average of 491 million dollars a year during the presidency of Gustavo Díaz Ordaz to only 110 million during Miguel de la Madrid's administration.

The same trend holds for the sector's principal components: the agricultural trade surplus was reduced by more than 40 percent, and the livestock surplus became a deficit, beginning with the administration of José López Portillo (Table 1).[4] Such a trend is explained by the differentiated performance of imports and exports; even though the latter have shown continuous growth during the entire period, the former have increased at a much greater rate (14 percent and 5 percent).

According to their intended purpose, the most frequently imported products—which from 1965 to 1987 encompass about 70 percent of agricultural and livestock purchases abroad—can be divided into four groups: a) foods for human consumption (beans, corn, rice and wheat); b) products for animal consumption including forage (alfalfa), grains (barley, oats and sorghum) and oleaginous plants (soya); other agricultural products (rubber); and d) livestock (bovine cattle and wool).

On the other hand, the main products exported account for more than 70 percent of sales of the Mexican agricultural and livestock sector abroad. These are indicated in Table 2 as follows: a) basic grains (beans, corn and wheat); b) traditional exports (cocoa, coffee, cotton, henequen and tobacco); c) fruits and vegetables (cantaloupes, grapes, oranges, pineapples, strawberries, watermelons, cucumbers, garlic, onion, tomato and squash); and d) others (sesame, garbanzo beans, honey and bovine cattle).

The value of sales and purchases abroad of the above products show that they have been substantially changed throughout the past 28 years. During Gustavo Díaz Ordaz' term, beans, corn and wheat were exported in considerable amounts; they accounted for almost 12 percent of agricultural exports. This situation was radically changed during the following presidential administration; increasing imports of these products grew to 26 percent of total imports during Miguel de la Madrid's presidency. Corn has been the most sought after commodity since the early 1970s. Imports of crops used in the production of animal foods have been added to those of grains. Such is the case of sorghum and soya, which jumped from representing 6.7 percent of the agricultural import bill from 1965 to 1970 to 30 percent during the last presidential term.

Even though agricultural and livestock sales abroad continued to be relatively diversified during the period in question, their composition has varied. Participation of traditional products became stagnant, but the weight of the components varied: cotton yielded its place as the leading

TABLE 1

TRENDS OF FOREIGN TRADE
(ANNUAL AVERAGES BY SIX-YEAR AND THREE-YEAR TERMS AND ANNUAL
VALUES IN THOUSANDS OF DOLLARS)

	Total	Agriculture & Livestock	Agriculture	Livestock
Imports				
1965–70	1,908,617	81,000	32,333	48,667
1971–76	4,984,433	476,833	363,500	113,333
1977–82	13,936,788	1,391,767	1,120,437	271,330
1983–88	12,595,989	1,702,431	1,291,943	410,487
1971–73	3,184,333	249,333	162,333	87,000
1974–76	6,784,533	704,333	564,667	139,667
1977–79	8,779,567	824,333	626,000	198,333
1980–82	19,094,010	1,959,200	1,614,875	344,326
1983–85	11,005,787	1,904,977	1,515,442	389,535
1986	11,432,364	1,337,318	900,195	437,123
1987	12,222,852	1,389,314	908,626	480,688
1988	18,903,359	1,773,023	1,396,514	376,509
Exports				
1965–70	1,205,967	571,833	477,500	94,333
1971–76	2,445,800	954,500	832,333	122,167
1977–82	12,738,033	1,559,120	1,416,991	142,130
1983–88	20,919,449	1,802,442	1,550,728	251,714
1971–73	1,701,233	786,667	643,333	143,333
1974–76	3,190,367	1,122,333	1,021,333	101,000
1977–79	6,528,200	1,656,333	1,486,667	169,667
1980–82	18,947,867	1,461,907	1,347,314	114,593
1983–85	22,723,957	1,630,427	1,434,058	196,369
1986	16,030,999	2,210,491	1,848,669	361,822
1987	20,656,187	2,041,036	1,752,601	288,435
1988	20,657,633	1,671,842	1,400,922	270,920
Balances				
1965–70	(702,650)	490,833	445,167	45,667
1971–76	(2,538,633)	477,667	468,833	8,833
1977–82	(1,198,755)	167,353	296,553	(129,200)
1983–88	8,323,459	100,011	258,784	(158,773)
1971–73	(1,483,100)	537,333	481,000	56,333
1974–76	(3,594,167)	418,000	456,667	(38,667)
1977–79	(2,251,367)	832,000	860,667	(28,667)
1980–82	(146,143)	(497,293)	(267,560)	(229,733)
1983–85	11,718,171	(274,550)	(81,383)	(193,166)
1986	4,598,635	873,174	948,474	(75,301)
1987	8,433,335	651,722	843,975	(192,253)
1988	1,754,274	(101,181)	4,408	(105,589)

Sources: Final Report, 1965–87, Tables 1, 2, 3; Banco de México, *Indicadores del Comercio Exterior, Cuaderno Mensual 120*. Dec. 1988.

export to coffee and the other crops decreased (cocoa and tobacco) or ceased to be exported (henequen).

In addition to coffee, sales abroad of some fruits and vegetables and livestock on the hoof have significantly increased their revenue share, e.g., tomatoes (which became the second most exported product during Miguel de la Madrid's term), cantaloupe and watermelon, cucumbers, onions, squash, garlic and calves.

III. DETERMINANTS: 1965–1988

A prior quantitative study indicates that supply and demand conditions of agricultural and livestock products, not their prices, were the variables with the greatest weight in the sector's external performance during the last two decades.[5]

Calculations of the factors that impel agricultural and livestock production by source of demand provide additional information on the process. Of the four components of the sector's total demand (final internal demand, import substitution, external demand and the effect of higher efficiency in the use of intermediate inputs), the first two weighed most in the changes that occurred in the sector's supply from 1975 to 1985.[6] In other words, domestic factors have been the most important to production.

It is therefore suggested that the evolution of international agricultural and livestock trade has depended, above all, on internal conditions of production and demand for its products.

Per Capita Production, Consumption and Traded Volumes

One way to analyze the effects of internal variables on the agricultural and livestock sector's balance of trade is through the study of changes in per capita production and in the proportion of imports and exports in domestic supply, taking into account the elasticities of domestic demand for food products.

The data show that the sector as a whole, as well as agriculture and cattle raising, has grown at a slower rate than that of the population from 1965 to the present. Moreover, the proportion of imports of agricultural and livestock products in internal supply has grown continuously.[7]

Evidence showing that cost elasticity for food and beverages by the lower-income population is greater than one and is positive at the national level,[8] plus the above data indicate that rising agricultural imports might result from sluggishness of supply in the face of increases in demand.

The evolution of the same variables at a disaggregated level supports this interpretation. Within the group of basic grains for human consumption, the volume of national production per capita of rice, corn and beans decreased during the period studied. This phenomenon, coupled with positive and high cost elasticity of these crops by lower-income groups, produces deficits and, consequently, a need for imports and their increased participation in internal demand.

Even though the evolution of wheat imports has been different, the data does not contradict the aforesaid. This is because the demand elasticity of its derivatives is positive and high and, in periods of decreased domestic per capita production, imports increased and vice versa.

A similar performance was observed in three imported commodities intended for animal consumption: per capita production of alfalfa, barley and oats increased from 1965 to 1985, and the volume of imports decreased.

In contrast, imports of sorghum and soya rose, as did their per capita production. Furthermore, the role of foreign purchases in domestic supply increased and, therefore, it can be said that the rise in the volume produced has been insufficient to satisfy a growing demand. Such a conclusion also rests on the fact that both sorghum and soya are used as inputs in the production of foods for hog raising and agriculture, and that the cost elasticity of national consumption of pork, poultry and eggs is high (0.77, 1.04 and 0.87, respectively).[9]

The data on exports show that there has not been any bias in favor of exports with regard to the more important products. This is because the per capita production of coffee, cucumbers, garlic, grapes, onions, squash and tomatoes increased, and, even though their export volume also increased, domestic supply of these products did not undergo abrupt change.[10] Furthermore, in the case of those goods whose per capita production declined, their volume of exports and their participation in domestic supply either decreased (cotton, henequen, oranges and strawberries) or have been stagnant since 1977 (tobacco).

Taking into account the fact that the elasticity of demand of the more dynamic export products is positive and usually high (1.46 for citrus products, 1.41 for other fresh fruits, 0.92 for soluble coffee, 0.5 for tomatoes, and 0.84 for other legumes and vegetables), the aforesaid shows that their domestic production has been enough to cover both internal and external demand.

In contrast, only five of the analyzed products showed a bias toward exports (cantaloupe and watermelon, garbanzo beans and sesame). This was because their per capita production decreased or became stagnant (honey and pineapple), while their exports and their participation in domestic supply increased.

Foreign trade in cattle is a separate matter, since calves bred in the northern states of Mexico and weighing from 100 to 250 kg. are exported to the United States and some are sent back fully grown. Considering that the balance of trade in bovine cattle has been very favorable to Mexico[11] and that the domestic cost of beef is of high elasticity, it is possible that northern cattle production is oriented towards the United States rather than the internal market.[12]

The preceding evaluation indicates that the Mexican agricultural and livestock sector has been undergoing a process of both depression and transformation. This is characterized by stagnant supply increasingly oriented towards the production of animal foods, cattle, fruits and vegetables, but detrimental to basic grains for the popular diet and the sector's balance of trade.[13]

The stagnation in agricultural production is mainly in corn and beans, which are typically produced in rainfed fields characteristic of peasant agriculture.[14] This phenomenon acts against nutritional self-sufficiency and is basic to the decline in the sector's commercial surplus.

Agriculture and the Style of Development

The process of stagnation and transformation of Mexico's agricultural and livestock industry is closely related to the economic development model followed by Mexico and, in particular, to the urban-industrial emphasis of state activity. This is shown by the continuous transfer of resources from the sector to the rest of the economy during the period of anti-agricultural bias of the economic policies followed from the 1950s to at least the late 1970s.[15]

One important aspect of the state intervention that has influenced the urban bias are the activities of the National Agency for Popular Subsistence (Compañía Nacional de Subsistencias Populares, CONASUPO). Studies of this government agency agree that its policy of guaranteed prices has not succeeded in systematically supporting producers of basic foods, and one study concludes that subsidies to corn and bean growers have been negative. In contrast, its supply function has meant strong support for urban consumption.[16]

It is therefore very probable that state intervention has discouraged peasant production of these two basic grains while encouraging more dynamic growers towards noncontrolled or more remunerative crops. Coupled with the state's policy of subsidizing food prices, this has produced the growing deficits observed and the need to import such grains. Most paradoxical of all is that the turn toward production of sorghum and soya has not led to self-sufficiency in these crops.

Other consequences of this type of development have been the depressed rural job market and the abandonment of land. Both have encouraged emigration, notwithstanding the great employment potential of agricultural activity and the growing problems of underemployment and poverty in large cities.

Available figures on paid rural employment indicate that it has grown at rates much below those of the Economically Active Population (EAP): from 1969–71 to 1983–85, the number of work years required for the production of the 50 most important crops increased by 1.1 percent, while the rate of the EAP rose by 4.1 percent. A similar process took place in livestock production.[17]

Stagnation of rural employment is caused by both the depressed labor-using peasant subsector and the process of reorientation of agriculture (corn, beans and cotton) towards the production of less labor-intensive crops (sorghum and oleaginous plants).

IV. AGRICULTURAL AND LIVESTOCK FOREIGN TRADE: 1977–1988

It is possible, however, that the evolution and determinants of the agricultural and livestock sector have changed during the past ten years, during which the Mexican economy experienced both boom and crisis as well as substantial modifications in economic policy.

Exchange and Trade Policies

There is a recent and popular hypothesis about the impact of exchange policy on foreign trade in agricultural and livestock products. This hypothesis, favored by those who consider prices to be the explanatory variable *par excellence* of economic performance, states that the devaluations of the peso in 1976 and, especially, from 1982–83 to 1988 promoted exports and reduced imports.[18]

The data show that, in fact, foreign sales of the agricultural and livestock sector (including forestry and fishing) increased by almost 10.8 percent in 1977 over the previous year, but so did purchases and at a much higher rate (74.6 percent), to the degree that the sector's favorable balance of trade was reduced by almost 20 percent.[19]

The recent period of liberalization of the exchange rate was characterized by annual fluctuations in agricultural and livestock trade, unforeseen by the argument about the effect of devaluations. The development of the sector's foreign sales and purchases that took place during the same time frame do not support the hypothesis either, since they both show tendencies of negative effects on the trade balance from any point of reference. For example, the value of agricultural and livestock imports and exports remained practically the same during the last year of the Miguel de la Madrid administration. In relation to the first, it rose in 1988 vis-à-vis 1982, and sales increased at a lower average rate than purchases during the six-year term (1.3 percent vs. 1.9 percent, respectively; see Table 1).[20]

The analysis contradicts the arguments of Martín del Campo, Rello and

Villa Issa about the positive effects of the peso's devaluations. Martin del Campo concludes that Miguel de la Madrid's exchange policy brought about the expected results in agricultural and livestock trade, especially in terms of export performance. However, he does this on the basis of increases in foreign sales of only some horticultural products, neglecting the net result that he himself reports—in other words, that the sector's balance of trade was negative during the period covered by his study.

Rello bases his argument on a comparison of the trends of the sector's balance of trade from 1980 to 1988. The problem here is that in addition to the fact that the tendencies toward improvement of agricultural and livestock trade from 1983 to 1988 are not clear, this argument only takes into account the one period during the administration of José López Portillo in which the sector's balance of trade experienced deficits.

Finally, Villa Issa's conclusion about the favorable effects of Miguel de la Madrid's exchange policy is also biased when it bases itself exclusively on the rise in exports during 1986 over the previous year.

It could be said that the devaluations did not have the expected effects because the trade liberalization measures followed by President de la Madrid did not discourage agricultural and livestock imports. However, the details of the process of deregulation of foreign trade indicate that the sector was not left unprotected. In fact, while tariffs on the most heavily imported products (grains and oleaginous plants) were kept controlled, those of inputs and capital goods used by the sector were freed.

Adding to this de la Madrid's decision to make the agricultural and livestock export quotas more flexible, it is possible to state that the administration's trade policy did not act against the potentially positive effects of devaluations.

Development and Determinants of the Agricultural and Livestock Foreign Trade by Product

A detailed study of the Mexican agricultural and livestock sector's performance must take into account its heterogeneity.[21] One way of doing this is to suppose that irrigated land is characteristic of entrepreneurial agriculture and rainfed land is characteristic of peasant agriculture.[22]

The disaggregated data on the dynamics of the sector during the period of Miguel de la Madrid with respect to that of José López Portillo indicate that purchases abroad of almost all the more important products continued to increase. The process included crops of different productive origin, and the increase in exports was localized.

Although there were the devaluations and the absence of a policy of less protection of agriculture during de la Madrid's administration, the country continued to depend on imports of the more important entrepreneurial, peasant and mixed crops—soya, corn and sorghum, respectively. The liberalization measures served only to promote exports of some products typical of irrigated, or entrepreneurial agriculture—vegetables, grapes, strawberries and bovine cattle (see Table 2).

This does not contradict the conclusion of the study of what took place after 1965, i.e., prices are not the most relevant variable in the sector's external performance.

Analysis of the correlation between the traded volumes of the principal products, internal and external prices and supply and demand in the last two presidential periods leads to a similar interpretation and provides additional elements for reflection. In the case of exports, the analysis shows that sesame seed was the only product during the two periods that had a positive and relatively high correlation between its international price and its volume of exports.[23] The influence of this variable occurs in other products, but in only one of the two presidential periods (coffee, cotton and garbanzo beans in José López Portillo's, and sesame seed in Miguel de la Madrid's). The same thing occurred with domestic prices: exports of sesame seed and tobacco had a negative correlation with its domestic price during the first period, and garbanzo beans and tomatoes in the second.

The influence of domestic production, even though it also varied from one presidential term to another, included more products (cantaloupe, watermelon, sesame seed and tobacco in the first; coffee, cotton, cantaloupe and watermelon in the second).

Finally, the results indicate that U.S. demand was relevant in accounting for the volumes of coffee exported during the two periods and for the volumes of cantaloupe, watermelon, garbanzo beans, tomatoes and strawberry exports during the de la Madrid administration.[24]

Concerning imports, the correlation analysis indicates the following: the relevant variable in foreign purchases of barley was its world price (with the expected negative sign during both presidential terms) and the domestic price for beans (with a positive sign during both administrations). This tells us that reductions in barley imports were possibly caused by increases in its international price, and cuts in bean imports by rises in its domestic price which fostered internal production.[25]

The case of wheat is different since the sign changed from positive to negative, even though the highest correlation during both administrations was that which takes into account its domestic price. This indicates that imports continued to rise despite increases in the grain's domestic price during López Portillo's term; however, such price increases stimulated domestic production into the first years of the de la Madrid administration, to the degree that imports diminished.

The high correlations of those products whose imports continued to rise during the crisis varied from one administration to the other. Moreover, the sign of high correlations was not as originally expected. Nevertheless, some interpretations can be proposed if lagged and nonlagged

TABLE 2

MAIN AGRICULTURAL AND LIVESTOCK IMPORTS AND EXPORTS
(THOUSANDS OF DOLLARS AND ANNUAL AVERAGE GROWTH RATES)*

	1965–70	1971–76	(Annual Averages) 1977–79	1980–82	1983	1984	1985
IMPORTS							
a) Foods for human consumption							
Rice	1,103	6,389	3,197	24,197	80	41,943	29,150
Beans	458	16,800	4,740	224,342	998	33,454	56,037
Corn	10,586	141,323	159,426	361,776	634,400	375,007	255,444
Wheat	3	57,138	100,904	154,904	59,657	41,360	31,669
b) Foods for animal consumption							
Alfalfa	554	1,021	345	2,096		1,216	1,000
Oats	824	883	62	1,861	59	120	79
Barley	1,882	12,586	7,499	16,281	10,495	10,930	4,423
Sorghum	2,319	35,625	103,514	313,117	433,884	363,254	264,391
Soy	3,120	39,718	162,736	214,444	217,801	403,397	275,157
c) Others							
Rubber	10,890	21,067	46,347	62,788	46,318	56,281	52,972
Bovine cattle	4,433	11,897	18,466	33,142	3,630	37,016	128,237
Wool	19,925	11,283	17,989	29,666	11,543	16,795	25,634
EXPORTS							1983-5
a) Basic grains							
Beans	7,583	6,143	20,477	4,466			14,497
Corn	47,784	6,800	2	389			615
Wheat	11,902	373	25	7			3
b) Traditional products for export							
Cotton	126,283	169,098	258,810	269,053			138,025
Cocoa	3,507	6,624	11,786	5,482			10,090
Coffee	64,537	166,961	461,543	366,720			433,938
Henequen	3,443	2,728	—	—			—
Tobbaco	6,547	22,450	34,240	47,707			24,492

c) Fruits and vegetables					
Garlic	1,841	1,813	6,841	7,960	6,439
Squash	165	542	13,372	22,991	17,259
Onion	2,062	3,086	13,381	35,715	29,257
Tomato	23,690	98,609	199,635	190,178	182,361
Cucumbers	2,336	5,168	34,253	63,510	45,696
Strawberry	4,390	8,130	8,387	2,454	3,066
Cantal & Watermelon	12,996	17,204	39,515	61,701	39,703
Oranges	3,189	3,178	2,991	1,732	809
Pineapple	371	620	2,160	1,982	1,132
Grapes	158	515	1,190	2,264	6,938
d) Others					
Sesame	1,074	2,589	26,285	20,673	12,133
Sesame seed	1,237	4,909	12,128	20,771	22,134
Garbanzo	802	13,224	62,406	48,219	30,115
Bovine cattle	24,361	65,766	120,647	79,847	150,371
Honey	5,014	16,598	30,104	29,807	35,993

Note: *Annual average growth rates estimated from the three-year, five-year and six-year terms, respectively.

Source: Final Report, Tables 4, 5, 25, 26.

TABLE 2 (continued)

	1986	1987	1988	80–2/77–9 %	86–5/80–2 %	86–8/83–5 %	83–8/77–82 %
IMPORTS							
a) Foods for human consumption							
Rice	373	710		49.90	−0.39	−61.13	0.54
Beans	82,910	17,990	13,624	116.29	−33.06	4.82	−10.41
Corn	165,527	283,630	393,819	17.81	3.11	−7.79	2.75
Wheat	20,108	36,636	137,281	8.95	−22.17	7.90	−7.47
b) Foods for animal consumption							
Alfalfa	157	323		43.43	−18.83	−24.49	−7.85
Oats	879	689		97.53	−45.93	73.73	−9.23
Barley	555	129		16.77	−11.95	−55.36	−7.75
Sorghum	78,102	61,677	138,267	24.78	2.48	−23.50	0.63
Soy	167,224	219,872	336,280	5.67	6.86	−4.20	3.31
c) Others							
Rubber	44,591	58,637	69,085	6.26	−3.75	2.07	0.01
Bovine cattle	65,872	33,475		12.41	11.18	−3.08	7.59
Wool	15,439	11,901	22,850	10.52	−9.52	−1.44	−2.84
EXPORTS			1986–8				
a) Basic grains							
Beans			29	−26.26	26.55	−71.14	−5.26
Corn			770	203.03	9.58	4.58	13.48
Wheat			1,204	−21.73	−18.38	239.57	43.57
b) Traditional products for export							
Cotton			86,584	0.78	−12.50	−8.90	−7.47
Cocoa			3,090	−14.19	12.98	−21.07	−2.67
Coffee			583,700	−4.50	3.42	6.11	1.89
Henequen			—	—	—	—	—
Tobbaco			23,739	6.86	−12.48	−0.62	−4.70
c) Fruits and vegetables							
Garlic			19,563	3.08	−4.15	24.89	5.80
Squash			27,068	11.45	−5.57	9.42	2.00
Onion			43,170	21.70	−3.91	8.09	3.96

Tomato	283,624	−0.97	−0.84	9.24	1.64
Cucumbers	61,810	13.14	−6.37	6.23	0.95
Strawberry	14,378	−21.79	4.55	36.22	4.42
Cantal & Watermelon	75,066	9.32	−8.44	13.59	1.15
Oranges	1,490	−10.35	−14.13	13.01	−6.95
Pineapple	826	−1.71	−10.59	−6.10	−7.22
Grapes	9,177	13.72	25.10	5.75	16.65
d) Others					
Sesame	10,931	−4.69	−10.11	−2.07	−6.86
Sesame seed	20,249	11.36	1.28	−1.76	2.33
Garbanzo	31,755	−5.03	−8.98	1.07	−5.15
Bovine cattle	179,850	−7.92	13.50	3.65	5.12
Honey	35,327	−0.20	3.84	−0.37	1.60

Note: *Annual average growth rates estimated from the three-year, five-year and six-year terms, respectively.

Source: Final Report, Tables 4, 5, 25, 26.

results are considered.

During López Portillo's term, the highest correlations between imports and domestic production of corn were positive without lag and negative with a one-period lag; during de la Madrid's period the only significant correlation was negative with lag. This could have been because the increase in the domestic supply of corn does not cause a decrease in imports until the following year.

The relation between imports of sorghum and domestic supply was positive and high during the López Portillo administration. This, and a similar result when considering the evolution of domestic demand, suggests that increases in the grain's production were insufficient to cover demand during the boom. The interpretation is confirmed by the unforeseen result of the high positive correlation between its imports and its international price (the continuance of that correlation during the subsequent administration means that imports of sorghum continued to rise despite increases in its international price).

Finally, the only high correlation for soya during López Portillo's term was its domestic price. The positive sign indicates that imports competed with internal production, or that price increases were not able to foster production enough to attain self-sufficiency. The change of sign during the last administration seems logical considering that increased production of this oleaginous plant was greater at the beginning of the term, and that its demand was possibly reduced by the crisis.

The product-by-product results of the analysis of the factors impelling production add to the analysis. These results show that from 1980 to 1985 import substitution was the most important factor in the production of corn, rice, wheat, beans, sorghum, barley and soya. However, the final domestic demand component continued to be positive in those commodities whose imports grew during Miguel de la Madrid's term (corn, sorghum and soya).[26] It can be stated, then, that notwithstanding the import substitution process experience of the first half of the 1980s, domestic production of these crops continued to be insufficient to cover demand.

Different from most agricultural products, the performance of the livestock and apiculture (bee keeping) trade was closer to that expected by the argument about exchange policy: exports of bovine cattle and honey rose during the devaluations period, and imports of wool decreased during the same time frame. However, purchases abroad of bovine cattle increased substantially; together with purchases of other livestock products, they increased the livestock trade deficit (see Tables 1 and 2).[27]

Since exports of livestock are made by entrepreneurial producers in northern Mexico, their evolution during President de la Madrid's administration does not contradict the view arguing for the localized positive effect of devaluations on such producers.

The Boom and the Crisis

Beginning in 1982, Mexico has experienced the deepest crisis of its post revolutionary era, as well as a radical change in government intervention.

With respect to policy for the agricultural and livestock sector, the Mexican Food System (Sistema Alimentario Mexicano, or SAM) stands out. This program of food self-sufficiency was put into effect by the José López Portillo administration during mid-1980 and abandoned by the end of 1982. One of its purposes was to promote rainfed or peasant agriculture to reduce the rising imports of basic foods and, especially, to attain self-sufficiency in the production of corn and beans by 1982.

It is worthwhile to compare imports projected by the SAM as based on historical trends against those that actually occurred. From 1981 to 1982, an average of 2.285 million tons of corn and 450,000 tons of beans were imported. The first figure is very close to the trend of 2.411 million projected for 1982, and the second is higher than the projected 317,000 tons. This indicates that the foreseen impact of the support granted to domestic production of these crops during the second half of López Portillo's term was not enough to recover self-sufficiency.[28]

A review of developments in the production of the main crops in irrigated or entrepreneurial lands, as well as in rainfed or peasant fields during the three three-year periods covering 1977 to 1985, is useful in analyzing the differentiated performance of agriculture during the boom and the first years of the crisis (Table 3).[29]

Production of basic foods was very dynamic in both types of agriculture during the period in which the SAM was in effect, and the same happened with coffee and sorghum. To these must be added two crops produced in rainfed lands (barley grain and sunflower) and three typical of irrigated agriculture (soya, cucumbers and tobacco).

Besides sorghum and soya, other crops intended for animal consumption showed high growth rates, but in localized form: forage barley and wheat in irrigated lands and forage corn in rainfed fields.

In contrast, the supply of vegetables, fruits and traditional export crops either became stagnant or declined.

Taking into account that grains and forage products are intended for domestic consumption and have been subject to state control, it can be concluded that when the SAM was in effect, production of these crops was encouraged and agriculture was oriented towards the domestic market.

On the other hand, the figures for the 1983 to 1985 period show reductions in agricultural supply, indicating that the sector suffered in the crisis. However, the slump's effect on rainfed and irrigated agriculture were different.

The rise in production of all crops destined for human consumption in

TABLE 3

AGRICULTURAL PRODUCTION VOLUMES
(ANNUAL AVERAGE GROWTH RATES)

	Irrigated		Rainfed		Rainfed & Irrigated
	80–2/77–9	83–5/80–2	80–2/77–9	83–5/80–2	86–8/83–5
		(percentages)			
Foods for human consumption					
Rice (m)	0.52	0.44	6.25	3.09	−1.39
Beans (r)	6.99	−8.60	6.14	2.37	−0.91
Garbanzo (m)	−14.44	3.47	−12.55	34.72	
Corn (r)	3.80	−0.41	4.85	2.30	−3.62
Wheat (i)	6.66	4.63	9.33	6.00	−0.65
Total	4.74	1.83	4.98	2.46	−2.70
Foods for animal consumption					
Alfalfa (i)	−3.26	0.02	10.62	−23.50	
Forage oats (r)	7.87	1.15	−2.95	5.79	
Forage barley (m)	5.87	−7.80	−3.80	−4.43	
Garbanzo (i, m)	−2.75	−5.21	−11.67	−16.45	
Forage corn (m)	−1.16	1.95	43.54	5.38	
Pastures (r)		24.01		210.63	
Sorghum (m)	2.01	0.23	6.81	1.99	−3.51
Forage sorg. (i)	−1.01	6.42	15.23	5.52	
Soy (i)	3.22	5.18	−12.88	20.75	−5.19
Forage wheat (m)	16.13	−18.21	0.93	−7.68	
Total	−1.33	1.48	8.00	48.67	
Vegetables					
Garlic (i)	−1.01	4.77	−2.68	−7.95	
Squash (r, i)	0.57	6.94	−14.49	−4.06	
Onions (i)	0.49	6.70	7.89	4.51	
Tomato (i)	0.53	3.65	−3.34	5.34	
Cucumbers (i)	3.41	4.00	21.39	−7.02	
Total	0.76	4.49	−2.45	3.70	
Fruits					
Strawberries (i)	−12.15	5.34	−16.59	47.42	
Cantaloupe (i)	−0.33	−1.60	3.62	16.19	
Oranges (r)	1.17	−8.66	−1.06	4.10	
Pineapple (r, m)	64.02	3.59	−0.65	−19.24	
Watermelon (m)	−2.63	0.37	−3.47	1.94	
Grapes (i)	6.51	0.16	2.88	−17.87	
Total	1.79	−2.69	−1.13	−0.30	
Oleaginous plants					
Sesame (m)	−11.06	9.15	−10.57	−8.34	−27.58
Cotton seed (i)	−4.55	−4.12	−12.38	−8.24	
Safflower (m)	−10.48	−14.37	−8.93	1.08	
Sunflower (r)	10.61	−8.07	7.09	7.72	−1.55
Total	−8.40	−9.69	−6.02	−1.58	
Traditional products for export					
Cotton (i)	−4.07	−4.07	−15.40	−4.95	−21.96
Cocoa (r)	6.30	18.31	0.36	1.93	
Coffee (m)	225.89	−63.78	6.55	6.66	
Henequen (r)			−2.15	−7.07	
Tobbaco (i)	3.45	−14.71	−8.15	−13.08	
Total	2.39	−10.21	−0.01	2.97	
Others					
Oats (r)	3.06	−0.64	−1.95	21.02	
Barley grain (r)	−0.68	−0.57	5.05	4.85	

Note: "r" indicates typical rainfed crops, "i" irrigated, and "m" mixed.

Source: Final Report, Tables 19, 23, 24.

rainfed zones did not become negative; and the same occurred with oats, sunflower, barley grain (peasant crops), coffee, forage corn and sorghum (mixed crops). In contrast, the only typically entrepreneurial crops whose production rose during the first three years of Miguel de la Madrid's term were wheat, soya, vegetables and some fruits.[30]

This observation leads to comment on Martín del Campo's hypothesis on the peculiar performance of agriculture during the crisis. The growth of agricultural and livestock production, within the context of a generalized depression of the Mexican economy during the first years of de la Madrid's administration, leads del Campo to suggest that the sector has displayed an anti-cyclical nature.

This review indicates that his interpretation, if true, would only apply to rainfed agriculture.[31] Nevertheless, his argument loses substance when taking into account that agricultural and livestock production collapsed during the second half of de la Madrid's presidential term.

In effect, the sector as a whole, as well as its agricultural and livestock components, remained practically stagnant during that period. According to the available data, domestic supply of crops subject to guaranteed prices (beans, corn, cotton, rice, sesame, sorghum, soya, sunflower and wheat) was reduced during the same time frame (see Table 3), to the degree that production volumes did not reach that obtained when the SAM was in effect. Livestock production had a similar experience, increasing in the first half of the presidential term and contracting in the second.[32]

An important factor in the sector's performance was state intervention. In general, the stabilization policy followed by the de la Madrid administration meant drastic reductions in public investment, subsidies and credit to the sector.

The evolution of guaranteed prices presents different characteristics and has prompted contradictory interpretations among specialists.[33] However, none deny the conclusion that it is since the second half of the de la Madrid presidential period that both the crisis and the stabilization policy have been having negative effects on the sector as a whole.

Existing data show that the contractionist policy toward agriculture deepened beginning in 1986. In fact, the ratio between guaranteed prices and the international price of beans, corn, rice and wheat, deflated with the index of raw materials related to agriculture, have been deteriorating continuously since 1986.

In addition, the volume of credit to the sector rose in 1985 only to fall again in the following years, and the same happened with the transferences and subsidies of the Secretariats of agriculture and energy.[34]

The relatively favorable domestic production performance of the main crops during the first three years of the crisis brought a decrease in imports since 1984, especially in 1985 and 1986. (This is the case of corn, sorghum and wheat in 1984, and of all the analyzed products in the next two years, with the exception of beans and bovine cattle; see Table 2).

The situation changed radically in the second half of President de la Madrid's term: the collapse of domestic production of corn, rice, wheat, sorghum and soya beginning in 1986 made the value of their imports rise in following years. Moreover, price freezing since early 1988 has depressed the profitability of production of basic foods even more, and an enormous amount of crops were lost to unfavorable climatic conditions during the same year.

With respect to exports, the figures show a notable reduction in value for most fruits and vegetables during the first three years of de la Madrid's administration in comparison to the previous three-year period, as well as a marked upturn during the second three years. In contrast, the value of the other main products for export became stagnant or decreased from the beginning of the term (the only exception was coffee, of which sales increased throughout the entire period; see Table 2).

Taking into account that fruits and vegetables are irrigated and that traditional products are of mixed provenance, it can be concluded that only farmer-entrepreneurs reacted positively to the process of gradual liberalization adopted by the administration.[35] Nevertheless, the economic policy's positive consequences were less than the negative consequences of the depression, at least in terms of the agricultural and livestock balance of trade, which reverted to a deficit in the last year of the presidential term (see Table 1).

V. ANALYSIS OF EFFECTS ON EMPLOYMENT AND AGRICULTURAL LIVESTOCK PRODUCTION, 1989–1994

The capacity of the agricultural and livestock sector to provide and generate employment is fundamental to development strategies of countries such as Mexico; analysis of the effects of alternative paths of growth and governmental actions contributes to the formulation of policy measures.

On the basis of Leontieff's model of open economy, two reference scenarios were created to simulate the variations in agricultural and livestock employment and production that would result from two different paths of growth of the Mexican economy during the presidency of Carlos Salinas de Gortari.

The first scenario, high economic growth, synthesizes the goals proposed by the Salinas de Gortari administration. It was constructed on the assumption that the economy will grow at an average annual rate of 2.9 percent during 1989–1991 and of 5.3 percent in the subsequent three years. In creating the second "low growth" scenario, the prolongation of stagnation was assumed—i.e., an annual growth rate of 1.4 percent during the six-year term, which is somewhat higher than that which took place from 1983 to 1988.[36]

With the purpose of studying specific aspects of the effects of policies toward the agricultural and livestock sector on its demand for wage labor and production, a special treatment was afforded to the sector's components, i.e., to the corresponding variables that form its vector of final demand. With respect to imports, effects were estimated for each of the reference scenarios assuming that all foreign purchases are liberated and increase at the average rate of the products that were subject to this policy change during Miguel de la Madrid's term, i.e., an average annual rate of 17 percent. With regard to exports, it was assumed that the economy grows at the rates planned by President Salinas, and that sales abroad of export products—tobacco, cocoa, fruits and vegetables, bovine cattle and apiculture[37]—will react favorably to promotion measures and increase at the highest historical rates—agricultural products at an annual average rate of 12 percent and livestock products at 75 percent.[38]

The results are overwhelming (see Tables 4 and 5). In general, the worst condition for the sector would be one induced by maintaining a high growth of its purchases abroad.

This can be seen by comparing two extreme cases: the results of the high-growth scenario with a 17 percent increase in imports with respect to the low-growth scenario with no policy changes. In effect, cumulative employment is the agricultural and livestock sector over the six years and generated by the first option would be lower by almost 5.7 million people with respect to that of the low scenario. The conclusion is valid even when considering that agricultural and livestock production induced by the first scenario would be higher, since the difference is minimal (in both cases, their participation in total generated production would be around 5.3 percent; see Tables 4 and 5, col. 3).[39]

The inconvenience arising from extending the need for external purchases is greater when comparing the effects of the reference scenarios with those deriving from increases in imports. This is because the generating of employment and production of the latter is much lower for the agricultural and livestock sector as well as for the economy as a whole (see Tables 4 and 5, col. 2).

In other words, the inverse relationship between imports and the generation of employment and products is so strong within the context of Mexico's agriculture and livestock sector that a condition of stagnation and low purchases from the exterior would be preferable to one of high rates of growth of products and imports.

The best situation would be that which would result from high rates of growth of domestic production and exports. For example, the employment generated from 1989 to 1994 in a situation of both economic growth and increased exports of the main products would be almost 35.2 million people. This means that about 3.4 million additional jobs would be

TABLE 4

DIFFERENCES IN EMPLOYMENT INDUCED BY ALTERNATIVE SCENARIOS AND POLICIES
(NUMBER OF PEOPLE)

Sectors	(1) High vs. Low	(2) High or Low vs. Imports	(3) Low vs. High-Imports	(4) Exports vs. High	(5) Exports vs. High-Imports	(6) Exports vs. Low
1 Corn	1,242,415	4,999,525	3,757,110	0	4,999,525	1,242,415
2 Rice	0	0	0	0	0	0
3 Wheat	5,788	391,745	385,956	0	391,745	5,788
4 Beans	614,122	1,284,809	670,687	0	1,284,809	614,122
Sum	1,862,326	6,676,079	4,813,753	0	6,676,079	1,862,326
5 Sorghum	1,055	921,993	920,938	0	921,993	1,055
6 Barley	107	3,043	2,935	0	3,043	107
7 Soy	5,434	540,674	535,240	0	540,674	5,434
Sum	6,596	1,465,709	1,459,113	0	1,465,709	6,596
8 Safflower	(334)	52	386	0	52	(334)
9 Sesame	14,870	0	(14,870)	0	0	14,870
10 Cotton	(116)	75,358	75,474	(373)	74,985	(489)
11 Sugar cane	2,408	0	(2,408)	0	0	2,408
12 Coffee	0	0	0	0	0	0
13 Tobbaco	189	7,282	7,093	609	7,891	798
14 Cocoa	1,162	0	(1,162)	3,744	3,744	4,906
15 Henequen	0	0	0	0	0	0
Sum	18,178	82,693	64,514	3,980	86,672	22,158
16 Other Agric.	978,289	601,341	(376,948)	3,152,054	3,753,395	4,130,344
Subtotal	2,865,390	8,825,822	5,960,432	3,156,034	11,981,856	6,021,424
17 Bov. cattle	146,333	28,930	(117,403)	199,954	228,884	346,287
18 Hogs	9,550	2,332	(7,218)	0	2,332	9,550
19 Sheep/Goats	32,461	83,326	50,865	0	83,326	32,461
20 Aviculture	205,869	13,101	(192,768)	0	13,101	205,869
21 Apiculture	5,588	55	(5,533)	24,445	24,501	30,034

22 Other Livst.	2,303	1,044	(1,260)	0	1,044	2,303
Subtotal	402,105	128,789	(273,317)	224,399	353,188	626,504
Tot Ag & Livst	3,267,495	8,954,611	5,687,116	3,380,433	12,335,044	6,647,928
23 Wood	2,474	11,837	9,364	0	11,837	2,474
24 Other forest	28,519	80,283	51,764	0	80,283	28,519
25 Game & Fish	54,373	1,445	(52,928)	0	1,445	54,373
26 Mining	523,578	163,043	(360,535)	0	163,043	523,578
27 Proc. Foods	3,220,574	1,791,124	(1,429,449)	0	1,791,124	3,220,574
28 Beb. & To- bacco	456,438	62,745	(393,693)	0	62,745	456,438
29 Textiles	904,311	277,559	(626,751)	0	277,559	904,311
30 Fertilizers	2,981	51,891	48,910	0	51,891	2,981
31 Machinery	672,903	3,702,285	3,029,382	0	3,702,285	672,903
32 Manufactur- ing	738,128	3,366,958	2,628,830	0	3,366,958	738,128
33 Construction	1,549,789	0	(1,549,789)	0	0	1,549,789
34 Electricity	31,262	5,085	(26,177)	0	5,085	31,262
35 Commerce	267,908	451,709	183,801	0	451,709	267,908
36 Com. & Transp.	387,660	850,138	462,478	0	850,138	387,660
37 Banking	396,977	38,393	(358,584)	0	38,393	396,977
38 Other Servs.	29,582,220	573,827	(29,008,393)	0	573,827	29,582,220
TOTAL	42,087,589	20,382,934	(21,704,655)	3,380,433	23,763,367	45,468,022

Source: Final Report, Table 28.

TABLE 5

DIFFERENCES IN PRODUCTION INDUCED BY ALTERNATIVE SCENARIOS AND POLICIES
(MILLIONS 1980 PESOS)

Sectors	(1) High vs. Low	(2) High or Low vs. Imports	(3) Low vs. High-Imports	(4) Exports vs. High	(5) Exports vs. High-Imports	(6) Exports vs. Low
1 Corn	60,698	162,346	101,647	579	162,925	61,278
2 Rice	3,226	1,796	(1,430)	30	1,826	3,256
3 Wheat	9,417	46,175	36,758	81	46,256	9,498
4 Beans	30,621	61,042	30,421	8	61,049	30,628
Sum	103,963	271,359	167,396	698	272,056	104,660
5 Sorghum	19,200	80,338	61,138	855	81,193	20,055
6 Barley	2,360	582	(1,778)	4	585	2,364
7 Soy	2,432	35,851	33,419	20	35,871	2,452
Sum	23,992	116,771	92,779	878	117,649	24,870
8 Safflower	3,946	2,270	(1,676)	37	2,307	3,983
9 Sesame	1,049	204	(845)	3	207	1,052
10 Cotton	12,242	10,835	(1,406)	43	10,878	12,284
11 Sugar cane	11,582	6,374	(5,208)	118	6,492	11,700
12 Coffee	9,797	5,454	(4,343)	90	5,544	9,887
13 Tobbaco	2,163	558	(1,605)	23	581	2,186
14 Cocoa	2,222	1,219	(1,003)	126	1,345	2,348
15 Henequen	782	294	(488)	5	299	787
Sum	43,783	27,207	(16,575)	446	27,653	44,228
16 Other Agric.	131,211	85,248	(45,963)	323,333	408,580	454,543
Subtotal	302,948	500,585	197,637	325,354	825,939	628,302
17 Bov. cattle	135,209	66,028	(69,182)	32,657	98,685	167,866
18 Hogs	37,266	20,269	(16,997)	331	20,599	37,596
19 Sheep/Goats	14,656	14,735	79	100	14,835	14,756
20 Aviculture	47,080	10,711	(36,369)	144	10,854	47,223
21 Apiculture	2,356	1,157	(1,198)	4,507	5,664	6,862

22 Other Livst.	3,893	1,790	(2,103)	84	1,874	3,977
Subtotal	240,459	114,690	(125,770)	37,822	152,511	278,281
Tot Ag & Livst	543,408	615,274	71,867	363,176	978,450	906,583
23 Wood	15,887	37,711	21,824	342	38,052	16,229
24 Other forest	10,393	24,593	14,200	43	24,636	10,436
25 Game & Fish	21,967	4,826	(17,141)	73	4,899	22,040
26 Mining	468,623	384,606	(84,018)	4,852	389,458	473,476
27 Proc. Foods	685,182	381,445	(303,737)	6,300	387,745	691,482
28 Beb. & To-bacco	158,838	22,119	(136,718)	133	22,252	158,971
29 Textiles	371,891	139,761	(232,130)	2,230	141,991	374,122
30 Fertilizers	10,279	39,417	29,138	5,679	45,096	15,958
31 Machinery	566,644	2,274,855	1,708,211	1,031	2,275,886	567,675
32 Manufactur-ing	1,226,266	2,803,982	1,577,716	27,324	2,831,306	1,253,590
33 Construction	378,620	0	(378,620)	0	0	378,620
34 Electricity	91,617	103,777	12,160	4,187	107,964	95,804
35 Commerce	503,261	666,701	163,440	12,592	679,293	515,853
36 Com. & Transp.	286,586	437,082	150,496	2,602	439,684	289,188
37 Banking	679,450	142,179	(537,271)	1,516	143,695	680,966
38 Other Servs.	3,977,111	240,058	(3,737,052)	1,954	242,012	3,979,065
TOTAL	9,996,022	8,318,385	(1,677,637)	434,036	8,752,420	10,430,058

Source: Final Report, Table 29.

offered compared to those that would be generated from a similar situation, but without promoting export activity, more than 6.6 million with respect to the low-growth scenario and 12.3 million in relation to the high-growth scenario with increases in imports (see Table 4, cols. 4, 6 and 5 respectively).

The results by product lead to similar conclusions but contribute elements of interest to the analysis. According to these results, the substantial growth in agricultural and livestock employment, induced by the recovery of growth, would be localized in corn, beans, fruits and vegetables,[40] and the continuous rise in exports would improve the demand for labor by producers of the last two crops and of bovine cattle. For example, the attainment of the growth rates planned by the Salinas administration would mean almost three million additional jobs in the production of corn, beans and "other agricultural products" with respect to those that would be created in a condition of stagnation. Another 3.4 million would be added if the economic recovery were to be accompanied by increases in exports of the main products sold abroad (cocoa, tobacco, fruits, vegetables, bovine cattle and honey).

The same would happen in two sectors closely related to that of agriculture and livestock: the processed food and tobacco industries, since the additional employment generated by them during the recovery would be of 3.7 million with respect to the stagnation condition (see Table 4, cols. 1 and 4).

In contrast, the effect on the demand for labor induced by products used to feed animals that would accompany recovery would be insignificant.

The findings on the effects of the alternative scenarios are also valid in the cases of agricultural and livestock supply and of employment and production of the economy as a whole; it can therefore be said that the ideal path for the coming years would be recovery of growth and increases in agricultural and livestock exports.

VI. TOWARD THE DEFINITION OF POLICIES TO PROMOTE INTERNATIONAL TRADE AND EMPLOYMENT IN THE AGRICULTURAL AND LIVESTOCK SECTOR

Secular depression, increasing domestic demand and an insufficient export capability have combined to cause the deterioration of the balance of trade of the agricultural and livestock sector.

Problems of supply come mostly from rainfed agriculture and are centered in the production of the basic foods of the Mexican diet: corn and, to a lesser extent, beans. Moreover, substantially increased production of sorghum and soya has not been enough to satisfy domestic demand for animal foods, nor have there been enough vegetables and coffee to meet export requirements needed to maintain the sector's surpluses.

The poor development of the sector and the unmet goals anticipated by the "interventionist" and "market-oriented" policies of the last two presidential terms do not mean, however, that the Mexican agricultural and livestock sector is incapable of recovering its role as an important component of Mexico's economic development. At worst, it should provide remunerative employment to the population and not be an additional component of the country's debt burden.

This calls for reflection on the elements of an effective agricultural and livestock strategy, which must take into account stringent budgetary limitations and continued liberalization, at least in the medium term.

A localized policy of support for the system of production of the basic grains of the Mexican diet is therefore proposed.[41] This would mean channeling the state's scarce resources towards the production of corn and beans in rainfed zones and leaving entrepreneurial producers to make their own decisions according to the market.[42]

Specifically: imports of the three basic grains of the Mexican diet—corn, beans and wheat—depend in great measure on the evolution of their domestic supply. After a period of boom, their supply again declined towards the end of Miguel de la Madrid's presidency because of the budgetary contraction and deterioration of their relative prices.

The impact of prices seems to have been the most influential in the case of the irrigated business crop: wheat. If we add to this the presence of a negative relationship between its domestic price and imports during de la Madrid's term, and if wheat producers act according to microeconomic precepts and are highly productive, liberalization might not be harmful.

This is valid even when taking into account the possible negative effect of such a measure on the employment offered by wheat producers, since the jobs lost would be much fewer than those that would be lost in similar situations affecting corn and beans.[43]

Supply of these last two crops is influenced by state resources and support and is characterized by the low productivity of their typical producers. If we add to this the fact that corn is the most imported agricultural product, the recommendation would be that the state channel resources towards the production of corn on rainfed lands, that it assign profitable prices and that it continue to regulate the product's foreign trade.[44] In other words, it would be preferable in this case to run the risks of intervention than to fall into a situation of increasing imports, which in the long run would be unsustainable because of the burden they would represent in terms of jobs and foreign exchange.

Most food for animal consumption, on the other hand, is obtained from irrigated or quality rainfed fields. Sorghum and soya stand out and require less labor than the crops with which they compete: corn, beans and cotton.

The weak and unexpected results of the quantitative research on these crops make recommendations risky. However, taking into account the characteristics of their production and the results of a previous regression study,[45] it can be said that imports of sorghum would not change substantially with the liberalization of its price and trade, and that, under the same measures, imports of soya could be reduced.

Production of fruits and vegetables is labor-intensive and typically entrepreneurial; their producers have reacted favorably to the exchange liberalization policy. If we add to this their potential for creating employment in a situation of increasing exports, it would not be unwise to let the producers guide themselves more and more by the market.

However, exports do not depend exclusively on domestic supply (seasonality and U.S. demand have a strong influence), and their sales face protectionist measures resulting from pressure by U.S. farmers. Since producers of fruits and vegetables are competitive in the international market,[46] the Mexican government should press for the multilateral and bilateral liberalization of their trade.

Recommendations for policy towards the traditional export products are much more difficult to formulate. This is due to the insufficiency of data, the heterogeneity of their producers, and the development of their external sales which differs from one crop to another. This notwithstanding, and without denying the need for detailed studies, it can be said that international demand is an important variable for the external performance of traditional products for export. The government would therefore face a strong constraint in promoting their sales; however, this does not mean that it should not make an effort so that at least the value of exports of labor-intensive crops is maintained.

Coffee deserves special mention, as it employs an immense number of workers and is one of the most important export crops. If we consider that its sales to the exterior have increased continuously and that, through the Mexican Coffee Institute (Instituto Mexicano del Café), the state intervenes in its production and marketing, it can be said that under conditions of favorable international demand, government promotion has in fact been effective.

Some aspects of bovine cattle exports are similar to those of vegetables (livestock is exported to the United States by entrepreneurial ranchers of northern Mexico), and so the previous suggestion for liberalization could apply to cattle as well. However, and as in the case of traditional products for export, the available studies and data are scarce, and bovine cattle production in the rest of the country is heterogeneous.

The formulation of policy measures is even more complicated because, different from export crops, the external market competes with the domestic. Moreover, consumption of red meat has been a luxury for low-income groups, and the imbalance between domestic production and the need for milk has made state intervention necessary in its production and supply.[47] Therefore, defining a strategy to promote livestock trade must take into account nutritional and income distribution considerations.

Finally, Mexican honey is a product of recognized quality in the international market, its exports depend in great measure on external demand, and it does not employ a large number of workers. This suggests that the government should limit its support of the product's international placement.

In conclusion, the study shows the advantages that would result if the current administration were to accomplish its goal of establishing the foundations of recovery; economic growth would increase productive employment in the agricultural and livestock sector and hence reduce the expulsion of the rural worker.

With regard to agricultural and livestock trade policy, Mexico's liberalization measures should be able to count on reciprocity from its commercial partners. In this respect, the government faces a dilemma in its bilateral and multilateral negotiations. Complete and immediate liberalization of trade in basic grains could bring about an increase in imports which, in addition to creating pressures on the balance of payments, would cause stagnation and encourage more migration. On the other hand, agreements on free trade in the fruit and vegetables market would stimulate export activity and, consequently, domestic supply and employment as well.

Nevertheless, state intervention in the production of grains is a generalized fact in the international economy, and a radical change is not foreseeable in the medium term. This argument must be stressed to offset pressures for adoption of unilateral liberalization measures by the Mexican government. Efforts should also be made to sensitize the international community, and especially the United States, to the pressures on the labor market and the balance of payments that would result from a lack of protection of poor rainfed agriculture.

NOTES

1. The study presents the principal results of research conducted at El Colegio de México. It was written at the Center for U.S.-Mexican Studies of the University of California, San Diego and translated by Santiago J. Rodriguez. The final report, with the same title and in the hands of the Commission for the Study of International Migration and Cooperative Economic Development for reference, is a complete version of the results. The section entitled "Trends: 1965–1988" corresponds to Part I of the Report (pp. 3–7); the next, "Determinants: 1965–1988," to sections II.2 and II.3 and to Part III (pp. 13–43); "Agricultural and Livestock Foreign Trade: 1977–1988" summarizes what is presented in pp. 8–13 and in Part IV (pp. 44–71); and the "Analysis of Effects . . . " and "Towards the Definition . . . " sections correspond to Part V (pp. 71–88). Ramón Blanno-Jasso, Associate Researcher of the project, made the quantitative analyses used in the reflections on structural interdependence and analyses of effects. However, the principal author is exclusively responsible for the interpretation. The collaboration of César Pérez Valdespino in editing the Final Report and in gathering data and calculations is appreciated. A summary of the results of the research on the period 1976–1988, made by Yunez-Naude and entitled "El Comercio Exterior Agropecuario Durante el Auge y la Crisis," is currently in the process of publication.

2. Unfortunately, livestock products are not treated systematically due to problems in the information; see Final Report, notes 38 and 47 and Table 13.

3. These are: 1965–70, Gustavo Díaz Ordaz; 1971–76, Luis Echeverría Alvarez; 1977–82, José López Portillo; 1983–88, Miguel de la Madrid Hurtado. The official data include agriculture, livestock and apiculture, forestry and game and fish.

4. It could be argued that the conclusion would have been modified if trade of processed products had been included. However, the available data indicate the opposite, see Antonio Yunez-Naude, "Factores Determinantes de la Balanza Comercial Agropecuaria de México, 1965–87." *Comercio Exterior,* no. 39, 1989, pp. 675–86, notes 2 and 3.

5. Made with annual data from 1965 through 1985 for seventeen of the principal traded products or the crops on which information is available for the entire period. They are: barley, beans, corn, rubber, sorghum, soya, wheat and wool, and cantaloupe and watermelon, coffee, cotton, garbanzo beans, tomatoes, sesame, strawberries, tobacco and honey. See Antonio Yunez-Naude, "Factores Determinantes."

6. See Final Report, pp. 13–9.

7. See Final Report, Tables 6–9.

8. Nora Lustig, "Distribución del Ingreso y Consumo de Alimentos: Estructura, Tendencias y Requerimientos Redistributivos a Nivel Nacional." *Demografía y Economía,* no. 50, 1982, pp. 107–145. The subsequent mentions of demand elasticities come from this source.

9. Rubber and wool are not included due to the lack of information on their domestic demand. In addition, domestic production of rubber is marginal and the

wool obtained in Mexico is of low quality, which is why there are strong restrictions on import-substitution.

10. Cocoa can be added, since even though its per capita production increased, its exports decreased.

11. Gonzalo Arroyo, *et. al.*, *La Pérdida de la Autosuficiencia Alimentaria y el Auge de la Ganadería en México*, *Vol. 2*, Mexico: Plaza y Valdéz, 1989, ch. 6 and Table 6.8.

12. This has been clearly observed since late 1987. The policy of freezing and controlling prices of the recent "Stabilization Pacts" has depressed the domestic price of beef and encouraged exportation. Consequently, the government has had to intervene to offset the reduced supply for the domestic market. To this must be added the growing deficits of a derivative of livestock activity: powdered milk (imports by the National Agency for Popular Subsistence [CONASUPO] have increased at an average annual rate of 10 percent from 1972 to 1988. "El Comercio Agropecuario," mimeo, CONASUPO).

13. The trend is seen in checking the figures on volumes produced, areas harvested and cultivated pasture lands. Compare Final Report, pp. 27–32 and Tables 11–16.

14. A characteristic of Mexico's agrarian structure is its heterogeneity, i.e., the coexistence of dynamic units of production (entrepreneurial) and family-type impoverished properties. See Final Report, pp. 11–12 and note 22, and Antonio Yúnez-Naude, *Crisis de la Agricultura Mexicana. Reflexiones Teóricas y Análisis Em-pírico*, Mexico: El Colegio de México y Fondo de Cultura Económica, 1988, pp. 184–200.

15. These transferences can be made through fiscal and credit means, as well as by pricing policies and by foreign trade, Final Report, pp. 35–37.

16. Oscar Vera Ferrer, *El Caso CONASUPO: Una Evaluación*, Mexico: Centro de Estudios en Economía y Educación, A.C., 1987, 239,32 and Tables 6.15 and 6.10.

17. Final Report, pp. 40–43, Tables 17 and 18, and Appendix V.

18. Compare, for example, Antonio Martín del Campo, "La Política Económica Reciente y la Agricultura," in J. Zepeda (ed.), *Las Sociedades Rurales Hoy*, Zamora: El Colegio de Michoacán-CONACYT, 1988; Fernando Rello, "La Agricultura con Pies de Barro (Estado y Campesinos en el México Actual," mimeo, 1989, pp. 159–161, and Luis Villa Issa, "Macroeconomic Policies and the Agricultural Sector: The Mexican Case (1940–1986)," mimeo, 1988.

19. Although in less overwhelming form, a similar conclusion is obtained when taking as reference the three-year periods of 1974–76 and 1977–79, Table 1 and Final Report, p. 9.

20. It could be argued that it is not valid to include 1988 due to the substantial change in economic policy decided upon since its first quarter and, especially, because the "controlled devaluation" of the Mexican peso, adopted in the same year, had negative effects on the agricultural and livestock trade. However, the same conclusions are reached when ignoring the events of 1988, Final Report, pp. 9–11.

21. Among other reasons, this is because economic behavior and the dynamics of its components are different and consequently, economic policy measures do not affect them equally.

22. In general, typical peasant crops will be those of which 70 percent or more were harvested on rainfed lands during the period 1977–1985, and as entrepreneurial those grown in the same proportion and in the same time frame, but on irrigated lands. The classification would be as follows: A) Peasant crops: barley grain, beans, cocoa, corn, garbanzo for animals, henequen, oats (grain and forage), oranges, pasture, pineapple, pumpkin and pumpkin seed, sesame and sunflower (up to 1982); B) Entrepreneurial crops: alfalfa, cantaloupe, cotton, cucumbers, garlic, grapes, onions, sorghum, soya, squash, strawberries, tobacco, tomatoes and wheat; C) Mixed crops: barley for animal consumption, coffee, garbanzo beans for human consumption and since 1983 for animal consumption, rice, safflower, sesame, forage corn, watermelon, pineapple (since 1983), sorghum, grain and forage wheat. Table 3 indicates rainfed or peasant crops with an "r", irrigated or entrepreneurial crops with an "i" and mixed crops with an "m". For details, see Final Report, pp. 33, 34, 44, 45, and Table 19.

23. The result on the factors encouraging production by source of demand for the period 1980–1985 is consistent, since it is the only export product for which external demand was the most important determinant of production, Final Report, pp.48–55 and Appendix I.

24. The estimates of the factors encouraging production lead to similar conclusions, Final Report. The results of a thorough quantitative analysis of the factors that influenced demand of the main exports of winter fruits and vegetables during Miguel de la Madrid's term do not contradict the argument about the low impact of the devaluation of the peso. Of the nine products studied (squash, tomatoes, cucumbers, strawberries, cantaloupe, watermelon, grapes, pinneaples and oranges), only squash and cantaloupe experienced the positive effect expected from the peso's devaluations during that period. In contrast, the other variables considered—U.S. demand and seasonality—were significant for most of the products: the first effect for tomatoes, cucumbers, cantaloupe, pineapple and oranges, and the second for tomatoes and cucumbers, as well as for strawberries, watermelon and grapes. Last, the study indicates the possible existence of trade barriers. See Alfredo Hernández Martínez, "La Demanda por Exportaciones de Frutas y Legumbres Mexicanas de Invierno a Estados Unidos: Un estudio de Casos," Master's Thesis, El Colegio de México, 1989.

25. Table 2. The data on the evolution of domestic production are in Table 14 of the Final Report.

26. In the case of rice, the effect of final demand was negative but close to zero, which is why beans were the only exception: imports decreased and the effect of domestic final demand continued to be positive. The case of rubber is not mentioned because it is not disaggregated in the agricultural and livestock matrix.

27. The results on the factors encouraging production support this because the most important effect for honey was external demand and was positive in the case of bovine cattle; see Final Report, p. 55 and Appendix I.

28. However, the evaluation of the SAM's effects and cost is a controversial subject (this is not due exclusively to ideological concerns about the issue of state intervention, but to other reasons having to do with the great variability of rainfall during the time SAM was in effect). If this evaluation compares what happened in 1981 with the program's goals for 1982, the conclusion will be favorable since the volumes produced, the areas farmed and the yields of rainfed corn amply surpassed the goals, and the bean picture was favorable. In contrast, the result is the opposite if the averages obtained in these variables during SAM's three-years (1980–82) are compared, since the only goal accomplished was that of yields, Final Report, pp. 55–59 and Table 22.

29. The comparison of the averages of the first two three-year periods is fortunate, since rainfalls were similar, while those of the last three-year period give an upward bias to the figures on production since 1983 and 1984 were normal years and 1985 was a good one.

30. It is important to mention that the number of paid agricultural workdays experienced positive growth rates: of an annual 0.9 percent during 1979–81 compared to 1974–76, and of 1.4 percent in 1983–85 in relation to 1979–81. This is explained by a generalized increase in the number of workdays in those crops whose production increased, and even in some in whose production became stagnant, Final Report, Table 17. This is interesting as it indicates that the sector, by offering a larger number of jobs during the first years of the crisis, could offset some of its effects.

31. The phenomenon could have been due to peasant producers' ability to fend off the first blows of the crisis, to their relative isolation from the rest of the economy or to the favorable weather from 1983 to 1985.

32. Final Report, Tables 24, 11 and 13 respectively.

33. Final Report, pp. 65–67.

34. Secretaría de Programación y Presupuesto, quoted by Julieta Medina Santos, *El Financiero*, 29 August 1989, and Roberto Escalante and Teresa Rendón, , "Neoliberalismo a la Mexicana: Su Impacto Sobre el Sector Agropecuario," *Problemas de Desarrollo*, October–December 1988.

35. Coffee is a separate case since, through the Mexican Coffee Institute (Instituto Mexicano del Café), the state intervenes in its production, processing and marketing. In addition, its exports depend heavily on world market conditions and international agreements, p. 25.

36. Final Report, pp. 73–75, table 27 and Appendix V.

37. The impacts on the employment of production of rice, henequen and coffee were excluded since the agricultural and livestock input-output matrix does not register any value in its final demand components. This is because national accounts considers these products as intermediate and subject to manufacturing. This is unfortunate, especially for coffee, which is the most exported product and employs a considerable portion of the agricultural workforce (8.5 percent, Final Report, note 105 and Table 17).

38. The estimates included another two cases with minor growth in imports and exports. They are not discussed because they lead to similar conclusions, Final Report, pp. 74–80.

39. The same cannot be said when considering the economy as a whole, since employment and production generated in the high-growth scenario with imports are larger than those generated in the low-growth scenario.

40. They are grouped in the agricultural and livestock matrix under the title "Other Agricultural Products," which also includes alfalfa, garbanzo, linseed, nuts, oatmeal, olives, potatoes and yams. Aggregating this component with fruits and vegetables is therefore an approximation forced by the way the different products were classified.

41. The subject of state intervention in storage, supply, distribution and processing will not be discussed, since it is being reviewed by the government and the World Bank. It is enough to say that the Carlos Salinas de Gortari administration should continue to target its subsidies only to poor producers and consumers.

42. The proposal is intended to stress the urgent need for a policy aimed at a certain type of producer and crop; this is not to say that certain support for producers of other labor-intensive crops on rainfed lands should be abandoned completely. Investment, credit and subsidies are obviously not enough in themselves to encourage production. Experience shows that such assistance is frequently diluted, since it does not reach the producer. This is due to the power structure in rural areas, to paternalism and to corruption. Thus, a basic component of agricultural development would be the active participation of the producers themselves in the processes of strategy formulation and decision making. See, for example, Gustavo Gordillo, *Estado, Mercados y Movimiento Campesino*, Mexico: Plaza y Valdéz, 1988, and Fernando Rello, "La Agricultura."

43. The available information on rice shows that, even though it is a mixed product, it has characteristics similar to those of wheat, and therefore the effects of liberalization would be comparable. See Final Report, Table 17, and CEPAL, *Economía Campesina y Agricultura Empresarial: Tipología de Productores del Agro Mexicano*, Mexico: Siglo XXI Editores, 1982, pp. 161–163.

44. The recommendation is similar to the policies followed during the period of the SAM. The differences would perhaps be that resources would not be squandered, it would be systematic, and its support would directly benefit producers with scarce resources. All this, together with an active involvement of peasant farmers, are necessary for them to become more efficient and competitive in the world market.

45. This shows that purchases abroad of sorghum depend much less on prices than on domestic demand, and that those of soya are influenced by trends in its domestic price (with a positive relation) and its international price (with a negative relation). See Antonio Yúnez-Naude, "Factores Determinantes de la Balanza Comercial Agropecuaria de México, 1965–87," *Comercio Exterior*, no. 39, 1989.

46. David Mares, "The U.S.-Mexico Winter Vegetable Trade: Climate, Economics and Politics," in Bruce Johnston, *et.al., U.S.-Mexico Relations. Agricultural and*

Rural Development. Stanford: Stanford University Press, 1987, pp. 288–318.

47. The disequilibrium is of such a magnitude that Mexico has become one of the world's largest importers of powdered milk.

9

Mexican Agriculture: The Potential for Export Production and Employment Generation in Rural Areas

*Amado Ramírez Leyva, Marcos Portillo Vázquez,
and Celia Sánchez Solano*

I. INTRODUCTION

This study seeks solutions to Mexico's international migration problem in agricultural export markets. It begins with the assumption that the primary cause of migration to the United States is rural underdevelopment, manifested chiefly by a lack of employment and low income levels. This fuels labor expulsion and drives workers to seek employment alternatives in urban areas or outside the country.

One solution to the problems that beset rural areas may be in the structure of production; an increase in agricultural exports would help alleviate these problems. However, agro-exports should be part of a general promotion strategy. This should be both complementary and diversified: complementary to the country's domestic needs and diversified with respect to exports and markets.

Two studies were conducted. The first selected 78 agricultural products with export potential, with projections to 1993, to reorient production toward export crops with high demand and favorable prices. It also identified the main importing countries to diversify the market. Finally, it identified the states that already produce these crops, determined the potential for increasing the area cultivated, and estimated the impact of such a change on rural employment.

The second study dealt specifically with the possibility of promoting these crops in three Rural Development Districts in the State of Zacatecas. This implied an evaluation of the impact of a change in current crop patterns. To accomplish this, an analysis was made of the economic potential for reorienting resources toward crop patterns that would more greatly benefit the region—patterns that would include agricultural products with good prospects in the external market. This entailed the following activities: the quantification and analysis of the use and efficiency of productive resources, a description of current crop composition and the determination of feasible combinations that would be more advantageous in generating income and employment in the area studied, and the identification of productive resources to reorient agricultural production and of crops with good export potential that can be grown in the Districts— crops that would also help generate greater income and employment.

II. PART I: POSSIBILITIES OF INCREASING AGRICULTURAL EXPORTS

This study explores the possibility of increasing agricultural export production to supplement rural employment and generate foreign exchange for the national economy.

Several contradictions are already inherent in the regions where agricultural export production has been intensified. One of the most serious effects is its propensity to generate competition for resources. Export production prompts a shift away from the traditional crops that are Mexico's basic foodstuffs. The rush to increase export crop yields gives rise to regional shortages of these basics; this ultimately affects the national food supply.

Closely associated with this problem is the lack of diversification in Mexico's export production. The range of export crops is narrow, as is the number of countries to which they are exported. This lack of diversification makes the country vulnerable to sudden price changes and other market constraints.

To correct these problems, Mexico must produce crops with good prospects in international markets; however, such crops must also be grown in areas of minimal resource competition. This would contribute to a complementary and diversified strategy of agricultural production in which products destined for the domestic market tend to seek an equilibrium with those destined for the external market.

This study can contribute to such a strategy, largely by identifying the export crops that should be promoted and their current production status in Mexico. Future studies will expand the discussion.

The following activities were conducted for this study:

1. Identification of agricultural products that show the greatest promise in export markets in terms of both volume and value. The 187 agricultural products with the most likely export potential and, consequently, the most attractive prices were identified; their market behavior was analyzed for the years 1960 to 1987.
2. Identification of the principal countries that produce, export and import these crops. This pinpoints current and potential competitors and buyers; this will, in turn, help orient the export process toward a market diversification strategy.
3. Identification of the states that produce, or have the potential to produce, selected crops. This process would enable Mexico to enhance the development and implementation of a production growth policy in states struggling with excess labor, unemployment and high migration rates.

This study's constraints are a consequence of its very nature. Designed to provide an assessment of potential rather than to make definitive recommendations, the prevailing conditions in the international markets and the state of domestic production of various crops are discussed, rather than conclusively evaluated. The discussion includes both domestic socioeconomic factors and current conditions limiting international trade.

Agricultural Export Production

Mexico is in the throes of a severe economic crisis, characterized by an inflationary process (which the government is attacking as a national threat), truly feeble economic growth and an increasing shortage of resources with which to stimulate such growth (reflected in the continuing budget deficit). The crisis has been exacerbated by a rising external debt and consequent debt service, as well as a drop in public investment and monetary reserves. However, its most serious manifestation is growing unemployment and deterioration of the quality of life of large segments of the Mexican population.

The question, then is: How can the agricultural sector contribute to solving the national crisis, especially if we acknowledge that the sector itself is part of the problem?

To resolve this dilemma, we must deal with two problems: (1) the nation's urgent need for monetary resources—specifically, foreign exchange to stimulate economic growth, and (2) the need for creation of employment to halt the increasing deterioration of the quality of life.

Employment is not only necessary for growth, but also basic to the quest for social justice. Employment in Mexico has declined drastically in recent years as a percentage of the economically active population (EAP). In 1981, the unemployment rate was 2.4 percent of the EAP, but by late 1988, it had grown to 23.4 percent; more than six million Mexicans were openly unemployed (see Table 1).

Open unemployment is greater in agriculture than in any other sector of the Mexican economy. About 20 percent of the rural *campesino* (peasant) population has steady work. The rest are classified as non-salaried or temporary workers. This lack of stable employment has seriously affected the quality of life in both rural and urban areas because unemployed rural workers flock to Mexico's urban centers and to the United States in search of jobs.

As unemployment grows, so does the number of new entrants into Mexico's job market each year. The EAP increases by an estimated 3.3 percent per year, creating an urgent need for economic growth. The Banco de Mexico has estimated that the country requires a minimum annual growth rate of 5.1 percent to absorb labor demand,[1] but Mexico has few financial resources with which to generate such growth. The national debt was $106.7 billion in 1988 and service on the debt was expected to

TABLE 1

POPULATION AND EMPLOYMENT TRENDS IN MEXICO
1981–1988

	1981	1982	1983	1984	1985	1986	1987	1988
Population (millions)	69.4	72.1	73.1	75.0	76.8	78.6	80.5	82.4
% Increase	2.8	2.7	2.6	2.5	2.4	2.4	2.4	2.4
EAP (millions)	20.7	21.4	22.2	23.0	23.8	24.7	25.6	26.5
Employment (millions)	20.2	20.4	19.6	20.1	20.6	20.3	20.3	20.3
Open Unemployment (millions)	−0.5	−1	−2.6	−2.9	−3.2	−4.4	−5.3	−6.2
Unemployment Rate (% of EAP)	2.4	4.7	11.7	12.6	13.4	17.8	20.7	23.4

Source: "México, Informe sobre la crisis," *Nexos,* 133, January 1989.

total $15.3 billion in 1989. Meanwhile, Mexico's international monetary reserves dropped from their previous high of $16.5 billion to approximately $8 billion in early 1989.[2]

Given these economic indicators, an increase in agricultural export production in Mexico makes sense, even though it implies certain risks. Reliance on export agriculture is inescapable, for the level of interdependence and international integration is rising as a result of worldwide market restructuring. Mexico plays an integral role in this process, particularly in view of its goal of modernization, which implies an opening of its economy. Whether we like it or not, global integration is taking place. It is therefore essential to analyze how this can be beneficial to Mexico.

Crops with Export Potential

Two basic factors must be explored: the potential for domestic production in its socioeconomic and agronomic dimensions, and the potential for exports.

Mexico is well endowed with natural resources and climatic and ecological diversity. These assets were fully evident in the Green Revolution, when Mexico successfully diversified its agricultural output to develop improved varieties of wheat. In fact, Mexico's ability to diversify its crops is one of its biggest assets, made possible by regions ranging from sea level to very high altitudes, and from deserts to temperate and tropical zones.

This regional variety opens the door to several possibilities. First, it permits the diversification of export crops. Second, it allows for increased export production within a variety of regions. With regional options,

Mexico can concentrate export production in sectors that will not have an adverse impact on the traditional crops that supply the nation's basic foodstuffs. In the choice of regions, we must bear in mind that the goal is not merely to generate foreign exchange, but to avoid unnecessary expenditures. High levels of agricultural imports, whether staples or raw materials, use up valuable foreign exchange.

Export marketing can be divided into two broad areas: the environment created by the trade policies of the developed country,[3] and the set of circumstances that favor agricultural products in the world market. The export outlook for Mexican crops is now bleak, given the growing protectionism of the developed countries, some of which are not only principal importers, but also large producers of some of these commodities. Nevertheless, there are possibilities for expanding the international market to include less developed countries that also need to import such products. Favorable international market conditions include a growing demand for agricultural products and an upward trend in their value. These conditions can be greatly affected by one other factor: other countries that produce and market the same crops. Other producers are potential competitors, exporters are current competitors and importers are potential customers.

Identifying Favorable Market Conditions

This study determined favorable market conditions on two levels: (1) by identifying crops with potential in terms of volume and value, and (2) by naming the countries engaged in marketing the crops so identified. To some extent, these countries determine market conditions.

Crop Selection Criteria. We applied the criteria of volume and value to production and to the export and import behavior of 187 crops suggested by the United Nation's Food and Agriculture Organization (FAO) for the 1960–1987 period.[4] This led to the selection of 78 crops which were divided into three groups with the following characteristics.

Group One
1. Noted for increased export volume.
2. Noted for increased export value.
3. Noted for decreased worldwide production (see Table 2).

Group Two
1. Noted for increased export volume.
2. Noted for increased export value.
3. Noted for stable worldwide production (see Table 3).

Group Three
1. Noted for increased export volume.
2. Noted for increased export value.
3. Noted for increased production (see Table 4).

TABLE 2

GROWTH RATE OF CROPS WITH POTENTIAL IN WORLD MARKETS, 1960–1987
DECREASING WORLD PRODUCTION
GROUP 1

	Production Volume	Export Volume	Export Value
1. Buckwheat	0.7	10.9	17.2
2. Potatoes	0.02	2.3	8.0
3. Sweet potatoes	1.0	11.1	5.0
4. Yautia	1.7	14.5	22.4
5. Taro	0.8	10.2	16.2
6. Chestnuts	− 0.7	2.7	10.8
7. Linseed	− 1.4	0.3	4.2
8. Asparagus	0.4	6.0	12.7
9. Spinach	1.5	2.6	6.6
10. Green Peas	1.3	3.1	10.0
11. Tangerines	4.7	7.4	11.8
12. Grapefruit	3.3	5.8	11.4
13. Quince	− 0.2	4.2	10.7
14. Figs	− 2.1	5.0	15.0
15. Alfalfa	0.6	8.1	14.0
16. Hops	1.5	2.4	7.7
17. Pepper	2.5	2.8	9.1

Source: Prepared from FAO data.

These crops were selected by two complementary methods. They were first identified by growth rates over the sample period and then graphically evaluated. This was needed to compensate for insufficient trend data since, in some cases, rates remain high for the entire period, even though productive activity may have dropped over the past decade. Graphic evaluation allows us to determine long-term production and export behavior in spite of periodic fluctuations.

Criteria for Identifying Participating Countries. Countries were classified as producers, exporters and importers.

We identified countries that produced selected crops during the 1960–1987 sample period. We ranked them by the percentage of their export share in 1987 to determine their relative importance as international suppliers.

Countries that imported the selected crops during the sample period were also identified. These were ranked by their percentage share of imports during 1987 to assess their relative importance in the volume of demand absorbed and to permit the identification of markets by region.

TABLE 3

GROWTH RATES WITH POTENTIAL IN WORLD MARKETS, 1960–1987
STABLE WORLD PRODUCTION
GROUP 2

	Production (Volume)	Export Volume	Export Value
1. Barley	3.1	5.5	10.1
2. Sugar Beets	2.2	2.6	7.5
3. Broad Beans, Dry	−0.9	3.3	9.4
4. Chickpeas for human consumption	−0.1	3.7	10.6
5. Walnuts	2.1	3.7	8.9
6. Lettuce	2.1	2.3	7.9
7. Beans, Green	1.9	0.1	6.6
8. Edible Mushrooms	5.8	5.6	11.5
9. Plantains	2.2	2.2	7.1
10. Oranges	4.0	1.3	6.7
11. Cherries	0.6	3.1	10.2
12. Peaches and Nectarines	1.7	2.8	9.6
13. Blueberries	4.0	0.2	6.6
14. Grapes	1.3	2.3	9.4
15. (Straw, Husks)	1.6	1.3	7.3
16. Natural Rubber	3.0	1.15	5.0

Source: Prepared from FAO data.

Implications of the Selection Criteria

That exports tend to grow in both volume and value implies the existence of unsaturated demand. The object is to sustain this trend and accompany it with an increase in international prices. To the extent that volume exceeds value, international prices will be more favorable, thus demonstrating an upward trend. To the extent that production decreases over time, there will be a concomitant decrease in market competition. However, when production stabilizes or increases, competition will tend to increase with supply.

These trends were observed in all crop groups. Production spiraled upwards in the third crop category; these contained the most common export—and most competitive—crops. They include various horticultural products, as well as coffee, cocoa beans and cotton.

The first and second groups included less common crops, which Mexico has not fully developed. These offer good potential because they are not widely produced and can be cultivated in areas not intensively entre-

TABLE 4

GROWTH RATES OF CROPS WITH POTENTIAL IN WORLD MARKETS, 1960–1987
INCREASING WORLD PRODUCTION
GROUP 3

	Production (Volume)	Export Volume	Export Value
1. Wheat	3.2	3.8	8.4
2. Yams	2.4	3.2	23.6
3. Beans	1.1	4.4	10.1
4. Dry Peas	0.6	14.5	22.4
5. Lentil Beans	3.1	6.2	12.4
6. Lupines	−0.6	43.0	44.2
7. Pistachios	9.4	4.5	11.9
8. Soy Beans	5.6	7.6	12.2
9. Coconut	1.9	4.8	9.5
10. Palm Oil	7.5	10.1	14.7
11. Sunflower Seed	3.9	9.8	15.1
12. Rapeseed	6.8	8.7	13.4
13. Sesame Seed	1.3	2.5	9.1
14. Mustard Seed	1.0	4.0	8.6
15. Melonseed	2.2	5.0	12.0
16. Cabbage	2.3	10.6	4.6
17. Tomatoes	3.7	2.7	8.8
18. Cauliflower	1.7	1.2	9.0
19. Pumpkins, Squash	1.0	15.0	21.3
20. Cucumbers, Gherkins	2.7	7.3	11.5
21. Eggplant	2.9	8.5	17.6
22. Chile, Peppers	3.4	8.0	15.8
23. Onions, Green	4.2	9.9	15.3
24. Onions, Dry	3.2	2.9	7.8
25. Garlic	3.5	6.2	10.8
26. Green Beans	0.8	6.3	12.1
27. Carrots	2.9	4.1	8.5
28. Pears	2.2	2.1	8.4
29. Apricots	1.9	1.5	8.2
30. Plums	0.9	2.1	9.0
31. Raspberries	2.9	3.3	10.0
32. Mangos	1.5	12.4	19.3
33. Avocados	3.6	18.5	29.1
34. Pineapple	4.7	6.7	13.4
35. Persimmons	1.4	9.6	14.2
36. Coffee	1.3	1.4	8.6
37. Cocoa Beans	1.6	0.9	8.7
38. Tea	3.6	2.4	6.0
39. Pimento Allspice	2.1	3.5	7.7
40. Cinnamon	3.8	5.6	9.4
41. Nutmeg, Cardamum	4.3	4.7	10.1
42. Anise, Fennel	3.1	4.0	10.1
43. Ginger	6.6	17.6	23.1
44. Cotton Fiber	1.7	1.0	5.4
45. Leaf Tobacco	2.0	2.0	6.8

Source: Prepared from FAO data.

preneurial in nature—i.e., they open possibilities in marginal agricultural zones, which means that marketing channels will have to be developed within these crop categories.

The relationship between production and export levels was also analyzed for each crop by examining the percentage produced for export, based on estimates made for 1987 and 1993, as Table 5 reveals. The analysis indicated that, as the percentage of export production increases, so does competition. This occurs because these crops are grown largely for export and are produced by countries that specialize in them or maintain stable marketing channels. Such is the case with crops like pepper, hops, linseed, grapefruit, barley and blueberries.

In exploring the relationship between production and export levels, we found that, when the percentage of export production is low, crops are grown mostly for domestic consumption in the producing countries. This implies that domestic production is inadequate. Included in this category are such crops as sweet potatoes, taro, figs, alfalfa, green pease, lettuce and sugar beets.

By analyzing the number of market participants, other trends became noticeable. First, a favorable competitive environment exists when importers outnumber producers and exporters. Second, the market is structured to include intermediaries who neither produce nor directly participate in the importing or exporting of the selected crops.

Study Constraints

The study had to contend with limited data on the production of various crops, and some statistics on reported crops are unreliable. To overcome these constraints, the initial number of agricultural products intended for analysis was pared down from 400 to 187 and limited to crops reported by the FAO. Thus, many agricultural products with possibly greater potential for international trade were excluded.

Data-gathering difficulties centered on inaccurate figures. Export and import totals for some countries exceeded 100 percent of cultivated crop volumes. This was because some countries do not report all crop volumes, which gives rise to inconsistencies.

A second constraint is the narrow scope of this work, which is to identify existing conditions and future marketing possibilities, not to provide definitive recommendations.

Finally, the study is limited by the abstraction that had to be made of many structural conditions, including socioeconomic factors, as well as trends in international trade.

TABLE 5

PERCENTAGES OF PRODUCTION EXPORTED
(PROJECTIONS FOR 1987, 1993)

First Group Crop	1987	1993	Second Group Crop	1987	1993
Pepper	99.3	97.2	Barley	44.4	46.4
Hops	40.4	46.4	Blueberries	21.6	33.6
Linseed	28.6	33.4	Plantain	17.8	13.2
Grapefruit	20.9	23.5	Dry Beans	10.6	14.7
Chestnuts	20.0	27.4	Walnuts	10.3	11.9
Tangerines	17.8	23.4	Peaches, Nectarines	8.4	8.9
Asparagus	12.3	20.0	Oranges	8.4	6.8
Yautia	10.8	15.7	Natural Rubber	7.6	7.0
Buckwheat	4.9	7.5	Cherries	5.4	5.7
Potatoes	2.1	2.5	Chickpeas	5.2	7.2
Quince	1.8	2.0	Edible Mushrooms	3.8	4.9
Spinach	1.4	2.2	String Beans	2.8	3.1
Green Peas	0.7	1.0	Grapes	2.1	2.6
Alfalfa for Forage	0.5	0.8	Straw, Husks	0.6	0.8
Figs	0.4	0.6	Sugar Beets	0.1	0.1
Taro	0.1	0.2	Lettuce	0.0	0.0
Sweet Potatoes	0.1	0.2			

Source: Prepared on the basis of FAO data.

Mexican Crop Production

This analysis is limited to groups 1 and 2 of the selected crops or those that offer the greatest potential for international trade.

The following factors of production were considered:

1. Identification of the principal states that currently produce the selected crops, based on the 1980–1985 production periods or, alternatively, the location of states that do not grow the crops commercially but have the potential to do so. Table 6 lists these states. The regional analysis will facilitate the formulation of production policies that can be oriented toward states with the most serious unemployment problems, as indicated in Table 8.
2. The maximum area under production each year. This provides data on the existing capacity in various producing states (see Tables 6 and 7).
3. The maximum potential production area. This is the maximum

area under production in each state in any given year. This parameter is useful in identifying the shortfall between maximum and minimum land usage, so that the maximum usage can serve as the production objective (see Table 6, col. 3).

4. Labor demand estimates, measured in increments in days worked per hectare. The figure varies according to the type of crop grown. It can be used to measure total labor demand for any given crop when production is increased to reach a region's maximum potential (see Table 6, cols. 2 and 3).

Mexico has the potential to increase its export production of the crops selected for this study, particularly given the wide variety that are already grown and the extent of the land already under cultivation. At present, Mexico's cultivated area for the crops selected is about one million hectares. There is potential for increasing this to 1.25 million hectares, as Table 7 indicates.

Impact on Rural Employment

Mexico's current production is not entirely destined for external market, nor should it be, given the need to satisfy domestic demand. The latter is strong enough to allow Mexico to increase agricultural production by at least the differential between the maximum cultivated area and the maximum potential area—roughly 250,000 hectares. This would also prompt an increase in labor demand, which would translate into 14,547,494 man-days, as shown in Table 7.

Increases in production for export could be targeted at states with the greatest employment needs in both the agricultural sector and the general economy. Nearly all selected export crops can be grown in the states with the greatest employment and migration problems, namely, Zacatecas, Guanajuato, Michoacán, Jalisco, Oaxaca and Guerrero.

Increased production could also significantly alleviate some of the urgent need for foreign exchange, so essential to economic growth. Mexico's economic problems are structural, and solutions must also be structural in nature. The agricultural sector has traditionally played, and will continue to play, an important role here.

Summary

By creating jobs in rural areas, Mexico can alleviate a national economic problem that demands priority attention. The lack of agricultural employment gives rise to a series of problems, including contraction of food production and supply-diminishing agricultural outputs, inability of rural populations to purchase industrial products, mass migration of rural populations to urban areas, the need to import food products (with the accompanying loss of foreign exchange) and disproportionate growth of

TABLE 6

MEXICAN PRODUCTION OF CROPS WITH POTENTIAL IN THE WORLD MARKETS, GROUP 1
(EMPLOYMENT OUTLOOK)

Crops	Principal Producing States	Max. Area Produced	Max. Potential Area	Days/ Hect.	Diff. Max.-Pot.	Potential Employment
Buckwheat	OAX, MEX, GTO, TLAX, MOR					
Potatoes	PUE, MEX, VER, CHIH, SIN, GTO, MICH, SON, BC, TLAX, NL, COAH, CHIS, DGO, HGO	81,845	97,644	54.6	1,579	862,625
Sweet Potatoes	MICH, JAL, GTO, GRO, YUC, CHIH, BCS, VER, MEX, ZAC	3,502	5,503	79.8	2,001	159,679
Yautia	TAB					
Taro	TAB, OAX, YUC, CHIS, JAL, VER					
Chestnuts	BCN, BCS					
Linseed	GTO, SON, JAL, TAM, SIN	6,326	6,326	4.7		
Asparagus	GTO, BCN, SON, NL, QRO, COAH, MICH	6,934	6,934			
Spinach	DF, PUE, GTO, TLAX, BCN, CHIS, DGO	698	1,375	677		
Green Peas	MEX, SON, PUE, SIN, GTO, VER, DF, JAL, TAM, OAX, MICH, QRO, ZAC, TLAX, BCN, HGO	20,083	27,273	122.1	7,190	877,899
Mandarins and Tangerines	VER, SLP, NL, YUC, TAM, JAL, SIN, OAX	15,288	17,324	65.0	2,036	132,340
Grapefruit	GRO, VER, NL, SIN, OAX, TAB, TAM, SLP, MICH, JAL, MEX, YUC, PUE	14,866	15,448	582		
Quince	CHIH, ZAC, JAL, SON, GTO, MICH, PUE, VER		1,556	1,556		
Figs	TAM, SON, OAX, TAB, CHIS					
Alfalfa	GTO, CHIH, HGO, PUE, DGO, SON, MEX, BCN, QRO, BCS, COAH, OAX, JAL, MICH, SLP, TLAX, AGS, NL, SIN, ZAC, VER, MOR	259,966	349,012	47.6	89,046	4,238,589
Hops	CHIH, NL	18	18	40		
Pepper	TAB, VER, OAX	1,794	1,834			

GROUP 2

Crops	Principal Producing States	Max. Area Produced	Max. Potential Area	Days/Hect.	Diff. Max.-Pot.	Potential Employment
Barley	COAH, HGO, NL, ZAC, VER, CHIH, GTO, MICH, TLAX, SLP, QRO	28,414	46,639	8.2	18,225	149,445
Sugar Beets	DF, PUE, YUC, GTO	318	415	97		
Broad Beans, dry	PUE, MEX, TLAX, VER, MICH, DF, HGO, ZAC, OAX, MOR, QRO, GTO	47,319	60,376	26.3	13,057	343,399
Chickpeas for human cons.	JAL, SON, SIN, BCS, OAX, SLP, MICH, TAM, GRO, BCN	93,996	137,208	28.6	43,212	1,235,863
Walnuts	MEX, TLAX, PUE, DF, QRO, DGO, MICH, OAX, CHIH, ZAC	954	954	36.6		
Lettuce	PUE, BCN, JAL, SLP, GTO, SON, HGO, DF, CHIS, QRO, SIN, MICH, MEX, ZAC, DGO	5,202	6,894		1,692	
Green Beans	SIN, MOR, TAM, PUE, JAL, GRO, MICH, SON, OAX	9,146	10,673		1,527	
Edible Mushrooms						
Plantains	VER, COL, CHIS, TAB, NAY, OAX, MICH, GRO, JAL, PUE	87,194	99,291	97.6	12,097	1,180,667
Oranges	VER, NL, SLP, TAM, YUC, TAB, HGO, SON, PUE, CHIS, OAX, COAH, QR, MEX, SIN, JAL	181,165	221,254	96.8	40,089	3,880,615
Cherries	CHI, ZAC	200	215	15		
Peaches and Nectarines	ZAC, CHIH* MEX, JAL, SON, AGS, NL, PUE, GRO, QRO, VER, OAX, SLP, GTO, MOR, NAY	38,195	46,594	90.0	8,399	755,910
Blueberries	JAL, HGO, VER, OAX					
Grapes	SON, AGS, BCN, ZAC, COAH, QRO, DGO, BCS, GTO, CHIH, SLP, JAL	76,995	79,528	127.3	2,533	322,450
Straw, Husks Natural Rubber	VER, OAX, TAB, CHIS	12,531				

Source: S.A.R.H.; Agricultural data 1987.

TABLE 7

EMPLOYMENT GENERATION THROUGH THE PRODUCTION OF CROPS WITH POTENTIAL IN WORLD MARKETS (GROUPS 1 & 2)

Crops	Maximum Area Produced	Maximum Potential Area	Days Per Hectare	Diff. Between Max/Pot	Employment in Maximum Area	Employment in Potential Max. Area	Potential Employment Demand
1. Alfalfa	259,966	349,012	47.6	89,046	12,374,381	16,612,971	4,238,589
2. Oranges	181,165	221,254	96.8	40,089	17,536,772	21,417,387	3,880,615
3. Chickpeas for human cons.	93,996	137,208	28.6	43,212	2,688,285	3,924,148	1,235,863
4. Plantains	87,194	99,291	97.6	12,097	8,510,134	9,690,801	1,180,667
5. Green Peas	20,083	27,273	122.1	7,190	2,452,134	3,330,033	877,899
6. Potatoes	81,845	97,644	54.6	15,799	4,468,737	5,331,362	862,625
7. Peaches and Nectarines	38,195	46,594	90.0	8,399	3,437,550	4,193,460	755,910
8. Broad Beans, dry	47,319	60,376	26.3	13,057	1,244,489	1,587,888	343,399
9. Grapes	76,995	79,528	127.3	2,533	9,801,463	10,123,914	322,450
10. Green beans[1]	9,146	10,673	122.1	1,527	1,116,726	1,303,173	186,446
11. Sweet Potatoes	3,502	5,503	79.8	2,001	279,459	439,139	159,679
12. Barley for forage/silage	28,414	46,639	8.2	18,225	232,994	382,439	149,445
13. Mandarins and Tangerines	15,288	17,324	65.0	2,036	993,720	1,126,060	132,340
14. Lettuce[6]	5,202	6,894	55.2	1,692	287,150	380,548	93,398
15. Spinach[1]	698	1,375	122.1	677	85,225	167,887	82,661

16. Grapefruit[2]	14,886	15,448	65.0	582	966,290	1,004,120	37,830
17. Pepper[4]	1,794	1,834	97.2	40	174,376	178,264	3,888
18. Sugar Beets[5]	318	415	33.5	97	10,653	13,902	3,249
19. Cherries[7]	200	215	35.7	15	7,140	7,675	5,385
20. Asparagus	6,934	6,934	122.1		846,641	846,641	
21. Quince[3]	1,556	1,556	57.0		88,692	88,692	
22. Walnut	954	954	36.6		34,916	34,916	
23. Linseed	6,326	6,326	4.7		29,732	29,732	
24. Buckwheat							
25. Figs							
26. Taro							
27. Edible Mushrooms							
28. Blueberries							
29. Straw, Husks							
30. Yautia							
31. Hops	18	18					
32. Chestnuts							
33. Natural Rubber	12,531	12,531					
Total	994,505	1,252,819		258,314	67,667,667	14,547,494	

Note: The days/hectare are taken as follows:

[1]Similar to chichpeas. [5]Similar to peanuts.
[2]Similar to mandarins. [6]Similar to onions.
[3]Similar to mangos. [7]Similar to olives.
[4]Similar to cocoa beans.

Source: S.A.R.H., Agricultural data, 1987.

TABLE 8

POPULATION AVAILABILITY, EMPLOYMENT, AND MIGRATION BY STATE

Population	Rate of Growth	Total EAP	Rural Population	Agricultural EAP	Migration to USA	Underemployment (by percent)
1. Mexico	1. Quintana Roo	1. D.F.	1. Oaxaca	1. Chiapas	1. Chihuahua	1. Sinaloa
2. D.F.	2. Mexico	2. Mexico	2. Chiapas	2. Oaxaca	2. Michoacan	2. Zacatecas
3. Veracruz	3. Baja Calif. Sur	3. Veracruz	3. Hidalgo	3. Zacatecas	3. Baja Calif.	3. Durango
4. Jalisco	4. Campeche	4. Jalisco	4. Zacatecas	4. Guerrero	4. Jalisco	4. Chihuahua
5. Puebla	5. Aguascalientes	5. Puebla	5. Guerrero	5. Michoacan	5. Guanajuato	5. Nayarit
6. Guanajuato	6. Morelos	6. Guanajuato	6. Tabasco	6. Tabasco	6. Sonora	6. Baja Calif.
7. Michoacan	7. Sinaloa	7. Michoacan	7. Morelos	7. Hidalgo	7. Guerrero	7. Queretaro
8. Nuevo Leon	8. Queretaro	8. Nuevo Leon	8. Tlaxcala	8. Puebla	8. Zacatecas	8. Michoacan
9. Oaxaca	9. Nuevo Leon	9. Oaxaca	9. Nayarit	9. Veracruz	9. Oaxaca	9. Guerrero
10. Guerrero	10. Veracruz	10. Chiapas	10. Puebla	10. Nayarit	10. Durango	10. Sonora
11. Chiapas	11. Yucatan	11. Guerrero	11. Veracruz	11. S. L. P.	11. D.F.	11. Morelos
12. Sinaloa	12. Coahuila	12. Chihuahua	12. S. L. P.	12. Durango	12. Coahuila	12. B. Calif. Sur
13. Tamaulipas	13. Colima	13. Tamaulipas	13. Durango	13. Campeche	13. Sinaloa	13. Jalisco
14. Chihuahua	14. Tabasco	14. Sinaloa	14. Michoacan	14. Yucatan	14. San Luis Potosi	14. Mexico
15. S. L. P.	15. Puebla	15. S. L. P.	15. Queretaro	15. Sinaloa	15. Nayarit	15. Coahuila

16. Coahuila
17. Hidalgo
18. Sonora
19. B. Calif.
20. Durango
21. Yucatan
22. Tabasco
23. Zacatecas
24. Morelos
25. Queretaro
26. Nayarit
27. Aguascalientes
28. Tlaxcala
29. Campeche
30. Colima
31. Quintana Roo
32. B. Calif. Sur

16. San Luis Potosi
17. Guerrero
18. Chiapas
19. Sonora
20. Tlaxcala
21. Baja Calif.
22. Jalisco
23. Guanajuato
24. Hidalgo
25. Tamaulipas
26. Michoacan
27. D.F.
28. Nayarit
29. Durango
30. Chihuahua
31. Oaxaca
32. Zacatecas

16. Hidalgo
17. Coahuila
18. Sonora
19. Baja Calif.
20. Yucatan
21. Durango
22. Morelos
23. Tabasco
24. Zacatecas
25. Queretaro
26. Nayarit
27. Tlaxcala
28. Aguscltes.
29. Campeche
30. Quintana Roo
31. Colima
32. B. Calif. Sur

16. Sinaloa
17. Campeche
18. Guanajuato
19. Colima
20. Aguascalientes
21. Yucatan
22. Sonora
23. Quintana Roo
24. Chihuahua
25. Baja Calif. Sur
26. Jalisco
27. Mexico
28. Tamaulipas
29. Coahuila
30. Baja Calif.
31. Nuevo Leon
32. D.F.

16. Quintana Roo
17. Colima
18. Queretaro
19. Guanajuato
20. Morelos
21. Sonora
22. Tlaxcala
23. Chihuahua
24. B. Calif. Sur
25. Jalisco
26. Aguascalientes
27. Tamaulipas
28. Coahuila
29. Mexico
30. Baja Calif.
31. Nuevo Leon
32. D.F.

16. Nuevo Leon
17. Mexico
18. Queretaro
19. Tamaulipas
20. Colima
21. Aguascalientes
22. Morelos
23. Puebla
24. Veracruz
25. Hidalgo
26. Yucatan
27. Chiapas
28. Tabasco
29. Baja Calif. Sur
30. Quintana Roo
31. Tlaxcala
32. Campeche

16. Tamaulipas
17. Guanajuato
18. Puebla
19. Colima
20. San Luis Potosi
21. Aguascalientes
22. Nuevo Leon
23. Hidalgo
24. Tlaxcala
25. Veracruz
26. D.F.
27. Tabasco
28. Oaxaca
29. Quintana Roo
30. Chiapas
31. Campeche
32. Yucatan

Source: S.A.R.H., Agricultural data, 1987.

the service sector, where the unemployed seek refuge.

To reactivate the economy, we recommend that strong support be provided for agricultural production. This implies a need to revitalize the agricultural sector. This would carry other benefits. It would help meet the ever-growing demand for agricultural products in both the domestic market, where demand and purchasing power have been constrained, and the external market. A second benefit would be in the lower rate of investment required by agriculture compared to industry, particularly given the sector's existing infrastructure for export production.

Since domestic demand is limited, agricultural reactivation should start with export production which, in turn, begins with a study of the possibilities of successful marketing. It is here that we hope to contribute criteria that will be useful in the design of an agricultural export policy.

Crops with Export Potential. Such an effort begins with the selection of crops that can be produced and promoted in Mexico and successfully marketed internationally. One way of identifying such crops is to observe international marketing trends in trade volumes and values. A product that will be successful in international markets can be defined as one that reflects a trend toward higher export volumes and values, where the rate of value increase is greater than that of volume increase. For such products, international prices tend to rise.

Price trends alone are not good indicators of exports. The international price of any given commodity may rise with a simultaneous drop in trade volume. This may result from either absence or saturation of the market or the existence of stable levels of production of high quality products within specialty markets with little room for expansion, as is the case with certain horticultural products. On the other hand, a trend toward higher trade volumes indicates better prospects for placing a product in the international market. If there is a simultaneous increase in value, the potential for improved prices is even greater. Nevertheless, a mere trend toward volume increases is not a sure indicator of success. If the value falls, the price is also likely to decline; or the decline in value may indicate that the international market is saturated.

Major Producers, Sellers and Buyers. After identifying the products with potential in the international market, we identified the countries that produce, export and import them. These transactions identify the competition for selected crops and indicate the demand response of other producing countries (with respect to the volume generated versus the total volume exported). By identifying the buyers of various agricultural products, Mexico should also be able to determine its geographic advantages and the potential for diversifying its agricultural markets.

Regional Production and Employment Generation. Finally, we identified producing regions where our selected export crops could be promoted and estimated the additional labor demand that would be generated by increasing agricultural output. Our work consisted of the following:

1. We calculated the growth rates of various export crops for the 1960–1987 period and then correlated that information with production rates for our 187 selected products.
2. We graphically represented these growth and production rates to observe crop behavior over the past several years and to detect behavior obscured by the growth rates.
3. We classified crops into three groups, of which Group 1 (with 17 products) represents those with the greatest export potential (see Tables 2, 3 and 4).
4. We identified the principal producing, exporting and importing countries for the selected crops and calculated their relative importance in terms of volume produced, exported and imported in 1987.
5. We determined the distribution, by state, of total population, as well as agricultural employment, unemployment and migration rates, to select potential producing states for the chosen crops. States with the most severe economic problems were given priority, as shown in Table 8.
6. We estimated the potential demand for rural employment that could be generated by raising production of the selected crops to the maximum potential area.
7. We prepared volume and value projections for production and exports for each selected crop through 1993. This depicted the potential demand and production increases.

Conclusions

Because the types of export crops grown in Mexico vary significantly, a variety of activities are needed to promote them in international markets. The crops we observed can be classified as follows:

1. Crops grown on a large scale that are already exported, such as grapefruit, green peas and grapes. These crops should be grown to the maximum extent possible since marketing channels have already been established. Furthermore, Mexico may be able to diversify markets for these products.
2. Crops grown on a large scale that are not exported in large quantities. These include potatoes, sweet potatoes, chickpeas, barley, lettuce, oranges and peaches. Potatoes and sweet potatoes also have the advantage of being able to grow in unirrigated areas.

These products show a potential for increased export production, which implies the need for a promotional campaign, as well as a search for markets and marketing mechanisms.

3. Crops produced only on small parcels of land, where the difference between current and potential production areas is minimal

or non-existent. Linseed, asparagus, spinach, tangerines, quince, broad beans, plantains and cherries fall into this category. Promotion of these products must be oriented toward both increased production and new markets and marketing channels.

4. Crops not currently grown in Mexico but that, nevertheless, show potential in both Mexico and in the international arena. These include buckwheat, chestnuts, pepper, mushrooms, blueberries (already in another category) and figs. They require production research and their production and marketing should be promoted.

5. Crops with international marketing potential produced in Mexico but currently grown in such small quantities that they must be imported: alfalfa, hops, quince (already in another category), sugar beets, walnuts and natural rubber.

Some areas require additional research, e.g., socioeconomic and political factors limiting export production in Mexico. This should find ways to encourage export production and, at the same time, determine how such production can redistribute income toward rural Mexico. This research must take into account producer organization, marketing structures that limit or promote integration into the international market and financing problems. It should also address the development of a promotional strategy for agricultural production, where priority is given both to regions of highest unemployment and those where natural resources can be maximized. This strategy must not promote crops that would displace current production. Its ultimate goal should be enhancement of the quality of life for rural populations.

Additional study is also needed on the international factors that might limit Mexican production. Among these are the current trend toward integrated common markets, which is part of the restructuring of world markets, the growing commercial protectionism in some countries and Mexico's present tendency to pass up many negotiating opportunities deriving from its position as a major international buyer.

III. PART II: METHODOLOGY AND RECOMMENDATIONS

This section evaluates a methodology that may be useful in formulating recommendations aimed at modifying current crop patterns in different areas of Mexico to enhance income and employment in the area studied-three Rural Development Districts (D.D.R.'s)[5] in the State of Zacatecas: Zacatecas (D.D.R. 182), Fresnillo (D.D.R. 183), and Jerez (D.D.R. 184).[6] In the context of the area's economic constraints and potential, this section assesses the viability of growing export crops identified in the previous section, with the goal of enhancing the likelihood that recommendations

contained in the current Policy of Integrated Rural Development be implemented by the state and federal governments.

Current agricultural production in these districts is analyzed in terms
of:

1. use and efficiency of productive resources;
2. crop composition and identification of the most feasible and
   advantageous combinations for generating income and
   employment;
3. productive resources for reorienting agricultural production; and
4. identification of crops with good export potential which also contribute to enhancing income and employment.

The importance of finding a feasible way to alter crop patterns from the
standpoint of income and job creation derives from the need to orient production in the medium- and long-terms toward agricultural products that
improve the profitability of agricultural activity.

The Problem

Parts I and II represent efforts to identify productive alternatives to the
problem of migration, starting with the assumption that one of the cata-
lysts for this phenomenon is the lack of job opportunities in rural areas.
Any employment promotion policy in the countryside, however, should
be productive in nature if the roots, rather than the symptoms, of the
problem are to be attacked. The question is, how can agro-exports contribute to the productive reactivation of rural areas? This must necessarily
take into account the low profitability of agricultural production—i.e.,
income-yielding alternatives must be found.

Part I identified 78 crops with favorable export prospects (i.e., international market demand) that would make it possible to reorient agricultural
output toward products with an existing market. This section seeks to
establish an alternative crop pattern that includes exportable products,
taking into account current production—particularly that of basic grains
—in the areas studied.

Nevertheless, any modification of crop patterns must also take several
conditions, such as the economic viability of the change, into account;
that is, it must determine which products will be most advantageous to
the region in terms of income and jobs. This requires a knowledge of the
current availability and use of resources to determine the potential for ef-
fecting changes toward income-yielding crops, including those for export, and to evaluate the impact of such change on rural employment.

Linear programming was used to identify feasible crop combinations
for reorienting agricultural production patterns as well as alternative uses
of resources. This method makes it possible to determine: the crop combinations and land area needed to maximize income; profit and job crea-

tion in each of the Districts under the present constraints of available land; the total number of times the crops are irrigated; the number of man-days and machine-hours used in the production of the crops grown in each District; and the amount of money spent on their production (variable costs).

Production in the Study Area

The State of Zacatecas is located in northern Mexico. It was selected because of the following characteristics (see Table 9):

1. Serious emigration problems, chiefly attributable to a lack of both attractive income and adequate job creation in rural areas, according to a diagnostic study conducted by the Program for Integral Rural Development (PRONADRI) district offices.
2. The need and the potential for implementing a crop diversification policy (48 crops are currently grown in the area).
3. The explicit intention of state and federal policy expressed in PRONADRI to undertake "medium- and long-term planning to include the possible diversification of crops that would reap greater benefits for producers."
4. The need to search for alternative income-yielding crops, particularly products destined for the export market. To deal with the Districts' problems and needs, the area's serious limitations (both agronomic and social) must be taken into account. Principal among these are:
   — the low level and poor distribution of precipitation, which implies the need for crops with a low demand for water;
   — a long frost period (this is advantageous to the production of fruit species that require a specific period of cold);
   — the limited availability of water for irrigation owing to improper use[7] by producers who employ inadequate irrigation practices, and an orientation toward crops with low profitability; this requires an exploration into alternative crops to reorient agricultural production; and
   — a lack of economic resources for infrastructure development and credit to producers. This requires an evaluation of current capital resource use and suggests the need to reorient it.

The study area selected has a total extension of 2,594,085 has., or 34.58 percent of the area of the State of Zacatecas. However, only 372,404 has. are used in agriculture (1989 figure)—i.e., 14.36 percent of the total— indicating under use of the land.

Most of the land used in agriculture is in unirrigated areas, which cover 279,355 has. (or 75 percent); 25 percent of the land is irrigated (Districts 182 and 183 have more irrigated land—30 and 25.5 percent, respectively). This points to a principal agronomic constraint in selecting alternative

TABLE 9

OBJECTIVES OF THE PROGRAM FOR INTEGRAL RURAL DEVELOPMENT (PRONADRI) FOR D.D.R.s 182, 183, & 184 IN ZACATECAS

General Aspects Problem: Insufficient job creation and lack of attractive income in rural areas—that is, lack of adequate absorption of excess rural labor.

Needs: To promote a policy to expand agricultural activities that encourage greater (and better*) resource use and changes in structural production to produce intensive labor absorption.

Objectives: "production, productivity, job creation, and social justice summarize the direction of the efforts to be undertaken in the coming years in a government-citizen relationship based on trust, . . ."

Constraints

D.D.R. #182
— Climate
— Period of frost
— Degeneration of subsoil
— Problems with crop production practices
— Failure to repair and maintain machinery
— Improper water use
— Labor shortages
— Low prices
— Inadequate and untimely credit

D.D.R. #183
— Topography
— Erratic precipitation
— Legal problems with land tenure
— Lack of timely economic resources
— Need to revise cost-benefit ratio
— Lack of medium- and long-term planning for regional crop selection
— Little crop diversification
— Inefficient use of water resources by producers

D.D.R. #184
— Topography
— Water shortage
— Poor use of irrigated area, owing to concentration of crops during spring and summer

Potential

D.D.R. #182
—Adaptation of vegetable and deciduous fruit species
—Resolution of agrarian problems
—Diversification of crops currently under production
—"Increased agricultural production, chiefly beans, vegetables, forage species and fruit crops, since these are the crops that generate more income for producers"
—Introduction of agricultural techniques and technology packages to modernize production systems

D.D.R. #183
—Exploitation of forest, forage, grazing and fruit crops
—Use of water runoff for agriculture
—"Creation of a production system to provide greater alternatives in the diversification of profitable crops"
—Increased production of basic foods to satisfy demand in the State, making rational use of potential

D.D.R. #184
—Adaptation of various crops: grapes, cotton, grains, legumes, vegetables, grasses and oleaginous species
—Increased food grain production, preferably beans and corn, boosting the productive capacity of campesinos living in unirrigated areas
—As a complement, increased vegetable, forage crop and fruit production
—Rational use of soil and water to extend agricultural frontiers; greater stress on the construction & rehabilitation of irrigation infrastructure support for basic grains, complementing them with vegetables, fruits and oleaginous species

Note: *Authors' addition.

Source: Programs for Integral Rural Development, 1987–1992, for Rural Development Districts 182 (Zacatecas), 183 (Fresnillo), and 184 (Jerez).

crops: the scarcity of water.

Of the agricultural products grown in the area, broadly classified as annuals and perennials, the latter have the greatest income yield: occupying just 7 percent of the area, they generate 20 percent of total crop value, yielding 2.94 pesos per peso invested. This is higher than the yield for annuals, although it should be borne in mind that this level of profit corresponds to a single year in production—that is, it does not take start-up costs into account (see Table 10).

This initial classification seems to indicate the need to promote perennial production. However, there remains the question of in what proportion and, especially, toward which specific crops should production be oriented. Further, what resources are currently available and how should they be used to direct production toward crops that yield greater benefits?

Production Alternatives with Resources Currently Available

The first step in this analysis is to study current production and determine how resources are used for a subsequent investigation of alternative crops through linear programming.

In the search for alternatives, we began with the assumption that a redistribution policy is really possible by maximizing income (to the extent that there is something to redistribute). Nevertheless, there is the possibility that what is good for the region is not good for the individual producer. Profit maximization, which implies greater net income for the producer, was also programmed into the search. Moreover, a program to maximize employment was designed to identify the crop combination that would generate the highest employment levels.

District 182. This District currently produces a total of 44 crops and, in this respect, is the most diversified of the three. Production covers a 144,722 ha. area, which generates an income of 287,078,509 thousand pesos. Its main feature, however, is a high concentration of land in a limited number of agricultural products (just five crops absorb 89 percent of the total area). These crops absorb most available resources—over 83 percent—but generate just 76 percent of the income. Through linear programming it was determined that:

1. For perennials, the cultivation of alfalfa, irrigated peaches, quince and grapes, in the proportions, would raise income from 23,645,822 to 26,956,790 thousand pesos. It should be pointed out that employment would fall by only 140,777 man-days (see Table 11).
2. Something similar happens with annuals, whose income from forage barley and potatoes alone jumps from 261,980 million pesos to 1,187,490 million pesos—a major difference. This production ratio substantially reduces employment, however, since

TABLE 10

RESOURCES USED IN THE PRODUCTION OF ANNUAL AND PERENNIAL CROPS
FOR THE THREE DISTRICTS AS A WHOLE
(percentages)

Crop	Area	Volume	Value	Cost	Man-Days	Irrig.	Mach.-Hrs.
Annuals	7	26.6	20.0	9.6	9.0	13.1	4.6
Perennials	93	73.4	80.0	90.4	91.0	86.0	95.4

Source: Table 2.

there is a surplus of 1,514,237 man-days (see Table 11).

3. For perennials, scarce resources are the total land available for production, the amount of irrigated land available, the amount of irrigation required and capital. For annuals, the only scarce resources are the amount of irrigation and machine-hours; land available for production, man-days and capital are in surplus; this means that there is a potential for cultivating other crops which, obviously, should include basic grains.

4. It is important to point out that the crops which maximize income in the area are precisely those which maximize profits, with the exception of grapes, which should be replaced by unirrigated peaches.

5. The crops that generate employment are those that also generate income—in this case, irrigated and unirrigated peaches and potatoes. Those would naturally be the most beneficial.

District 183. Thirty-nine crops are currently grown in this District, whose characteristics are similar to those of District 182. Land use is concentrated in a few agricultural products. The six main crops occupy 87 percent of the total land area; they are equally demanding of resources, absorbing over 80 percent of man-days, machine-hours and capital, as well as 58 percent of the irrigation. At the same time, they generate only 66 percent of the income.

Crop programming yielded the following results:

1. For perennials, growing only alfalfa and irrigated and unirrigated peaches in the proportions indicated in Table 5 would raise income from 28,071 million pesos to 34,133 million pesos. The employment level, however, would fall by 44,224 man-days (see Table 11).

2. For annuals, the production of forage maize and potatoes in the required proportions would considerably boost the level of income from 167,091 million pesos to 1,591 million pesos. However, employment would drop by more than 1.5 million man-days (see Table 11).

3. The crops that maximize income also maximize profit; that is, they are good for producers; only grapes should be replaced, in this case with unirrigated peaches.
4. Scarce resources in this case would be: for perennials, the land available for cultivation and the amount of irrigation required; for annuals, water and machine-hours. This leaves land, man-days, the amount of irrigation required and machine-hours available, and a surplus of both irrigated and unirrigated land, labor, and capital that could be used in the production of other crops.
5. With respect to employment-generating crops, irrigated and unirrigated peaches are among those that also generate income. Crops like these leave land available for other employment-generating crops, such as cauliflower and grapes.

District 184. With 32 crops currently recorded, this is the district with the least diversification. Of the three districts, however, it is the greatest producer of perennials. Its resources are highly concentrated, with five main crops absorbing 88.1 percent of the total land area, 84 percent of the man-days, 93 percent of machine-hours and 78 percent of the costs. These crops, however, produce just 48.5 percent of the District's income, a relatively low figure.

Crop programming yielded the following results:

1. For perennials, the production of irrigated and unirrigated peaches alone (increasing land area only for irrigated peaches) would raise income from 66,637 million pesos to 78,690 million pesos, while preserving current employment levels (see Table 11).
2. For annuals, just forage oats and potatoes are recommended, which would raise income from 45,591 million pesos to 181,216 million pesos (see Table 11).
3. The crop combination that would maximize both employment and income is irrigated and unirrigated peaches.
4. Scarce resources are: for perennials, man-days and irrigated land; for annuals, the amount of irrigation required and capital. This leaves a surplus of resources that can be channeled toward other production.

The contradiction between the search for maximum income and higher employment levels should be noted since employment drops as income rises. The implications of an increase in profitability are obvious, hence, the need to encourage alternative activities to boost employment in rural areas.

Export Crop Potential

None of the basic grains (principally maize, beans and wheat) were selected as possible alternatives by the income and employment-maximization models. Therefore, the use of surplus resources for their pro-

TABLE 11

OPTIMUM PATTERNS FOR INCOME GENERATION

Selected Crops	Area Planted With Current Pattern	Area Planted With Optimum Pattern	Value of Production With Current Pattern	Value of Production With Optimum Pattern	Resource Use With The Optimum Pattern
District 182— Perennials			23,645,822	26,956,790	2) area
Alfalfa	394	1,030			3) water 4) 14,077 man-days
Irrig. Peaches	180	522			5) 25,801 Mach.-hrs. 6) capital
Quince	2	296			7) irrig. area
Grapes	862	4,904			
District 182— Annuals			261,980,018	1,187,480,000	3) water 2) 39,852.8 has.
Unirrig. Forage Barley	512	74,075			4) 1,514,237 man-days
Potatoes	506	24,043			5) mach.-hrs. 6) 13,813,000 thous. Mex. $
					7) 15,837.5 has.
District 182— Total			285,625,840	1,310,268,000	3) water 2) 33,315.6 has.
Unirrig. Peaches	3,830	16,659			5) mach.-hrs. 4) 1,319,395 man-days
Unirrig. Forage Barley	506	68,724			6) capital 7) 15,837.5 has.
Potatoes	506	26,022			
District 183— Perennial			28,071,166	34,133,660	2) area 4) 44,224.5 man-days
Alfalfa	377	1,565			3) water 5) 34,193.8 mach.-hrs.
Irrig. Peaches	117	1,004			7) mach.-hrs. 6) 137,016 thous. Mex. $
Unirrig. Peaches	3,491	3,491			
District 183—Annuals			167,091,369	1,591,937,000	3) water 2) 69,722.6 has.
Unirrig. Forage Maize	825	68,439			5) mach.-hrs. 4) 1,640,636 man-days
Potatoes	57	26,582			6) 3,504.763 thous. Mex. $
					7) 7,643 has.

Item	(1)	(2)	(3)	(4)	Constraints
District 183—Total			195,162,536	1,721,386,000	2) 49,386 has. 4) 1,732,714 man-days 6) 318 thous. Mex. $ 7) 6,490 has. 3) water 5) mach.-hrs.
Unirrig. Forage Maize	825	64,530			
Potatoes	57	30,304			
District 184—Perennial			66,637,599	78,690,390	2) 936.7 has. 3) 11,243.5 times irrig. 5) 15,414.5 mach.-hrs. 6) 181,881 thous. Mex. $ 4) man-days 7) irrig. area
Irrig. Peaches	2,685	4,767			
Unirrig. Peaches	8,144	7,654			
District 184—Annuals			45,591,983	181,216,600	2) 21,865.7 has. 4) 954,817.3 man-days 5) 943,438.1 mach.-hrs. 7) 4,653.6 has. 3) water 6) capital
Unirrig. Forage Oats	5,062	43,260			
Potatoes	2	4,973			
District 184—Total			112,229,582	308,071,600	2) 44,709.7 has 4) 518,938.7 man-days 5) 1,320,627 mach.-hrs. 3) water 6) capital 7) irrig. area
Irrig. Peaches	2,685	9,964.2			
Unirrig. Peaches	8,144	24,356			
Potatoes	2	4,429.8			

Note: 2) Total available land area
3) No. times irrigated
4) man-days utilized
5) machine-hours
6) Production costs (capital)
7) Irrigated land area available

Source: Programming results.

duction is a possibility. There is also the problem of marketing the surplus deriving from augmented production of the selected crops. This brings up the issue of export crop promotion—that is, where could such crops be produced (see Table 11) and where could the surplus deriving from changes in crop patterns be marketed?

In this respect, 30 of the 78 crops with favorable export prospects are currently grown in the study area (26 in District 182, 22 in District 183, and 20 in District 184). Ten were selected as maximizers of income, profit, or employment (see Table 12).

Marketing channels for surplus agricultural products are needed to encourage production of export crops which would not only generate foreign exchange and benefit the entire zone, to the degree that the crops are income maximizers. Most of the crops selected (especially alfalfa, barley, peaches, quince, potatoes and grapes) belong to Group 1 or 2 and have the greatest export potential in terms of volume and price. Coupled with declining world production (Group 1) and stabilizing production (Group 2), competition in the external market would not be too overwhelming.

Promotion of the crops selected should be a short-term measure. From a medium- and long-term perspective, concentrating production in just a few crops is counterproductive because of their vulnerability to changing market conditions. An effort should, therefore, be made to increase production of other crops with good export potential for which natural production conditions already exist. One possibility is shown in Table 12, which lists crops with the above characteristics. The table also provides data on the income level per hectare that should be attained before attempting to use these products to change or displace current crop patterns and become part of the income-maximization effort. We recommend those that require a proportionally lower level of income-generation (based on current income per hectare) and that may be promoted in the District which meets this condition.

Implementation of a Change in Crop Patterns: Potential and Constraints

The first constraint on any concrete change in crop patterns toward those selected by the models derives from the nature of this study. This research is essentially an analysis of economic alternatives, of better uses of resources in the study zone, which sets aside the agronomic problem that the recommended changes would imply. Our recommendations are therefore indicative in nature. Despite this constraint, we believe that the information provided will help orient agricultural planning in a more income-yielding direction.

A second constraint is the difficulty of marketing agricultural production since the producer must face a host of problems, e.g., strong price variations resulting from over-supply at certain times of the year, lack of

TABLE 12

INCOME AND EMPLOYMENT GENERATING CROPS PRODUCED IN DISTRICTS 182, 183 AND 184 OF ZACATECAS WHICH HAVE FAVORABLE EXPORT OUTLOOKS

District 182 Surface Crops hectares	District 183 Surface Crops hectares	District 184 Surface Crops hectares
394 Alfalfa[1] I,G	377 Alfalfa[1] I,G	2,685 Irrig. Peaches[2] I,G,E/I
512 Unirrig. Barley I,G	1 Cauliflower[3] E,E/I	8,144 Unirrig. Peaches[2] I,G,E/I
10,878 Dry Chillies[3] I,E,E/I	117 Irrig. Peaches[2] I,E,E/I	2 Potatoes[1] I,G
69 Cauliflower[3] E,E/I	3,491 Unirrig. Peaches[2] I,G,E/I	227 Vid[2] E,E/I
180 Irrig. Peaches[2] I,G,E/I	1,206 Vid[2] E,E/I	
2 Quinces[1] I,G		
1,074 Nopal T. E,I		
506 Potatoes[1] I,G,E/I		
862 Vid[2] I		

Note: I) Crops selected for income generating model.
G) Crops selected for earning generating model.
E) Crops selected for employment generating model.
E/I) Crops selected for employment and income generating model.
[1]Group I crops with export potential.
[2]Group II crops with export potential.
[3]Group III crops with export potential.

financing, heavy presence of intermediaries and lack of marketing organization. In other words, the main difficulty lies in marketing the production,[8] since the market is highly uncertain, owing to a lack of buyers, drastic price fluctuations and high transportation costs (especially for vegetables). Production, therefore, should be initially oriented toward the consolidation of markets to make change possible.

The third constraint is the low or non-profitability of basic grains, which were not selected by the models. Alternative crops should, therefore, be found and surplus resources and support measures used to stimulate their production.[9]

Conclusions

Changes in crop patterns toward higher income-yielding products have a negative impact on employment levels. In most cases, such changes lead to job losses; hence, surplus resources should be used to promote employment-generating crops. Resources for production in the zones studied are highly concentrated in beans, maize, peppers, peaches and oats. These crops account for over 80 percent of the area in production in the three districts. However, their share of the value generated is far less.

While searching for alternative uses of resources, it was found that greater regional income can be generated with fewer resources but more crop variety (assuming that surplus resources are available in all the models for all crops. Basic grains are not among these, however, a problem that should be addressed through other measures.

This alternative pattern includes ten crops with good export prospects selected in Part I. It addresses the issues posed by the Program for Integral Rural Development concerning the promotion of medium- and long-term planning for agricultural production, the search for crops with higher income yields and the scarcity of resources, from water to capital, within the study areas.

The study areas currently produce 32 crops that, though not selected by the models, show good export potential. They could be promoted as part of a crop diversification policy that would make it possible to address the price fluctuations inherent in the international market (see Table 10). Some crops with good export potential are not presently grown in the Districts. The possibility of cultivating these products should be explored.

The main problem facing agriculture, and any change in crop patterns, is marketing, i.e., where to sell. Therefore, official support efforts should concentrate on establishing contacts in the external market, diversifying markets whenever possible.

One alternative is to obtain futures contracts for agricultural production.

Studies should be undertaken to evaluate how producers' associations could be integrated into the process of modifying crop patterns. Ways should also be sought to promote income redistribution that could result from changes in crop patterns, since raising average income levels will not necessarily redistribute income.

Our analysis should be expanded in further studies to include other dimensions we did not address. These studies should:

1. use historical price and yield series to provide greater support for their conclusions; and
2. take international price levels into account to derive potential income per hectare. This would help orient production toward exports and indicate possible marketing margins, as well as permit the integration of new crops into an optimum pattern.

Similar studies should be conducted in other parts of Mexico to orient production toward certain crops that are not profitable in some areas.

NOTES

1. Banco de México, *Requerímientos de financiamiento externo para la economía mexicana en crecimiento* (Mexico City, 1989).

2. *El Financiero*, 17 January 1989, p. 23.

3. We abstracted existing conditions in the international context.

4. Information on 187 crops provided by FAO for 1960–1987 (magnetic tape).

5. Rural Development Districts are the basic operational units of the programs organized and implemented by the federal government and the states in behalf of rural areas.

6. These were chosen as the most important in terms of their potential for agricultural development.

7. Ruvalcaba Limon, Domingo. "Uso y Manejo del Agua de Riego en Zacatecas." Professional Thesis, Chapingo, Mexico.

8. SARH. "Comercialización Agropecuaria en Zacatecas." Mimeo.

9. Measures under consideration in the present Program for Rural Modernization currently promoted by the government.

10

Tourism and Absorption of the Labor Force in Mexico

Daniel Hiernaux Nicolas
and Manuel Rodríguez Woog

I. TOWARD A REDEFINITION OF TOURISM

Tourism is defined in a variety of ways.[1] Because of the many variables that affect the phenomenon, most characterizations are neither sufficient nor comprehensive. Many models of tourism lack a theoretical basis, which has led authors such as Aramberri to charge that "the phenomenon of tourism continues to be poorly understood and even more poorly theorized."[2]

There are three basic approaches to studying tourism: the statistical, the marketing-oriented and the sociological. The first is based on the analysis of statistics gathered according to the World Tourism Association definition: the ". . . tourist is the visitor who spends at least a night but no more than a year in the chosen country and whose principal motive is pleasure, business or some other tourist endeavor."[3] This definition basically attempts to standardize the criteria and methods for measuring the phenomenon on an international scale, for comparison purposes. An additional, complementary definition is that of the "international visitor," the person who is visiting a country other than that of his permanent residence. The latter includes two categories: the international tourist who fits the earlier definition and the international excursionist, i.e., the traveler who crosses the border but remains less than 24 hours in the country visited. These definitions, however widely disseminated, are ambiguous, both with respect to the nature of the tourist's trip and the quantification problems created; this is particularly true in the case of Mexico.[4]

In contrast, marketing studies define tourism as a demand for services associated with transportation, lodging, food, recreational activities, etc.[5] In its economic, social, political, cultural and environmental context, this mode of analysis results in an extremely selective treatment of the activities related to the trip, whether for tourism or other purposes. In other words, this viewpoint reduces tourism to its strictly commercial aspect.

Sociological studies introduce another dimension into the analysis of tourism: the linkage with leisure and free time. This, rather than the simple purchase of services, is the heart of tourism. Sociological studies include anthropological and political science analyses with a broad spectrum of approaches that range from radical criticism of tourism because it tends to alienate the indigenous population, to identification of tourism as a manifestation of a new society "the global village."

Our position, which has been detailed in several publications,[6] can be summarized very briefly. Tourism is, first of all, a concept found in modern societies. While economic analyses have underscored its economic impact, it should be considered essentially a societal phenomenon. Tourism is a social reality, a manifestation of social behavior adopted by the majority of social sectors in developed societies and by a substantial portion of the middle and upper-classes of developing countries.

Tourism reflects new needs within the population, whether spontaneous or media-induced through advertising. Tourism is also a potent stimulus to economic activity. It should be stressed that our position differs sharply from that of those who subscribe to the marketing viewpoint, which confuses tourism with its manifestations. We consider tourism a social phenomenon, which therefore creates demand in diverse areas of the economy, generates growth of productive units to satisfy this demand, and helps to establish certain models of domestic and international economic activity, but which can in no way, however, be considered an economic activity in itself.[7] Tourism also serves as a stimulus to new social relationships, environmental changes and modifications in political relations among countries. These dimensions are as important as the economic features of tourism.

Tourism has to be related with issues like leisure and free time and must therefore be analyzed as one of the socially acceptable and economically induced ways of occupying free time. In our work, we stress both the economic essence of tourism as well as its geographic impact. This orientation, though influenced by sociological and spatial considerations, does not downplay the existence of other dimensions or the need for other, complementary approaches to the topic.

II. THE MEXICAN TOURISM MODEL

Tourism in Mexico is a complex phenomenon involving the many factors previously mentioned. The evolution of the key characteristics of tourism (occupation, investment, etc.), overlap extensively, and this overlapping constitutes a true "Mexican tourism model." This model does not preclude contradictions in the historical development of tourism or existing antagonisms among its agents, nor does it overlook significant questions about the future of Mexican tourism. It suggests that a "certain" vision of tourism has gradually been imposed on the country and assimilated by most social and economic sectors involved in the activities.

In developing a comprehensive view of the Mexican tourism model, the historical development of tourism in Mexico should be taken into account.[8] First, the evolution of tourism has been intimately linked to economic development in the United States during the post-World War II period. In its initial phase, an increasing number of foreign tourists entered Mexico. From 1949 to 1959, the annual figure rose from 323,000 to 746,000.[9] Most came from the United States. During that decade, Mexico made a tangible effort to develop its highway network, and provided access to the main tourist centers of Veracruz and Acapulco, as well as to Mexico City, the site of fine pre-Colombian ruins and a rich colonial heritage.

During the 1970s, the foundations were laid for the eventual evolution of the current Mexican tourism model. This decade coincided with the emergence of "golden hordes" of developed country tourists.

The Great Tourist Flows

Except during certain periods, the influx of international tourists has continued to grow. About 4.78 million foreign visitors arrived in 1983, increasing to 5.69 million in 1988. This growth resulted from the undervaluation of the peso, a resurgence in the U.S. economy, and an easing of the regulations that govern both the entry of foreign capital into Mexico and the provision of some tourist services, particularly airlines, according to the liberalization of the Mexican economy.

Visitors from the United States account for 85 percent of the country's total inbound tourism. Mexico, together with Canada and Europe, constitutes one of the more attractive destinations for the U.S. tourist. Mexico benefits from a significant location advantage for U.S. tourists, similar to that of Spain with respect to Northern Europe.[11] However, in contrast to Spanish tourism, where travel occurs chiefly by land, 67.2 percent of Mexico's international visitors in 1987 used air travel as the principal mode of transport, compared with only 55 percent in 1977.

Various developments explain this situation. They include the increasing popularity of mass access to air transport through the introduction of charter flights and the growing role of tour operators in the global demand for services. The latter provide low-cost packages that include transportation, hotel accommodations, food and, occasionally, recreational services.

Although Mexico enjoys locational advantages, vast tracts of northern Mexico offer no particular attractions and constitute natural barriers for U.S. and Canadian travelers. The intimidating prospect of having to cross these vast, inhospitable distances in a private vehicle has consequently served as an inducement to fly. Therefore, it is unrealistic to imagine that Mexico will achieve the levels of inbound tourism attained by Spain, which benefits from an urban continuum and major tourist attractions that start at its border with France.

To complete the overview, tourist flows from two other sources must be considered: domestic tourism and outbound tourism (Mexicans traveling outside the country). The propensity of Mexicans to travel abroad is intimately linked to their domestic economic situation. The oil boom years facilitated the outward flow of Mexican tourists, whose numbers reached 3.96 million in 1981. One result was an unexpected deficit in the tourism balance. In 1982, the volume of outbound tourists fell drastically. As a result, the tourism foreign exchange balance recovered. There is always a latent tendency for outbound tourism to increase.[12] This depends on middle class purchasing power, since the middle class—the dominant social stratum in this type of tourism—is highly influenced by consumption patterns in developed countries. The 1988 statistics show a 19 percent increase in outbound tourism.

Domestic tourism, by contrast, is a complex phenomenon whose official measurement is imprecise. In 1987, an estimated 33.7 million domestic tourists used hotels—the equivalent of about one-half of the nation's population. This measurement is approximate, since the frequency of travel is not known. Moreover, it is highly probable that domestic tourism is under recorded. Characteristics of the country—such as the high percentage of urban population of recent rural extraction and the maintenance of strong family ties—suggest that major contingents of leisure travellers seldom use tourist services and facilities, making it difficult to document their number.

Domestic tourism has largely been channeled toward the principal metropolitan centers—Mexico City, Guadalajara and Monterrey, which welcomed 6.1 million domestic travelers in 1987; beach resorts such as Acapulco, with an influx of 1.2 million domestic tourists; and other tourist centers in the interior. The latter have been gaining importance as alternate tourist destinations in response to the country's economic crisis.

Economic Impact of Tourism

One of the variables used to measure the impact of tourism on the economy is the money spent by the tourist. The amount of money spent, in turn, is influenced by a tourist's length of stay. The average length of stay in Mexico decreased from 12.3 days in 1970 to 9.7 days in 1987. The decline has been gradual and is similar to travel patterns in developed countries. It reflects a growing tendency to take a greater number of trips for shorter periods, to take winter vacations, or to take advantage of the gradual elimination of vacation constraints imposed by the school calendar as birth rates decline.

The average daily expenditure of the foreign tourist in Mexico shows a strong increase, rising from $15 in 1979 to $43 in 1987. There is a significant difference between tourism by land, where the tourist takes more time to travel but spends far less per day, and tourism by air, where the length of stay is briefer but the daily expenditure greater. However, the average daily expenditure is clearly below what is needed to defray the cost of tourist services. There are two possible explanations for this: expenditures, and therefore the tourism balance, are underestimated; or, a sizable portion of travel costs are paid in advance to tour operators outside the country. In this case, local expenditures would be additional expenses incurred by tourists.

The average daily expenditure for outbound tourism is $37, which is not far below the $43 for inbound tourism. Outbound tourism generates a stay of 10.3 days when travel is by air, which is nearly two days more than the average for inbound tourism. This ratio is significant in explaining which social sectors are able to travel outside of Mexico.

Estimates by the Bank of Mexico indicate that tourism has traditionally generated a surplus in the balance of payments. In 1988, the surplus was $1.349 billion. This positive balance served as the chief official argument for assigning priority to the promotion of tourism.

The hotel trade and restaurants in Mexico contribute 3 percent of the gross domestic product (GDP). This figure, virtually constant since 1970, is an understatement in that it fails to include various related activities, such as transportation and recreational services. Furthermore, the impact can be more significant at the regional level, since certain states, such as Quintana Roo and Guerrero, are much more dependent on tourism for their gross product than the nation as a whole.

In terms of employment generation, official estimates indicate that the industry generated 522,000 direct and 1.3 million indirect jobs in 1987. We will return to these figures later.

State Involvement in Tourism

In recent years, the state, through an extensive regulatory framework, has played a decisive role in promoting tourism. This began with the inclusion of the term "tourist" in the country's population law and the subsequent development of various legal instruments to regulate the industry. Until a few years ago, however, the state neglected the formulation of a legal framework, but played a direct role in the development of tourist activities. Direct intervention took several forms. It included conducting publicity campaigns abroad to encourage tourism; direct intervention in the concept, design, construction, operation and promotion of tourist centers (Cancún, Ixtapa, Loreto, San José del Cabo and, more recently, Huatulco); direct investment in hotels and support for other projects; and finally, by obtaining international loans and channeling domestic investment toward credit lines managed by the *Fondo Nacional de Fomento al Turismo* (National Fund for The Promotion of Tourism—FONATUR) for hotel construction.

Basic Features of the Mexican Model and Its Recent Evolution

Tourism in Mexico is influenced by rising developed-country demand for tourist services; the growing internationalization of multinational corporations into hotel chains, airlines and major tour operators; the intensive modernization of hotel facilities to provide deluxe services; and the increase in technology which confers advantages to huge economic conglomerates over small, family-owned hotels. Despite the increase in the absolute number of visitors to Mexico and the fact that Mexico is the most significant and renowned tourist destination in Latin America, the country's share of world tourism was only 1.52 percent in 1987.[13]

International and domestic tourism are profoundly different. International tourists—even those with modest incomes—can obtain high levels of service at modest cost; domestic tourists, due to the economic crises, are increasingly unable to take advantage of high-quality facilities. Although such facilities are currently available and are used almost exclusively by foreign tourists, they generate sizable benefits to Mexico. The influx of foreign exchange is considerable; it is about the same as foreign exchange remitted by Mexicans working without documentation in the United States. Fixed capital investment in tourism facilities is substantial, although it has not been estimated either in this study or in official statistics. In view of these activity characteristics, there is the need to reach a broader understanding of tourism and its impact—not only from an economic perspective, but also from the social, political and environmental perspectives as well.

Mexico's tourism model is changing. First, there has been a renewed involvement of private investment, some from the corporate sector. The state, in line with its privatization policies, has increasingly stepped out of the picture; it has already withdrawn from the hotel industry and other direct investments. There are now more opportunities for foreign capital, which is benefitting from greater flexibility in the regulations that govern foreign companies and capital investment in Mexico. New projects (essentially private but with the blessing and indirect backing of the state) are spearheaded by the restructuring and, in all likelihood, the greater internationalization of tourism in Mexico. Other developments, such as the rapid growth of "time-sharing" projects and the opening of new air routes, create a changing picture in constant need of reevaluation.

III. TOURISM AND JOBS

The employment generated by tourism is significant and on the upswing. As the country struggles to emerge from its nearly decade-long economic crisis, it is important to clearly understand this source of job creation. The task is far from simple since the statistical sources for an analysis of job-creation in tourism are few and out of date. This study draws on hybrid sources: selective surveys, qualitative information and exploratory studies of specific aspects of the problem. Conclusions are therefore tentative and need further study.

Conceptualizing Tourism to Analyze Job Creation

The study of job creation through tourism involves the analysis of four main areas of activity and their economic interdependence.[14] These four areas are transportation, food, lodging and recreational activities. Their interdependence has led companies like Club Mediterranée, for example, to provide an integrated service encompassing all activity groups. Transportation and lodging serve as primary activities, with food and recreation subordinated to them.

In selecting a travel option, a tourist chooses services from each area. A personalized tourism sequence is created as a function of resources, social aspirations and the influence of advertising. In Mexico, an airline package, including deluxe hotel, meals and entertainment, has become increasingly important; whereas others activities—camping, for instance—is a less attractive option.

Tourism-generated employment can best be studied by focusing on each area of activity and by giving a different direct job creation weight to each facet of an activity. Each has a different multiplier for indirect employment as well as a differential impact on other areas. In the case of packaged tours, it is clear that the impact on job creation is greater in the preparation and organization of the trip in the tourist's home country than at the destination. It has also been shown that deluxe hotels do not generate as much employment as the traditional hotel industry under family management.

Direct and indirect employment are affected by a tourist's preconceived ideas about suitable trip sites and potential activities at the destination. Direct employment is understood to be jobs derived from the sale of goods or services to the tourist, while indirect employment is work generated in response to the demand created to support direct services.

An analysis of the manner in which job activities are related is a creative way of focusing on the issue of job creation. Unfortunately, little information is available for such studies. Nevertheless, we have made an attempt to separate tourism-related job creation into various activities, although it is not possible to integrate the data into the different related activity sequence.

The Contribution of "Input-Output" Analysis:
The Multiplier Effect on Employment in the Tourist Industry

This paper does not analyze the 1970, 1975 and 1980 input tables or discuss their methodological problems (although the main report to the Commission includes such analysis). The results, although relevant, are limited, mainly because tourism was not considered as such. In part, this is because output-input tables intuitively regard the tourist sector as a chain of activities. Some countries have attempted to elaborate an input-output tourism sub-matrix, but this has yet to be done for Mexico.[15] Our analysis is limited to the multiplier effects in two areas: hotels and restaurants. It is a partial analysis, of course, because it ignores recreational services, an essential facet of tourism, as well as transportation. In the longer version of this study, attention was devoted to these two sectors.

For every job created in hotels and restaurants, indirect employment increases over time. The 1970 input-output table shows an employment multiplier effect of 1.78 (one direct job generates 1.78 indirect jobs). The multiplier rises to 2.31 in 1975 and 2.81 in 1980. If this trend had continued, a current ratio of 1 to 3 would not be out of the question.

For its purposes, the Secretariat of Tourism uses a multiplier of 1.5, a value far below the one in our study. The official multiplier was obtained in studies FONATUR made of Cancún during the first phase of its development. This very limited case does not allow for induced demand, and hence, for the employment created in all sectors.

Our estimate may be overstated. Indeed, the data on hotels and restaurants include employment not necessarily related to tourism (salesmen, for example). In other areas that generate direct and indirect employment, however, such as personal services, amusement or transportation, there is definitely a tourist service component—one that we have not been able to differentiate. The multiplier effect, whether under- or overstated, is highly significant. Tourist activities generate considerable aggregate demand and substantial employment in almost all areas of the economy. Further, these are not isolated activities since they are open to influence from other sectors.

Estimating Direct Employment

Labor absorption by tourism is measured in this study through a 1986 job creation survey of the Secretariat of Tourism (SECTUR).[16] The data were reprocessed in order to assess regional differences.

We first classify tourist centers inventoried by SECTUR into eight categories based on different tourism variables, such as number of rooms, type of facility, local tourist attractions, etc. The classification also takes into account other complementary variables of a socioeconomic, demographic and spatial nature. (See Table 1). The patterns of these variables vary across categories, thus revealing interesting geographic differences.

The estimates also rely on a description of related activities derived from a variety of sources. These include a list of hotel facilities by number of rooms, category and location. The National Tourism telephone directory, which lists the producers of goods and services related to tourism, has also been used. All of these sources introduce methodological shortcomings. Businesses without phone service are not included, nor are the jobs created by constructing secondary residences, accommodations in

TABLE 1

CLASSIFICATION OF TOURIST CENTERS IN MEXICO

1. Historical	Guanajuato, Oaxaca, San Miguel de Allende, Taxco, Zacatecas.
2. Medium-sized Cities	Aguascalientes, Campeche, Coatzacoalcos, Colima, Córdoba, Cuernavaca, Chihuahua, Durango, Hermosillo, La Paz, León, Mérida, Minatitlán, Morelia, Orizaba, Pachuca, Poza Rica, Puebla, Querétaro, Saltillo, San Cristobal de las Casas, San Luis Potosí, Tampico, Tapachula, Tepic, Tlaxcala, Toluca, Tuxpan, Tuxtla Gutiérrez, Villahermosa, Xalapa.
3. Metropolitan Areas	Ciudad de México, Guadalajara, Monterrey.
4. Border Towns	Ciudad Juárez, Ensenada, Matamoros, Mexicali, Nuevo Laredo, Reynosa, San Felipe, Tijuana.
5. Traditional Beaches	Acapulco, Bahía Kino, Cozumel, Guaymas, Isla Mujeres, Manzanillo, Mazatlán, Puerto Vallarta, Veracruz.
6. Planned Beaches	Cancún, Ixtapa-Zihuatanejo, Los Cabos, Loreto.
7. Archeological & Cultural Sites	Chichén-Itzá/Uxmal, Palenque.
8. Spas and Recreational Sites	Catemaco, Cuautla, Fortín de las Flores, Ixtapan de la Sal, San Andrés Tuxtla, San Juan del Río, Tequisquiapan, Valle de Bravo.

Source: Authors' processing, based on miscellaneous sources.

family homes, and all other forms of informal lodging. Ours is an exploratory examination of a topic whose various complementary facets merit a more detailed assessment. These instruments also fail to capture the employment effects associated with nonhotel tourist lodgings (e.g., secondary residences, family homes).

The labor market survey conducted by SECTUR in 1986 lacks a conceptual basis. It contains a sample of 1,362 respondents distributed among 19 tourist centers throughout the country. With all of its limitations, it represents the best data base currently available. We reprocessed the survey by type of activity and by tourist center. The geographic breakdown diminishes the statistical representativeness of the findings as compared with the overall sample. The disaggregation, however, allows for a more revealing analysis than more global studies.

Table 2 presents employment indicators by type of activity and tourist center. In the hotel industry, the ratio of direct employment per room falls as the quality of hotel facilities declines. This may reflect the fact that lower-quality hotels do not offer related services, such as restaurants or bars, in addition to lodging. Such services are integrated into the direct employment ratio for the better hotels. The figures also reveal sharp differences in employment by type of tourist center. Total direct job creation can be estimated by relating the employment indicators to the number of

TABLE 2

EMPLOYMENT INDICATORS BY ACTIVITY

TYPE OF ACTIVITY	TYPE OF TOURIST CENTER							
	Hist.	Med.	Metro	Border	Trad. Bch.	Pl. Bch.	Arch'/ Cult.	Spa
Travel Agencies & Airlines	6.00	10.80	11.69	2.00	12.60	12.18	nd	nd
Car Rental	13.00	5.25	10.50	10.00	10.38	12.95	nd	nd
Boat & Motorcycle Rental	nd	nd	nd	nd	18.00	19.50	nd	nd
Taxis	15.00	25.00	73.63	nd	32.00	nd	nd	nd
Handicrafts & Boutiques	4.40	8.00	2.78	3.35	4.20	3.85	nd	nd
Miscellaneous Businesses	4.90	8.80	2.15	2.75	4.97	5.85	nd	nd
Restaurants & Bars	13.27	12.53	27.35	11.65	18.03	17.70	nd	nd
Related Misc. Services	11.90	9.07	20.70	20.20	13.30	10.10	nd	nd
Deluxe Hotels	na	na	1.15	na	1.70	1.55	na	na
5* Hotels	1.49	1.33	0.84	1.09	1.07	0.99	na	na
4* Hotels	0.92	0.83	0.54	1.35	1.15	0.83	na	na
3* Hotels	0.41	0.91	0.26	0.30	0.54	0.68	na	na
2* Hotels	0.44	0.26	0.23	0.21	0.27	0.63	na	na
1* Hotels	0.27	0.19	0.18	0.23	0.34	0.23	na	na

Source: Authors' processing, based on the Tourism Labor Market Survey, SECTUR, 1986.
Note: It is important to point out that the data on hotels is computed per room and not
        per facility, whereas in the other cases, businesses and services, the data corre-
        sponds to companies or facilities as a whole.
nd.: no data; na.: not applicable

business concerns.

Table 3 presents the results of these calculations. Information was not
available for employment by airlines and other modes of transportation.
Nevertheless, 658,056 jobs were directly created in 1988. This figure is derived by applying the 1986 ratios to the figures on number of enterprises
in 1988 on the assumption that no changes had occurred in the interven-
ing years.

The 658,056 jobs created in 1988 are 25 percent above SECTUR's estimates. Our estimating technique appears to be more precise than official
methods. It includes a greater number of activities in the linked tourism
sequence and is based on data from more recent surveys.

The comparative results are particularly revealing. Contrary to the
usual claims, the hotel industry is not the main source of job creation in
tourism—one of the key objectives of official tourism promotion pro-

TABLE 3

TOTAL DIRECT EMPLOYMENT IN TOURISM IN 1988 PER TRIP
(IN CENTERS RECORDED BY SECTUR)

TYPE OF ACTIVITY	JOBS	PERCENT
Travel Agencies & Airlines	16,650	2.53
Car Rental	4,118	0.63
Taxis	57,254	8.70
Handicrafts & Boutiques	28,854	4.38
Miscellaneous Businesses	11,640	1.77
Restaurants & Bars	182,434	27.72
Related Misc. Services	266,147	40.45
Deluxe Hotels	17,860	2.71
5* Hotels	21,281	3.23
4* Hotels	27,343	4.16
3* Hotels	13,510	2.05
2* Hotels	5,925	0.90
1* Hotels	5,040	0.77
SUBTOTAL HOTEL INDUSTRY		13.82
TOTAL	658,056	100.00

grams—since its share in total direct employment is under 14 percent. The central dynamics of the hotel industry are not found in employment, but rather in its ability to support other tourism activities. Within the industry, luxury hotels generate most jobs: four- and five-star hotels account for about 73 percent of hotel employment—roughly 10 percent of total direct employment in tourism.

Jobs in surface transportation, travel agencies and airlines, account for 10 percent of total direct employment, a relatively low figure. The greatest relative job creation is in services, restaurants and bars. These account for 40 percent of total direct employment. This is a logical outcome of the growth of the service sector in developing economies.

Table 4 presents direct employment estimates and the number of tourist centers by state. As expected, the highest job concentration, 33 percent of the total, is in Mexico City. The Federal District continues to be the favored stopover for tourists and nontourists alike, reflecting the country's economic, administrative, political and geographic centralization. Mexico City is followed by Guadalajara and Monterrey, the country's second and third largest cities and the state capitals of Jalisco and Nuevo Leon; Jalisco also has a major beach resort, Puerto Vallarta, which has 2 percent of total employment.

A significant group of states generates 3 percent to 6 percent each of total direct employment. These include Baja California Norte, Chihuahua, Guerrero, Quintana Roo, Sinaloa, Tamaulipas and Veracruz. Two

TABLE 4
DIRECT EMPLOYMENT BY STATE (1988)

	DIR. EMP.	%	NO. CENTERS
Aguascalientes	6,569.37	1.00	1
Baja California Norte	21,709.23	3.30	3
Baja California Sur	2,694.60	0.41	3
Campeche	327.70	0.05	1
Coahuila	628.91	0.10	1
Colima	7,671.26	1.17	2
Chiapas	7,238.19	1.10	3
Chihuahua	29,422.38	4.47	2
Distrito Federal	217,190.35	32.99	1
Durango	5,460.08	0.83	1
Guanajuato	11,021.99	1.67	3
Guerrero	42,234.49	6.42	3
Hidalgo	2,938.34	0.45	1
Jalisco	64,449.16	9.79	2
Mexico	2,936.98	0.45	3
Michoacan	7,331.17	1.11	1
Morelos	7,491.35	1.14	2
Nayarit	3,132.33	0.48	1
Nuevo Leon	69,378.05	10.54	2
Oaxaca	6,886.12	1.05	1
Puebla	12,923.44	1.96	1
Queretaro	5,894.84	0.90	3
Quintana Roo	21,204.52	3.22	3
San Luis Potosi	7,217.70	1.10	1
Sinaloa	22,738.76	3.45	3
Sonora	2,841.65	0.43	1
Tabasco	4,828.72	0.73	2
Tamaulipas	20,261.49	3.08	3
Tlaxcala	969.67	0.15	1
Veracruz	28,194.75	4.28	12
Yucatan	12,261.06	1.86	2
Zacatecas	2,259.24	0.34	1
TOTAL	658,307.89	100.01	70

Source: Authors' table and projection to 1988, based on the Tourism Labor Market Survey, SECTUR, 1986.

subgroups can be clearly differentiated: those border states with a major urban center and states with either a traditional or modern beach resort. Despite major investment in Cancún, Quintana Roo accounts for only 3.2 percent of total direct employment, demonstrating a lack of correlation between the amount of investment and the ability of capital-intensive tourist centers to absorb workers. In contrast to Quintana Roo and Guerrero, which benefited from heavy investments aimed at creating jobs, Veracruz ranks fifth among states in tourist-related job creation but has received little official support. Table 4 shows that beach resorts account for just 17 percent of total jobs created, despite having received the greatest share of government support.

Indirect employment generated by tourism is not likely to follow the same geographic pattern as direct employment. In other words, indirect employment is not generally found in the same place, neighborhood, town, state, or even region as are the direct jobs engendering them. The reason is obvious: the Mexican economy has little regional self-sufficiency. Most regions are highly dependent on production and supply centers concentrated in large metropolitan areas, while benefits resulting from regional economic activity accrue to the more developed regions and sometimes even to foreign countries.

The Nature and Impact of Employment in Tourism

The quantification of direct and indirect employment is a first step toward an understanding of tourism's labor absorption. Some of the features of this employment must also be emphasized. Its seasonal nature is one of the most important characteristics of the tourist industry and is related to high and low tourist seasons. These could be quantified by examining direct and indirect employment fluctuations. Seasonality accounts for the temporary nature of workers' contracts, a feature of the sector that is documented in the Tourism Labor Market Survey. Seasonal employment is most often related to the major beach resorts and the more expensive hotels. If appropriate data on the informal economy were available, they would likely reveal much higher rates of temporary employment than in the formal economy. Tourism complements other low-skill occupations held by workers during the low season.

Two other significant features of tourism employment are high rates of female participation and the weak participation of local labor pools, except in the most unskilled positions. The implications for the social and regional development of areas surrounding tourist centers are clear: few employment opportunities exist for more skilled labor. Tourist centers act as magnets for migrants from nearby regions.[17] Tourism has also impacted on urban settlement patterns. Jobs are concentrated in specific areas, while the balance of urban spaces focuses on other activities or house tourist industry workers.

Tourism, as a service sector, tends to favor the development of informal activities. In order to assess some of these activities, a pilot study of 67 street vendors was conducted in Acapulco.[18] This was a limited survey, of course, since it focussed only on the most visible members of the informal economy. The pilot survey did not address other important informal activities, such as money laundering, drugs, illegal gambling, prostitution or illicit rentals. The results of the survey are revealing. They suggest that street vendors are generally less informal than is generally assumed.

They have licenses, sell in broad daylight and have open relationships with formal sector suppliers. The state knows who they are, acknowledges them and sometimes exploits them. Street vendors essentially cater to domestic tourists, an indication that formal and informal activities complement each other. Domestic tourists buy from lower-priced street vendors in response to the higher prices charged by formal establishments. Paradoxically, hotel owners are those most opposed to allowing street vendors on the beaches.

IV. CONCLUSIONS AND RECOMMENDATIONS

Two primary conclusions flow from our analysis of employment in Mexico's tourism sector:

1. Tourism, or the sequence of related tourism activities, is a main contributor to employment generation and thus to improvement in standards of living.
2. Direct employment is substantial and, contrary to what has been assumed in earlier studies, most tourism jobs arise from activities unrelated to lodging. In fact, other activities satisfy most of the tourist's needs. The key elements of tourism are the countless recreational activities, rather than travel and lodging. The former generate a good deal of economic activity and employment.

A review of the input-output tables confirms the official view that tourism demands few imports. On the contrary, it favors the development of linkages to other branches of the domestic economy. Tourism should be encouraged, not only because of its cultural, social and economic impact, but also as a major stimulus to economic activity in other branches of the economy. This confirms the importance of tourism as a priority in national development.

The ability of tourism to create a significant number of jobs through activities unassociated with the hotel industry should be exploited to promote new, nontraditional production sectors with a strong development potential. The potential for job creation in tourism is an important reason to reconceptualize and redesign Mexico's population distribution policy. In fact, tourism could be used as an important element in the spatial reordering of both Mexican society and its economic activity. To accomplish this, Mexico should ensure that tourism activities not lead to the further strengthening of the country's key cities at the expense of the regions where tourism has developed.

Additional study is needed on this topic to design a comprehensive strategy transcending narrow sectoral bounds. Such a conceptualization could lead to substantial improvement and consolidation of labor absorption through tourism-related activities.

Our findings indicate that Mexico should:
1. Redefine the role of tourism in the national economy, revise sectoral and inter-sectoral policies and re-establish new quantitative and qualitative objectives for tourism development.
2. Diversify tourism's offerings by a reconceptualization of market segmentation and the identification of different types of tourism. Mexico should also assess the development potential of new tourist sites by reevaluating the national tourism inventory and revising the classification criteria. This should include a reevaluation of tourist attractions. Moreover, the fiscal incentives policy must be modified, tourism should be diversified and a detailed analysis of unregistered modes of domestic tourism undertaken.
3. Create an information system for tourism. The information deficit could be remedied through the construction of a tourism input-output table; selecting a system of variables to define the phenomenon, studying tourism activity sequences, investigating the operation of tourist centers, assessing the impact of tourism on diverse social groups and conducting studies on migration and the regional impact of tourism.
4. Reorient foreign investment. Foreign investment should be channeled toward nontraditional areas of tourism in need of capital. Hotel investment should be limited because the demand is less pressing and the direct and indirect effects of job creation less tangible.
5. Promote domestic tourism through special incentives, expanding the number of destinations and assessing the profitability of investments in the various tourism-related activities. This should stimulate capital flows to these tourist developments.
6. Reconceive employment generation in tourism as a sequence in order to take advantage of job creation opportunities in the field of tourism.

In order to take full advantage of the capacity of the tourist sector to absorb labor, it is necessary to promote key linkages in the tourism sequence as well as complementary activities. Support mechanisms for informal sector activities related to tourism should also be developed so that Mexico can make better use of inter-sectoral linkages.

NOTES

This study was conducted under the supervision of Mexico's National Population Council and received logistical support from the Secretariat of Tourism (SECTUR). We would like to express our gratitude to the Mexican government officials who lent us their support. Furthermore, our very special thanks go to Dr. Sergio Díaz Briquets of the Commission and Dr. Sidney Weintraub and Dr. Chandler Stolp, of the University of Texas at Austin, who devoted many hours to reviewing the preliminary document and providing us with highly relevant observations.

1. See Manuel Rodríguez Woog, "El conocimiento científico del turismo: reflexiones y consideraciones generales," in Daniel Hiernaux Nicolas (ed.), *Teoría y praxis del espacio turístico*, (México: Universidad Autónoma Metropolitana Unidad Xochimilco, 1989); and Daniel Hiernaux Nicolas and Taeko Shimizu Kano (book in progress), *Hacia una definición del fenómeno no turístico*.

2. Julio Aramberri, "El paraiso . . . perdido? Sobre algunas teorías del turismo," *Estudios turísticos*, Instituto Español de Turismo, 80, (Winter 1983), pp. 77–93.

3. Organización Mundial de Turismo, "Suplemento Metodológico de las Estadísticas sobre Viajes y Turismo Mundiales" (Madrid: O.M.T., 1985).

4. In Mexico, the term "tourist" is defined in the General Population Law, Article 42, which states, "The tourist is deemed to be the non-immigrant who enters the country temporarily for recreational or health purposes, to take part in artistic, cultural, or sports activities that are neither remunerative nor lucrative, for a maximum period of six months, non-extendable."

5. See Fabio Cárdenas, *Comercialización del turismo* (México: Ed. Trillas, 1986); and Miguel Acereza, *Administración del turismo* (México: Ed. Trillas, 1987).

6. See references to Note 1, and Sergio Molina, Manuel Rodríguez Woog, and Felipe Cuamea, *Turismo alternativo: Un acercamiento crítico y conceptual* (México: Ed. Nuevo Tiempo Libre, 1986).

7. Roberto Boullón, *Planificación del espacio turístico* (México: Ed. Trillas, 1985), pp. 24–29.

8. Alfonso Jiménez, *Turismo: Estructura y Desarrollo* (ed.), Interamericana, 1984; and Gloria Caballero, *Historia legislativa del turismo en México* (ed.), (México: Instituto Mexicano de Investigaciones Turísticas, 1965).

9. Throughout this work, we used the most frequently publicized official statistical sources on Mexican tourism in addition to our own research. Our secondary sources included:
• Secretariat of Tourism: miscellaneous statistical sources, 1984–1989.
• Banco de México: "Indicadores del sector externo," "Encuestas de turismo receptivo, egresivo y transacciones fronterizas," miscellaneous editions.
• Instituto Nacional de Estadística, Geografía e Informática (INEGI): "Manual de estadísticas básicas del sector turismo," miscellaneous editions; input-output tables and national account systems, miscellaneous years.

10. Louis Turner and John Ash, *The Golden Hordes* (London: Constable, 1975).

11. Georges Cazes, *Les Aménagements Touristiques au Mexique* (Aix-en-Provence, France: Centre des Hautes Etudes Touristiques, Etudes et Mémoires, 38, 1980).

12. This phenomenon, particularly interesting and potentially unhealthy for Mexico's net tourism balance, has a high income elasticity, according to 1988 SEC-TUR data. There is no doubt that improvement in certain socioeconomic sectors brought about by the growth in several areas (e.g., the in-bond and automotive export industries and imports of consumer goods, among others) provided the resources for an increase in the number of outbound Mexican tourists.

13. Manuel Rodríguez Woog, "Análisis de la situación del turismo en México," *Capital, Revista de Bursamétrica*, December 1989.

14. The concept of a sequence of "related productive activities" has been developed by several Latin American authors and applied to a number of sectors. Its most innovative feature is to describe the economy in terms of linkages between economic activities that cater only partially to the tourist industry. These activities are then related to different sectors of the economy, such as manufacturing, transportation, and marketing structures, in an effort to understand flows rather than to produce a static analysis. This represents an important contribution to the study of tourism.

15. See, among others, Manuel Figuerola Palomo, "El turismo en el sistema de cuentas nacionales de la economía," *Estudios Turísticos*, Instituto Español de Turismo, 85 (Spring 1985), pp. 3–14.

16. Secretaría de Turismo, *Encuesta del Mercado Laboral Turístico, 1989;* miscellaneous reports; and work carried out in 1986.

17. Daniel Hiernaux Nicolas, *Politiques de Développement et Gestion de l'Espace dans le Port Industriel de Lázaro Cárdenas, Mexique*, Paris, 1984. Doctoral thesis in Latin American Studies, specialization in Geography and Urban Development, Institute of Advanced Latin American Studies, University of Paris III. Unpublished.

18. "El sector informal en Acapulco: encuesta a vendedores ambulantes," survey conducted under the direction of Daniel Hiernaux Nicolas, with students from the Master's Degree Program in Tourism Studies, Universidad Autónoma de Guerrero, Plantel Sur, Acapulco, 1989.

11

Nature-Oriented Tourism
in the State of Guerrero, Mexico:
Issues and Recommended
Policies for Local Economic Development

Art Pedersen and Héctor Ceballos-Lascurain

I. INTRODUCTION

The purpose of this study is to present the issues involved in using nature-oriented tourism as a tool for rural economic development in the state of Guerrero, Mexico, and to suggest a series of policies and recommendations to develop such a program.

To carry out this grass roots approach to tourism development, this study examines alternative markets based on outdoor recreation activities within the specialty travel market. These new markets are compared to the more traditional tourism markets, and the issues that affect their relationship are discussed. The study briefly examines Mexican tourism policy at the national and state levels. It assesses several sites that have the physical resources for alternative tourist potential and examines the local issues of tourism development. From the information collected, it determines how international, national, state and local issues will both encourage and limit an alternative tourism program for rural Guerrero. The study then proposes a series of measures for incorporating alternative tourism markets into the state's development strategy.

II. BACKGROUND INFORMATION

The Growth of the Specialty Travel Market

In the last fifteen years there has been steady and continued growth in the travel industry's specialty travel markets. The specialty travel market is composed of tourists who travel for a specific purpose and participate in or practice a particular sport or hobby, e.g., mountain climbing, photography, archeology, opera, architecture, etc. They travel because it offers them a chance to pursue their interests in a unique, exotic or more physically challenging setting. They may go with a tour company specializing in their chosen activity, on a well-organized expedition, or they may travel with friends.

While the number of specialized tourists is relatively small compared to traditional markets (according to one report 3 to 5 percent of international travel expenditures, excluding airfare[1]), their number is growing. This is evidenced by the increasing number of travel agencies offering specialized tours and outings. A 1987 study found the number of new tour operators advertising in the *Specialty Travel Index Magazine* had increased 22 percent between the 1986 Fall/Winter issue and the 1987 Spring/Summer issue.[2]

Outdoor Recreation

Among the most popular of the specialty travel markets is the outdoor recreation market. Outdoor recreation activities range from hiking and camping, and hunting and fishing, to river rafting and bird-watching. It is most popular in the developed countries: the United States, Canada, Western Europe, Australia and Japan, countries which fuel the foreign travel markets.[3]

Participants in outdoor recreation are numerous. Their numbers grew rapidly with the increased discretionary income and rising living standards of the 1960s and 1970s. In the United States, it is expected that total participation in all forms of outdoor recreation will triple by the year 2000. Wilderness-related outdoor recreation is predicted to show an even greater level of increase, over 800 percent by the year 2000.[4]

The popularity of this market has generated an increase in the number of people traveling to foreign countries to participate in outdoor pursuits. One study found that outdoor oriented tour operations (described as "nature-oriented operators"), consistently account for about 23 percent of all specialty tour operators advertising in the *Specialty Travel Index Magazine*.[5] Of the 98 nature-oriented tour operators in the 1987 edition of the *Specialty Travel Index Magazine,* the study found 27 percent to be new entries.[6] When interviewed, 80 percent of the tour operators felt the demand for this kind of travel will increase in the next five years.[7] The same study also found that in 1986, 81 percent of these nature-oriented tours were to developing countries.[8]

Tourists engaged in outdoor activities produce significant revenues in the United States. In 1980, 2.3 million U.S. salt-water fishermen spent a total of $2.4 billion. Eighty-eight percent of this figure went for equipment, lodging and transport, and the remainder for fees, licenses and related expenses.[9] In Texas, deer hunting is a $1 billion industry.[10]

The gross national product of several countries is heavily based on the international markets related to outdoor recreation. Tourism connected with viewing wildlife in Kenya's National Parks contributes greatly to its foreign exchange earning. Rwanda's tourism industry, based on its famous mountain gorilla population, is that country's third-ranked foreign exchange earner. Nepal's foreign exchange is strongly tied to the revenue produced by mountain trekking tourism and climbing expeditions. Costa Rica's Corcavado National Park generates an estimated $1 million a year.[11] Figures show that the diving industry of Bonaire brings in about $5 million annually and revenues from Tobago's Buccoo Reef/Bon Accord Lagoon Restricted Area brings $510,000 per year.[12] Ecuador's Galapagos Islands attract 25,000 foreign tourists each year, a figure that includes half of all U.S. and European tourists visiting Ecuador. (That number could be higher, but, due to the sensitivity of the ecosystem, the number of tourists permitted to visit the Islands is limited.)[13]

Defining the Market

The market created by the growth in specialty travel and outdoor recreation has been difficult to define. In the past, similar activities have been grouped together under one tourism definition depending on the types of activities they encompass. These have been labeled with several names. For example, the "adventure travel" market includes sports such as mountain climbing, trekking and river rafting; the "natural history" market includes birding and wildlife observation. In an attempt to place all these outdoor recreation activities in one broad category, the name "ecotourism" was suggested. This includes natural history and adventure travel, as well as cultural and archeological activities. Nature-oriented tourism has also been used to categorize the outdoor recreation market.

Travel that uses natural resources as an attraction has been further broken down into "soft nature-oriented travel" and "hard nature-oriented travel."[14] Soft refers to nature-oriented travel which is not scientifically serious. Hard nature-oriented tourism refers to serious or dedicated practitioners, for example, serious amateur naturalists or those engaged in scientific research. Hard and soft also refer to the physical rigorousness of the activities and the trip. For example, a mountain climbing trip to Nepal or trekking in Thailand would be considered under the category hard due to the physical discomfort and effort needed in these activities. A bird watching trip with clients staying in a comfortable lodge would be put under the soft category.

The categories are further obscured by the additional breakdown of the market into nonconsumptive and consumptive tourism. Consumptive activities are those that use and do not replace natural resources. Nonconsumptive tourism, on the other hand, does not exhaust or negatively effect a resource. For example, hunting is called a consumptive activity and bird watching is nonconsumptive.[15]

The diversity of activities and definitions in the market have led to some confusion and some controversy. Specifically, there is a gray area regarding what is considered acceptable within the category of consumptive activities. The debate stems from the fact that some members of conservation organizations interested in tourism are strongly against sport hunting and fishing. For example, at the first Ecotourism Conference, held in Merida, Mexico in 1989, there were discussions on whether or not sport fishing should be considered an ecotourism activity. The topic of sport hunting, because it was so controversial, was not even discussed. (The authors of this study, who are not hunters and who are members of conservation organizations traditionally not in favor of hunting, feel that any suggestion of hunting, even as an aid to conservation, will alienate some members of these organizations.)

Realistically, both hunting and fishing can be profitable tourism markets and aid conservation. Many hunting and fishing organizations contribute to and initiate conservation activities. In Mexico, the hunting, fishing and conservation organization, Ducks Unlimited, is a major force in wetlands conservation projects. There are other examples of hunting programs being used profitably. In New Mexico, the Mescalero Apache Reservation generates the funds for its conservation work through hunting permits and guide fees.[16] In Africa, big game hunting has generated much foreign exchange. In both Zimbabwe and Zambia, poaching has been slowed through safari hunting programs that funnel profits back into surrounding communities. These safari hunting programs represent one of the few success stories where local communities directly benefit from tourism.[17]

For the purpose of simplification, this study will refer to all the outdoor recreation markets previously mentioned as nature-oriented tourism. This definition will include those specialty travel activities that utilize natural resources and wildlife. The activities include nonconsumptive natural history activities such as bird-watching, nature photography and visiting ruin sites, as well as adventure travel activities such as river rafting, caving and mountain climbing. It will also include some consumptive activities such as sport hunting and fishing because they have the potential to generate large sums of foreign exchange for Mexico and other developing countries and because many hunting and fishing organizations are active conservationists.

Opportunities for Rural Development

The number of tourists traveling to rural areas in developing countries to participate in outdoor activities has generated interest in tourism's potential role as an aid to rural economic development. Because this tourism is based on the continued health of the local natural resources, it can also act as an incentive to maintain natural resources and thus mitigate certain environmental problems.

Nature-oriented tourism offers certain communities an opportunity to benefit from the popularity of natural attractions. Outstanding natural areas, such as parks and protected areas, are usually ringed by any number of rural communities. In theory, if a program is planned and implemented correctly, tourists on their way to and from the attraction will use the services of the local communities. Patronage of local restaurants, shops and guide services by the incoming tourists can generate employment and inject additional revenues into the economies of these small towns. If these services do not exist, they have the potential to be developed.

Nature-oriented tourism is not necessarily limited to those rural communities with outstanding natural resources. Other communities may be able to develop popular recreation activities. This is particularly relevant for communities near population centers which can develop activities that are in demand by the residents of nearby towns and cities. Farm and forest land in these areas may have the potential to serve as habitat for wildlife resulting in the possibility of the development of a bird watching or hunting market. A stream may be able to be stocked for fishing, and trails may be developed for horseback riding.

Most of the interest in nature-oriented tourism as an aid to solving environmental problems comes from conservation organizations such as the World Wildlife Fund/Conservation Foundation. In the past, international conservation organizations viewed tourism as incompatible with conservation. However, these organizations are now considering tourism's potential as an incentive to halt negative environmental impacts on parks and protected areas. In most countries, parks and reserves protect both wildlife and important watersheds. These areas are commonly threatened by conflicts with the surrounding communities, usually over control of park resources, i.e., lumber, agricultural land and game animals. Deforestation and poaching on park land are common problems. Many in the conservation community believe that if local people see an economic value in preserving a nearby natural area, they will be less likely to destroy it. If, for example, some of the revenue produced by a park goes to the people living nearby, they will be more willing to regard the park as an economic resource to be protected rather than exploited for lumber, farmland and other resources.

Even for parts of the countryside without official parks or protected areas, some tourism specialists see the possibility of nature-oriented tourism as a component of programs aimed at halting destructive environmental practices. If, for example, communities profit from a tourism program, e.g., bird watching, that uses a nearby wooded area, it is possible that forest land will be maintained intact. If no alternative economic activity exists, the forest will most probably be cut for timber and farmland. Forest cover is generally important to the local watershed, and if it is cut in many areas this results in soil erosion, loss of arable land and water supply and crop failure. The key is that people must see a connection between the economic benefit and the natural resource; for example, poaching of big game was reduced in Zimbabwe because locals saw economic gains from profits funneled back to them by safari hunters.[18]

The Use of Parks and Protected Areas in Nature-Oriented Tourism Development

Much of the nature-oriented tourism industry utilizes attractions that are within the boundaries of national parks and protected areas.

There has been criticism by some environmentalists that using parks and protected areas for economic development can encourage destructive management practices. Critics of an economic justification to parks and protected areas have argued that if the area is not generating revenues through tourism, government policy toward the area could change. In their search for revenue producing activities, officials may decide on policies that open up the resource to mining, timber production or some other environmentally destructive industry. They warn that if a country's goal is to increase tourism through its park system, there is also the temptation to tolerate negative tourism impacts even at the long-range expense of the resource. Park personnel may be under pressure and forced to permit the overuse of the resource. Even if park personnel desire to control the number of tourists entering an area, because of the lack of manpower and equipment, the park service simply may not be able to deal with the increasing human pressures. In Africa's game parks, the impacts of tourism have had negative effects on the habitat of several species of larger mammals. In the long term, the impact will have an effect on the quality of the resource and eventually on the number of tourists visiting the park.[19] Left unchecked, a country like Kenya stands to lose much of the foreign exchange produced by game parks if a balance is not struck between its financial needs and the long term environmental health of its parklands.

On the other hand, a natural resource controlled by the government may, without clear policy or good reason, restrict tourists or tour companies from entering the area. This may lead to a valuable source of foreign exchange going untapped. Also, if there is the commonly found park/community conflict over the right to use park resources, without a tourism program and without benefits accruing to the locals, the conflict will continue and hope for the preservation of the resource for the long-term will be diminished.

Since the beginning of the 1980s, most international conservation organizations have supported the idea that long-term preservation of a park requires that surrounding communities benefit economically and environmentally from the resource. At the present time there are only a few community-oriented tourism programs utilizing natural areas. The two previously mentioned government-run safari hunting programs in Africa have funneled profits from hunting fees back to the surrounding communities, thereby reducing the poaching of endangered species. In Thailand, locals have been used as trekking guides inside Thai National Parks, a program that has helped to mitigate some of the conflicts between the parks and the local communities.[20]

III. FACTORS AND GROUPS DRIVING THE NATURE-ORIENTED TRAVEL MARKET

Background information on the nature-oriented tourist market is needed to assess a community's tourist potential and to determine the existing opportunities for its participation in the market. The following section provides an overview of the market by describing nature-oriented tour operators and their clients. Planners who consider the tourism market can help form broad guidelines from which they can work to identify and plan the development of a site and a marketing strategy to promote it.

The Activity Market

Nature-oriented tour operators offer their clients an extensive list of activities. This varied activity market gives tourist developers a wide range of opportunities. This is especially true for a country as diverse in natural resources as Mexico. A 1987 study of U.S. based nature-oriented tour operators found that the most offered activities were (in order of popularity): trekking/hiking, bird watching, nature photography, wildlife safaris, camping, mountain climbing, fishing, river rafting/canoeing/kayaking and botanical study. Other nature-oriented activities promoted by the tour operators were: horseback riding, cultural and archeological study, deep sea activities, spelunking, boat trips to uninhabited islands, orchid study, butterfly watching and four-wheel drive excursions. The study found that the tour operators interviewed visit Mexico most frequently for bird watching and botanical study.[21]

Profile of the Nature-Oriented Tourist

Each nature-oriented activity has a hard and soft component and a tourist's motivations for participating in an activity are varied. For this reason it is difficult to group all nature-oriented tourists together for the purpose of listing common characteristics. However, several frequently seen characteristics have been identified, providing a limited profile of nature-oriented tourists.

Research shows that the nature-oriented tourist is willing to travel to developing countries and even to experience undeveloped areas at a grass roots level. These motivations differ from many traditional tourists seeking a classic, resort-based "fun in the sun" holiday. Another principal difference is the concern with luxury. Many nature-oriented tourists are more willing and often prefer to use rustic accommodations. This is not to say that all are willing to rough it. Many nature-oriented tour operators use luxury hotels, but during the same trip they also may use rustic, but clean, locally owned accommodations in the small communities adjacent to a national park or protected area.[22]

On the other hand, bird watchers and natural history tourists on organized tours tend to be older, and wealthier and generally require a higher level of comfort. The Massachusetts Audubon Society reports that their groups prefer accommodations that are simple and clean, for example, a small inn, motel or pension. Clients prefer that the atmosphere of the facility should fit into the local environment and the natural area. Overnight stays in very rustic conditions are acceptable for these groups, if they permit the group to see a particularly attractive area. While hot water is preferred but not absolutely necessary in warm areas, food is important to the groups and clients want a choice of local and American food available at all meals.[23]

Tourism professionals in several developing countries believe that it is the hard or dedicated tourists that most tend to direct economic activity to remote communities. This group is more tolerant of primitive facilities and infrastructure than other type of tourists. However, many feel that soft tourism is the largest part of the nature-oriented tourism market. If this is the case, this group will demand more sophisticated infrastructure, something that most rural communities lack.[24]

Non-Host Country-Based Tour Operators (Outbound Operators)

An essential element in nature-oriented tourism and community development is the use of local services. Whether local services are used depends largely on the business practices of nonhost-country or outbound tour operators. The 1987 study on nature tourism found that 40 percent of U.S. nature-oriented tour operators used rural or village accommodations. Of seven operators in the study who use luxury accommodations, five use them in combination with camping, village areas and other hotels.[25] The total number of clients served by these operators is small compared to the number served by the mass-tourism firms. Thirty-two nature-oriented tour companies in the United States reported firm sizes from 20 to 3,000 clients per year. Tour groups tend to be small, between four and 25 persons, and many operators deliberately keep them so, believing that limiting group size assures their clients of a more personalized experience.[26]

Inbound Operators

Outbound tour operators generally employ host-country inbound operators to handle their ground arrangements. Inbound operators are used by the tour companies to arrange the facilities, transport guides and itineraries within their country. Inbound operators are usually travel professionals with their own agency in the capital city arranging the trip packages for the outbound operators who sell the programs to individuals or groups within their countries. The inbound operator is usually upper-middle-class and well-educated. Expatriates from the United States or Europe who reside in the country are sometimes found in this line of work. While a foreign tour operator will use the guides of the inbound operator, they will often also have a non-host country guide acting as the overall coordinator of the trip and the liaison between the clients and the in-country staff.

Guide Services

Inbound operators generally do not hire local rural people as guides. Because of the requirements for the job, most guides hired by the inbound firms live in the capital city and are well-educated and well-traveled. Operators look for people who are bilingual, familiar with the area's fauna and flora and skilled in the necessary activities (e.g., river rafting, first aid and an array of other skills). Many guides who are involved with natural history tours are university graduate students with experience in the biological sciences.

The situation for guides can change as the outdoor activities become "harder." Wilderness trekkers and foot safaris will use local inhabitants as guides because of their excellent route finding abilities and knowledge of the area and the people. Sherpas in Nepal and jungle guides in certain areas of Thailand are used to assist the main guides of the inbound operators. Generally, however, rural locals, if they are used by firms, are usually delegated to lesser paid auxiliary roles, such as pack animal managers, cooks, boat operators, porters or trackers.[27] In some areas, country people do operate independently of inbound operators. For example, in Huaraz, Peru, local campesino families work as trekking guides and provide mules for the treks as well as for climbing expeditions.

IV. TOURISM DEVELOPMENT IN MEXICO AND THE STATE OF GUERRERO

Government Plans and Priorities

Historically, the Mexican government has concentrated its efforts on developing traditional mass-tourism markets. These markets are based on the popularity of large beachfront resorts like Cancun and Ixtapa, or well-established traditional destinations such as Taxco. According to the Mexico Secretary of Tourism, Carlos Hank Gonzalez, the government's efforts in the next six years will be directed toward maintaining and developing these traditional areas and not, except for the Bahias de Huatulco in Oaxaca, constructing any major new resorts.

In Guerrero, government efforts for tourism development focus on the triangle formed by the three major resorts, Acapulco, Zihuatanejo/Ixtapa and Taxco, the Triangulo del Sol. These efforts include completing construction of an expanded highway from Acapulco to Chilpancingo, plans for a new road from Mexico City to Chilpancingo and the construction of a new hotel complex at Puerto Marquez, essentially an extension of Acapulco. The development strategy also includes the search for new attractions that will keep tourists at these areas for greater periods of time.[28]

Much criticism has been directed at this mass-tourism market in developing countries such as Mexico.[29] Critics charge that these projects principally benefit land owners and those with the financial means to enter the market. Although employment opportunities are generated, proportionally few economic benefits filter down to local populations and the revenues are "leaked" out of the communities, a term used to describe the revenues lost to pay for imported food and materials. Locals can lose jobs to outsiders newly attracted to the area. There are also the well-documented social, economic and environmental problems associated with large-scale tourism. Such problems include increased crime, inflation and pollution.

While this criticism is valid, there are reasons why countries like Mexico emphasize mass-tourism and will continue to do so. The mass-tourism market has proven to be an important source of foreign exchange revenue. In spite of criticism that much of tourism's profits are leaked out of countries to pay for imported food or materials, evidence suggests that developing countries retain at least 50 percent of tourist expenditures made in the country. An indirect factor that has locked governments into those policies favoring high-volume, large-scale projects is the cycle created by the desire for more foreign exchange and the need to pay for the expensive infrastructure demanded in resort areas.[30]

There are also proven employment benefits to mass-tourism. One researcher wrote that, "Official sources in Mexico have estimated that about a million families are employed, at least partially, in the production of handicrafts and that at least 50 percent of the handicraft production is sold to nonresident tourists. For the families involved, this extra income (estimated at $192 million) has been important in raising their level of economic well-being above subsistence."[31]

Community Organization in Guerrero

Understanding the working of rural communities is a major factor in effective nature-oriented tourism planning. Much rural land in Guerrero is held under the communal land tenure system of the *ejido* or *bienes comunales*. In both the *ejido* and *bienes comunales*, the land is cooperatively worked by the local people. A percentage of the profits is shared by all members for some agreed upon community need. Both systems have extensive bureaucracies and represent numerous competing interests.

Ejidos and *bienes comunales* can be organized as tourism production units authorized by the Agrarian Reform Ministry. They can request an *aununcia* from the Ministry giving them the authorization to engage in tourism activities and receive credit. The state government of Guerrero through the state's economic development Secretariat contains the Instituto de Empresas del Sector Social, INDES, which supplies this credit that is specifically meant for *ejidatarios* and workers. Two kinds of loans are given: the AVIO, for basic equipment such as boats, motors, agricultural tools, etc. and the REFACCIONARIO, for the construction of roads and physical infrastructure. INDES also has the capability of and the responsibility for carrying out market surveys and research for rural communities.

In the past, *ejidos* have not proven to be effective in carrying out programs involving local participation and the administration and management of tourist businesses. The land tenure system has an extensive bureaucracy causing decision-making to be slow, the administration of programs cumbersome and conflicting interests common. An Inter-American Foundation founded *ejido* (cooperative) tourism project near Puerto Vallarta, Mexico, failed because of a combination of outside pressures and internal conflict. In this project, an *ejido* unit constructed several small cottages with the hope of renting them to tourists coming to this popular Mexican resort area. Internal feuding among *ejido* members stopped the project when outside interests contacted *ejido* members with offers to buy land.[32]

A state-funded, *ejido*-owned hotel project at Punto Tracones (near Zihuatanejo/Ixtapa in Guerrero) has also met with problems. In this project, *ejido* members lacked the administration and hotel management skills to effectively run the business. In an attempt to salvage the project and find a solution beneficial to the *ejido*, the state's Secretariat of Economic Development is attempting to locate an investor who will lease the hotel from the *ejido*, (2 million pesos monthly with a renewable six month contract) and hire a professional manager to turn the business around.[33]

V. LOCAL COMMUNITY ISSUES

Site Identification and Assessment of Communities with Nature-Oriented Tourism Potential

To look at the issues in developing a local nature-oriented tourism program, several sites in the state of Guerrero were examined. To identify sites, the authors utilized the following process:

Interviews. Interviews were conducted with Mexican and U.S. professionals in the fields of tourism, ecology, conservation and economic development. During the interviews, participants were asked to identify those areas of the state that they thought had exceptional natural areas with the potential for outdoor recreation and attracting tourism.

Review of U.S. Guidebooks. Guidebooks, specifically those geared to outdoor recreation activities, often mention areas with good tourist potential, sometimes unknown to government officials and those not active in the sport. The authors studied guidebooks directed at specific activity markets, e.g., *Skin Diving Mexico,* more traditional tourism markets, e.g., *Fodor's Mexico,* and *The American Express Guide to Mexico* and those geared to independent, adventurous travelers, e.g., the *South American Handbook.*

Site Visits. From both the interviews and guidebooks, 37 sites were identified. The list was by no means complete, and a more extensive overview of the state could have been carried out if time permitted. The sites were then visited to estimate their tourist potential. When assessing the sites, several factors were considered:

1) *The recreational resources and potential of an area.* Whether there are suitable resources for nature-oriented tourism. Whether the site has some unique quality or offers some activity that would be sufficiently attractive to a nature-oriented tourist, e.g., the existence of interesting wildlife, canoeable rivers and lakes, hunting, fishing, hiking possibilities, etc. Whether the site is maintained in a relatively natural condition.
2) *The site's accessibility.* Whether access to the site is feasible or could be developed and/or if there is a means of acceptable transportation.
3) *The facilities and infrastructure available.* This includes any accommodations, roads, trails, camping areas, etc. that the area can provide for tourists.
4) *The area's land tenure situation.* The land tenure situation in the area and how it will effect tourism development. Is the area under park or protected area status, private or cooperative land ownership, etc.?
5) *The security of the area.* Is it safe to travel in the area? For tourists this can be actual or perceived security of an area.

During the visits, the authors attempted to gain a better understanding of the issues that would determine the feasibility of a tourism project, and to determine the more subtle or hidden social and economic issues that may act as constraints in site development. As a follow-up, additional interviews were conducted with government officials, for example, the head of the Reforma Agraria, to determine government attitudes regarding a given tourism proposal, and to attempt to sort out, at a higher level, any government issues impacting the areas being studied.

A Description of the Site and Comments on Tourism Development

Based on the visit, a number of sites were identified as having suitable resources for nature-oriented tourism activities. Most of the 37 sites, due to low recreational potential, did not qualify as sites that would attract international and domestic tourists. If a site had recreation possibilities suitable for domestic tourism but did not have some outstanding quality that would attract a foreign nature-oriented tourist, it was dropped from the list. A number did have good potential and of these three were selected for further examination. Two, Ixcateopan and Puerto Vincente Guerrero, were selected because they seem to offer opportunities for several outdoor activities. They also have easy access. Because the road system and transportation opportunities in Guerrero revolved around the resort towns of Taxco, Acapulco, and Zihuatanejo/Ixtapa, these two areas were close enough to Acapulco and Taxco and to their transportation routes that they could draw on the tourism markets there. The third area, a portion of the Sierra Teotepec west of the capital Chilpancingo, was selected because it has exceptional and endangered natural resources that would prove an attraction to nature-oriented tourists.

Area: Ixcateopan. Ixcateopan is a small, charming village 45 km outside Taxco. The local church houses the supposed remains of the Aztec emperor Cuauhtemoc. There is also a small museum just off the square outlining the struggle between the indigenous Mexican tribes and the conquistadores.

The area is a natural extension of any tour of Taxco. Ixcateopan's overall aesthetic qualities, its attractive woods and farmlands, its historical significance, and its closeness to Taxco all make it an area that could be developed for recreation. While there is adequate public transportation for independent travelers, because of the limited accommodations in Ixcateopan, the most feasible strategy for a larger volume of visitors would be through an arrangement with a hotel in Taxco. Tourists would use the hotels as a base, and the hotels would arrange transportation to the area.

For a community-based recreation business, horseback riding is recommended for Ixcateopan. Many people in the area already own their own horses and it is an activity that locals could organize without excessive amounts of capital. Horseback riding tours could be sold to the Taxco hotels as an add-on activity to their recreation programs.

Two factors that were mentioned by the President of the local PRI organization as being important in starting a tourism program in the community were the systematic maintenance of the road from Taxco and the availability of government credits. He mentioned that the Economic Development Secretariat provides credit for the construction of small hotels, cabins and restorations, etc.

Area: Sierra Teotepec. The Sierra Teotepec is a large, mountainous area west of Chilpancingo. It is one of the last remaining cloud forests on the Pacific side of Mexico. Although access to certain areas of the Sierra is difficult, the recreational value in terms of bird-watching, hiking, camping and hunting is high. Because the area contains several species of neotropical birds and Mexican endemics, it has all the qualities of an attractive bird-watching site. White-tailed deer would be the principal game animal.

Much of the Sierra and its remaining forests act as an important watershed for surrounding communities and farms. The whole general area is made up of both *ejido* land and land under control of *bienes comunales*. The Olmiltemi area, an extension of this Teotepec cloud forest just west of Chilpancingo, contains a state park protecting the watershed which supplies the drinking water to the state capital in Chilpancingo. There is only occasional and sporadic protection of the area. Officials have been unable to prevent members of local *ejidos* from entering the area to graze cattle and cut trees. Fires and poaching are also reported.

The growing of crops related to the drug trade (e.g., poppies) is common in this part of the Sierra. Because of the drug production, people are suspicious of outsiders and many are well-armed. Conflicts among rival drug owners are not uncommon. Overall, because of the security problems, either real or perceived, developing tourist travel to the Sierra would be problematic for the short-term.

Area: Puerto Vicente Guerrero. Puerto Guerrero is a small fishing village 150 km north of Acapulco and 80 km south of Zihuatanejo/Ixtapa. This coastal area holds good potential for sport fishing and skin diving.

Members of the community generally belong to the one local *ejido*, which contains two fishing cooperatives. The cooperatives own small motor boats that could be rented out to visiting tourists. Because boat rentals are inexpensive, compared with resort standards, fishing and skin diving in the area could be very competitive with expensive Acapulco and Zihuatanejo/Ixtapa. The area is also close enough to these resorts for inexpensive add-on day trips. Because there is a contingent of marines stationed in the community making regular patrols and handling security matters—unlike other beaches along the coast—crime is not a problem.

VI. RECOMMENDATIONS FOR A NATURE-ORIENTED TOURISM PROGRAM

The following section recommends policies and a practical strategy to develop and implement a nature-oriented program in the state. While these recommendations are based on the situation in Guerrero, many could be applied to the development of a nature-oriented tourism program in other areas of the country.

Part 1: Recommended Government Policies

Develop policies and programs for a segmented approach to marketing tourism in the state. Current tourism policies provide limited incentives for the involvement of tourism professionals in alternative markets. Tourism professionals continue to base their strategies around either developing the mass-tourism resorts or attempting to increase the time visitors stay at these resorts.

To focus solely on mass-tourism does not allow consideration of a more segmented approach to marketing. This approach need not be directed only at nature-oriented travelers, but could also include those interested in other markets, such as tourists interested in native handicrafts. To start the process, an integrated effort on the part of tourism, nature resource and community development specialists is needed.

Coordinate information better between tourism and natural resource professionals. To plan a nature-oriented tourism program effectively, coordination is needed between tourism and natural resource professionals. Although their work gives them different orientations, both groups have expertise needed for the development of this type of program.

Generally, for site identification, those working in the ecology and conservation fields have a better understanding of the type of natural resource that would best appeal to the nature-oriented traveler, especially the foreigner. For example, the ecologists and conservationists surveyed in this study identified all of the hunting and fishing sites and all of the bird watching sites in the state. It is no surprise that they also knew those more isolated and natural areas of the state that would appeal to foreign nature-oriented tourists. They were also more aware of the potential of the nature-oriented markets for both domestic and foreign tourism. Several told of a growing interest in outdoor activities and ecology in Mexico and mentioned the small but growing number of bird watchers in Mexico City. All identified the Sierra Teotepec as a unique biological area and a good location for bird watching. Several agreed on the excellent potential in coastal sport fishing.

State officials, on the other hand, tended to identify areas in and around the main tourist destinations. This is understandable considering these areas have the greatest demand and are the most important revenue generators for the state. They identified, for example, the town of Ixcateopan. When asked to identify natural areas, however, they identified sites good for domestic tourism, but lacking sufficient wild and untouched areas to attract foreign nature-oriented tourists. For example, they identified two municipal parks as possible tourist sites but upon examination it was determined these did not have sufficient undisturbed natural areas to appeal to international tourists. They also failed to realize that the parks lacked nature trails and the kind of isolated camping that U.S. and European tourists enjoy.

Tourism professionals must be made aware of the differences between planning for mass-tourism markets and nature-oriented travel. Each area needs to be considered on the basis of the activities it has to offer the tourist and the specific market needs of those activities. For example, a planner must consider whether the activity is physically hard or soft. Then the planner must consider the degree of comfort that would be generally acceptable for the different nature-oriented activity markets. This has particular importance in determining a site's accessibility and infrastructure needs. For example, while access is a key factor in the development of a mass-tourism attraction, accessibility can sometimes be more flexible with nature-oriented sites. Areas with excellent natural attractions like the Sierra Teotepec, but with difficult access, need not be overlooked by tourism planners nor excluded outright. An area that is deemed inaccessible to the typical tourist does not necessarily mean it is devoid of recreational value for the nature-oriented tourist. In nature-oriented tourism, the visitor is generally more willing to endure some discomfort if the end point in the trip fulfills his or her expectations.

Planners should consider the possibility of using unsophisticated infrastructure facilities. Few governments and even fewer rural communities will have the resources to attempt to build a tourism program with well-developed facilities and infrastructure. Depending on the market they are trying to attract, some may have adequate funds for start-up facilities. An example for Guerrero might be well maintained, safe camping areas along the coast. Facilities need not be costly. Both photographic and hunting safaris in Africa use large, inexpensive tents to house tourists. The Corbet Game Reserve in India also used large canvas tents for years, for tourists interested in seeing one of the country's last tiger populations. These are only a few examples of the possibilities of low-cost infrastructure development. The only prerequisites are that the attraction is outstanding, there is wholesome food and the accommodations, even if rustic, are clean. This is supported by data presented to the Commission by Hector Ceballos-Lascurain in "Design Guidelines for Ecotourism Physical Facilities."

Provide maintenance and protection for the state's parks and protected areas and coordinate their development with tourism. A key ingredient to the long-term development of nature-oriented tourism is a system of maintained protected areas. In general, Mexican national parks and specifically the parks in Guerrero face serious problems. The lack of resources and management of these areas affects the state's potential to attract nature-oriented tourists. In Guerrero, the parks are underutilized, have insufficient staff or no staff at all for protection and have serious human impact problems such as illegal hunting, deforestation, overgrazing and man-made fires. Part of the problem with the Sierra Teotepec area is that although a large part of the Sierra is designated a park and natural area, there is little protection and few resources for its management. If these areas were given sufficient management resources and protected, security would be less of a problem to visitors and simple infrastructure could be developed.

Utilizing parks and protected areas as tourist destinations can help break this cycle of underutilization and lead to a better-developed park system. Pressures on park services arise because park systems do not have either the infrastructure, the staff or the budget to manage and control an area. Increased foreign tourism generated from these areas demonstrates to officials the importance of parks and a park service. In the long term, the revenue producing capability of the park service may allow it more leverage in lobbying for an increased budget and additional staff.

Implement policies whereby parks and protected areas benefit local communities. To develop a sustainable park system some benefits must accrue to the surrounding local communities. Many rural people see little value in setting aside large tracts of land as preserved, untouchable areas. If a national or state park system is to endure, local people must see some benefit from its existence. Policies that can help safeguard the long-term integrity of the area include, for example, the hiring of locals for the construction of park infrastructure and maintenance of park facilities. Depending on the recreation activities of the park, locals should be used as guides. Some locals should be hired as rangers. Food for park personnel should be purchased in the local communities. Some of the revenues generated from the park should be used to provide health or educational benefits to the community. If parks and protected areas protect important watersheds, locals should be made aware of that and of the important role played by parks in protecting the environment. There should be a community environmental education campaign taking place at the same time to convince people of the long-term need for sound environmental practices.

Environmental limits must be set and controlled. The long-term health of a nature-oriented tourism program is dependent on policies and actions that safeguard the environment of an area. If governments plan to institute nature-oriented tourism programs, they must also accept and insure a degree of control over the environmental integrity of the resource. If they do not, the resource will suffer and eventually lose its popularity as a favored destination.

Controlling environmental impacts will be easier to accomplish in state and national parks than in communities. An example of the difficulty in controlling impacts on community property is the Inca Trail, a popular trekking route to Machu Picchu in Peru. The route is not under government protection and has, because of the number of trekkers, serious sanitation and garbage problems. This condition has detracted from the scenic value of the trail and will eventually limit tourism to the area. (In the past few years the area has also had security problems which have affected the flow of tourism.)

Implement community tourism projects slowly. Ideally, a community tourism project should be planned at the level at which tourism can be absorbed both socially, economically and environmentally. Much has been written about the destruction of the social fabric of traditional communities due to large-scale tourism projects. Economically, a slow-growth tourism policy implies a tourism threshold for a community's economy. This means that a program should be designed to match a community's ability to supply the necessary labor and inputs without suffering the usual negative impacts of inflation and food shortages which destroy the benefits to the local population. Environmentally, a resource must maintain those qualities that first attracted nature-oriented tourists to the site. If the site is too heavily impacted it will lose its desirability and nature-oriented tourist demand will decline.

Although most planners know that tourism in communities must be introduced slowly, the policy is difficult to carry out. If a tourism program proves to be popular, a small trickle of tourists can turn into an excessive number with the resultant environmental, economic and social problems becoming difficult to control. If the project's success attracts politically and financially more powerful interests, there can be a push for increased exploitation and moves to wrest control of businesses from members of the community. This has begun to occur on Taquile Island in Bolivia's Lake Titicaca. The Islanders have started a small community tourist business based around crafts. They also provide transportation for the tourists to the Island. As tourism grows in popularity, powerful mainland operators are beginning to compete with the Islanders' tourist transportation system using faster and safer motorboats.[34] In Zaire, a World Wildlife Fund project with a community tourism component based on viewing mountain gorillas and chimpanzees also confronted outside interests. In this community pressure came from a large, politically well-connected firm wishing to monopolize business and funnel the revenues from the park tourism back to their own pockets.[35]

While overuse has been a problem facing many tourism projects, underuse may be a more frequent problem encountered in small community tourism projects. There is a good chance that such projects may be unable to generate enough tourism to justify the expenses incurred in developing a tourism program. Unless a resource is exceptionally attractive or has other advantages, such as being near a resort town like Taxco, attracting sufficient tourists may be difficult. Because of the lesser numbers of tourists involved in nature-oriented tourism, the industry may not generate the quantities of revenues needed to sustain communities. A policy of slow implementation will help permit verification of the site's tourism potential. This will prevent the waste of scarce resources on projects that are not successful. It will also be less likely to create unrealistic expectations in the community.

The problem of underuse is illustrated by a project cited in the past as an example of community-based tourism. The project is based on tourism cooperatives formed in the Casamance region of Senegal. While the project did well in terms of community control, economic benefits were minimal. In spite of low prices, beds went unfilled, only five part-time jobs were created, and cash receipts to the villages were low. The government is now hesitant to support similar projects elsewhere.[36]

Increase the security in tourist areas. The security issue is a major problem facing state tourism development. The problem is mentioned in several U.S. guidebooks which contain warnings about drug trafficking in the mountains and the problems of robbery and assault in the coastal areas adjacent to Acapulco. Whether real or perceived, this problem will cause limitations in the development of the full potential of certain areas and activities. The security problem will almost certainly impede sport hunting in some parts of Guerrero. The military and the police would be reluctant to have firearms enter problem areas. Because of the current conditions, hunting may be limited to areas where the government can be assured of controlling the hunting, the weapons and the ammunition.

Use guidebooks for advertising. Advertising can be a problem for small tourism projects. However, with the proliferation of guidebooks, inexpensive promotion is possible. Guidebooks will accept and publish information about a new tourist area at no charge to the state; this publicity can help increase the flow of tourists to a community.

The *South American Handbook*, geared toward independent, adventurous travelers, is the type of guide that can aid tourist development in small communities. For example, in 1976 a brief description of Taquile Island (in Lake Titicaca) was published in the *Handbook*. Shortly afterwards, foreigners began arriving from the mainland both to buy indigenous handicrafts and because of their attraction to the Taquilenos Indian culture. Seeing a profitable market, the Taquilenos pooled their savings and rapidly developed a community tourism industry. They are now involved in the transport system to the island and control the handicraft and restaurant businesses.[37]

In this case, the island resource was exceptional enough to capture the curiosity of a foreign writer. Other areas may be attractive but not have the dramatic setting or unique culture to attract journalists. To insure that the information from the communities does get into the guides, government officials should be responsible for transmitting this information to the editors.

There is little information on Guerrero outside of the main destinations of Taxco, Acapulco and Zihuatanejo/Ixtapa in guidebooks on Mexico. Of the guidebooks reviewed by the authors, Ixcateopan was mentioned only once and little detailed information was given on how to get there. With the exceptions of the sport fishing and skin diving businesses in Acapulco and Zihuatanejo/Ixtapa, there is little information on recreation possibilities in the state. One guide had two sentences on bird watching possibilities on the coast. One guide mentioned sport fishing possibilities outside of the major resorts. Skin diving was mentioned once, but only in the areas around Zihuatanejo/Ixtapa and Acapulco. One guide did briefly mention skin diving possibilities at the southern Costa Chica, below Acapulco.

Develop a program to train outdoor guides. Although Mexico does have a tourist guide licensing program, the official training is geared toward leading cultural tours having to do with art, history, anthropology and archeology. It would not be difficult to include in the national curriculum a licensing tract for those interested in becoming a guide for outdoor recreation activities. Depending on the activity, the training should be expanded to include natural history subjects and some of the adventure activities such as white water rafting, mountaineering, trekking and other activities in which Mexico has some potential.

Research the feasibility of developing a state hunting program. Of all the activities mentioned as having potential in the state, hunting would be the most controversial and therefore the most problematic. It is also associated with the generation of sizeable profits for those involved in the business, e.g., guides and outfitters.

Deer hunting in Guerrero has several advantages as an activity. A principal advantage is that deer can live on farmland and coexist with cattle. The ideal white tailed deer habitat is an interspersed pattern of woodlands and fields, the pattern of land use in much of the state. Ixcateopan and the Sierra Teotepec also have extensive oak forests, and acorns are a principal food for deer. Ixcateopan and communities in the Sierra ideally could develop and maintain deer herds and benefit economically from the hunting. Environmentally, deer hunting could offer an incentive and help prevent rapid destruction of forested land in communities using farming and cattle as an economic base.

Many existing barriers impede its development. Any hunting program takes years to develop. It takes coordination with wildlife management specialists and outfitters, as well as the expertise of community development workers. It involves local control of the number of animals hunted as well as programs for the maintenance of the animal population. While

Mexico has excellent wildlife management specialists who could be used as consultants, at the present time there are no game wardens in the state to control poaching. There also appear to be no commercial hunting outfitters operating in Guerrero, and outfitters either in Mexico City or the surrounding areas would have to be convinced to bring clients to the areas to hunt. Also remaining is the security problem and the army's probable reluctance to permit weapons, even for legal hunting.

Another impediment to attracting foreign hunters to Guerrero and to Mexico is that the Mexican hunting regulations for foreigners frequently change and the process of obtaining a license is difficult and time-consuming. Recently, for example, a regulation has been made requiring all foreign hunters to have a Mexican guide. Unfortunately, there are not enough Mexican guides to cover the foreign demand.

One hope for the program is that the domestic market in Mexico City may be sufficient to make an impact on the tourist industry of the state. If this is the case, well-regulated areas outside of the main tourist resorts may possibly be developed.

Part 2: Short-Term Recommendations for Implementing a Nature-Oriented Tourism Program in Guerrero.

Guerrero has several obstacles to overcome in the development of a nature-oriented travel market. Guerrero's main limitation is with its natural areas and parks and their attractiveness, accessibility and security compared with other natural areas outside the state. Any natural area, in the interior of the state and outside the main tourist triangle of Taxco, Acapulco, Ixtapa/Zihuatanejo, suffers from those limitations. Until the state takes action to develop its parks and the natural areas in the interior, the area has to rely on other strategies to develop this market.

Because of the limitations faced by natural areas outside the Tringulo del Sol, the state's strongest resource for developing community-based, nature-oriented tourism is its well-known resorts. For the short term, the most feasible way to promote outdoor recreation activities is as add-on attractions from these resorts to the surrounding communities. With this plan, tourists would visit the surrounding communities for the day, participate in the activities they offered and return to the resort in the evening. This approach ties in with the government's strategy of trying to find ways of inducing visitors to stay for longer periods of time in the resort areas and at the same time it will hopefully benefit rural communities. Because the approach uses the resort, it insures the availability of acceptable hotel facilities for a wide range of tourists as well as simply providing a large market from which to draw.

Concentrate on those activities that make existing community resources available to tourists. To start the program, have tourists pay for those resources that communities can offer with little skill training on their part. Experience has shown that problems can develop when responsibility for complex activities, such as hotel management, are given to community members who may not have adequate training. Examples of activities where few skills are needed are the sale of hunting leases on communal land, boat rental for sport fishing and skin diving and renting horses for recreational trail riding. In Puerto Vicente Guerrero, whose potential lies in fishing and skin diving, boats owned by the *ejido* could be rented to fishermen and divers coming from Acapulco. Members of the *ejido* could be hired as boat captains and crew. Ixcateopan could offer horseback riding and hiking for tourists coming from Taxco, and tourists could hire horses owned by the villagers for trail riding. This approach will help insure that some benefits go directly to the community. Furthermore, planners should initially avoid large infrastructure projects which might result in community conflicts over how profits should be divided. Renting or hiring only those resources with established ownership will lessen the chances of dividing the community.

Identify community members willing to participate in the tourism program. State functionaries carrying out the tourist development program must go to the towns both to ask town members if they want tourism and to identify specific individuals willing to offer their services or willing to hire out their equipment. In Puerto Vicente Guerrero, those willing to work as boat captains and crew should be identified. A reliable contact person in the *ejido* should be found to be in charge of boat rentals. In Ixcateopan, community members willing to rent horses should be found. A number of people should be identified so that if one is busy or not available others can be contacted. Community tourism activities like this should be carried out through the direction of a separate community chamber or *camara* of tourism.

This kind of system can work. In a community close to Corcovado National Park, in Costa Rica, several people were found who were willing to provide transportation to the park for tourists. Because transportation to the park is difficult, or expensive if one flies in, there is an existing market for the community to fill. This information was then published in a guidebook to the park and the guidebook distributed in the capital city.[38]

Provide guidebooks and state tourist brochures with the necessary tourist information about the recreation opportunities in the communities. To start the flow of tourism, government officials should provide foreign and domestic guidebooks with sufficient information so that tourists will know how to get to the area and who to contact in the community to arrange the activity. This includes the names of individuals, their addresses and the fee they would charge. Information should also be publicized in state tourist brochures recommending areas to practice outdoor activities, for example, areas for sport fishing. Even with the limited infrastructure these areas should be publicized as long as a description of the area paints an honest picture of what is available or not available for tourists. In addition, government officials should actively pursue free editorial advertisement by informing, at home and abroad, specialty travel publications and major newspapers of the state's attractions.

Offer credit to rural communities for equipment. Ample coordination between the Secretariat de Desarollo Economico and the state's tourism department needs to be developed to provide loans for community tourism opportunities. Government officials working for INDES must be made aware of the nature-oriented tourism markets to assure that the potential for these projects won't be overlooked.

For the short term, government officials should avoid offering credit to *ejidos* for complex organizational projects like hotels. Based on the experience of *ejido* hotel projects, it would be a mistake for government officials to give credit to *ejidos* for this purpose. Instead there should be loans for equipment rather than for infrastructure projects. (For example, money for sport fishing, skin diving and safety equipment for the rented boats in Puerto Vicente Guerrero and money for replacement tack for a trail riding business in Ixcateopan.)

VII. CONCLUSION

At present there is an increasing number of governments and nongovernmental organizations considering the possibilities of nature-oriented tourism. International nongovernmental organizations, the conduits for most of the money for conservation projects, are concentrating their efforts around parks and protected areas. While this is encouraging, there remains the question of how much effort these institutions will place on making it a prerequisite that some of the benefits from this tourism go to the communities.

This is not easy to carry out. Not every community can benefit from a rural tourism program, and many issues must be addressed to insure long-term success of the program: Will parks really be protected? How will the program be managed so as not to negatively impact either the natural resource or the community? Will tourism provide enough benefits for the communities? Can they be induced not to return to short-term, environmentally destructive practices? If a successful program is started, will well-connected business people usurp community efforts? In addition, governments have yet to explore the whole range of possibilities for involving the international nature-oriented tourism industry in rural tourism development: Can foreign tour operators be induced to use more community resources? Are they willing to help train and hire community members as guides? Will they help publicize the conservation needs of an area in their promotional materials? These are issues for the future as future projects are developed and implemented.

Countries like Mexico have little to lose in attempting to implement such programs. The destruction of forests and important watersheds is a shadow hanging over rural community development. Erosion and the loss of arable soil is an increasing problem in the countryside. Many of those parks and protected areas helping to preserve important resources seem to be under siege. Aside from agriculture and forestry programs, there are few opportunities that may provide an economic alternative to destructive environmental practices. Nature-oriented tourism can be a viable, environmentally sound component in a program of rural community development.

APPENDIX 1
LIST OF PEOPLE INTERVIEWED FOR THE STUDY

1. Sam Taylor, U.S. AID Representative in Mexico, U.S. Embassy, Mexico City, Mexico.

2. Lic. Mario Melgar, Secretary of Social Development for the State of Guerrero.

3. Public Officers of the Community of Ixcateopan, Guerrero, Mexico.

4. Arq. Adrian Cordero, Secretary of Urban Development and Public Works of the State of Guerrero, Mexico.

5. Ing. Morelos Vargas, Federal Delegate of the Secretariat of Agriculture and Hydraulic Resources (SARH), for the State of Guerrero, Mexico.

6. Lic. Jose Eduardo Rangel, Federal Subdelegate of Agrarian Issues, for the State of Guerrero, Mexico.

7. Lic. Jose Luis Minute, Federal Delegate of the Secretariat of Agrarian Reform, for the State of Guerrero, Mexico.

8. Carmen Catelan Romero, Manager of the El Serano Sawmill, operated by Ejido de Yextla, Sierra Teotepec, Guerrero, Mexico.

9. Felipe Valentin, employee of Forestal Vicente Guerrero, La Cruz Nueva (near El Jilquero), Guerrero, Mexico.

10. Paulino Leyva, Ejidatario of Ejido Papanoa, Puerto Vicente Guerrero, Guerrero, Mexico.

11. Alfredo Cisneros, in charge of the Registro Civil of Papanoa, Papanoa, Guerrero, Mexico.

12. Prisciliano Bravo Avellaneda, President of the Surveillance Council of the Comisariado Ejidal of Papanoa, Papanoa, Guerrero, Mexico.

13. Professor Gildardo Rojo Salazar, Director of the Center for Marine Technical Studies, Papanoa, Guerrero, Mexico.

14. Felix Gutierrez, Manager of the Hotel Papanoa, Papanoa, Guerrero, Mexico.

15. Nicolas Perez Gutierrez, Municipal Head of Puerto Vicente Guerrero, Playa Escondido, Guerrero, Mexico.

16. Marcelo Barajas, Comisario Ejidal of Papanoa, Playa Escondido, Guerrero, Mexico.

17. Pedro Alvarez Sutter, Vice President of Ducks Unlimited of Mexico (DUMAC), Acapulco Chapter, Acapulco, Guerrero, Mexico.

NOTES

1. Gabriela Goldfarb, "International Ecotourism: A Strategy for Conservation and Development?", Report to the Osborn Center for Economic Development, World Wildlife Fund-Conservation Foundation (Washington, D.C., Spring 1989), p. 8.

2. C. Denise Ingram and Patrick B. Durst, "Nature-Oriented Travel to Developing Countries," Forestry Private Enterprise Initiative Working Paper No. 28, Southeastern Center for Forest Economics (Research Triangle Park, North Carolina, October 1987), p. 16.

3. John Pigram, *Outdoor Recreation and Resource Management* (New York: St. Martin's Press, 1983), Chapter 1.

4. Pigram, *Outdoor Recreation*, p. 9.

5. Ingram and Durst, "Nature Oriented Travel," p. 16

6. Ingram and Durst, "Nature Oriented Travel," p. 16

7. Ingram and Durst, "Nature Oriented Travel," pp. 12–16.

8. Ingram and Durst, "Nature Oriented Travel," p. 12.

9. Rodney A. Salm and John R. Clark, *Marine and Coastal Protected Area: A Guide for Planners and Managers* (Gland, Switzerland: International Union for the Conservation of Nature, 1984), p. 268.

10. James Gramann, "Trends in Texas Lease Hunting," *Texas Tourism Trends*, Vol. 1, No. 1 (September 1988), pp. 6–7.

11. Patrick B. Durst, "Nature Tourism: Opportunities for Promoting Conservation and Economic Development," Presentation to the International Symposium on Nature Conservation and Tourism Development, Surat Thani, Thailand (22–26 August 1988).

12. Tom Van Hot, "The Economic Benefits of Marine Parks and Protected Areas," from a paper prepared for NOAA, Sanctuary Program Division, United States Department of Commerce (Washington, D.C., 1986), p. 8.

13. Durst, "Nature Tourism."

14. Jan G. Laarman and Patrick B. Durst, "Nature Travel in the Tropics," Forestry Enterprise Initiative Working Paper No. 23 Southeastern Center for Forest Economics (Research Triangle Park, N.C., June 1987), pp. 5–6.

15. The differences between consumptive and nonconsumptive can be subtle. Any disturbance of a habitat, even by tourist birdwatchers can cause a negative impact on a species (e.g., whooping crane observation at Aransas Wildlife Refuge, Texas). While this is nowhere as dramatic as killing wildlife with a weapon, wildlands managers are aware that any outdoor recreational activity has, in varying degrees, an impact on both the environment and on wildlife. With any form of

outdoor recreation it is an overriding concern to manipulate and manage the trade-offs between the natural environment and the desires of visitors.

16. Conservation Department, Mescalero Apache Reservation, New Mexico. Interview with several Department members (June 1988).

17. Tom McShane, World Wildlife Fund, Washington, D.C., phone conversation (February 1989).

18. McShane conversation.

19. Wesley R. Henry, "Patterns of Tourist Use in Kenya's Amboseli National Park: Implications for Planning and Management," *Tourism Marketing and Management Issues*, ed. Hawkins et al. (George Washington University: Washington, D.C., 1980), pp. 43–57.

20. Warren Y. Brockelman, "The Role of Nature Trekking in Nature Conservation," Paper presented at the International Symposium on Nature Conservation and Tourism Development, Surat Thani, Thailand (22–26 August 1988).

21. Ingram and Durst, "Nature Oriented Travel," 1987, pp. 3–5. The sample of tour operators for this study was taken from the *Specialty Travel Index* magazine. Some activities, such as hunting, fishing and skin diving, may concentrate their marketing efforts in other publications. Other firms may not use the magazine. By studying other sources, a planner may conclude that the activities could be ranked in a different order of popularity.

22. Ingram and Durst, "Nature Oriented Travel," p. 12.

23. Ray E. Ashton Jr., "The Requirements of the Ecotraveler and How These Can be Used to Preserve the Ecopreserve," Paper presented to the first conference on Ecotourism (Merida, Mexico, April 1989), p. 3.

24. Laarman and Durst, "Nature Travel and Tropical Forests," p. 9.

25. Ingram and Durst, "Nature Oriented Travel," p. 12.

26. Ingram and Durst, "Nature Oriented Travel," pp. 8–12.

27. Ingram and Durst, "Nature Oriented Travel," p. 12.

28. Interview with Mr. Ignacio O. Ortiz Ocampo, assistant to the Municipal President of Taxco, February, 1989.

29. A critical look at tourism and development is found in E. de Kadt, "Tourism-Passport to Development?" (Oxford: Oxford University Press, published for the World Bank and UNESCO, 1977).

30. Goldfarb, "International Ecotourism," 1989, p. 15, citing from *The Great Escape? An Examination of North-South Tourism*.

31. G. Donald Jud and Walter Krause, "Evaluating Tourism in Developing Areas:

An Exploratory Inquiry," *Journal of Travel Research*, Vols. 15–16 (1976–78), pp. 8–9.

32. Reports and letters from Inter-American Foundation Project (ME-091), Inter-American Foundation, Rosslyn, VA.

33. Lic. Angel Aguirre, Secretary of Economic Development of the state of Guerrero, Mexico and Lic. Ernesto Velez, Director of the Instituto de Emprersas del Sector Social, private interview, Chilpancingo, Guerrero, Mexico, 12 April 1989.

34. Kevin Healy and Elayne Zorn, "Lake Titicaca's Campesino-Controlled Tourism," *Direct to the Poor, Grassroots Development in Latin America*, ed. by Sheldon Annis and Peter Hakim (Boulder and London: Lynne Rienner Publisher), pp. 45–57.

35. Goldfarb, "International Ecotourism," p. 34.

36. Goldfarb, "International Ecotourism," p. 32, citing from *The Great Escape? An Examination of North-South Tourism*.

37. Healy and Zorn, "Lake Titicaca."

38. Art Pedersen, "Ecotourism, An Alternative for the Sustainable Development of the Osa Peninsula, Costa Rica," Report to Project BOSCOSA, a World Wildlife Fund-Conservation Foundation Project, San Jose, Costa Rica (September, 1988).

12

Mexican Perceptions on
Rural Development and Migration of
Workers to the United States
and Actions Taken, 1970–1988

Jesús Tamayo and Fernando Lozano

I. INTRODUCTION

How is it possible that for 25 years, until the 1990s, there has been no agreement between the governments of Mexico and the United States on the question of the migration of Mexican workers to the United States? Why has the Mexican government had no explicit policy with regard to the emigration of its workers, in spite of the regional and national relevance of that phenomenon? The Mexican authorities' reluctance to get involved in actions or bilateral agreements had its origin in Mexico's experience during the years of the Bracero Program (1942–1965); the lack of an explicit policy has, indeed, been a policy in itself.

During the 23 years of the Bracero Program, the hiring of Mexican workers followed a clear cycle of ups and downs. As the number of people hired decreased, especially from 1960 on, the number apprehended by the Border Patrol grew considerably; that is, there would seem to have been an increase in undocumented migration (see Table 1).

The end of the Bilateral Agreement on Migrant Workers in 1965 was the start of a new stage in the migration of Mexican workers to the United States. On the one hand, it reduced to a minimum the flow of legal migrants; on the other, it was the start of double-talk in speeches by Mexican officials. They welcomed home the people who had ceased to be legally employed by the Americans and said that they would create new jobs in order to avoid the exodus of workers. The Mexican government not only disapproved of the Bilateral Agreement (which it considered unilateral), but also announced a package of actions oriented toward coping with unemployment in the border cities. In essence, it would use surplus labor along the Mexico-U.S. border. President Díaz Ordaz started to implement the policy in 1965 and began to permit the operation of in-bond (*maquiladora*) plants in Mexican territory. This program was one of the government's main strategies for coping with the unemployment along the border that derived from the termination of the Bracero Program.

At the same time as the bilateral agreement on seasonal work came to an end, the decline in Mexican agriculture began. The slowing down of agriculture led to unemployment in the rural areas that made the problem of unemployment in the border region look pale by contrast. Some people perhaps foresaw that the agricultural decline might also encourage migration to the United States.

Since 1970, the different Mexican administrations have attempted—with varying degrees of decisiveness—strategies for increasing activity in the rural areas and, implicitly, raising employment in the agricultural and stock-raising sector. When it was necessary, they pointed out that such strategies also were intended to stem or slow down emigration to the north.

TABLE 1

BRACEROS AND EMIGRANTS DEPORTED FROM THE UNITED STATES

Year	Braceros	Emigrants Deported
1942	4,203	10,603
1943	52,098	16,154
1944	62,170	39,449
1945	120,000	80,760
1946	82,000	116,320
1947	55,000	214,543
1948	35,345	193,852
1949	107,000	289,400
1950	67,500	469,581
1951	192,000	510,355
1952	197,100	531,719
1953	201,380	839,149
1954	309,033	1,035,282
1955	398,650	165,186
1956	445,197	58,792
1957	436,049	45,640
1958	432,857	45,164
1959	437,643	4,732
1960	315,846	39,750
1961	291,420	39,860
1962	194,978	41,200
1963	186,865	51,230
1964	177,736	41,589
1965	20,286	48,948
1966	8,647	89,683
1967	8,647	107,695
1968	0	14,520
1969	0	189,572
1970	0	265,539
1971	0	348,172
1972	0	430,213
1973	0	609,673

Source: U.S. Dept. of Labor and Dept. of Justice. Taken from J. Bustamante, *Espaldas mojadas, materia prima para la expansión del capital norteamericano.* Cuadernos del CES No. 9 first reprinting, Mexico City, 1983.

The most serious limitation that the government encountered in promoting development was the country's economic and political instability, which was implicit in the exhaustion of the Mexican model. This exhaustion caused a slide into the morass of administrative inefficiency, a crisis in 1976 and 1982 and an economic slump in the 1980s. This may be the reason that the Mexican government has not attempted to reduce or stop the emigration of workers, and seems far from wanting to reverse the trend. In spite of statements made for domestic and external consumption, the Mexican government has avoided formulating an active policy in this respect, probably because it did not want to upset the status quo or affect the precarious economic and social stability that the migration of seasonal workers has brought to various regions of the country. This is the angle from which the Mexican government perceives the emigration of its workers; it would be too much to ask it to be objective about it.

II. THE ECHEVERRIA AND LOPEZ PORTILLO ADMINISTRATIONS, 1970–1982

Rhetoric on Migration

In late 1970, when Luis Echeverría took over the presidency, the Mexican government appeared to want a bracero agreement similar to the one that had been in operation up to 1965. The Mexican proposal contained three basic points:

1) Both parties should set an annual quota.
2) Both parties should agree on equitable treatment for workers.
3) The United States should grant greater representative capacity to Mexican consular officers, so that they might protect migrant workers better.[1]

The Mexican initiative did not prosper; on the contrary, a radically different strategy soon developed. In 1974, in the middle of his term, President Echeverría announced to President Ford the Mexican government's refusal to sign a new bracero agreement. He stated that the main responsibility for the exodus of workers was Mexico's, and indicated he would devote more resources to the countryside so as to keep the peasants "down on the farm."[2]

In 1975, in his fifth state of the union message, Echeverría was to ratify that position: "The solution to the bracero problem depends then on our own efforts. The peasants must have access to a decent life in their own country. To the extent that we achieve this, the mirage of emigration will diminish little by little. But as long as this phenomenon exists, we shall continue to struggle to prevent our compatriots from being the object of abuses that run counter to the most basic human rights."[3] On repeated occasions, President Echeverría spoke of *"the need to create more jobs in the countryside in order to prevent the exodus of workers to the United States."* He stressed that, to achieve this goal, a great economic effort would have to be made.[4]

By assuming Mexico's responsibility for the exodus of workers to the United States, Echeverría recognized that the flow was a safety valve to lessen the pressure built up because of unemployment. Probably this admission was due to the fact that the development programs promoted during his six-year term were directed toward creating jobs, above all, in rural areas.

Although at the beginning of his administration (1976), López Portillo accepted that emigration to the United States had to do with unemployment in Mexico, he changed his position little by little to a defense of the workers' human and working rights. Concurring with Echeverría's argument, López Portillo maintained that it was not convenient to set up a new bracero agreement. He was also inclined to ask for U.S. investment in order to create jobs in Mexico. He repeatedly stated that Mexico should export goods, not people. In a well-known 1977 interview with a New York paper, López Portillo pointed out that: "It is difficult to be the neighbor of someone so powerful. But even 'a good neighbor' should recognize that more economic aid, better assistance for Mexico, and fairer terms of trade might represent an attempt to show gratitude for the considerable subsidy represented by the labor that Mexican emigrants have contributed to the prosperity of the southwestern states [of the United States]."[5]

The rhetoric of both presidents was similar (although Echeverría's frequently denounced the ill treatment that undocumented Mexicans received in the United States). What is certain is that in neither of the two presidential terms, in spite of the arrogant tone of their declarations, was there any *ex profeso* program for stemming the tide of migration, or for fostering the creation of jobs in the regions where the push factor to the United States was highest. There were, indeed, general development programs that—when necessary—served to show the government's concern about rural unemployment and, by extension, about the emigration of labor to the United States. The largest of them was PIDER.

Development and Employment Programs

PIDER: Rural development. The Programa de Inversiones Públicas para el Desarrollo Rural (Public Investment Program for Rural Development, PIDER) was an important strategy established during the Echeverría administration in order to promote the development of agriculture and, consequently, raise employment levels.[6]

PIDER originated in 1973; its declared aim was to endow the rural areas of the country with the public works and services necessary for their economic and social development, create permanent and well-paid jobs that would make it possible to keep the people in their *place of origin* and contribute to the well-being of rural society. It announced that its priority investments would be productive ones, and that they would go to "microregions" and *rural* communities of between 300 and 3,000 inhabitants. No contribution was expected from the communities themselves.

PIDER existed for two presidential terms. During its first stage, from 1973 to 1976 (the Echeverría administration), the program spent (or, according to official rhetoric, "invested") 5,116.3 million pesos, distributed in the following fashion: 42 percent on projects to support production; 39 percent on productive projects; and 19 percent on projects of benefit to the whole society. The productive projects were in agriculture, fruit growing, infrastructure for fishing, rural industries or technical assistance. The projects to support production were roads, electricity and warehouses; those for social welfare were health centers, drinking water, classrooms and housing. Table 2 shows the regional distribution of the investment carried out during PIDER's first four years.

Beginning with the López Portillo administration in 1977, PIDER changed its rhetoric. The buzzword was no longer rural investment, but comprehensive development. The new general objective was "to promote the process of self-sustaining development in the rural communities, through the organized participation of their inhabitants, in order to generate and retain economic surpluses, channel them toward productive investments and guarantee them access to minimum standards of living."[7]

In its second stage, regional distribution of investment was as shown in Table 3. Investment in the period 1977–1981 was 47 percent for productive projects, 42 percent on support for production and 11 percent for social welfare projects.

Of the almost 30 billion pesos invested over the period 1977–1981, 85 percent were from domestic sources, and only 15 percent from foreign loans, taken out with the International Bank for Reconstruction and Development (IBRD), the Bank for InterAmerican Development (BID) and the International Fund for Agricultural Development (IFAD).

During the years in which PIDER was in operation (1973–1981), foreign loans, according to official declarations, were no more than 422.5 million dollars, granted as shown in Table 4. The relatively low amount of international loans assigned to the program ($422.5 million) is rather surprising; certainly it is insignificant in comparison with Mexico's external debt, which by 1981 had already reached $75 billion.

TABLE 2

PIDER INVESTMENT CARRIED OUT IN THE LARGEST STATES, 1973–1976

State	Investment (Million Pesos)	%
Jalisco	558.4	10.9
Oaxaca	340.8	6.7
Guerrero	330.0	6.4
Michoacán	269.2	5.3
Chiapas	244.7	4.8
Zacatecas	211.7	4.1
Sinaloa	208.3	4.1
Subtotal	2,163.1	42.3
Rest of the states	2,953.2	57.7
Total	5,116.3	100.0

Source: Ministry of Planning and Budget, Comprehensive Program for Rural Development (PIDER), Report 1977–1981.

TABLE 3
PIDER INVESTMENT

State	Investment	%
Sinaloa	1,710.4	5.8
Zacatecas	1,648.1	5.6
Jalisco	1,463.8	5.0
Oaxaca	1,445.8	4.9
Guerrero	1,441.2	4.9
Chiapas	1,327.6	4.5
San Luis Potosí	1,161.8	4.0
Subtotal	10,198.7	34.7
Rest of the states	19,167.0	65.3
Total	29,365.7	100.0

Source: Ministry of Planning and Budget, Comprehensive Program, Report 1977–1981.

A U.S. specialist has asserted that the bulk of international financing in the seventies—mainly that granted by the World Bank (IBRD)—was siphoned off to large-scale commercial agriculture in areas with high productivity.[8] The type of microregions in which PIDER operated (with communities of no more than 3,000 inhabitants, later raised to 5,000) were certainly not the most important objective for foreign financing. This perhaps explains the relatively low share of foreign loans in PIDER's total resources.

The PIDER funds were allocated or assigned to various federal government agencies. In the López Portillo administration they were allocated as shown in Table 5. The relative importance of agricultural and hydraulic works, rural roads and loans are self-evident.

With regard to employment, which was one of PIDER's main objectives, the official figures tell us that, from 1977 to 1981, 39.132 million days of casual labor were created during the building of infrastructure works; "it is calculated that with the maturing of the productive projects 35.280 million such days per year will be created, *equivalent to 147,000 permanent jobs* if one considers 240 days work a year per job."[9]

TABLE 4
FOREIGN LOANS TAKEN OUT BY PIDER, 1975–1981

Year	Million Dollars
1975	110.0
1977	120.0
1980	17.5
1981	175.0
Total	422.5

Source: Ministry of Planning and Budget, Comprehensive Program, Report 1977–1981.

TABLE 5

PIDER INVESTMENT CARRIED OUT BY AGENCIES, 1977–1981

Agency	Million Pesos	%
Min. Agriculture & Water Resources	8,093.5	27.6
Min. of Human Settlements & Pub. Works	5,227.7	17.8
Rural Bank (BANRURAL)	2,765.2	9.4
State governments	2,104.1	7.2
Federal Electricity Commission	1,689.8	5.8
Ministry of Planning & Budget	1,169.1	4.0
Ministry of Agrarian Reform	1,146.3	3.9
Subtotal	22,195.7	75.6
Other agencies	7,170.0	24.4
Total	29,365.7	100.0

Source: Ministry of Planning and Budget, Comprehensive Program, Report 1977–1981.

PIDER was not oriented toward areas or states with the highest migration of workers. In all the states, with the exception of the Federal District, public works were financed by this program. Resources within each state were distributed on the basis of a prior determination of microregions. *However, it would appear that the rate of migration to the United States was not considered in the definition of the territories and communities where investments would be made.* The state of Zacatecas, for example, although it was one of the states receiving the most PIDER resources, did not receive any support in two regions that, without doubt, have the highest number of people emigrating to the United States, both in absolute and in relative terms: Juchipila Canyon and the Jérez regions.

Two other big government programs, COPLAMAR and SAM, were set up during the López Portillo administration that, although only indirectly oriented toward rural economic development, did affect employment and consequently may have influenced the rate of rural emigration.

COPLAMAR and SAM: Welfare and Productivity. In 1977, López Portillo set up a General Coordinating Office for the National Plan for Depressed Areas and Marginalized Groups (Coordinación General del Plan Nacional de Zonas Deprimidas y Grupos Marginados, COPLAMAR), whose objective was to coordinate the actions of various federal agencies in the rural areas and to foster the organization of the peasants. COPLAMAR therefore made a series of important studies that explained the situation prevailing in the marginal areas of Mexico, almost all of which were rural.[10]

COPLAMAR planned and carried out various actions in marginal rural areas on health care, education, food supplies, improvement of rural housing, drinking water, road building, creating jobs, organizing people for work, bringing electricity to rural areas, agro-industrial development and support services for the peasant economy, ranging from loans to technical assistance and marketing.[11]

The limitations of a program of this nature are obvious, since in spite of the relevance of COPLAMAR's actions and the noble thoughts behind them, "they are far from covering the problem of marginalization in Mexico in its full extent. [Since COPLAMAR fights] . . . against social and economic conditions that have prevailed far too long, sometimes centuries, and it is clear that the efforts made in the last four or five years—however important they may be in relative terms—cannot hope to eradicate the problem."[12]

COPLAMAR always maintained the aim of creating rural jobs, but it did not set any specific goals on this subject. Therefore, it is difficult to evaluate or have any idea of its impact on job creation.

In the case of the Mexican Food System (Sistema Alimentario Mexicano, SAM), a government agency set up in the second half of the López Portillo administration, job creation was also an indirect aim. Its objectives were to increase the production of staple foodstuffs and return to reasonable levels of self-sufficiency in food for the country (this had been lost since the mid-1960s). It also aimed to provide support for Mexico's impoverished masses. SAM's first public declaration on consumption goals and strategies for the production of foodstuffs was made on 1 March 1980, at a time when the output for staples was at one of its lowest levels in 15 years, due partly to the serious drought in 1979.

In spite of its being a program that was very articulated with regard to its objectives and goals, according to some analysts, the SAM did not have sufficient resources. It was assigned 4 percent of the Ministry of Agriculture and Water Resources' total budget in 1980 and 12.5 percent of the Program of Infrastructure for the Development of Agriculture and Stock Raising's budget.[13]

In the period covering the two presidential terms that we are now examining (1970–1982), an annual rate of growth of employment of 4.4 percent was achieved—higher than that foreseen in the Comprehensive Development Plan 1980–1982—and the rate of outright unemployment was also lowered below the goals set. Such changes were certainly not the result of the action of PIDER, COPLAMAR or SAM; they were evidently the result of the growth in oil production. Looking back on them, these programs appear to us to be populist actions—for local consumption—by administrations that were relatively affluent, but still obliged to talk of equality. Agricultural output and employment therefore had no economic or political priority, nor did they become a state strategy.

Government Research

The Interministerial Commission. In 1972, the Echeverría administration set up the Interministerial Commission for the Study of Surreptitious Migration of Mexicans to the United States. It was made up of the Ministries of Labor and Social Security, the Interior, and Foreign Affairs. This commission carried out the first surveys on the northern border among workers deported by U.S. authorities (1972, 1974 and 1975). The objective of these surveys was to pinpoint the characteristics of Mexican undocumented workers who migrated to the United States. They attempted to determine the profile of migrant workers, their migration routes, and the characteristics of their insertion into the U.S. labor market.[14]

Although the number of workers surveyed was relatively low (between 1,300 and 2,800 in each survey), the results reveal important features.

According to the first survey (2,794 interviews), the flow of migration in September 1976 was made up predominantly of men (99 to 1), for the most part young, unmarried men, 23 percent of whom were completely illiterate and another 47 percent hardly knew how to read and write. There were two basic causes for their migration: the search for better wages, and lack of employment in Mexico. Sixty-five percent replied that they worked only occasionally and had never found permanent work in Mexico. More than half of the interviewees—nearly 6 out of 10—declared that they worked in agricultural and stock-raising jobs or that one of these had been their main activity in Mexico; consequently, the majority of the workers (54 percent) were employed in agriculture in the United States. In the following years, this migration pattern underwent significant changes.

The commission proposed to the federal executive a plan that mainly had to do with measures for consular protection. It does not seem to have suggested any actions oriented toward stemming the flow of migration from the areas with the greatest push factors.

The ENEFNEU. The López Portillo administration (1977–1982) sponsored a group of researchers from the Colegio de México and the National Center for Information and Labor Statistics (Centro Nacional de Información y Estadísticas del Trabajo, CENIET), an agency of the Ministry of Labor and Social Security, to examine the problem of undocumented emigration. Their findings substantially altered the Mexican government's perception of the problem.

In late 1976 and early 1977, CENIET did the preliminary work on the biggest survey ever made in Mexico: the National Survey on Emigration to the Northern Border and to the United States (Encuesta Nacional de Emigración a la Frontera Norte y a Estados Unidos, ENEFNEU). The survey was carried out in December 1978 and January 1979. The interpretation of the results led to some conclusions that, because of their political implications, were only unofficially adopted by Mexican civil servants involved in these matters. Some of the conclusions follow:[15]

1) The flow of migration is made up mainly of people who worked in Mexico before going abroad.
2) Migration to the United States is no longer predominantly from rural areas, since large contingents of urban workers have joined in the movement.

3) Migrant workers are not the "poorest of the poor", nor do they come from "marginal" areas.

4) The volume of the flow and the quantity of undocumented Mexicans in the United States are not as high as U.S. sources claim.

The ENEFNEU was a godsend to a government that hardly wanted to appear responsible—even if by omission—for the flow of migrants. Thus it was proven that emigration to the United States was not a safety valve for the pressure of unemployment. Its determining factors were to be found, rather, in the structure of the international economy. Therefore, ignoring the mass emigration of Mexicans entailed no political costs.

Unfortunately, the Mexican government's actions were once again superficial. López Portillo paid some attention to the problems resulting from the migration movement—occasional abuses of undocumented Mexicans—but he shied away from making emigration a national problem, a question of state.

A Proposal from the Academic Community. In 1977, J. Bustamante, an expert on migration matters with a good deal of influence in government circles, and adviser to the president on undocumented workers during the Echeverría administration, proposed a set of measures oriented towards creating jobs in Mexico. According to Bustamante, at that time rural unemployment was one of the main reasons for the emigration of undocumented workers. He proposed the following: "[We] should select strategic sites among the regions with the greatest emigration in the country (north-central region of the country), to set up agricultural production units, or semi-industrialized products, and *maquiladoras* to act as intermediaries between the central and the border area for manufactured goods produced with Mexican raw materials from the Center of the country."[16] He proposed an international agreement between Mexico and the United States in which the latter would buy the output of the labor-intensive units. In his opinion, "the importing of these products by the United States should not be considered a trade operation, but rather a measure for keeping undocumented migrants in their place of origin."

In the hiring of workers, preference would be given to those who had not been apprehended by the INS after a certain date, and to those residing in the geographical areas with the most migration to the United States. "The form of ownership of the units [would be] private, but collectively controlled by the group of workers in the unit, to whom the Mexican government would provide loans."

After an experimental phase lasting two years, U.S. imports would be extended for another three. The fourth year would be a period of transition to shift from exports, as in the initial program, to the marketing of the products in the national market on the border or to regular export programs.

Bustamante emphasized that the production units should offer the migrant:

1) equal or better probabilities of getting a job in them than in the United States; emigration without a visa should reduce the probabilities of being employed by the production units;
2) income high enough that it would not be worthwhile to run the risk of going to the United States without documents.[17]

In spite of the importance of this proposal, as far as we know, its feasibility was never explored. Bustamante himself did not insist on promoting programs for employment or for keeping workers from emigrating. His proposals progressively became demands for consular protection and accusations of ill-treatment of undocumented workers.

III. THE PRESIDENCY OF MIGUEL DE LA MADRID HURTADO, 1983–1988

The administration of Miguel de la Madrid inherited the immediate impact of the crisis of September 1982. His planners soon drew up an emergency scheme and, shortly afterwards, the National Development Plan 1983–1988.[18]

Shortly after the beginning of his presidency, an employment program was set in motion that aimed to create between 500,000 and 700,000 emergency jobs in 1983. This program also proposed to train workers (it was hoped that anyone trained by the program could find a job in the modern sector of the economy once recovery was consolidated) and to create jobs through social welfare. The emergency program operated mainly in urban areas selected for their high rate of unemployment.

The Regional Employment Programs (PREs)

From 1984 on, in all the states, Regional Employment Programs (Programas Regionales de Empleo, PREs) became widespread. These were the natural outcome of the emergency program.[19]

The PREs' official objective was to protect the levels of employment and productive activity, to see to the most urgent cyclical aspects with regard to demand for labor and to improve the population's standard of living. All of this was to be done through useful, low-cost public works with deadlines of no longer than a year in both rural and urban areas.

The action of the PREs was carried out through the following:

1) The allocation of resources to the countryside, through labor-

    intensive works for building rural or village roads, small production projects and conservation of and infrastructure for water resources;

2) the Program of Scholarships for Training Workers (Programa de Becas de Capacitación para Trabajadores, PROBECAT);

3) the Program of Social Service by Students from Higher Education Institutions in the Mexican Republic (COSSIES);

4) the Ignacio Ramírez Scholarship Program; and

5) The Program for Involving Women in Development (PINMUDE).

During the de la Madrid administration, the resources channeled through PREs reached 265 billion pesos, which represented 9 percent of the resources of the Development Agreements (Convenios Unicos de Desarrollo, or CUDs).[20]

Of the PRE resources, 50.5 percent was channeled to Nuevo León, Jalisco, the State of México, Puebla, Oaxaca and Yucatán, where the programs generated 42.5 percent of the temporary jobs. The states with the least share in invested resources, according to the studies made by the Ministry of Planning and Budget, had recorded lower levels of unemployment, due perhaps to a greater relative economic expansion in recent years. In this group were Aguascalientes, Baja California Norte, Baja California Sur, Campeche, Tabasco and Veracruz. In these states only 10 percent of the total of jobs were generated.[21]

Officially, the PRE reports point out that "during the period 1983–1988, 900,000 temporary jobs were created."[22] President de la Madrid, in his last state of the union message, gave a slightly higher figure: "the Regional Employment Programs made it possible to create a million jobs from 1983 to 1987".[25]

In absolute terms, the orientation of the PREs toward urban areas was obvious. This is perhaps due to the urgency of attending to urban unemployment problems deriving from the 1983 and 1984 depression. Although in certain states rural employment programs were carried out, Table 6 clearly demonstrates the attention paid to urban centers such as Guadalajara, the part of the Mexico City metropolitan area that belongs to the State of México and Monterrey. When one considers the figures for jobs created relatively, it is clear that the PRE's greatest impact was in Quintana Roo, Baja California Sur, Morelos, Campeche and Nuevo León (Tables 6 and 7).

The regional employment programs were oriented toward creating temporary jobs. It would seem that the creation of permanent jobs was left to the Regional Development Programs (Programas de Desarrollo Regional, PRD). Following the objectives of the old PIDER, PRD also supported productive projects. (Strictly speaking, the PRDs received the majority of the federal resources channeled to the states through the Development Agreements.) In any case, there does not seem to be any

TABLE 6

JOBS CREATED BY THE REGIONAL EMPLOYMENT PROGRAMS IN EACH STATE,
1984–1987

State	1984	1985	1986	1987	Total	%
Jalisco	34,765	13,597	9,562	17,889	75,813	10.3
State of Mex.	33,242	10,576	11,093	20,690	75,601	10.2
Neuvo León	30,707	18,033	6,774	14,396	69,910	9.5
Oaxaca	12,769	15,475	2,306	8,115	38,665	5.2
Morelos	27,376	2,576	1,110	393	31,455	4.3
Puebla	16,490	3,148	5,683	4,454	29,775	4.0
Tamaulipas	17,277	2,876	3,237	4,968	28,358	3.8
Michoacán	15,644	5,691	2,115	2,066	25,516	3.5
Yucatán	13,815	3,745	2,965	3,452	23,977	3.3
Chiapas	14,327	1,944	2,008	3,710	21,989	3.0
Veracruz	11,504	4,487	53	4,537	20,581	2.8
San Luis P.	9,361	3,798	2,947	4,470	20,576	2.8
Chihuahua	10,598	3,253	3,766	2,781	20,398	2.7
Hidalgo	12,002	2,853	1,780	3,074	19,709	2.7
Guerrero	6,867	5,539	4,307	2,986	19,699	2.7
Coahuila	8,256	3,843	3,255	3,266	18,620	2.5
Baja Calif.N.	11,772	2,403	1,961	2,217	18,353	2.5
Guanajuato	7,297	2,578	3,960	4,073	17,908	2.4
Queretaro	7,757	2,965	2,488	3,296	16,506	2.2
Sonora	9,261	3,085	2,199	1,750	16,295	2.2
Durango	4,705	4,136	1,797	4,217	14,855	2.0
Quintana Roo	8,103	3,381	1,479	1,590	14,553	2.0
Tabasco	6,405	2,090	1,959	2,966	13,420	1.8
Sinaloa	8,435	1,639	1,482	1,558	13,114	1.8
Tlaxcala	5,668	3,159	1,720	2,380	12,927	1.8
Campeche	6,431	3,148	1,115	1,566	12,260	1.7
Zacatecas	3,687	2,311	1,612	4,522	12,132	1.6
Nayarit	6,055	1,865	2,108	1,707	11,735	1.6
B. Calif. Sur	5,363	1,436	1,083	781	8,663	1.2
Aguascalientes	4,454	1,050	1,127	1,079	7,710	1.0
Colima	1,048	2,786	716	1,983	6,533	0.9
Federal Dist.						
Total	371,441	139,466	89,767	136,932	737,606	100.0

Source: Ma. de los A. Moreno Uriegas and M. Sandoval Lara, "El empleo regional 1983–1988, balance de una polítića descentralizada," *El Economista Mexicano*, vol. 20, nos. 2 and 3 (April 1988, Jan. 1989).

record of permanent jobs created in that six-year presidential term.

In order to evaluate the scope of the regional employment programs adequately, we should compare the figures for jobs created by them with the corresponding information on the labor force, unemployment and underemployment in Mexico in the years that the programs were in operation. Our first impression is that such programs played a mainly political role. They did not make any significant contribution to relieving the problem of unemployment among workers in Mexico, aside from the official trumpet blowing about fulfilling goals and results.

TABLE 7

RELATIVE SHARE OF JOBS CREATED BY REGIONAL EMPLOYMENT PROGRAMS
COMPARED WITH ECONOMICALLY ACTIVE POPULATION

State	EAP (1980)	% (1)	Jobs 1984–1987	% (2)	2/1
Quintana Roo	79,341	0.42	14,553	2.0	4.8
B.Calif.Sur	69,954	0.37	8,663	1.2	3.2
Morelos	303,838	1.62	31,455	4.3	2.7
Campeche	134,423	0.72	12,260	1.7	2.4
Nuevo León	803,764	4.29	69,910	9.5	2.2
Tlaxcala	174,965	0.93	12,927	1.8	1.9
Querétaro	224,435	1.20	16,506	2.2	1.8
Yucatán	367,825	1.96	23,977	3.3	1.7
Colima	108,754	0.58	6,533	0.9	1.6
Nayarit	210,188	1.12	11,735	1.6	1.4
Jalisco	1,413,854	7.54	75,813	10.3	1.4
Aguascal.	159,943	0.85	7,710	1.0	1.2
Baja Calif.N	403,279	2.15	18,353	2.5	1.2
Tamaulipas	624,497	3.33	28,358	3.8	1.1
Oaxaca	858,283	4.58	38,665	5.2	1.1
Durango	357,163	1.90	14,855	2.0	1.1
Tabasco	327,502	1.75	13,420	1.8	1.0
Zacatecas	300,963	1.60	12,132	1.6	1.0
Hidalgo	505,091	2.69	19,709	2.7	1.0
San L.Potosí	532,115	2.84	20,576	2.8	1.0
Coahuila	483,898	2.58	18,620	2.5	1.0
Sonora	484,277	2.58	16,295	2.2	0.9
St. of Mex.	2,410,236	12.85	75,601	10.2	0.8
Chihuahua	664,707	3.54	20,398	2.8	0.8
Chiapas	734,047	3.91	21,989	3.0	0.8
Michoacán	872,775	4.65	25,516	3.5	0.8
Puebla	1,081,573	5.77	29,775	4.0	0.7
Guerrero	719,154	3.83	19,699	2.7	0.7
Sinaloa	568,427	3.03	13,114	1.8	0.6
Guanajuato	978,013	5.22	17,908	2.4	0.5
Veracruz	1,796,219	9.58	20,581	2.8	0.3
Total	18,753,503	100.0	737,606	100.0	1

Note: Percentages may not add to 100 because of rounding.

Source: INEGI-Ministry of Planning and Budget, 10th General Census on Population and
Housing, Mexico City, 1980, and Table 5.

Miguel de la Madrid's Perception

During the six years of the de la Madrid administration there were few
speeches made about the migration of Mexican workers to the United
States. Neither was any mention made of the need to keep workers in
their place of origin. Presidential speeches for all intents and purposes
lacked the rhetoric of the two previous terms.

Miguel de la Madrid's position on Mexican emigration to the United

States, and the emigration of Central Americans to Mexico, is summed up by the following:

1) to fight for the respect of the human and working rights of foreigners in Mexico, refugees from Guatemala and other countries, and Mexicans in the United States;
2) to strengthen consular protection to help Mexicans in the United States;
3) to offer solidarity and support to Mexicans who, because of U.S. migration policy had, or would have, to return home.

The position assumed by the Mexican government when the changes in U.S. immigration law were approved in November 1986, and again when they were put into effect in May 1987 illustrates the official interest in this subject. Although the Mexican government understood that the United States was exercising its sovereign right to modify its laws, it considered this amendment a unilateral response to the phenomenon of international migration. Thus, the Mexican government decided to address the defense of human and working rights of undocumented Mexican workers in the United States by reinforcing consular protection and other support mechanisms.[24]

The Mexican government also thought that the consequences of the modification in the status quo for migrants would negatively affect not only Mexico but also the United States. This was spelled out in a naive presidential declaration one day after the amendment, "in any case, we shall see what the reactions of the Americans are when their costs price them out of the market."[25]

Surveys and Hearings

The ETIDEU. During the Miguel de la Madrid administration, the National Council on Population (Consejo Nacional de Población, CONAPO) made a survey on the northern border. The Survey on the Northern Border of Undocumented Workers Deported by the U.S. Authorities (Encuesta en la Frontera Norte a Trabajadores Indocumentados Devueltos por las Autoridades de Estados Unidos de América, ETIDEU) was carried out in December 1984. Its objective was "to bring up to date our knowledge of the phenomenon of migration to the United States, and to generate data comparable with the results of earlier studies on the subject in order to analyze the evolution of this phenomenon".[26] The ETIDEU did not have the magnitude of the ENEFNEU, since it consisted solely of a survey of 9,631 individuals. However, it is the most recent survey of its kind.

The ETIDEU showed that migrants continued to be predominantly male, although the share of women had grown to one woman for every nine men. The Mexican agricultural sector continued to be the main supplier of labor, although the secondary sector was already contributing a comparable quantity. Three-quarters of the flow was composed of wage earners. Almost half of the men went into the primary sector in the United States, whereas the women mainly went into domestic service. Almost a third of the people interviewed had had some primary schooling, and a significant number had reached secondary school. Only 15 percent replied that they did not know how to read and write. Seventy percent of the interviewees replied that they had had a job in Mexico before leaving for the United States. The number of undocumented workers in industrial activities and services had grown a good deal since the ENEFNEU; those hired for agricultural work had dropped to 45 percent. Finally, with regard to the origin of the workers, the increasing importance of two states—Oaxaca and Guerrero—stood out. Although they had been present in an earlier survey of migration to the United States their share had been minimal.

Although the results of the ETIDEU reaffirmed to a large extent the trends already observed in the surveys coordinated previously by the CENIET, they also showed a clear modification in the migration pattern from Mexico to the United States. Possibly these changes reflected modifications in the U.S. labor market, especially changes in the characteristics of demand, which in turn influenced the characteristics of the Mexican labor joining that market. It is highly probable that the changes in the migration pattern were due more to the peculiar conditions of the Mexican labor market in the early 1980s.

Senate Hearings in 1984 and 1985. In December 1984, the Senate of the Republic set up a Public Hearings Commission to examine the situation of Mexican migrant workers. This commission organized 16 public hearings in different regions. Over almost a year (from December 1984 to November 1985), members heard testimony from more than 230 persons. The commission examined the situation of the migrant worker, both domestically and abroad.[27]

Contrary to what some expected, in the conclusions drawn from these hearings, only vague mention was made of the Mexican system's responsibility for the emigration of its labor force. There was only one abstract comment on the need to keep the workers in their place of origin. The commission concluded that the emigration of Mexican workers to the United States had a "binational" origin. Therefore, there was an obvious "need to have a joint approach to it." It added that, "in practice, the flow of migrants can be conceived as a response to the needs of employers and bosses, who have fixed the rules both for the reception and the expulsion of our migrant compatriots."[28]

Policy recommendations stressed the idea that emigration of workers to the United States is contrary to the national interest, "because it weakens our own economic development." However, no suggestions were made about how to use this labor for the country's benefit, how to keep the people at home or how to promote development in the countryside. The commission report merely pointed out the need to "make the plans for comprehensive rural development more dynamic, within the spirit that inspires our constitution, supporting the agricultural workers with truth and efficiency."[29]

It would seem that, as the economic depression in Mexico became more acute, it was increasingly difficult to admit the Mexican development model's responsibility for the erosion of the national agricultural system; on the contrary, there was a greater tendency to stress the importance of outside circumstances.

IV. CARLOS SALINAS, 1988–1989

Carlos Salinas As Presidential Candidate

In his presidential campaign, Carlos Salinas made some unusually frank statements about the emigration of Mexican workers to the United States. According to Salinas, in 1988, expected economic growth would lessen the flow of migration to the United States, as long as that growth offered new opportunities to all Mexicans, including migrant workers. First, he promised to defend migrant workers from the abuses of the Mexican authorities. Salinas did not denounce the abuse that undocumented workers are subject to in U.S. territory, as Echeverría and—to a lesser extent—López Portillo had. He referred only to the extortion of migrants by the Mexican police.

According to candidate Salinas, "The migration flow can only go down if we recover growth that will enable us to offer full opportunities to all Mexicans. Until this happens, I promise to act energetically on two fronts: attacking the extortion that migrants are subject to within Mexico, with energetic action on the part of the federal authorities, and studying in depth the proposal to create a special attorneyship for the defense of migrants."[30]

During Salinas's campaign, his statements on migration to the United States and migrant workers were made on the northern border (Chihuahua and Baja California) and in Zacatecas. In the latter, Salinas said that "Zacatecas should stop being a labor-exporting state. . . . The great challenge for Zacatecas is to create jobs."

He continued, "It seems important to me to analyze the facilities that can be given to emigrants who come back home and the additional employment opportunities that should be offered to those who want to stay. . . . We should offer greater employment opportunities to young Zacatecans, so that they know that in their own state—which they love deeply— they can find prospects for a better life; likewise, we should try to help avoid the obstacles that prevent many Zacatecans who live outside the country (and who wish to return) from doing so; and who thus confirm, by their action, that they continue to consider Zacatecas as their home region and Mexico as their homeland that they love and respect."[31]

Salinas's concern on the subject is obvious, as is his knowledge of migration and its consequences for the country.

The National Development Plan and the PRONASOL

President Salinas has ratified the ideas he expressed as a candidate. The solution to Mexico's social problems depends, he has declared, on Mexico's economic growth in the next few years.

One of the guidelines of the National Development Plan (NDP) 1989–1994 refers to the creation of productive jobs and the protection of the workers' standard of living. The authors of the NDP hold that, "in order to promote a sufficient number of well-paid jobs for a population of working age that is growing at a pace of over 3 percent [a year], it is necessary to recover the dynamism of our economic activity, even though this may be a slow process. In order to satisfy the demand for jobs among the generations that will be entering the labor market, . . . the Mexican economy must achieve rates of growth of around 6 percent a year."[32] That is to say, the increase in employment and real wages will depend on the increase in the demand for workers, which, in turn, will be fueled by economic growth, productivity gains and the drop in transfers abroad.

It would be hard to disagree with the NDP's proposals; however, we are not clear about the means proposed for achieving even such plausible objectives.

Another important part of the NDP strategy is the wiping out of extreme poverty through the National Solidarity Program (Programa Nacional de Solidaridad, PRONASOL). It has been announced that this program will be oriented toward the native Indian peoples, peasants with few resources and working-class urban groups who are the hardest hit by the problems of the big cities. "The areas that will receive particular attention are food, regularizing the ownership of land and housing, justice, opening and improving educational facilities, health care, bringing electricity and drinking water to the communities, agricultural infrastructure and the conservation of natural resources, all this through recuperable investment projects, both in the countryside and in the cities."[33] Local labor is supposed to be used in the public works promoted by PRONASOL, with the aim of multiplying social benefits in the communities themselves.

At the time of writing, however, there are still no specific goals set for any of the areas mentioned.

In short, the present government has made few statements on migration to the United States, and there are still no specific actions oriented toward stemming the flow of labor.

V. FINAL NOTE WITH REGARD TO ZACATECAS

The Zacatecas Plan

Although the emigration of workers is a characteristic of Zacatecas, in the most far-reaching document on state planning, the Zacatecas Plan 1986–1992, there is only brief mention of it. The plan admits that migration to the United States is one of the state's three economic supports, together with agriculture and mining: "Agricultural and mining activities and the income from migrant workers constitute the economic base for Zacatecas."[34]

The annual reports by Gov. Genaro Borrego explain the state's official view on emigration to the United States. According to him, migration has decreased in recent years, although it is not known by how much. "Due to present conditions in the state, the migration flows of Zacatecans toward our northern neighbor are tending to drop. However, we are fully aware of the fact that the phenomenon is still present and, on occasion, under unacceptable conditions. We, both people and government, are struggling to root out as far as possible the causes that motivate some of our compatriots to leave their land and their loved ones."[35]

VI. CONCLUSIONS

In our opinion, Mexican administrations, perhaps concentrating too much on macroeconomic policies, have neglected the regional dimensions of development and have ignored problems such as the emigration of workers to the United States.

The rural or regional development programs that we have reviewed in this section have had a more rhetorical than real effect on the concrete economic growth strategy followed by the Mexican administrations in the second half of this century. From the PIDER scheme through COPLAMAR and SAM, up to the present, the good faith of their promoters aside, these programs have to a large extent served to hide the political and discretionary allocation of resources under development-type rhetoric.

There is little doubt that emigration has relieved demographic, economic and political pressures in Mexico, particularly in rural areas. Perhaps for this reason, the different administrations not only have not attempted to reduce it or stop it, but at times have seemed far from wanting to reverse the trend. Officially, the migration of Mexican workers to the United States has been assumed to be a deficiency of the system that must be combatted by rural or regional development programs. One should not, therefore, be surprised by the lack of success in this struggle.

In spite of the declarations made for local consumption (and now for foreign consumption, too), the facts seem to show that given the economic benefits implicit in the remittances of migrant workers, Mexican administrations have preferred to abstain from formulating an active policy in this respect. This absence of policy is probably due to the desire not to alter the status quo; that is to say, to an intention not to affect the economic, political and social "stability" that seasonal emigration has brought to various regions.

If our presumption is correct, the Mexican government will be in no hurry to define an economic policy oriented toward stemming the migration of its workers to the United States. It is well known, however, that the government is hesitantly beginning to pay attention to the emigration of workers. This process will not be easy; it demands that the government assume that a good deal of the macroeconomic equilibrium, so dear to government technicians and politicians, depends to a large extent on the poverty-stricken half-castes who, socially speaking, are so looked down upon.

Mexicans are not alone in this blindness. Both Mexico and the United States are good examples of the difficulty of seeing oneself as one really is and recognizing internal weaknesses: the emigration of labor for Mexico; the consumption of drugs for the United States. Paradoxically, the agent responsible for making Mexico wake up to reality with regard to migrant labor is the U.S. government, an efficient promoter of border and migration controls. We should be grateful to it.

NOTES

1. Mónica Veréa, *Entre México y los Estados Unidos: los indocumentados*, (Mexico City: El Caballito, 1982), p. 145.

2. Veréa, *Entre México*, p. 114.

3. Luis Echeverría, *Quinto informe de gobierno*, 1975.

4. "Se deben crear más fuentes de trabajo para evitar la emigración del labrador a E.U.," *El Día* (26 August 1976).

5. "Gap between Earnings", *The Nation*, (26 March 1977), quoted by Veréa, *Entre México*.

6. The information in this section was taken mainly from Ministry of Planning and Budget, Comprehensive Program for Rural Development, PIDER, Report 1977–1981, Mexico City.

7. Ministry of Planning and Budget, Comprehensive Program 1977–1981, p. 14.

8. Wayne Cornelius, "La nueva mitología de la emigración indocumentada a los Estados Unidos", in *Indocumentados: mitos y realidades*, (Mexico City: Colegio de México, 1979).

9. Ministries of Planning and Budget, Comprehensive Program 1977–1981, p. 26.

10. COPLAMAR, Mínimos de bienestar (Mexico City, 1979), vol. 6; see also, *Necesidades esenciales de México: situación actual y perspectivas al año 2000*, (Mexico City: Siglo XXI, 1982), vol. 5.

11. COPLAMAR, *Necesidades*; see also Geografía de la Marginación, (Mexico City: Siglo XXI, 1985), p. 9.

12. COPLAMAR, *Necesidades*.

13. Luisa Paré "La política agropecuaria 1976–1982" *Cuadernos Políticos*, no. 33; See also *Nueva antropología*, no. 17 (May 1981).

14. Interministerial Commission for the Study of Surreptitious Migration of Workers to the U.S.A. Survey results unpublished, not dated.

15. National Population Council, CONAPO, *National Population Program*, 1984–1988 (Mexico City, 1985).

16. Jorge Bustamante, "Emigración indocumentada a los Estados Unidos," in *Indocumentados* (Mexico City: Colegio de México, 1977).

17. Bustamante also proposed an agreement between the two countries to regulate the migratory status of undocumented Mexicans in the United States. In the same style that years later the IRCA was to use, this program proposed legalizing the migratory status of those who were working or who had had a job one year before the regularization measure was decreed: Bustamante, "Emigración."

18. In the National Development Plan a drop in product of between 2 and 4 points was predicted for 1983 (this was a stage of necessary adjustment, after the economy had had an average growth of over 6 percent per year during the 12 previous years); in the medium-term a slight recovery in economic activity, of between zero and 2.5 percent was predicted for 1984 (the stabilization stage), and growth of between 5 and 6 percent during the period 1985–1988 (recovery stage). This meant increases of the order of 3.5 percent to 4 percent in job creation and increases in real wages no lower than productivity gains after the initial adjustment period (Federal Executive, National Development Plan 1983–1988, Mexico City, 1983).

19. The information on the Regional Employment Programs was obtained from Ma. de los A. Moreno Uriegas and M. Sandoval Lara, "El empleo regional 1983–1988, balance de una política descentralizada," *El Economista Mexicano*, vol. 20, nos. 2 and 3 (April 1988, Jan. 1989).

20. The Development Agreements, or CUDs, are a political-administrative figure to consolidate investment expenditure in a certain state over a given period. This a tricky way of presenting total public investment, be it federal, state or municipal, in a particular territory. The agreement is, mainly, a political tool in the process of planning public spending, especially on the geographical allocation of spending. The federal government, the state governments and the direct beneficiaries all participated in the agreement.

21. Moreno and Sandoval, "El empleo," p. 37.

22. Moreno and Sandoval, "El empleo," p. 37.

23. Miguel de la Madrid, *Sexto informe de gobierno 1988*.

24. CIDE/Regional Studies Program, "Importancia de la ejecución o puesta en marcha de las modificaciones a la Ley Migratoria estadounidense (enmienda Simpson-Rodino): Algunas respuestas políticas posibles," August 1987 (restricted document prepared for the Ministry of Planning and Budget, Mexico City).

25. *Excélsior* (6 May 1968).

26. CONAPO, "Survey on the Northern Border among Undocumented Workers Deported by the U.S. Authorities, ETIDEU, December 1984, Statistical results," Mexico City, 1986.

27. 53rd Legislature, Senate of the Republic, "Migrant Workers, Conclusions," Mexico City, 1985.

28. 53rd Legislature, "Migrant Workers," p. 24.

29. National Meeting of IEPES on the Northern Border, Chihuahua, 25 March 1988, in C. Salinas de Gortari, *Campaign Speeches*, vol. 9.

30. Salinas, "Campaign Speeches," vol. 8, p. 231.

31. Salinas, "Campaign Speeches," vol. 8, pp. 231, 243 and 254.

32. Office of the President, *National Development Plan, 1989–1994.*

33. Office of the President, *National Development Plan, 1989–1994.*

34. Constitutional Government of the United States of Mexico/Constitutional Government of the State of Zacatecas, *Zacatecas Plan 1986–1992,* p. 23.

35. Genaro Borrego, *First Annual Report,* 1987.

About the Editors and Contributors

Jesús Arroyo Alejandre is director of the Institute for Economic and Regional Studies at the University of Guadalajara. He has a Ph.D. in regional science from Cornell University and did his master's studies at the London School of Economics. He teaches in the University of Guadalajara's Economics Department. His field of research is internal and international migration in relation to regional and urban development. His main publications are: *El Abandono Rural*, University of Guadalajara, 1989 and *Migración a Centros Urbanos en una Región de Fuerte Emigración: El Caso del Occidente de México*, University of Guadalajara, 1986.

Ramón Blanno-Jasso is associate director of the Departamento de Estudios Econométricos of the Subsecretaría de Planeación (Secretaría de Agricultura y Recursos Hidráulicos, SARH) and tenured professor at the Universidad Autónoma Metropolitana (UAM-Azcapotzalco). He also teaches economics at the Centro de Investigación y Docencia Económicas and is a specialist in input-output analysis. He has lectured on econometrics, economic theory, and national accounts. He has written numerous quantitative analyses of the agricultural and livestock sector for the SARH and is responsible for the creation of an agricultural and livestock database for that agency.

Héctor Ceballos-Lascurain is an architect. He is a graduate of the Instituto Tecnologico y Estudios Superiores de Monterrey. He is an ecotourism specialist and a consultant to the Mexican Ministry of Tourism, the World Wildlife Fund and the International Union for the Conservation of Nature. He has served as Director General of Standards and Technology of the Ministry of Urban Development and Ecology (SEDUE). He has also worked extensively on the planning of the Sian Ka'an Biosphere Reserve in Quintano Roo, Mexico and the Grey Whale National Park in Guerrero Negro, Baja California, Mexico.

Wayne A. Cornelius is the Gildred Professor of U.S.-Mexican Relations and the founding director of the Center for U.S.-Mexican Studies at the University of California, San Diego. He holds a Ph.D. in political science from Stanford University and for eight years was on the faculty of the Massachusetts Institute of Technology. He has been engaged in field studies of rural-to-urban migration within Mexico and Mexican migration to the United States since 1970. He has published widely on Latin American urbanization, immigration issues and the Mexican political system. His most recent books are *Mexico's Alternative Political Futures* (coedited with Judith Gentleman and Peter Smith; Center for U.S.-Mexican Studies, 1989) and *Mexican Migration to the United States: Process,*

Consequences, and Policy Options (coedited with Jorge Bustamante; Bilateral Commission on the Future of U.S.-Mexican Relations, 1990). He is currently writing a book on Mexican migration and U.S. immigration reform, to be published in 1991 by Stanford University Press.

Sergio Díaz-Briquets is with Casals & Associates, a consulting firm in Washington, D.C. He was research director of the Commission for the Study of International Migration and Cooperative Economic Development, created by Congress. Earlier he held appointments with Duquesne University in Pittsburgh and with the Population Reference Bureau in Washington, D.C., and was a program officer with the International Development Research Centre (IDRC) in Ottawa, Canada. Díaz-Briquets has been a consultant to the U.S. Agency for International Development, the World Bank, and other international development agencies. Holder of a Ph.D. from the University of Pennsylvania, Díaz-Briquets is the author of several books on a variety of development-related topics, including *The Health Revolution in Cuba* (1983), and coauthor of *Social Change and Internal Migration* (1977). Most recently he edited *Cuban Internationalism in Sub-Saharan Africa* (1989).

Daniel Hiernaux Nicolas received his Ph.D. in geography from the University of Paris III, France. Among other public administration posts held in Mexico, he was general manager for urban and regional planning at the Fondo Nacional de Fomento al Turismo, FONATUR. He presently serves as a research professor at the Universidad Autónoma Metropolitana, Xochimilco, in Mexico City and as chief researcher at the Centro de Investigaciones y Documentación de América Latina (CREDAL)—the laboratory of the C.N.R.S., the National Center for Scientific Research of France. He also serves as associate director of Redes de Investigación para el Desarrollo, S.C. (REDES).

Adrián de León Arias is director of the Center for Mexican-U.S. Studies at the Institute for Economic and Regional Studies, University of Guadalajara. He completed his master's degree in international economy and politics at the Centro de Investigación y Docencia Económicas—CIDE (Center for Research and Teaching of Economics). His areas of study are Mexican-U.S. relations and regional economic development.

Fernando Lozano took his degree in agricultural engineering, majoring in rural sociology, at the Autonomous University of Chapingo. He taught at the National School of Anthropology and History and did research at the Center for Research on Rural Development. Since 1983 he has coordinated the Department for the Analysis of Labor Markets in the Ministry of Planning and Budget. There, he designs studies on the employment of labor in rural districts and the migration of undocumented workers to the United States from central Mexico. He is at present doing post-graduate work in demography.

Alejandro Nadal Egea is member of the Center for Economic Studies and coordinator of the Science, Technology and Development Program (PROCIENTEC) at El Colegio de México. He obtained his law degree from the National Autonomous University (UNAM) and a Ph.D. in economics from the University of Paris-X (Nanterre). His interests include general equilibrium theory and the analysis of technical change and resource management. Since 1982, he has taught the history of economic thought in the Master of Arts program of the Center for Economic Studies.

Art Pedersen is an outdoor recreation specialist. He is a graduate of the Lyndon Baines Johnson School of Public Affairs of The University of Texas at Austin. He has served as a consultant to the Texas Economic Development Commission and with the Costa Rican Park Service. He has also worked as a consultant to Project BOSCOSA, a World Wildlife and Conservation Foundation sponsored program. As a member of the BOSCOSA team, he developed a practical nature-oriented tourism plan for the Osa Peninsula in Costa Rica.

Marcos Portillo Vázquez is director of the Department of Agricultural Economics at the Autonomous University of Chapingo. He has broad experience in both teaching and research, focusing on agricultural policy, and has directed a number of projects on agricultural production planning.

Amado Ramírez Leyva is a professor and researcher in the Department of Agricultural Economics at the Autonomous University of Chapingo, Mexico's leading agriculture research institute. He has worked primarily on conceptualizing issues pertaining to technology in agricultural development. His work also addresses problems in agricultural policymaking and the role of the federal government in the agricultural sector.

Manuel Rodríguez Woog has a degree in tourism from the Universidad Autónoma de Baja California, Tijuana, with specialized studies in regional development, tourism and development and planning. He was a researcher and board member of the Centro de Estudios Superiores en Turismo of Mexico's Secretariat of Tourism from 1981 to 1989. He is currently a research professor at the Universidad Cristobal Colón in Veracruz and associate director of Redes de Investigación para el Desarrollo, S.C. (REDES).

Celia Sánchez Solano is professor-researcher at the University of Chapingo's Department of Agricultural Economics. Her research centers on the problems of adapting technology in marginal areas and those in which productive resources are scarce.

Jesús Tamayo studied architecture, majoring in housing, at the National Autonomous University of Mexico. He has a master's degree in urban development from El Colegio de México. He was a researcher at the Center for the Research and Teaching of Economics (CIDE), where he founded and directed the Regional Studies Program; at present he holds the post of technical secretary of that center. He is author of *Zonas Fronterizas (México-Estados Unidos)* and various articles and essays on subjects having to do with his specialty. He has been a visiting fellow at the University of California, San Diego, and Fulbright scholar at the University of Texas, Austin. Since 1985 he has been director of the Center for Social Research on Regional Development, CISDER.

Basilia Valenzuela Varela is a researcher at the Center for Mexican-U.S. Studies at the Institute for Economic and Regional Studies, University of Guadalajara. She has her master's degree in Regional Development from the Colegio de la Frontera Norte. Her areas of research are population movements, international migration and tourism in relation to regional development.

David C. Warner is professor of public affairs at the LBJ School of Public Affairs at the University of Texas at Austin. He is a graduate of Princeton

University, received a master's in Public Administration and a Ph.D. in economics from Syracuse University. He conducted postdoctoral study in health policy at Yale University. He has taught at Wayne State University, Yale, and the LBJ School. He has published extensively in the areas of health, mental health policy and finance, and on the health of Mexican Americans and border health care. During the 1988–89 academic year, he held the Sharpe Fellowship and during 1989–90, he held a fellowship from the Wilbur Cohen Professorship. Both endowments helped provide research assistance for chapter four.

Sidney Weintraub is Dean Rusk Professor and director of the Program for U.S.-Mexico Policy Studies at the Lyndon B. Johnson School of Public Affairs at the University of Texas at Austin. He is also a Distinguished Visiting Scholar at the Center for Strategic and International Studies (CSIS). As a career diplomat (1949–1975), he was an assistant administrator of the Agency for International Development, Deputy Assistant Secretary of State for international finance and development, chief of the AID mission in Chile under the Alliance for Progress, and chief of commercial policy in the State Department. Dr. Weintraub also has authored numerous books and monographs focusing on Mexico-United States relations, including *Mexican Trade Policy and the North American Community* (1988), *Industrial Strategy and Planning in Mexico and the United States* (Westview, 1986), *Free Trade Between Mexico and the United States?* (1984), and *A Marriage of Convenience: Relations Between Mexico and the United States* (1990). He is co-editor with Luis F. Rubio and Alan D. Jones of *U.S.-Mexican Industrial Integration* (Westview, forthcoming).

Patricia A. Wilson is an associate professor in the graduate program in community and regional planning, School of Architecture, in the University of Texas at Austin, where she directs the joint master's program in Planning and Latin American Studies. Dr. Wilson holds a Ph.D. in regional development planning from Cornell and a B.A. in economics from Stanford. She has published numerous articles on regional development planning in Latin America, focusing on Peru and Mexico. She authored *Problemática Regional y Política Central en el Peru* (Universidad del Pacífico, 1983) and co-edited *Regional Development and the New International Divison of Labor* (Kluwer Nijhoff, 1983). She is author of a forthcoming book entitled *The New Maquiladoras; Export-Led Development and Local Linkages.* Dr. Wilson has also done consulting work for the U.S. Department of Commerce, Economic Development Administration and U.S. AID.

Antonio Yunez-Naude is professor and researcher at the Centro de Estudios Económicos (El Colegio de México), holds a Ph.D. in economics from The London School of Economics and Political Science and is a "National Researcher" for the Sistema Nacional de Investigadores de México. He has been awarded fellowships from the Consejo Nacional de Ciencia y Tecnología, the Ford Foundation and the U.S. government. He is currently on sabbatical leave as a visiting research fellow at the Center for U.S.-Mexican Studies of the University of California–San Diego with Fulbright and Center fellowships. He has written several books and articles on the problems of economic development in Mexico, such as: *Crisis de la Agricultura Mexicana* (El Colegio de México and Fondo de Cultura Económica); *Energy Efficiency and Conservation in Mexico* (coauthor, Westview Press); "Factores Determinantes de la Balanza Comercial Agropecuaria de México" (*Comercio Exterior*); and "Theories of the Exploited Peasantry: A Critical Review" (*Journal of Peasant Studies*).